FAR EAST AIR OPERATIONS 1942-1945

DESPATCHES FROM THE FRONT

The Commanding Officers' Reports From the Field and At Sea.

FAR EAST AIR OPERATIONS 1942-1945

Introduced and compiled by
Martin Mace and John Grehan
With additional research by
Sara Mitchell

Pen & Sword
AVIATION

First published in Great Britain in 2014 by
Pen & Sword Military
an imprint of
Pen & Sword Books Ltd
47 Church Street
Barnsley
South Yorkshire
S70 2AS

ISBN 978 1 78346 212 4

A CIP catalogue record for this book is available from the British Library.

Printed and bound in England
By CPI Group (UK) Ltd, Croydon, CR0 4YY

Pen & Sword Books Ltd incorporates the Imprints of Pen & Sword
Aviation, Pen & Sword Family History, Pen & Sword Maritime,
Pen & Sword Military, Pen & Sword Discovery, Pen & Sword Politics,
Pen & Sword Atlas, Pen & Sword Archaeology, Wharncliffe Local History,
Wharncliffe True Crime, Wharncliffe Transport, Pen & Sword Select,
Pen & Sword Military Classics, Leo Cooper, The Praetorian Press,
Claymore Press, Remember When, Seaforth Publishing and
Frontline Publishing.

For a complete list of Pen & Sword titles please contact:
PEN & SWORD BOOKS LIMITED
47 Church Street, Barnsley, South Yorkshire, S70 2AS, England
E-mail: enquiries@pen-and-sword.co.uk
Website: www.pen-and-sword.co.uk

CONTENTS

INTRODUCTION

Japan's sudden and explosive entry into the Second World War completely changed the military situation in the Far East. The Japanese advance westwards was supported by strong air forces and, as the Japanese marched into Burma in late December, the battle for control of the skies over Rangoon began in earnest. This battle forms the basis of the early passages of the first despatch in this volume.

Air Vice-Marshal Stevenson commanded a small Allied Air Force (American Volunteer Group, Royal Air Force and Indian Air Force) consisting of just thirty-seven combat aircraft. There was only one battery of anti-aircraft guns for airfield defence other than Browning machine-guns. Apart from this weakness, the nature of the Burmese countryside, with its high jungle-covered mountains crossed with scarcely any roads, meant that the installation of radar and telephone communications was all but impossible. The defending aircraft therefore had no warning of any attack and this greatly hampered Stevenson's ability to counter Japanese incursions.

Nevertheless, Stevenson called for reinforcements and began to build airfields to accommodate the expected arrivals. Using lots of local labour, a hard, dry paddy field could be converted into a landing strip for bombers or fighters in a day. Reinforcements began to arrive but not in the numbers that Stevenson had said were necessary for the defence of Burma. Even when squadrons of aircraft arrived, the lack of spares and workshop facilities meant that only a small percentage of aircraft were airworthy at any one time.

On 1 January 1942, the Japanese air force deployed for operations in Burma was reckoned by Stevenson to be around 150 strong. By 14 February both sides had received reinforcements. This brought Stevenson's numbers up to fifty-three aircraft, those of the Japanese to 200. The latter increased still further and by the time Rangoon fell, on 7 March, the Japanese could count something in the region of 429 to 500 aircraft.

Despite this overwhelming disparity the Japanese fighters, of which there were three types deployed over Burma, were no match for either the Curtiss P-40s or the Hawker Hurricanes. Stevenson's problem, though, was that without early warning, his fighters could be caught on the ground where they were defenceless. To quote Stevenson's own words: "Fighter for fighter we were superior and it was only when heavily outnumbered, and without warning and proper airfield facilities, that the enemy were able to get a decision. Their bombers were 'easy meat' for our fighters if interception took place, while our bombers were satisfactory for their task, though light on range and much inferior to the enemy in bomb lift and numbers."

The first waves of Japanese attacks upon Rangoon were delivered by some sixty or seventy bombers with around thirty escorting fighters. A second series of attacks were undertaken between 23 and 29 January 1942, with the enemy despatching a total of around 218 aircraft, most of which were fighters, in a bid to eliminate Stevenson's small force. In the air battles of those six days, the Allied fighter force claimed a total of fifty Japanese bombers and fighters destroyed.

So heavy were the Japanese losses, they were forced to revert to night bombing until, on 24 and 25 February, they made a final attempt to win air superiority over Rangoon. On those two days, they launched attacks with 166 bombers and fighters, but sustained the heavy loss of at least thirty-seven aircraft. On the second day, the 25th, the P-40s of the American Volunteer Group claimed no less than twenty-four aircraft shot down. This ended the Japanese efforts over Rangoon.

"Such wastage had been inflicted on the enemy," Stevenson proudly boasted, "that thereafter he never attempted to enter our warning zone round Rangoon until the city was captured and the air bases in his hands." We have come to think of the Battle of Britain as epitomising the David and Goliath struggle of the RAF against the *Luftwaffe* yet the Battle of Rangoon stands comparison. The Allied Air Force can undoubtedly be compared to "The Few".

The latter part of Stevenson's despatch deals with the air support for the British Army as it withdrew from Rangoon and then all of Burma. This includes the disaster at Magwe where, in two days of attacks, seventeen aircraft were destroyed or badly damaged where they sat on the ground.

Following the withdrawal from Burma, Allied forces in India were re-structured and on 16 November 1943, South East Asia Command was formed. Air Chief Marshal Peirse became Allied Air Commander-in-Chief, South East Asia.

Peirse had two main tasks upon taking up his new role. The first was to integrate the American, Indian and British air forces into a single, effective command. The second was to prepare for the re-invasion of Burma with the preparation of the air bases that would enable his command to provide support to the 14th Army when it began its drive eastwards. That support was to begin with a strategic bomber offensive to destroy enemy air forces and installations, selected rail, road and river communications, and depots and maintenance facilities.

Compared with the situation that Stevenson had found in 1942, Peirse had under his command forty-eight RAF and seventeen USAAF squadrons when he took over – a figure to rise even further over succeeding months. Against this the Japanese had just 250 aircraft.

The odds had swung decisively in favour of the Allies, and perhaps the most significant element of this was when Supermarine Spitfires first flew over the Bay of Bengal. Aerial superiority, from that moment onwards, was assured. The enemy continued to send fighter sweeps over the Arakan, but, Peirse claimed, the Spitfires were able to inflict casualties upon them in the ratio of eight to one. The degree of superiority enjoyed by the Allied air force throughout the period covered by his despatch is indicated by the number of enemy sorties were sighted or plotted. These amounted to just 2,700, which was less than three per cent of the number of Allied sorties in that same time.

Supplying the troops of the 14th Army as they pushed into Burma was another of Peirse's responsibilities and to facilitate this he formed the Troop Carrier Command in December 1943. It was, however, the Japanese that attacked into the Arakan early in 1944, and the Troop Carrier Command, with scarcely any warning, had to take supplies to troops cut off by the sudden enemy attack.

Peirse's despatch also covers the creation of the Air Commandoes, the operations in support of the Allied troops at the Battle of Imphal, including the air evacuation of casualties. Peirse also details the operations of the bomber offensive in this single despatch covering his tenure as Allied Air Commander until that position was handed over to Air Marshal Sir Guy Garrod.

Garrod's was only a temporary appointment and there is no published despatch detailing his time in command. He was replaced by Air Chief Marshal Sir Keith Park on 23 February 1945.

Park opens his first despatch on a triumphant note, declaring that "a fanatical and over-confident enemy has been driven back from his foothold in India at Imphal over 800 miles, which included the complete rout of the enemy's field army in the open plains of Burma and culminated in the occupation of Rangoon". He ascribes this success to air power, both in driving the enemy from the skies and supporting the ground forces. Park also states that the Burma campaign should be marked in the history of warfare "as a triumph of air power and air supply".

After detailing just how that triumph was achieved, Park ends by explaining one of the more unusual operations performed by his command – the supply and return of ballot papers from the troops serving in the Far East for the July 1945 General Election in the United Kingdom. More than 30,000 ballot papers were received, distributed right across the Indian Ocean and the Indian sub-Continent, and collected for despatch back to the UK. That truly is a demonstration of air supremacy.

This non-combatant role of the RAF is also a feature of the second and final despatch from Sir Keith Park. Whereas the first part of this despatch records the successful pursuit of the Japanese out of Burma and Malaya, the latter part concerns the relief of the Allied prisoners of war – Operation *Mastiff*.

As Park explains, it was only through the rapid supply of sustenance to these prisoners, many of whom were too weak to stand, that saved them. Only air power, Park believed, could have penetrated these vast territories throughout South East Asia with the speed required to initiate that essential relief.

The value of this last despatch, which is more than 40,000 words long, is that it covers an almost forgotten campaign. Whilst so many histories focus upon the Battle of Britain and the bombing campaign against Germany, the operations in South-East Asia, particularly after the end of the fighting in Europe, are generally overlooked. This despatch, and those that preceded it, provides a comprehensive account of a war fought in the most difficult of conditions over enormous distances.

To give the reader some indication of the achievements of the RAF in the closing stages of the war, Park explains that the "mercy missions", as he describes them, to drop Red Cross parcels and send in medical teams to the starving prisoners deep in the Asian jungles, involved distances which were the equivalent of a trans-Atlantic crossing. Seventy-five per cent of these fights were successful.

Park concludes by analysing the lessons learnt from operations in South-East Asia. These operations demonstrated that an army could march for a thousand miles through some of the worst country in the world so long as air superiority was guaranteed. As we now accept, whoever controls the sky, controls the battlefield – and that was proven emphatically in the war against Japan.

*

The objective of this book is to reproduce these four despatches as they first appeared to the general public some seventy years ago. They have not been modified or edited in any way and are therefore the original and unique words of the commanding officers as they saw things at the time.

The only change is the manner in which the footnotes are presented, in that they are shown at the end of each despatch rather than at the bottom of the relevant page as they appear in the original despatch. Any grammatical or spelling errors have been left uncorrected to retain the authenticity of the documents. Where words are no longer legible, due to the passage of time, this has been indicated in the text.

John Grehan and Martin Mace
Storrington, 2014

LIST OF ILLUSTRATIONS

the railway line between Monywa and Sagaing in central Burma on 18 July 1943. (HMP)

11 Chindwin air drop: The crew of a 40mm Bofors anti-aircraft gun of the 11th East African Division watch as an RAF Dakota drops supplies on the western side of the Chindwin River, 8-11 December 1944. (James Luto Collection)

12 The 2,760 ton Japanese transport *Angthong Goo* on fire after an attack by Liberators of 159 Squadron in the Gulf of Siam, 4 June 1945. (HMP)

13 Paddle steamers and similar low draught vessels were often used by the Japanese as headquarters or accommodation on some of the Burmese rivers; they were moored to the river bank and camouflaged. It is once such vessel that is pictured here under attack between Kyaukpadaung and Muale during November 1943. (HMP)

14 The aftermath of a Beaufighter attack in the Minhlayathaya area on 16 December 1943, with four or more native craft left burning on the shoreline. The original caption states that "they burst into flames immediately and emitted dense smoke showing them to be carrying an inflammable cargo, probably petrol or oil", for the Japanese. (HMP)

15 A series of images which illustrate the dangers of the "minimum altitude bombing" often undertaken by the Allied air forces in the Far East. They were taken by a RAAF aircraft during an attack on camouflaged Japanese ships in Hansa Bay, New Guinea, on 28 August 1943, and show the consequences of following the preceding bombing aircraft too closely, without allowing sufficient time for its bombs to explode. The top left picture shows bombs from a preceding B25 dropped but not exploded. A second 'plane is coming in low from over the land, with smoke from gunfire. In the top right picture, a bomb dropped amidships from the first attacker is exploding under the second. The violence of the bomb's explosion, see bottom left, blasts the wing and tail off the second B25, catapulting it into the sea. The image bottom right shows the moment that the stricken bomber hits the water. (HMP)

1

AIR VICE-MARSHAL STEVENSON'S DESPATCH ON AIR OPERATIONS, BURMA AND BAY OF BENGAL

1 JANUARY TO 22 MAY 1942

General Headquarters, India,
New Delhi, India,
28th September, 1942.

From: General Sir Archibald P. Wavell,
          G.C.B., C.M.G., M.C., A.D.C.

To: The Chiefs of Staff, London.

I forward herewith two copies of a report by Air-Vice-Marshal D.F. Stevenson on Air operations in Burma and the Bay of Bengal from January Ist (the date on which Air-Vice-Marshal Stevenson assumed command) to May 22nd, I942 (the date when the forces from Burma completed evacuation to India).

Air-Vice-Marshal Stevenson's report emphasises the remarkable work performed by a small air force in defence of Rangoon, and the difficulties which the Air Force, in common with the Army, suffered through lack of the necessary resources for the defence of Burma. I have already commented on these in my Despatch[1] of July Ist, I942, on the Burma operations and I have nothing further to add.

In paragraphs I22 to I3I Air-Vice-Marshal Stevenson refers to certain telegrams addressed to ABDA Command to which he received no reply. From the records of

ABDA Command it appears that both these telegrams were received with very considerable delay, and not until instructions had been received transferring Burma back from ABDA Command to the command of the C.-in-C. India. Also Air-Vice-Marshal Stevenson had included the proviso that "failing immediate instructions am putting this plan into action commencing today". By the time, therefore, that these telegrams were received command had passed from ABDA and Air-Vice-Marshal Stevenson had presumably already taken action. No reply was therefore necessary.

Please pass one copy of this report to Air Ministry.

A.P. WAVELL,
General.

Despatch on Air Operations in Burma and the Bay of Bengal covering the period January 1st to May 22nd, 1942, by Air Vice-Marshal D.F. STEVENSON, C.B.E., D.S.O., M.C.

AIR OPERATIONS IN BURMA AND THE BAY OF BENGAL, SPRING, 1942.

INTRODUCTION.

1. The following is a report on the air operations carried out by a small Allied Air Force (American Volunteer Group, Royal Air Force and Indian Air Force) against the Japanese Air Force in Burma and the Bay of Bengal and the subsequent movement of the R.A.F. and I.A.F. to India whence operations against the Japanese continue.

2. In reading this Despatch the following chronological summary may be of assistance:-

1941.

Dec. 9th	– War declared by Japan.
Dec. 23rd	– Struggle for air superiority over Rangoon commenced.

1942.

Jan. 18th	– Mergui and Tavoy evacuated.
Jan. 29th	– Japanese thrust through Tenasserim towards Rangoon commenced.
Feb. 15th	– Singapore fell.
Feb. 25th	– Last Japanese effort failed to establish air superiority over Rangoon.
March 7th	– Demolitions at Rangoon commenced, Rangoon evacuated

	and General Alexander's Army commenced withdrawal up Prome Road.
March 2Ist	– Japanese inflicted severe reverse on R.A F. Wing at Magwe.
April I2th	– Air operations based in India and Assam in support of the Army commenced.
May 20th	– General Alexander's Army withdrawn to India and Air operations against the enemy in Burma continue.

3. On the I2th December, I94I, I was informed by the Air Ministry that I was to take over Command of the Air Forces in Burma. It was proposed to reinforce Burma with a force of 4 Fighter Squadrons, 6 Bomber Squadrons and I G.R. Squadron with the object of making a front in Burma should the Japanese campaign against Malaya prove successful. On the I4th December I left England. I met the Commander-in-Chief in India, General Sir Archibald Wavell, and the Air Officer Commanding-in-Chief, Air Marshal Sir Patrick Playfair, on the 28th December in Delhi, where the land and air situations were explained to me.

PART I
AIR SITUATION ON MY ARRIVAL IN BURMA AND CONSEQUENT REQUEST FOR REINFORCEMENT.

4. On the Ist January, I942, I flew to Rangoon to take over command from Group Captain E.R. Manning. He met me at Mingaladon aerodrome and I proceeded to Group Headquarters. It was necessary to make an appreciation of the air situation as a first step.

5. During the first seven days of January I visited the airfields in Burma, the Station, Squadron and Detachment Commanders and met the Military and Civil Authorities. The Governor of Burma was H.E. Sir Reginald Dorman Smith, G.B.E., the Army in Burma was under the command of Lieutenant-General T.J. Hutton, C.B., M.C., while the Senior Naval Officer at Rangoon was Commodore C. Graham, R.N. – Commodore Burma Coast – who succeeded Capt. J. Hallett, R.N., up to that time N.O.I.C. Rangoon.

6. I found that the air garrison of the country comprised one Squadron of the American Volunteer Group, armed with P.40's at a strength of 2I I.E. based at Mingaladon, and No. 67 R.A.F. Buffalo Squadron of a strength of about 16 aircraft, also based at this Sector Station. Apart from the personnel of 60 Squadron – whose aircraft had been retained in Malaya – and the Communication Flight equipped with aircraft of the Moth type belonging to the Burma Volunteer Air Force, there was at that time no further aircraft in the country. Reinforcing aircraft for the Far East were, however, flying through Burma to Malaya and the Dutch East Indies.

7. The American Volunteer Group, whose primary role was the defence of the

Burma Road, under the command of General (then Colonel) C.L. Chennault, was based at Kunming. A Squadron of the A.V.G. had been detached by the Generalissimo Chiang Kai-Shek for the defence of the Port of Rangoon, the only port through which supplies for China, could be passed.

8. Control of the R.A.F. in Burma had been somewhat chequered. Up to the I5th December, I94I, it was organised as Burgroup – later 22I Group – under A.O.C. Far East. On the I5th December I94I, this Group was transferred to the command of the C.-in-C. India. Almost immediately after my arrival in Burma 22I Group became Norgroup under the command of General Wavell, Supreme Commander South-Western Pacific Command, though remaining under the C.-in-C. India for administration. After the fall of Javar Norgroup reverted again to the Command of C.-in-C. India.

9. *Airfield lay-out and topography.* – Geographically, Burma is a cul-de-sac with a long tongue of jungle escarpment reaching South from Moulmein to Victoria Point. The Port of Rangoon therefore provided the only means of maintaining an Air Force in Burma, since on the West, Burma is cut off from India by the dense jungle escarpments of the Arakan Yomas, in the North by the Naga Hills, in the East by the Karenni Hills, while the Pegu Yomas, a mountain range, divides the waters of the Sittang and the Irrawaddy which flow almost their entire distance through Burma to Rangoon and the Gulf of Martaban. Thus there were two Valleys in which airfields could be made.

I0. The main line of airfields ran from Victoria Point to Moulmein, to Rangoon and Mingaladon and then up the Valley of the Sittang through Toungoo to the East, through Heho and Namsang and up to Lashio in the North, a total distance of some 800 miles. This line of aerodromes faced the enemy air force based in Thailand and because the territory to the East and South East of this line of air bases was mountainous country covered by jungle, through which there were few if any communications, it followed that situated here adequate R.D.F. and telephone warning of the approach of enemy aircraft attempting to attack our bases was impossible. Had Toungoo, Heho and Namsang been situated with their attendant satellites in the Irrawaddy Valley, warning would have been possible and satisfactory as long as the communications in the Sittang Valley remained in our hands. This fact gravely influenced the air campaign.

II. In general, the aerodrome development and construction undertaken on behalf of the Far East Command by the Government in Burma showed an extremely good state of affairs. Indeed, remarkable. All airfields had one or two all-weather runways fit for modern aircraft of the heaviest type. Accommodation for personnel, P.O.L. and bombs and ammunition were available and all-weather satellites were provided for most airfields. Moreover, at this time of the year the paddy fields were hard and, provided labour was available, a runway suitable for fighter or bomber aircraft could be prepared in a week. Thus airfield accommodation for a considerable air force was available in Burma. The weakness of the lay-out, however, was, as already stated, that the four main airfields between Toungoo and Lashio (inclusive) had little or no warning.

I2. *State of Warning of Air Attacks.* – It was hoped, however, to develop our telephone system in the Karenni Hills and the Valley of the Salween, and with R.D.F. to bring warning to a state where it would be practicable to base bombers and fighters at all these airfields. We asked India for the necessary equipment and personnel, including a W/T screen of 35 posts.

I3. *Airfield Accommodation.* – Consequently, from the point of view of airfields, there was nothing to prevent the reception of considerable reinforcements as long as we held Rangoon.

I4. As regards communications, a good telephone system connected all our airfields, while point-to-point wireless was in course of being put in to parent Stations.

I5. *Burma Observer Corps.* – I found the Burma Observer Corps under the command of Major Taylor to be, over the area covered, an efficient warning system. As long as main centres of communications and telephone lines were not closely threatened by land attack the system functioned devotedly and satisfactorily.

I6. In respect of aerodrome defence I found that outlying Station airfields such as Tavoy and Mergui had garrisons while detachments of troops for land defence and anti-sabotage precautions had been provided at occupied airfields.

I7. *A.A. Defence.* – A.A. defence was weak, with an initial strength of but one battery of locally raised troops, whose equipment had only arrived at the end of December, I94I. The later arrival of British and Indian light and heavy batteries rendered it possible to organise a weak scale of defence for the important vital points. Although the A.A. defence did yeoman service they were never in sufficient strength to provide adequate defence for all the vital points and areas – let alone our airfields. Except for a weak airfield detachment the A.A. Artillery was deployed in defence of vital points in Rangoon and of our troops so that some cover against enemy bomb attacks in forward areas could be provided. Later during the withdrawal they provided such close protection as was practicable for our columns. General Alexander has remarked upon this phase of the operations in his Despatch.

I8. *L.A.A. Defence.* – For light automatic defence against low-flying aircraft, detachments of the B.A.F., each equipped with I0 to I2 .5 Browning machine guns on A.A. mountings, were stationed at Mingaladon and Zayatkwin and later at Magwe. They were manned entirely by Burmese personnel mainly of the I2th Burma Rifles. Their training was of necessity hurried and their numbers were generally much under strength. Elements of the R.A.F. regiment arrived too late to be of much service although they were in action at Akyab.

I9. *Headquarters' Staff.* – The position as regards Headquarters and Station Staffs was not good. Only a nucleus H.Q. staff existed and Mingaladon was the only airfield having a Station H.Q. All other airfields had care and maintenance parties.

20. A store holding unit and an explosives depot existed but there was no repair organisation.

Air Appreciation – Strength of the Air Force in Burma.

2I. On the I4th January I completed my appreciation of the situation. Copies of this paper were forwarded to Headquarters, ABDA Command, India and the Air Ministry.

The object of this paper was to appreciate the likelihood of a determined attack being made by Japan on Burma and from this to deduce the form and scale of air attack; and thus the fighter force necessary to secure our interests against this attack and the bomber counter-offensive force that would also be necessary. From this it will be noted that I considered that the Japanese Air Force would attempt a "knock-out" blow against Rangoon in the event of the fall of Singapore and that the scale of attack might reach as much as 600 aircraft a day at maximum intensity.

22. *Air Defence.* – The air defence system necessary to secure our interests in Burma against an attack of this kind required that the fighter force should be on a 14 Squadron basis – 9 beyond the 5 Squadrons already on programme. (These 5 Squadrons were 67 Squadron and the 4 Squadrons of 267 Wing, which had been allocated in the first place to India for Burma – Trooper's telegram 57543 of 12.12.41.) One of these Squadrons – 232 Fighter Squadron – was later diverted from Burma. The fact that the Hurricane force comprised only 3 (which only reached a strength of 2 Squadrons) instead of 4 Squadrons during the initial phase of the campaign, had a serious effect on the operations.

23. Further heavy and light A.A. Artillery was necessary together with a Balloon defence for the City and Port of Rangoon. More R.D.F., G.C.I, and Observer Corps and W/T. posts were required for strengthening the warning system.

24. *Bomber Counter-offensive.* – As regards the Bomber offensive, I considered that the 7 Squadrons on programme would be sufficient (i.e. 60 Squadron already in Burma plus 6 reinforcing Blenheim Squadrons promised from the Middle East – Trooper's telegram 58315 of 16.12.41) until vigorous attacks against Japan from bases in China became necessary.

25. *Security of Sea Communications.* – The 1 Hudson Squadron on programme, provided we had a force of 2 Torpedo Bomber Squadrons to call on at seven days' notice would, I considered – together with the Bomber force – go a long way to secure our line of sea communications from attack by Japanese war vessels in the Northern portion of the Bay of Bengal and the Gulf of Martaban. Apart from one or two patrol craft there were none of H.M. ships present in these waters. Thus the burden of anti-submarine protection, anti-bomber security and the attack of enemy surface vessels in the Bay and the Gulf would rest for some time on the Bomber, G.R. and Fighter aircraft of my command.

26. *Reinforcement requested.* – After agreement in the Joint Commanders' Sub-Committee I accordingly telegraphed ABDA Command and the Air Ministry requesting reinforcements to the scale (A.418 of 18/1) recommended in my appreciation. On the 20th January ABDA Command (00186 of 20/1) informed the Air Ministry that while the reinforcements asked for were undoubtedly required, it was not known whether they would have to be found from the aircraft allotted to the South Pacific theatre. The full position was asked before agreement to allocate from the total pool was possible; – since the need in the Southern Malayan theatre was more immediate than that in Burma.

27. *Proposals for immediate Fighter reinforcement.* – On the 2nd February the Deputy Chief of the Air Staff telegraphed the Air Ministry's proposals for

reinforcements for Burma in the immediate future (Webber W.446 of 2/2). This approved an immediate reinforcement of 2 further Hurricane Squadrons, bringing the programme to 6 Hurricane Squadrons in all, but assumed that we should be able to re-equip 67 Squadron, with Hurricanes. There were never enough Hurricanes to do that. After the fall of Singapore on February 15th the Chiefs of Staff diverted these 2 Squadrons (30 and 26I Fighter Squadrons) to Ceylon. Thus the total Fighter force actually available throughout the air campaign in Burma was reduced to 3 Hurricane Squadrons.

28. *Initial Equipment of Hurricane Squadrons and the Hurricane Flow.* – The inability adequately to equip our Squadrons with Hurricanes and to maintain them during air action had a serious effect on the air campaign. For example, it led to a situation in which it was only possible for 6 Hurricane II's to take the air against the first heavy attack on our airbase at Magwe on 2Ist March – and except for I aircraft every Hurricane II in the Command was present at Magwe on that day.

29. The requirement initially to equip I7, I35 and I36 and to re-equip 67 Squadron was a total of 80 Hurricanes (i.e. I6 I.E. plus 4 I.R. per Squadron). Additionally, a flow of at least 24 per month was necessary to meet minimum war wastage. Therefore over the campaign which lasted three months, the total requirement was at least I28. During this period a considerable number of our Hurricanes due for Burma were diverted to Singapore. Thus of this total requirement only a proportion arrived in Burma and of these a number were obsolescent, worn-out Hurricane I's.

30. *Hurricane Effort.* – Consequently the maximum number of Hurricanes reached in action with the enemy was about 30 Hurricanes, i.e. the equivalent of 2 instead of 4 Squadrons. This strength, moreover, fell away rapidly due to lack of reinforcing aircraft, proper operational facilities and absence of spares, and was on IIth February I5 serviceable Hurricanes, and on 5th March only 6.

3I. *Maintenance, Spares and Tool Situation.* – With the exception of 2 Hurricane "pack-ups," no spares for the Hurricane II's arrived in the country before the fall of Rangoon. Consequently, aircraft becoming unserviceable for lack of small parts remained so unless requirements could be provided from the cannibalisation of other unserviceable aircraft. There was a great shortage of tools and rotol kits, while the lack of air screw-blades was serious. Moreover, since the equipment of our R.S.Us, and A.S.Ps. did not arrive before the fall of Rangoon, there was no proper organisation for the repair and salvage of aircraft. This factor exercised a considerable influence on our small fighter force and contributed towards the critical shortage of serviceable Hurricanes at Magwe on the 2Ist March.

32. *A.V.G. Maintenance.* – The A.V.G. Squadron at Rangoon usually had 2I P.40 aircraft of which about I5 would be serviceable. Later in March this figure fell to I0 or 7. But here again the shortage of replacement aircraft, spares, and proper maintenance for the A.V.G. reduced the effort available. The maintenance crews of the A.V.G. did remarkable work in maintaining their aircraft, often under bombing attack. As the A.V.G. were short of trained personnel, R.A.F. personnel were attached to them.

33. *Bombers.* – As regards Bombers, the D.C.A.Ss. telegram indicated that of the

7 Squadrons promised, we should only have 3 in the immediate future. This assumed that Blenheims would be available to equip 60 Squadron. There were never enough Blenheims to do that. The aircraft, personnel and "pack-up" of II3 Squadron arrived in January and early February. The aircraft of 45 Squadron (Blenheim) also arrived but were unaccompanied by personnel or "pack-up." There was a great shortage of tools and spares. Additionally, the R.S.U. and A.S.P. organisation did not arrive in time. Consequently, the average daily bomber effort of the combined Blenheim force stood at about 6 aircraft a day. Thus throughout the campaign, we had the equivalent of one Bomber Squadron available for operations instead of 7.

34. *General Reconnaissance.* – In respect of G.R. aircraft, No. 4 Indian Flight equipped with Wapiti and Audax aircraft arrived in Burma at the end of December. This was later replaced by No. 3 Indian Flight which was armed with an I.E. of 4 Blenheim I's. After the fall of Singapore, I39 Squadron en route for Java was held up in Burma and, equipped with Hudsons commencing at 6 I.E., undertook our G.R. requirements. There were no personnel or Squadron equipment and the Hudsons were maintained by No. 3 and No. 4 Indian Flights.

35. *Army Co-operation.* – 2 Squadrons armed with Lysanders, No. I Indian A.C. Squadron and No. 28 A.C. Squadron, were made available for operations in Burma.

36. Constant requests were made for the re-equipment of these Squadrons with modern aircraft. The Mohawks, however, were not available and the Lysanders were retained until the Squadrons returned to India.

37. *Indian Air Force.* – The units of the Indian Air Force referred to above proved their war efficiency and gallantry on active service. In addition to a number of tactical reconnaissances, No. I Indian Squadron's Lysanders provided 4I bomber sorties against enemy aerodromes and direct support targets. The standard of accuracy achieved in bombing was satisfactory. No Lysanders were shot down by enemy fighters. The G.R. aircraft and, in particular the Blenheim I's of No. 3 Flight, carried out a considerable number of reconnaissances in the Preparis Channel and the Gulf of Martaban.

38. *P.R.U.*[2] – Up to half-way through January there were a few Buffaloes in 67 Squadron with the necessary range. They undertook long reconnaissance. When these were finished we were without long reconnaissance until in the first week of February. 2 P.R.U. Hurricane en route for Java remained in Burma. These were attached to Hurricane Squadrons and met our P.R.U. requirements on an outline basis only.

39. *Balloons.* – An advanced party of 274 Balloon Wing arrived and reconnaissance of sites commenced. The Balloon Wing, which was diverted from Basra, did not arrive in time and, in consequence, balloon defence was not available.

40. *R.D.F. Warning.* – Of the considerable programme of R.D.F. in Burma (3 chain stations 2 C.O.L. and 2 G.C.I.) only one C.O.L. set was in the country, the balance not having arrived. This one was at Moulmein, but its arc of observation there was ineffective. It was therefore moved out for the defence of Rangoon. It was later moved to Magwe. No spares of any kind existed for this set but local arrangements were possible to keep it in action until it left Rangoon. The lack of adequate R.D.F. equipment of the M.R.U. or Chain Station and C.O.L. type exerted a critical influence

on the air battle in Burma, since *early warning* of low flying fighter attack and high flying bomber attack was an essential quality of successful air operations. Without such warning an air force inferior in numbers – as ours constantly was – faced annihilation as indeed later happened at Magwe.

41. To summarize under this heading: Of the Air Ministry programme of 6 Fighter Squadrons, 7 Bomber Squadrons, 2 A.C. Squadrons and I G.R. Squadron for the defence of Burma – for various reasons – principally that of time – only the mixed equivalent of 2 Fighter Squadrons, I Bomber Squadron, 2 A.C. Squadrons and one-third G.R. Squadron joined action with the enemy in the campaign. Of 7 R.D.F. Stations only I existed.

42. As regards other units, the following arrived:-

H.Q. 267 (Fighter) Wing.
No. 60 R.S.U.
No. 39 A.S.P.
No. 7 S. and T. Column.
No. 258 A.M.E.S.

The R.S.U. and A.S.P. had no equipment, and the A.M E.S. arrived so late that it was turned round at Rangoon, sited to defend Akyab, and finally withdrew to Calcutta where for many critical weeks it remained our primary means of warning for oversea attack.

43. Personnel for Group H.Q. Staff gradually arrived and Station H.Qs. Zayatkwin, Toungoo and Magwe were formed.

Co-operation.

44. *Co-operation between the Services.* – As regards the co-operation between the four Services, I have to record that Sir Reginald Dorman Smith, H.E. the Governor, was always ready to assist me with wise advice and his Government was at my service with active and energetic help so long as was practicable.

45. General Hutton's Headquarters and mine lay close together at Rangoon. I gratefully record the good feeling and understanding he extended to the R.A.F. which made possible close co-operation. We usually met each morning and evening to review the situation, and to agree action. At these meetings there was an interchange of important telegrams which had been received or despatched by us. The same cordial relations continued when General Alexander took over on the 5th March.

46. Our co-operation with Commodore Graham, R.N., and earlier Capt. Hallett, R.N., was all that could be desired. Although there were none of H.M. ships present in the close defence of Rangoon and Tenasserim, there were many maritime tasks to be undertaken from day to day by aircraft and the few patrol craft that were available.

47. *Co-operation with A.V.G. and the American Air Force.* – I took the earliest opportunity of meeting Colonel (now Brigadier-General) Chennault in Kunming on the 31st January. At this meeting we discussed and agreed the principles on which the A.V.G. Squadron in Burma would be used in air-battle. As always, his primary requirement was good warning. He was quite clear that if I was unable to provide

this for the A.V.G. the Squadron would have to be withdrawn to China. I have to record my appreciation of the way in which General Chennault wholeheartedly maintained the Squadron at the highest practicable level in pilots and P.40's from his fast dwindling resources in China. On the 18th January so bad were these that he issued instructions for the Squadron to be withdrawn to China. The Supreme Commander was informed and the Generalissimo, Chiang Kai-Shek, after the representations of the combined Chiefs of Staff, agreed to the retention of the A.V.G. in the defence of Rangoon. Elsewhere I have remarked upon the admirable gallantry and fighting characteristics of the 3 Pursuit Squadrons of the A.V.G. – who fought over Rangoon in turn – an admiration felt not only by the R.A.F. but by the Army also. The co-operation between the A.V.G. and the Hurricanes was close and cordial.

48. When bombing operations in Burma were later carried out from India, a small force of American Army Air Corps long range bombers closely co-operated.

49. *Co-operation with the Chinese.* – I took the first opportunity of visiting the Generalissimo, Chiang Kai-Shek, on the 30th January. The Generalissimo very kindly gave me an interview on this day at which he promised to maintain I Squadron of the A.V.G. in the defence of Rangoon as long as this was possible. It is a matter of great regret to the R.A F. that towards the end of the campaign in Burma it was impracticable on account of shortage of aircraft and the effect of the air battle for the R.A.F. to give adequate support to the Chinese Armies deployed in Burma.

PART II
STRENGTH AND EQUIPMENT OF THE JAPANESE AIR FORCE ENGAGED IN BURMA.

50. *Enemy Air Effort.* – In the opening stages, from the Ist January onwards, P.R.U. reconnaissance and information from other sources put the enemy air force within close range at I50 plus, bomber and fighters – an effort of (say) I00 plus. They were disposed as follows:-

Prachaub Girikhan	10
Mesoht }	
Tak }	40+
Bangkok	70+
Lampang }	
Chiengmai }	30+

Our effort on the 3Ist January was 35 plus.

5I. Reinforcement of the enemy air force took place during February. The strength of the enemy air force which joined action with up rose to 200 plus – an effort of (say) I40 plus

disposed at:-

Bhisanuloke	20 +
Bangkok	30 +
Nagorn Sawan	20 +
Tak and Mesoht	20 +
Moulmein	30
Chiengmai	40 +
Lampang	40 +

Our effort on February I4th was 53 plus.

52. Singapore fell on the I5th February and Rangoon on the 7th March. During this period and up to the 2Ist March the enemy had again brought up reinforcements, bringing his total air force, based largely on our airfields in the Rangoon area South of Tharrawaddy and Toungoo, to 400 plus – an effort of (say) 260 plus. This was the opinion of the Intelligence staff at Burwing. I considered it on the high side.

53. Some corroboration for this, however, is provided by the fact that intelligence from China and other sources has since indicated the presence in Burma and Thailand of some I4 air regiments of the Japanese Army Air Force. This would comprise a force of 420 to 500 plus aircraft.

Our total effort on March 2Ist when the Magwe action commenced was 42, of which I4 were at Akyab.

54. *Japanese Fighter equipment.* – Of Japanese fighter equipment there were three types: the Army 97 with a fixed undercarriage; the Army 0.I (an Army 97 with slightly improved performance and a retractable undercarriage) and the Naval "O" fighter. The former two were manoeuvrable with a top speed of 270 miles an hour at I5,000 feet and a climb of 2,500 feet per minute. Armament consisted of 2 machine guns. No self-sealing tanks and no armour were fitted. Similarly, the Navy "O" had neither armour nor self-sealing tanks. It had, however, two 20 millimetre machine guns in addition to 2 machine guns of the Vickers' type. This aircraft was much superior in performance to the Army 97, having a top speed of 3I5 miles an hour at I0,000 feet, a good climb and good manoeuvrability. It was, however, slightly inferior to the P 40 and the Hurricane II, particularly at medium heights. At heights above 20,000 feet the Hurricane II was definitely superior.

55. All three types were convertible to long range fighters with a radius of over 500 miles. Two jettisonable petrol tanks were fitted. Even without such tanks both types were superior in range to our short range interceptor fighter having a radius of action of over 250 miles instead of the I35 miles of the Hurricane II.

56. *Japanese Bomber equipment.* – In respect of bombers, the Army 97 heavy bomber was mostly employed. It had a cruising speed of about 200 miles an hour, a radius of action of 700 miles and a service ceiling of 25,000 feet. With a full load of petrol its lift was I½ tons of bombs – a formidable bomber. Indeed such range and bomb lift placed great flexibility in the hands of the enemy air command. This type was used for day bombing and occasionally for night bombing operations, and had a crew of 7. No self-sealing tanks nor armour were fitted.

57. Although air fighting frequently took place over scrub or jungle country, 32

crashed enemy fighters and bombers were located on the ground up to the fall of Rangoon. Technical examination of these – although many were burnt or otherwise destroyed beyond recognition – established the quality of equipment about which little was previously known.

58. *Effect of equipment.* – Thus the enemy with their long range fighters were able to reach out over great distances and to destroy our first line aircraft on the ground. There were decisive instances of this kind in the Malayan campaign. Consequently unless airfields, both for bombers and fighters, had a good warning system – i.e. a time warning the equivalent of at least 50 miles – the enemy fighters, achieving surprise, would come in and by deliberate low flying attacks and good shooting could be relied upon to cause great damage to first line aircraft, if not indeed to destroy them all. This form of attack could well be met by a good ground defence, including an adequate number of Bofors (predictor controlled), automatic weapons and P.A.C., but in the campaign in Burma we were extremely weak in these forms of defence.

59. As regards bombers, such range and bomb lift gave the enemy a wide choice in the selection of objectives and great flexibility. If warning of such attacks, particularly those carried out at high altitude, was not adequate, a bomb lift of considerable weight, accurately aimed, could be expected on the objective. Operating in formations of not less than 27, such a pattern of some 27 tons of small light A P. and H E. bombs causes great damage to first line aircraft and P.O.L., even though dispersal and anti-blast protection has been provided. If such protection is not provided results may well be decisive and the provision of such protection requires time and labour – two needs that in the hurried movement of war may not be available.

60. *Comparison of Air equipment.* – Thus we were much inferior to the enemy; in the first place in numbers, in the second place in the vital factor of restricted range in our fighters, in the third place range, bomb lift and speed of our bombers. The enemy, on the other hand, suffered the grave disadvantage of not having armour and self-sealing tanks, both characteristics of all our types, while from the point of view of the air battle, the Hurricane II was a much superior fighter to the Army 97, slightly superior to the Naval "O" and quite decisive against such ill-defended bombers as the Army 97. The P.40 was comparable to the Hurricane II, particularly in medium altitude fighting. With its fine clean dive and armament of .5's it could be relied upon to do as much damage or more to the enemy than the Hurricane II – especially as the air battle usually took place at medium altitude heights below 19,000 feet.

6I. As regards bombers, the Blenheim with its power-operated turret gave a good account of itself against enemy fighters – only on one occasion was a Blenheim known to be shot down by enemy fighters. This, however, was mostly due to the provision of fighter escort to bombing raids or careful routeing which would give the bomber formation the best chance of avoiding enemy fighter interception.

62. *Conclusion.* – To sum up on equipment, fighter for fighter we were superior and it was only when heavily outnumbered, and without warning and proper airfield facilities, that the enemy were able to get a decision. Their bombers were "easy meat" for our fighters if interception took place, while our bombers were satisfactory for

their task, though light on range and much inferior to the enemy in bomb lift and numbers.

PART III
THE AIR SUPERIORITY BATTLE OVER RANGOON.

63. *Situation.* – From the initial attack carried out by the Japanese air force on the 23rd December against Rangoon and the second attack which followed 48 hours afterwards, in which the bomber formation on both occasions numbered between 70 and 80, with escort of some 30 fighters, it was obvious to me that I had against me at close range a Japanese air force of about I50 plus. A severe set back had been inflicted on the enemy in these two attacks by the P.40's of the A.V.G. and the Buffaloes of 67 Squadron and not less than 36 enemy first-line bombers and fighters were claimed as destroyed on these two days. The situation, therefore, that faced me on my arrival on Ist January was that I must with my small but growing fighter force defend the base facilities at Rangoon, the docks, the convoys arriving and departing and the air bases at Mingaladon and Zayatkwin. If these could be preserved from a damaging scale of day bombing attack, we should be enabled to secure our interests hereabouts and to get in our land and air reinforcements and maintenance. Additionally, I should have to be prepared to aid the Army in any operations they undertook with both fighter and bombing action.

64. *Plan.* – Thus my general plan was to keep my fighter force concentrated in the Rangoon area, to accept such enemy bombing attacks as might be made on any other objectives in Northern Burma, to fight the enemy in the defence of the base and lean forward to hit the enemy wherever and whenever I could with my small but total force.

65. To achieve this, against a numerically superior and constantly growing air force, I must do all I could to reduce the scale of air attack on the Rangoon area, yet still be able to meet attacks on the bases in sufficient force to inflict a high casualty rate proportional to the scale of attack – thus making such attacks in this area abortive and wasteful for the enemy.

66. *Reduction of the scale of attack.* – To reduce the scale of attack I therefore commenced to lean forward with a portion of my fighters, and by using advanced air bases like Moulmein, Tavoy and Mergui to attack enemy aircraft wherever found. Further to weaken him I must spread my bombing action in daylight to widely dispersed but important objectives such as Chiengmai, Mehohngsohn and Chiengrai in the North and in the South his aerodrome and railway communication system running down the Eastern coast of the Malaya Peninsula from Bangkok to Singora. As Singora was a main base for Japanese operations in Malaya this action was especially favourable. Thus I hoped to make him disperse his fighters by forcing protection for these widely separated points and so weaken him in the central sector opposite Rangoon. I gave instructions accordingly on 2nd January.

67. *Offensive Fighter and Bomber action.* – Such enemy airfields as Chiengmai,

Mehohngsohn, Lampang, Rahong, Mesoht, Prachuab Girikhan, Jumbhorn and Kanchanburi were searched and attacked if enemy aircraft were present. Later when in enemy hands Moulmein, Mingaladon and Highland Queen were attacked and loss inflicted on the enemy. Hangars, M.T., launches, enemy troops and trains were also attacked.

68. *Results.* – Attacks in pursuance of this policy during the campaign resulted in the P.40's and Hurricanes and Buffaloes claiming 58 enemy bombers and fighters destroyed on the ground. In addition, a large number were damaged but could not be computed. Furthermore, attacks by bombers taking part in the air superiority battle also accounted for a considerable number. Such, however, is the difficulty of assessing results by bomber attack that no claims were made; but from the strike of the bomb lift and its position either amongst or close to enemy aircraft concentrations on the ground, further considerable losses must have been inflicted on enemy first-line aircraft.

69. This was a handsome contribution towards the air superiority battle in Burma and reduced the scale of air attack against Rangoon and our troops.

70. But this form of action was later reduced in effort, since General Chennault at this time was not anxious to undertake offensive operations with the P.40's against ground targets on account of the shortage of equipment. The Buffalo Squadron was reduced to two or three serviceable aircraft with engines too worn out to permit of flying far over jungle country. The Hurricanes with an effective range of I35 miles were unable to reach anything but the closest enemy objectives.

The Air Battle.

7I. The air battle over Rangoon lasted from 23rd December, I94I, until 25th February I942. The weight of enemy attack was directed intermittently against air bases at Rangoon with the object of destroying our growing fighter force and achieving air superiority over Rangoon to the point where it would be possible for him to undertake unrestricted day bombing operations on a destructive scale.

72. During this period of about 8 weeks, 3I day and night attacks were made – one in great weight. After sustaining serious losses – 38 claimed destroyed – in the first 3 attacks terminating on the 4th January, the enemy resorted to night bombing, his scale of effort varying between I or 2 heavy bombers up to I6.

73. *Scale of attack brought to rest.* – Between 23rd and 29th January a second attempt was made to overwhelm our small fighter force, the enemy putting in a total of 2I8 plus – mostly fighters. In the air battle of those 6 days our fighter force claimed a total of some 50 enemy bombers and fighters destroyed. He at once went back to night operations and continued these until his third and last attempt to achieve air superiority over Rangoon on the 24th and 25th February. On those two days, when he put on a scale of attack of I66 bombers and fighters, he sustained the heavy loss of 37 fighters and bombers which were claimed destroyed with 7 probably destroyed. On the second day, the 25th, the P.40's of the A.V.G. claimed no less than 24 aircraft shot down. This terminated the air superiority battle over Rangoon.

74. Such wastage had been inflicted on the enemy that thereafter he never

attempted to enter our warning zone round Rangoon until the city was captured and the air bases in his hands.

75. *Result.* – This had a critical influence on the course of our land operations and on the security of our convoys bringing in final reinforcements. These and the demolition of our oil and other interests in the port and the final evacuation by land or sea were completed without interference from enemy bomber or fighter aircraft.

76. Thus up to the last moment the P.40's of the A.V.G. and the Hurricane force were able to provide a state of absolute air superiority over this wide and vital area against a considerable weight of air attack.

77. *Conclusion.* – To sum up on the air superiority battle over Rangoon, for a force of I Squadron of P.40's of the A.V.G., a half Squadron of Buffaloes and the equivalent of 2 Squadrons of Hurricanes commending to arrive in January and continuing to half-way through February, a claimed loss of I30 enemy bombers and fighters was inflicted on the enemy with 6I claimed as probably destroyed – the greater proportion falling to the guns of the A.V.G. Counter-offensive action by our fighters and bombers to reduce the scale of attack had inflicted a loss of not less than 28 enemy aircraft destroyed on the ground, not counting those destroyed by our bombing attacks. Air superiority was achieved over Rangoon and maintained until it fell on 8th March. The A.V.G. – first in the field – fought with ready devotion and resolute gallantry.

Fighting Tactics.

78. In regard to the major tactics employed in the air battle over Rangoon, in the first place the warning was good. As long as the telephone lines remained in our hands the Burma Observer Corps provided this with high war efficiency. The R.D.F. set from Moulmein had been sited in Rangoon looking over the main avenue of enemy approach. Thus enemy plots were accurate and frequent until the line of the Sittang was threatened.

79. *Fighter deployment.* – Fighters in the correct proportion could be deployed against the enemy scale of attack. The A.V.G. and the Hurricanes fought together. The Wing leader system was introduced. The pilots of the A.V.G. had considerable flying experience. Some of the pilots, particularly the leaders in the Hurricane force, had considerable war experience against the G.A.F. Consequently, the force fought well together. In the operations room there were two R/T. sets for the control of the air battle on different frequencies – one for the American fighters and one for the Hurricanes.

80. The general principles of fighting the air battle were agreed between myself, the Wing leader and the Commander of the A.V.G. Pursuit Squadron, and the major tactics employed were those generally exercised in the Western theatre; the single point of difference being that on account of the manoeuvrability of the Japanese fighter (which was the only advantage it had over our aircraft), the best method of attack was a dive, taking advantage of height and the sun, breaking away in a half roll or aileron turn before resuming position to carry out the attack again.

8I. Enemy escorted bomber raids were met on first interception, the bombers were attacked with a suitable proportion of our forces while the fighters were attacked and drawn off by the remainder. Against the fighter formations of (say) 40 to 60 plus, which so frequently appeared at height with the object of drawing up our fighters and shooting them down before they got their height, the P.40's and the Hurricanes leant back on Rangoon and delivered their attack when the enemy fighters either lost height, with the object of carrying out a ground attack, or turned for home.

82. Throughout this air action from the 2Ist January onwards the fighter force in addition to defending Rangoon had also to meet its commitments over the battle area, providing security for our bombers and carrying out ground attacks on enemy concentrations in support of the Army.

83. *Night Fighting.* – As regards night bombing, there were no facilities for night interception. Although the enemy bombers were operating without flame dampers, and at first with navigation lights burning, the P.40's and Buffaloes were not able to intercept. On the arrival of the Hurricanes, trained in night fighting, however, some success was achieved. On the first night an enemy bomber was shot down in flames at 9,000 feet over the aerodrome at Mingaladon, the aircraft, with bombs, exploding close to the airfield. Two further successful night interceptions were made, both enemy aircraft being shot down in flames. With pilots at constant readiness throughout the hours of daylight, however, it was impossible in view of our limited resources to put the Hurricanes up each night.

84. I have no doubt that on moonlight nights – and the enemy bombed on no other – considerable success would have been obtained from the "fighter night" system, had Rangoon held.

85. *Assessment of Fighter Results.* – There was a little feeling in the A.V.G. on the assessment of results. Consequently I held a meeting with the A.V.G. Squadron Commander, and the Wing leader and Squadron Commanders, at which it was agreed that the standard of assessment should be that obtaining in Fighter Command at home. Colonel Chennault was informed. Combat reports by pilots were initialled by Squadron Commanders. The claim was then admitted. Previous claims by the A.V.G. for aircraft destroyed in the air were agreed at this meeting.

PART IV
THE LAND BATTLE – AIR OPERATIONS IN SUPPORT OF THE ARMY IN TENASSERIM.

86. *Situation at Sea.* – After the fall of Singapore and Java the Japanese had command of the sea in these waters. There was no effective naval force of ours based in the Bay of Bengal. Thus the littoral of Burma was thereafter under the threat of sea-borne invasion unopposed by the Navy. Consequently, reinforcement by sea of the Japanese Army in Burma took place unmolested after the fall of Rangoon. This was a vital factor in the defence of Burma.

87. The Joint Commanders' Committee telegraphed on several occasions pressing for the provision of ships and material to provide some further local defence at least for the Port of Rangoon and for light craft to support our operations on the coast of

the Gulf of Martaban and Tenasserim. No ships were, however, available and none arrived – except those which escorted our convoys.

88. *The Land Situation.* – The land situation, which influenced air operations, has been fully described in the Despatches of Lieutenant-General Hutton and General Alexander. It is not proposed further to remark on this except in so far as it is necessary in order to make clear the influence of air superiority fighting and bombing action on land operations and vice versa. I should, however, make the point that until Mergui and Tavoy fell on January I9th, I assumed the security of Burmese territory from attack by the Japanese Army based in Thailand.

89. *Daily Planning of Close Support Operations.* – Bomber and fighter action in support of the Army during the land campaign up to the fall of Rangoon was decided each evening at a general staff and air staff Conference held at my Headquarters. General Hutton and I met morning and evening to agree joint action and review the changing situation. Subsequently, the programme was adjusted according to the requests made by the I7th (Indian) Division, to which an Air Liaison Officer had been attached. Communication was by W/T. and telephone. In general, the system worked satisfactorily.

90. *Tenasserim unsatisfactory for Bombing Operations.* – Close support bombing operations in the close jungle country in Tenasserim and to the East of the River Sittang was an unsatisfactory task for the R.A.F. At the request of the Army we undertook bombing operations in jungle country where it was impossible to see the enemy or to see our troops, – indeed difficult to see anything except the tops of the trees. In such circumstances not only is the objective not seen but it is impossible for navigators to pin-point their target with accuracy since there are no suitable land marks. The situation is made more difficult still by the knowledge in the mind of the crew that our positions were frequently outflanked by the enemy and therefore there was always the chance that our troops and the enemy were intermingled near the objective. When attempts were made to give bombing objectives in forest clearings, crews often found on arrival that such clearings were overgrown with scrub and consequently the same difficulties arose. As, however, our forward troops in the jungle on the Kawkareik position and during the battle of Tenasserim had reported the enemy's promiscuous bombing of the jungle to be effective and as having considerable moral effect, I did not hesitate, while realising the risk to our own troops of bombing in such densely wooded country, to continue the task in order to do our best to help the Army.

9I. Further obvious difficulties arose from the bombing point of view. For example, the enemy was frequently disguised in captured uniforms and native dress. This made recognition difficult. Moreover, they captured some of our transport during actions, while the native bullock carts, launches and private cars left behind and other vehicles were used freely. This made it difficult, and sometimes impossible, for crews to recognise the enemy in the open. Unsatisfactory, therefore, as the "bomb line" method was in such circumstances of cover, communications and moving battle, it had to be adopted as our primary security against the risks of attacking our own troops.

92. *First requirement – Army support.* – The fundamental requirement for the

support of the Army in Tenasserim was the maintenance of air superiority over the Port of Rangoon, and the bases and supply depots in this vicinity. This secured the line of communication from serious bombing attack in the form and scale best calculated in this campaign to bring about a critical if not disastrous situation. Consequently I kept my small fighter force concentrated in the defence of Rangoon with the satisfactory results noted above.

93. *Security of Bombers and Fighter support for Army.* – From day to day, however, security for our bombers acting in support of the Army was necessary, since few as they were their destruction by enemy fighter action would have brought about a serious situation. Consequently, each day a careful appreciation of the air situation was made and a portion of the fighter force was thrown off from the Rangoon defence to undertake the Army support role. Indeed, when a particularly favourable ground target presented itself, I accepted the risk of an attack on Rangoon, and all fighters, with what bombers were available, were thrown in to support the land battle. The point here is that where the command of the fighters and bombers is undivided, such operations are practicable and close co-ordination between fighter and bomber operations can be readily achieved.

94. *Bombing of Bangkok.* – The aircraft and crews of II3 Squadron had arrived during the first week in January. The night of their arrival the enemy base at Bangkok, the main enemy base in Thailand, was attacked by I0 low flying Blenheims. II,000lbs. of bombs were dropped on the dock area in the centre of the town and fires were started. The Squadron was then withdrawn to Lashio to enable aircraft inspections to be carried out after its long desert flight. Owing to the shortage of tools and spares, it was the I9th January before the Squadron was in action again.

JAPANESE OFFENSIVE BEGINS.

Mergui and Tavoy.

95. On the afternoon of the I8th January the situation at Mergui and Tavoy suddenly deteriorated and I was informed by the B.G.S. Burmarmy that instructions had been issued for the evacuation of Mergui. I accordingly ordered the withdrawal of our refuelling parties from both aerodromes, and as Tavoy was closely invested, an attempt was made to evacuate our detachments by air. On arrival of the aircraft the following morning the aerodrome was, however, in the hands of the enemy. Both detachments were safely evacuated by sea.

Action at Kawkareik.

96. Concurrently with this, reconnaissance beyond the Kawkareik position on the track through Mesoht and Raheng had disclosed some, but not unusual activity. We had also destroyed a number of enemy bombers and fighters on both these forward landing grounds. The country was densely covered with jungle and unsuitable for air action since movement on the ground could not be seen from the air.

97. On the 20th the enemy commenced their attack on the Kawkareik position. Air action in support of the troops holding this position was difficult, since no clear picture of the whereabouts of the enemy or our own troops was possible. Accordingly the enemy forward landing ground and base depots at Mesoht was attacked by bombers and fighters. Two enemy aircraft were destroyed on the aerodrome. Reconnaissance was carried out over this position and towards Tavoy in the South with the object of locating our own troops and the enemy.

98. The withdrawal from the Kawkareik position to Moulmein took place on the 22nd January. On the 2Ist and 22nd the Blenheims attacked Raheng aerodrome and village and Mesarieng, dropping some 6,000 lbs. of bombs on each raid. Fighter escort was provided with the object of clearing the air for short periods over the Army front and providing support for the bomber operations. Moulmein was bombed by a strong formation of enemy escorted bombers which was intercepted by the escort of our bomber raid on its outward journey – an occasion on which our attempt to choose the right time proved correct. Seven enemy bombers and 9 fighters were destroyed in this air action. Reconnaissance was continued over the battle area.

The Action at Moulmein.

99. On the 30th January the Japanese attacked Moulmein. Our forces were disposed holding Moulmein and the right bank of the Salween from Pa'an, southwards, with one Brigade in the Bilin area. During the period between the 23rd January and the 30th, frequent low visual reconnaissance by fighters was carried out covering the battle area and the coast of Tenasserim together with Japanese lines of communication. Information obtained, however, was sketchy owing to the nature of the country and the fact that, in open country, the enemy lay close in the day time and moved by night. Our available bomber force – an average of about 6 a day – with the aid of such fighters as could be spared from the defence of Rangoon, acted in support of our land forces in the area.

100. Our bombers and fighters attacked enemy aerodromes, M.T., and the enemy line of communication, through Kawkareik, Myawaddy and Mesoht, while the enemy main base at Bangkok was attacked again on the nights of the 24th, 27th and 28th. In these operations a total of 42,I00 lbs. of bombs were dropped.

I0I. Limited escort to our ships coming into Rangoon, anti-submarine patrols and G.R. reconnaissance in the Gulf of Martaban were carried out from day to day.

I02. The fighter support which was provided over the Army forward positions each day on a limited scale had accounted for at least 7 aircraft shot down and I3 damaged (to end of January). Our losses were slight.

I03. The main objective of the Japanese air force, outside the Rangoon area, during this period, was Moulmein, which was attacked on 7 occasions between the 3rd and 22nd January. The first attack was carried out by 9 fighters, and the later ones by bombers, in pairs by night, and in formations up to 27 in number by day with fighter escorts of up to I5 aircraft, the chief target being the aerodrome.

The Action on the Bilin.

104. From the 30th January until the 15th February, when the 17th Division took up a line on the Bilin River, all available bombers were employed in direct Army support with the maximum number of fighters it was practicable to spare each day. Bombing operations took the form of support to our hard pressed detachments. Attacks were made on river craft on the River Salween and off Moulmein with both bombers and fighters. The fighter effort available was employed in attempting to intercept at this great distance from its base the enemy raids on our forward positions, and providing security for our bombing operations. During this period river craft, batteries, enemy concentrations, troops, landing stages, railway stations and barracks and stores were attacked. A total weight of 70,136 lbs. of bombs were dropped on these objectives, with successful results. Most of the bombing was carried out from a low altitude and, in consequence, the results could be seen, provided objectives were not in the jungle. The raids were carried out on such places as Kado, Martaban, Pa'an, Moulmein, Minzi, Heinze, the Thaton Road and the Dunzeik Road. The fighter effort diverted from the Rangoon defence in support of the Army and bombing operations was usually from 6 to 12 per day and sometimes sorties were repeated.

105. During this period the Japanese air force continued night activity against Rangoon on a small scale up to the 8th February. Daylight operations, apart from support of their land forces, comprised 4 attacks on Toungoo aerodrome by raids of 6 to 15 bombers on the 3rd and 4th February. From the 8th to the 12th enemy bombers attacked our troops between Pa'an and Thaton, but generally with little effect.

The Battle of the Sittang.

106. The withdrawal to the Bilin River commenced on the 15th February, and this position was attacked by the Japanese on the 17th. On the 18th the River had been crossed and the withdrawal to the Sittang position commenced. On the 22nd our forces had reached the right bank of the Sittang.

107. During this period air operations continued at the maximum intensity practicable in support of the Army. The air battle of Rangoon still continued. With the loss of Moulmein we lost our forward air base in this area. Consequently, air operations, both fighter and bomber, were carried out from the main airbase at Rangoon. Furthermore, with the capture of territory by the enemy, our warning system in Tenasserim was rapidly rolled up. Now warning of the approach of enemy raids over Tenasserim was impossible. For the defence of Rangoon we still had observer posts to the East of Rangoon, while our R.D.F. set provided some warning. But the interception of enemy aircraft supporting the Japanese Army was impracticable unless such attacks took place when our fighters were present over the line.

108. The Supreme Commander, General Sir Archibald Wavell, visited the command during the last week of January and on the 5th February. At these meetings I explained the air situation and our urgent need for reinforcements, particularly the acceleration of the 2 reinforcing Hurricane Squadrons which had been promised and

for an allocation of 24 Hurricanes per month from the flow. As regards bombers, I asked for 2 further reinforcing Blenheim Squadrons, for I6 Blenheims to equip 60 Squadron and for I2 Blenheims a month from ABDA Command flow of maintenance aircraft, and additionally for the Mohawks to re-equip the 2 Lysander Squadrons. General Wavell said that he would do what he could to meet these requirements, but explained the pressing need for air support in Malaya and the N.E.I.

I09. During the period I6th to 23rd February the maximum effort that could be put forward by the bombers was I02 sorties, in which 89,992 lbs. of bombs were released in low flying attacks on the enemy, accompanied by machine gun fire. Such objectives as the railway station at Moulmein, troop concentrations and M.T., river traffic and aerodromes were bombed. Direct hits on such things as trains and paddle steamers in Sittang were observed. Fighter support for the Army and the security of our bombers continued.

Air Action on the Bilin-Kyaikto Road.

II0. For the first time in the campaign the enemy provided a satisfactory bombing target. On the 2Ist an enemy column of some 300 or more vehicles, ox-carts and M.T. was reported on the road between Bilin and Kyaikto. The "bomb line" ran North and South through Kyaikto. The total fighter effort of the Rangoon defence and what bombers were at readiness were ordered to attack at I6.25 hours. The first sortie off was one of I2 P.40's at I6.30, closely followed by 8 Hurricanes at I6.40. A total of 38 fighter sorties and 8 Blenheim sorties were engaged in the attack. Direct hits were reported on M.T. and horse transport accompanied by many fires. The village of Kyaikto through which the column was passing was also set on fire. At I6.25 hours the Army Headquarters moved the "bomb line" to a line running North and South 2 miles West of Kyaikto.

III. The enemy had during the afternoon of the 2Ist penetrated through the village of Kyaikto and moved along the road running North to Kimmun. That afternoon their infantry were seen by the Duke of Wellingtons West of this road (and North of the Kyaikto Road). Their thrust that night at the Sittang Bridge took place up this road when they worked round our left flank and attacked the Bridge in the rear of the I6th and 46th Brigades. It is evident that although our air attack in some weight on the enemy's main column could not have entirely prevented his attack from developing, it must have reduced its scale and intensity.

Alleged bombing of own Troops.

II2. There was an incident reported on this day and remarked upon in Army reports. It is alleged that our troops at Mokpalin were bombed and machine gunned by some Blenheim aircraft between I2.00 and I5.00 hours. The facts are that at the request of Army Headquarters 8 Blenheims bombed Kawbein (near Bilin) in the morning and landed back at their base after mid-day. After an exhaustive enquiry, in which I have taken the opinion both of Officers who were in the air and on the ground, I have failed to reach a firm conclusion that our aircraft did, in fact, bomb our own troops at this time and place. The enquiry is complicated by such statements as "the attacking aircraft were identified by roundels on the underside of their wings" – our Blenheims have roundels on the upper side of the wing but certainly not on the underside, and the possibility that the Japanese used captured Blenheims during this campaign should be considered. There is, moreover, a great similarity between the plane silhouette of the Japanese Army 97 medium bomber and the Blenheim, and there must have been a number of enemy bombers flying over Mokpalin about this time because the enemy effort was concentrated on the Sittang area, a few miles to the West of Mokpalin. Since, however, the country between the Rivers Sittang and Bilin is closely covered in jungle, I consider it not improbable that some crews by mistake may have bombed the wrong objective. The enemy effort reached on this day a total of 90 fighters and 12 bombers in action in the Sittang area. The Sittang Bridge was the scene of the heaviest attacks.

II3. In the meantime, Mandalay had its first attack by 10 bombers on the 19th.

II4. *G.R. Escort for Shipping.* – Such escort to shipping, G R. reconnaissance and coastwise search in the Gulf of Martaban as was practicable was carried out with the slim effort available. Fighter support against bomber attack was provided once our convoys came in range.

II5. To extend the range of our reconnaissance for this purpose and to give forewarning of enemy naval movements in the direction of the Andaman Islands it was decided to locate reconnaissance aircraft at Port Blair. The construction of a landing ground in the Andaman Islands presented some difficulty, but after considerable work it was possible to construct a runway of 800 yards at Port Blair. The only type of reconnaissance aircraft available that could be operated from such a base was the Lysander and 2 of these aircraft were fitted with long range tanks and flown over escorted by Hudsons on the 11th February. These aircraft were able to carry out reconnaissance until the Andamans were evacuated.

II6. Daily coastal reconnaissance was also carried out throughout the campaign against possible Japanese attempts to attack our Army by landing behind them. Such an attack did happen on one occasion – at night.

II7. This concludes the air operations carried out in support of the Army in Tenasserim.

Air Directif – ABDA Command.

II8. On the 17th January air directif 0087 from Headquarters, South Western Pacific, was issued to Norgroup. This gave our primary tasks as:-

(*a*) To secure the arrival of reinforcements and to protect the Port of
Rangoon, and

(*b*) *To* reduce the scale of air attack on Malaya.

Subsequent directifs received from ABDA Command related more to the battle in the South Western Pacific than to operations that could be based in Burma.

PART V
AIR OPERATIONS COVERING THE
EVACUATION OF RANGOON.

II9. In February it seemed to me that the troops available in Burma might be unable to hold the country against the form and scale of land attack which the Japanese were exerting through Tenasserim. This question was discussed in the Joint Commanders' Committee on several occasions. Our forward air bases at Mergui and Tavoy had fallen. The Moulmein airfields had been captured. Our warning system East of the Sittang was in enemy hands.

I20. At this time the fighter force and bomber squadrons building up in Burma comprised the only Allied air force between the Japanese and India, indeed between the Japanese and Middle East. Had we had time to establish and consolidate the forces in passage from the U.K. and Middle East comprising personnel, equipment, maintenance and warning system, there would have been a good chance of presenting a firm front to the enemy air force with their inferior equipment. On the other hand, if the Port of Rangoon fell into enemy hands in March or April, the flow would stop, and there was a grave possibility that our air force might well be destroyed piece-meal in Burma before it was strong enough and had time to organise. Such a defeat in detail could be of no help to the Army in Burma and would uncover India at a critical time.

I2I. The question therefore arose as to whether plans should not be prepared to prevent the annihilation of our force by moving our base to India and providing it with strong mixed Wings in Burma maintained from India. Thus dispersed, air support could be given to the Army in Burma and bombers based in India could support operations in Burma. Such action, moreover, would contribute to the air defence of India in her critical and naked sector.

I22. On the I2th February I therefore telegraphed ABDA Command, A 677 of I2/2, indicating that in the unlikely event of the loss of Rangoon administrative plans might be necessary to enable fighter equipment to be withdrawn, and requesting a directif as to whether the R.A.F. units should proceed with the Army North towards China or whether they should proceed in the direction of India for the defence of Calcutta and North Eastern India. I pointed out that if they were withdrawn to the North there was no adequate warning on the airfield line Toungoo-Heho-Namsang-Lashio and that the forces there located would therefore be open to fighter attack without warning when on the ground. If withdrawn to Calcutta they could provide a strong defence. R.D.F. cover could be provided. Once separated from Rangoon (the only point through which maintenance for an air force could pass) the force instead of building up to its planned size would become a wasting force. In China there were few or no facilities for operating our bombers and fighters, whereas with lay-back bases in India and forward bases and strong detachments in Northern Burma, bomber and fighter action in support of the Army could continue. No reply was received to this telegram.

I23. On I5th February Singapore fell.

I24. On the I8th February, General Hutton sent off his telegram 0.749 of I8/2 which indicated the possibility that the enemy might penetrate the line of the Sittang and that the evacuation of Rangoon might become an imminent possibility. Consequently, in view of this serious situation, I telegraphed my appreciation in which I set out the factors of the air situation and indicated three courses of action. Firstly, to remain with the Army during the move northwards towards China. In these circumstances the R.A.F. units would have become a wasting force, since maintenance would be difficult if not impossible once Rangoon had fallen, while heavy losses for small return would be inevitable in the event of reinforced enemy scale of attack. Secondly; to withdraw the air force to India when Rangoon was closely threatened. The final course was to leave a mixed force of I Hurricane Squadron, I Blenheim Flight and I Army Co-operation Flight, withdrawing the remainder of the force to India. No reply was received to this telegram.[3]

125. On the 20th February instructions were given for the withdrawal of the I7th Division behind the River Sittang. A meeting was held at Government House at which General Hutton and I were present. The G.O.C. stated that he had instructed the Commander of the 17th Division to fall back behind the Sittang. He outlined the steps that he proposed to take in this situation in regard to commencing the evacuation scheme of Rangoon and the establishment of Rear Headquarters at Maymyo.

126. Our Rangoon air bases were closely threatened. The warning facilities except for limited R.D.F. and Observer Corps observation had practically gone. As a result of this meeting the G.O.C. despatched his telegram 0.792 of 20/2.

Decision to organise base landing grounds in India with mixed Wings in Burma.

127. I therefore telegraphed Headquarters ABDA Command indicating the situation described at this meeting. There was no time to be lost. General Hutton agreed with me that the only course open to us to maintain our effort in support of the Army in Burma – once our airfields and warning at Rangoon had been lost – was to establish base landing grounds in India, operational landing grounds at Akyab and Magwe with advanced landing grounds in the Rangoon area to provide what fighter and bomber support could be given. Failing immediate instructions to the contrary, I proposed in my telegram putting this plan into action.

128. Arrangements were accordingly made to leave a mixed Wing one Hurricane Squadron, one Blenheim Squadron and half an Army Co-operation Squadron, organised as a mixed Wing, with one Squadron of the A.V.G. in Upper Burma, based at Magwe, one mixed Wing of one Hurricane Squadron, one Bomber Squadron and one G.R. Squadron at Akyab and to build up and feed these two Wings from a base organisation in India.

129. The decision which set the size of the Wing left at Magwe was based on the amount of maintenance in the country on the 20th February. It was calculated by the staff that there was sufficient maintenance in this mixed Wing for a period of three months. As regards Akyab, access by sea was still open and maintenance therefore would be satisfactory. There was no overland communication between Magwe and Akyab. The route from India in the North down the Manipur Road had not been completed.

130. The decision to base the force in Northern Burma at Magwe was made because it lay behind two lines of observer corps telephone lines, one down the Valley of the Salween towards Rangoon and the other down the Valley of the Irrawaddy. It was proposed to attempt to evacuate the R.D.F. set if Rangoon fell. By this means it was hoped to provide sufficient warning at Magwe to secure the base against anything but the heaviest scale of attack. Since Singapore had fallen on the 15th February the weight of the Japanese air force could now be turned towards Burma. I therefore expected that if Rangoon fell, with the considerable number of airfields now prepared in the Rangoon area, heavy reinforcement of Japanese aircraft would be flown in at will to Burma. The enemy would have control of the communications and the free use of the Port of Rangoon and thus a large air force could be maintained.

131. I received no reply to my telegram.[4] Action was commenced. I had received a personal telegram from Air Headquarters, India on the 19th in which the A.O.C.-in-C. informed me that if the necessity arose he had prepared a plan for the withdrawal of my force to India. On the 20th we requested air transport to be flown to Magwe, whence it would work a shuttle service between Magwe and Akyab. Onward transport of personnel from Akyab would be by sea. The personnel to be evacuated numbered some 3,000, the majority of whom were in the Rangoon area. A proportion were moved by sea, the remainder by air.

132. On the 21st the Postmaster General reported to me that the telephone system in Rangoon would cease functioning at 18.00hours that day. Except, therefore, for our single R.D.F. set – worn-out and of the wrong kind – there would be no warning for the defence of Rangoon and our airfields. Arrangements were at once made to man the observer centre in the Central Telegraph Office with R.A.F. personnel. This limited warning continued until within a few days of the fall of Rangoon.

133. Beyond the general statement by the Army that in the event of the evacuation of Rangoon they would proceed to the North and generally in the direction of China, there was always the element of doubt as to whether they would proceed to China or fall back towards the Manipur Road and so towards India. Rear Headquarters had been established at Maymyo and stocks were being back-loaded up country to the Mandalay – Maymyo area. The initial line of withdrawal, I had always been informed, would be along the Prome Road, a road 150 miles in length.

134. Our air bases in general lay on the other main route to the North – up a Valley of the Sittang. The main railway system ran through this Valley to Mandalay and branched to Myitkyina in the North, and Lashio in the N.E. The Burma Road lay along the same route to Mandalay and Lashio.

135. In consequence, from the air point of view the Prome route was unsatisfactory since there were no air bases of any kind of withdrawal between Rangoon and Mandalay suitable for the operation of modern fighters and bombers with high wing loading – except Magwe, and that had no accommodation, no pens and no dispersal. Indeed the only other aerodromes were at Myitkyina, 600 miles to the North (runway incomplete) and Meiktila – our depot of the future – where a runway was finished. But Meiktila was rather too much to the North and East to be effective in the initial stages and had only slight warning facilities.

136. I had foreseen the possibility of having to operate my mixed fighter and bomber effort in what might well be – and later proved to be – a tense situation, in which the Army would be attempting to withdraw along this single line of communication. There would be no opportunity of dispersing off the road and no cover from air attack. Accordingly, I had a series of strips cut into the hard paddy land along this line of communication and on the Ist March, when the C.-in-C., India, visited Rangoon, I was able to report that I was prepared to operate on this route.

137. But operating a numerically inferior force from such landing grounds against a weight of air attack without adequate warning was a risky and fortuitous operation. Thus I had grave doubts about our ability to maintain ourselves in being. But when and if this situation arose we should have done our best to secure the Army against enemy air action.

138. Against this threat, therefore, the location of our "kutcha" strips had been kept as secret as possible and a very useful number had been prepared in the vicinity of Mingaladon and towards the North and West up the Irrawaddy to Prome.

139. At night all first-line aircraft, bombers and fighters, were flown off the parent airfields at Mingaladon and Zayatkwin to "kutcha" strips. Thus the location of our fighting force, when based on such temporary airfields, was not readily obvious to the enemy. Pilots and air crews were motored into their accommodation. They arrived at the "kutcha" strip before dawn the next morning to fly their aircraft. This we found the only method of ensuring secrecy of the strips and the security of equipment from the damage caused by night bombing. With large numbers of small bombs the enemy's night bombing of Mingaladon was accurate and effective. If Rangoon were to be evacuated when the warning had entirely gone, I proposed to guard the security of my fighters by the use of these strips, and evacuate the parent airfields. The bombers on account of their range could operate from Magwe and refuel and rearm in the forward area, but the fighters with an extreme fighting range of 135 miles would have to be brought back along the Prome Road in steps of some 50 miles so that security could be provided for our retiring columns.

140. All preparations practicable were made to improve the warning system at Akyab and Magwe, but with the time and resources available this proved to be a hopeless task. Furthermore, much work was necessary at Magwe to make it a satisfactory base, and labour was difficult to get. The provision of satellite "kutcha" strips was, however, undertaken to provide dispersion. Magwe, although it had a runway still under construction, had been a civil air port and, since it lay in the back area of Burma was not intended in the general plan to be an operational aerodrome. Anti-blast protection in the way of pens or dispersal arrangements had not been started. Had, for example, Toungoo been situated where Magwe was, it would have been a different story and the situation in regard to P.A.D. measures would have been much more satisfactory for the operation of a mixed Wing.

141. Final preparations to continue to fight the battle over Rangoon, and for the withdrawal to the North, were taken in hand at once. Rear Headquarters was opened up at Magwe on 22nd February with forward Headquarters in Rangoon.

Formation of " X" Wing.

142. To control the fighter action and the bombing offensive action in support of the Army throughout this phase, I formed an "X" Wing Headquarters under the command of Group Captain Noel Singer, D.S.O., D.F.C., with a strong staff, reasonable communications, and good mobility. The role of "X" Wing was to maintain air superiority over Rangoon until the demolitions of the oil interests at Syriam and Thilawa, the docks, power stations, munitions and stores had been completed and until the Army had withdrawn from the area and thereafter to provide air superiority over the area in which the Army was moving, until it reached Prome.

143. The detachments on Toungoo, Heho, Namsang and Lashio would continue in operation to enable limited air action to take place in support of the Chinese, while a landing ground was' prepared at Mandalay to serve Rear Headquarters at Maymyo. A scheme was drawn up to enable detachments to be withdrawn from forward aerodromes should the situation necessitate – with preparations for the evacuation of equipment, stores, etc. Arrangements had been made with Army Headquarters that in these circumstances all petrol and oil would be handed over to the Army for the use of the Armoured Brigade and M.T. columns.

144. On the 23rd February the Sittang Bridge was blown. Except on the days on which the enemy had thrown the weight of his attack against the Rangoon defence, his bombers and fighters flew over their forward troops advancing through the jungle. Air action was carried out against our troops intermittently on most days. As explained previously, we did the best with the slim fighter resources available to support the Army in this respect.

145. On the next two days, the 24th and 25th, the final attack was made by the Japanese Air Force on the Rangoon defence system with the object of attaining air superiority over the area. As noted elsewhere, this failed in a signal manner and severe casualties were inflicted on the enemy. Thereafter, until the fall of Rangoon, his fighter force was occupied purely defensively over the area in which his advance was taking place, formations of up to 40 plus, operating each day. When possible, therefore, in order to keep them on the defensive, bombing operations were carried out in the area in which the enemy fighters were working. We attempted to make interceptions but with no great success, since their fighter effort was only over the area of operations at certain times. On the 23rd, however, a message was received from the 17th Division and interception did take place in which 2 enemy aircraft were shot down.

146. Our fighter effort which had built up to no less than 44 – Hurricanes and P.40's – on the 17th February, dwindled away after the air battle on the 24th and 25th and after our air operations over Tenasserim to a low mark of under 10 on the 28th February, due to the lack of maintenance, spares and the number that were "shot up" in the air battle. The figure, however, gradually increased again to 27 on the 4th March, but fell to an average of about 17 aircraft from this date until the 10th March.

147. As regards bombers, the effort built up to 16 on the 17th February and fell away during the battles in Tenasserim to a low mark of under 5 on the 25th February for exactly the same reasons as described above. It built up, however, to 12 aircraft

on the 28th February and to an average of about I0 serviceable from that time until the I0th March.

The Battle of Pegu.

I48. On the 23rd February I visited the I7th Division at Pegu with General Hutton. The Armoured Brigade had now arrived and was mostly deployed in this area. The enemy used the hours of darkness to cross the Sittang and pressure was exerted against our forces at Waw on the 26th February. Between this time and the 5th March the battle developed.

I49. On the 4th March General Alexander arrived at Magwe. He flew down with me to Rangoon. I accompanied him on his visit with General Hutton to the I7th Division at Pegu. The enemy had engaged our forces round Pegu and an infiltration in strength, accompanied by light tanks, had taken place to the North through the jungle country of the lower Pegu Yomas in the direction of the Prome Road – our line of communication. This movement was observed by low flying Hurricanes on reconnaissance. The 63rd Brigade had been accepted and General Alexander planned the last stand in the defence of Rangoon. Throughout this action which terminated on the 8th March with the completion of the demolition and the final evacuation of the Port of Rangoon, an interesting air situation arose.

I50. It was of paramount importance that the last vital demolition on a big scale should be completed without the interference of hostile aircraft and that the movement of the Army which was disposed astride the Pegu Road and in Rangoon should be enabled to give last cover to demolition parties and to withdraw as planned through the cross-road at Taukkyan and North up the Prome Road. The Army was tied to the road on account of the nature of the country and the fact that it was mechanised.

I5I. As already noted, the air actions over Rangoon on the 24th and 25th had inflicted severe casualties on the enemy air force. From that day until the evacuation of the Army from Rangoon had been completed, until all our convoys and ships had left the Port in security and until our demolition parties had been withdrawn, no enemy bomber attempted to enter what had previously been our warning zone round the airfields of Rangoon, i.e., roughly a circle 40 miles in radius from the centre of the town.

I52. I can only assume that when their last effort to establish air superiority failed, the enemy air force were determined not to incur further wastage until Rangoon fell. Consequently the demolitions and the withdrawal of our forces from Rangoon took place in a state of absolute air superiority.

I53. As regards the enemy effort in the battle of Pegu, air attacks took place against Maymyo, Toungoo and Bassein, whilst considerable activity was maintained over the battle area.

I54. On the 2nd March I gave instructions for the R.D.F. station, which had been made mobile to move to Magwe, to provide some R.D.F. warning for our new air base. Consequently, when the telephone observer corps system collapsed there was no warning in the area except that provided by observation from military points and airfields.

155. To offset this to some extent a "Jim Crow" Hurricane was kept over Rangoon by day.

156. During this critical phase, fearing that my fighter force might be caught on the ground and destroyed by surprise low flying fighter attack, I had moved them out to a newly prepared "kutcha" strip at Highland Queen from which offensive fighter patrols were maintained. To give the impression that the force was still at Mingaladon, wrecked aircraft fuselages and dummies were parked in the readiness position on the runways.

157. During this critical phase to the 7th March, the bomber effort was directed against the enemy wherever he could be found. The fighters accompanying the bomber raids came down to shoot up enemy objectives. 96,800 lbs. of bombs were released, and a considerable number of fighter offensive and protective sorties carried out. Such objectives as enemy troop concentrations, trains, boats on the Sittang and M.T. columns were attacked with satisfactory results. The bombers operated from Magwe aerodrome using Highland Queen and John Haig as advanced bases.

158. General Sir Archibald Wavell, now Commander-in-Chief, India – to which Command Norgroup had reverted – visited Burma on the 1st and 2nd March. A meeting was held at Magwe on the morning of the 1st March in which the Commander-in-Chief reviewed the land and air situation. At this meeting H.E. the Governor, General Hutton and myself were present. I described the air situation and the need for reinforcing Hurricanes and Blenheims. With Rangoon now closely threatened, with our warning non-existent, with a slender fighter force of 20 serviceable Hurricanes and a few Buffaloes, with the A.V.G. force standing at 4 serviceable aircraft at Magwe, it was a position in which I said we should be unable to deny the enemy fredom of air action; while our bombing effort in support of the Army would be limited to the efforts of our quickly dwindling force of 16 bombers.

Attack on Highland Queen.

159. On the 6th, an enemy formation of about 20 plus aircraft which was flying over the Japanese troops advancing through the jungle towards the Prome Road over-shot its mark and, by accident and without warning, arrived flying low over Highland Queen where our fighters, some bombers and some G.R. aircraft were on the ground.

160. Fortune attended us on this occasion. The enemy shooting was bad and some Hurricanes were able to take off. Although no claims were made there were indications that 2 enemy fighters were damaged or destroyed. Two aircraft of ours were destroyed on the ground. The anti-aircraft defence of the aerodrome went into action satisfactorily. This was a raid which might well have been a decisive end to our small air force.

161. I immediately issued instructions for all aircraft to fly in from Highland Queen to Mingaladon, whence our last sorties were carried out.

162. Infiltrations by boat had taken place up the River Rangoon. Offensive action by our fighters was taken but movement continued by night. On the afternoon of the 6th March I left Wing Headquarters, Rangoon, and flew to my Headquarters at Magwe.

163. Our fighter force had for some days been split between Magwe and the forward bases round Rangoon, Highland Queen and Mingaladon. The Hurricane force which was then standing at about 15 aircraft was a mixed one comprising commanders and pilots of 17, 135 and 136 Squadrons, and operating from the forward bases was maintained from Magwe, where maintenance inspections were carried out. The P.40's of the A.V.G. which had done such sterling work were now suffering from acute unserviceability due to lack of spares and replacement aircraft. I therefore placed them in the defence of the air base at Magwe. This made good my promise to General Chennault that I would not employ them at airfields without adequate warning.

Evacuation of Rangoon.

164. I had been with General Alexander until 14.00 hours. He had told me of his decision to evacuate Rangoon, and the code word for blowing demolitions and evacuation was issued just before midnight on 6th March. With his agreement I moved Headquarters "X" Wing from Rangoon to Zigon, the first "kutcha" strip from which we would operate in support of the Army's withdrawal along the Prome Road. A small party of Officers and airmen were left behind to complete the demolition of the operations room and the facilities at Norgroup Headquarters. They were then to go on to Mingaladon and help to complete the demolitions at this airfield. This party came out with the Army.

PART VI
AIR OPERATIONS COVERING WITHDRAWAL
UP THE PROME ROAD.

165. There was a heavy haze on the 7th and 8th, which interfered with observation by fighters, made worse by the great pall of smoke from the burning oil which rose to a height of 15,000 feet and was blown North over the area of operations as far as Tharrawady. General Alexander's force failed to dislodge the road block at Mile 22 on the 7th, but on the morning of the 8th was able to overcome this resistance, and the withdrawal of our Army commenced North up the Prome Road.

Operations from Zigon.

166. The rough surface of Zigon proved unsatisfactory for Hurricanes. I had to decide whether to risk damaging Hurricanes – which when damaged might not be repaired – or to operate the fighters from Magwe where their range would not have enabled them to provide security over our troops. The following day from Zigon the fighter effort was maintained.

167. The column of our withdrawing Army was reported by aircrews to be some 40 miles long, mostly M.T. vehicles and tanks – an admirable target for enemy bomb action in country where there was little or no cover from air attack and no possibility of getting off the long straight tarmac road.

168. But the state of air superiority finally established on 25th February still continued. Fighter patrols were carried out over the line from Zigon to Rangoon. The Army, without molestation from the enemy air force, was thus able to take up and consolidate its position on the Petpadan – Tharrawaddy line.

169. As regards fighter sweeps to secure the withdrawal, the Hurricanes at Zigon carried out about I2 to I8 sorties a day until "X" Wing had withdrawn from Prome to Magwe on the IIth March. It was then disbanded on the formation of Burwing at Magwe. Group Captain Singer, who arrived on the I2th March, took over the command of Akwing, which was then in formation at Akyab.

170. Operations from Zigon resulted in the tail unit of a Hurricane giving way on an average of I in every 5 landings. A bamboo skid was fitted to the tail of the Hurricane which then took off and landed at Magwe for repair. 2 Buffaloes were badly wrecked by the aerodrome surface and were eventually burnt. I Blenheim and I Lysander were also rendered unserviceable, but were repaired and flown out before the airfield was left.

171. The sole Japanese air attack driven home at this time was directed against the town of Tharrawaddy, where the bomb lift of I0 bombers was disposed of on civilian quarters causing a number of civilian casualties.

172. G.R. Reconnaissance in the Gulf of Martaban and the Bay of Bengal continued and escort was provided for the last convoy which carried detachments and demolition parties. All ships got safely away.

Operations from Park Lane.

173. The range for fighters was now shortened and, consequently, "X" Wing moved to Park Lane, a "kutcha" strip North of Prome. This move was completed on the night of the 9th March. The enemy did not locate and attack the fighters at Zigon or Park Lane.

174. Fighting continued and on the 25th March the Army had taken up their position on the Prome line, with the Ist Bur. Division's move from Toungoo to Allanmyo in progress.

175. During this period, from the 7th March to the 2Ist March, the bomber force was either held in readiness for close support of the Army or attacks were made in order to reduce the scale of air attack and so aid the fighters in their task of security. Attacks on enemy objectives in support of the Army were also carried out. A total of 3I,500 lbs. of bombs was released with good results on such objectives as troop concentrations, aerodromes, road and railway communication and river craft. Constant reconnaissance was carried out over the entire front towards Rangoon and in the Valley of the Sittang, while a close watch was kept on our old air bases in the Rangoon area and at Moulmein for signs of the arrival of the enemy air force and reinforcements. Some effort, however, was wasted because bombers available were held standing by for objectives which the Army did not provide.

176. The enemy attacked Toungoo on the I7th March and carried out reconnaissance of our airfields up the Burma Road, Tangan, Namsang, Nyaumglebin and Meiktila – obviously searching for our air force.

Formation of Burwing.

177. Burwing, comprising No. 17 Hurricane, No. 45 Bomber Squadron, the elements of an Army Co-operation Flight, 1 weak A.V.G. Squadron and the R.D.F. Station, had been formed at Magwe under the command of Group Captain Seton Broughall. This was a fully mobile mixed Army support force which, by instructions from Air Headquarters, India, was placed under the operational control of General Alexander on the 18th March.

Air Directif – 9th March.

178. On the 9th March I flew to Akyab to meet Air Marshal (now Air Chief Marshal) Sir Richard Peirse, the Air Officer Commanding-in-Chief, Air Forces in India.

179. The Air Officer Commanding-in-Chief issued a Directif in which I was told to maintain my two mixed Wings at Magwe and Akyab and to support the Army in Burma and to organise the air defence of Calcutta, Asansol and Tatanagar in India, and of Digboi oil installation in Assam; also to continue from India offensive bombing operations in support of the Army in Burma. Additionally, a further role of the force was reconnaissance and the attack of enemy surface vessels in the Bay of Bengal in aid of the security of our sea communications.

Formation of Akwing.

180. My Headquarters were moved from Magwe to Akyab on the 12th March, where I commenced forming Akwing. On the 17th this Wing comprised 135 Squadron, armed with obsolete Hurricane I's and 1 Hurricane II, a G.R. Flight and a small air communications detachment. It was proposed to make good the warning (R.D.F.) and to build the Wing up with 1 Bomber Squadron (113 Squadron) when Blenheims became available from flow and 1 G.K. Squadron (139 Squadron) when Hudsons became available.

181. On the 17th March I flew to Calcutta to meet the Commander-in-Chief and the Air Officer Commanding-in-Chief. My Headquarters was in process of opening in Calcutta.

PART VII
REVERSE INFLICTED ON MIXED
WING AT MAGWE.

182. On the 22nd March I returned to Burma to inspect Akwing at Akyab and Burwing at Magwe. On landing at Akyab I received a telegram from Group Captain Seton Broughall to say that the enemy had attacked Magwe in force the previous day. This was immediately followed by a signal telling me that heavy attacks had recommenced and closing the aerodrome to approaching aircraft. He reported that nearly all the first-line aircraft had been written off or damaged and asked for approval to move to Lashio and Loiwing to refit. I telegraphed agreement and flew on to Mandalay where I arranged for Group Captain Seton Broughall to meet me.

The Bomber Attack at Mingaladon.

183. Examining this action in full detail:- On the 20th March reconnaissance carried out by Burwing had disclosed concentrations of the enemy air force taking place in the Rangoon area. More than 50 aircraft were reported on our old airfield at Mingaladon. Group Captain Seton Broughall decided to attack the following morning in an effort to reduce the scale of attack in Burma which his intelligence staff had put at 400 plus in all. A raid of ten Hurricanes and nine Blenheims of 45 Squadron accordingly took off. The Blenheims were intercepted by enemy Naval "O" fighters 40 miles North of Rangoon and fought their way in to Mingaladon. The Bomb lift of 9,000 lbs. with stick adaptors was dropped on the runways among the enemy aircraft. The formation fought their way back to Tharrawaddy. During this gallant engagement in which 18 enemy fighters were encountered the Blenheims shot down two enemy fighters and claimed two probably destroyed and two damaged. Most of our aircraft were shot up but none were shot down. There were no casualties to personnel except one pilot wounded.

Low Flying Fighter Attack on Mingaladon.

184. The Hurricanes carried out a low flying attack. Nine enemy fighters were claimed as destroyed in air combat while 16 enemy bombers and fighters were destroyed or damaged on the ground. This was a magnificent air action. Some Hurricanes were badly shot up while one crashed on our side of the line through lack of petrol, following combat. O.C. Burwing intended to repeat the attack that afternoon, but while final preparations were being made for this sortie, the enemy commenced their considerable attack on the air base at Magwe.

185. It should be appreciated that on this day at Magwe all serviceable operational aircraft, fighters and bombers, of my command were present with the exception of one Hurricane II and nine worn-out Hurricane I's, ex O.T.U., at Akyab.

Enemy Attack on Magwe Begins.

186. Over a period of some 25 hours, commencing at 13.23, Magwe was attacked in force by the enemy. In all, the scale of attack reached about 230 fighters and bombers, which included 166 Army 96 and 97 medium and heavy bombers. It is calculated that a great weight of bombs, some 200 tons, were accurately released in patterns during this attack.

187. Similar attacks had been carried out against Rangoon without decisive effect. But at Rangoon there was good warning and the number of fighters available against such attacks was usually 20, rising on occasion to the high figure of 45.

Fighter Effort.

188. 21 fighters were present at Magwe when attacked, but as a direct result of the air action which had been fought over Mingaladon in the morning, the number of serviceable aircraft at readiness to take to the air was only 12. It should here be mentioned that the leaders and many of the fighter pilots at Magwe had been at two minute readiness day after day, from dawn to dusk, for a period of some eight weeks.

Warning.

I89. The only observer corps system remaining to the East and South-East was the observer post belt as far South as Toungoo and Prome on the main line of communication, reporting through Mandalay, and a chain of posts on the railway line Pyinmana-Kyaukpadaung which reported direct to Magwe operations room over an R.A.F. W/T. link. There was no observer corps system to the West and North-East of Magwe – an outflanking avenue used by the enemy during this attack. The R.D.F. set was of wrong type, its arc of observation was to the South-East. The equipment had given three months hard service and no spares had been available. The warning was weak and unreliable.

The Enemy Air Action.

I90. At I3.00 hours on the 2Ist March, a report was received of a single unidentified aircraft approaching and two Hurricanes were sent off to intercept, but were unable to make contact. At I3.23 hours the approach of an enemy formation was confirmed and all available fighters took off. But they numbered only four Hurricanes and six P.40's. At I3.30, 2I bombers escorted by ten fighters attacked, bombing and machine gunning the airfield. Our fighters intercepted and destroyed four enemy aircraft with one probable and one damaged, but the weight of the attack got home and considerable damage resulted in which communications were destroyed.

I9I. The enemy followed this up with further raids at I4.I0 and I4.30. In all the scale of attack was 59 bombers and 24 fighters that day.

I92. On the 22nd March, plots of movements were received from the R.D.F. set at 08.04 and 08.II hours. Immediately afterwards there was a temporary breakdown of the W/T. link which, combined with interference, prevented the reception of plots in the operations room until the enemy attack had developed at 08.45 hours. Two Hurricanes had been sent off to intercept a high flying enemy reconnaissance aircraft heard over the airfield at 08.30. They had not yet made contact when at 06.47 hours 27 bombers with an escort of ten plus fighters appeared over the aerodrome, followed a quarter of an hour later by a second wave of 27 bombers also with fighter escort. As no warning of these raids had been received, no further fighters were sent off to engage. The two Hurricanes already in the air engaged the Japanese formation and damaged two.

I93. Considerable damage was sustained. The runways were rendered unserviceable, communications were broken down and a number of aircraft, both bombers and fighters, were destroyed on the ground.

I94. Immediately afterwards, the Commander of the Second Pursuit Squadron, A.V.G. reported to Group Captain Seton Broughall that in view of the absence of warning and the scale of attack he was compelled by the terms of his instructions from General Chennault to withdraw his remaining flyable aircraft to refit. At this stage of the action only three P.40's and three Hurricanes remained flyable, the Hurricanes alone being operationally serviceable. The A.V.G.'s P.40's withdrew to Loiwing that afternoon followed by their ground party.

I95. At I3.30 hours reconnaissance aircraft were again reported approaching and two of the three remaining Hurricanes were sent up but failed to intercept. While they were returning to land at I4.30 the enemy again commenced his attacks with two waves of 27 and 26 bombers respectively, each accompanied by fighter escort. This terminated the enemy's attacks.

I96. Great damage had been done and 9 Blenheims and at least 3 P.40's were destroyed on the ground, 5 Blenheims were unserviceable, while 3 Hurricanes had been destroyed in air combat. The remaining 20 aircraft (6 Blenheims, 3 P.40's and II Hurricanes) were flyable but unserviceable due to normal un-serviceability or damage from enemy action. These aircraft, except the P.40's, were flown out to Akyab.

I97. This grave reverse to Burwing – the R.A.F. detachment in Upper Burma – was the result of our weakness in fighters, the weakness of the warning system at Magwe and the complete absence of aircraft pens and bad dispersal arrangements at this airfield so hurriedly occupied. There has been a good deal of criticism of the subsequent hasty move of Burwing from Magwe, while it had an adverse effect on the morale of both the Army and the civil population.

I98. The convoy left Magwe for Lashio and Loiwing early on the morning of the 23rd. Salvage and refuelling parties were left behind.

I99. On the nights of the 22nd and 23rd respectively, I met General Alexander and Group Captain Seton Broughall at Maymyo. It was confirmed that Burwing would be withdrawn to Lashio and Loiwing – the only remaining aerodrome where fair warning existed – for refitting.

200. In the meantime it was proposed to try and make good the warning at Magwe, to put it into a proper state of defence and fit for Burwing to return there for operations. As the convoy had already left Magwe I issued instructions for the R.D.F set to be turned round and sent back to Magwe and for the salvage and working parties at Magwe to be strengthened.

20I. Loiwing was the only airfield left with reasonable warning and therefore the proposal to leave Magwe and to refit at Loiwing was not unsound despite the great distance of the latter airfield from the area in which the Army was operating. By use of the advanced landing grounds, limited support could be given to the Army until the defence at Magwe was satisfactorily completed and the aerodrome reoccupied. At Lashio warning was weak.

202. As events turned out it would not have been possible to reoccupy Magwe since the airfield fell into enemy hands 3 weeks later and the organisation of the warning system and the provision of works – for which only limited labour then existed – could not have been done in time. Additionally, the observer corps belt in the Sittang Valley and the Valley of the Irrawaddy was gradually being rolled up and with it any warning from this source.

Enemy Action – Akyab.

203. The enemy had also found our small force at Akyab. A similar action took place which commenced on the 23rd, was repeated on the 24th and on the 27th. Our fighters

intercepted on 2 occasions inflicting a loss of 4 enemy aircraft destroyed and 3 probably destroyed for a cost of 6 Hurricanes.

204. Although warning was received on the 27th, low flying enemy fighters caught our small force unprepared on the ground on this occasion. 2 Hurricanes got into the air and engaged, I being shot down. 7 Hurricanes were destroyed on the ground and a Valencia. Instructions had already been issued by Air Headquarters, India, to withdraw Akwing from Akyab to Chittagong as warning was so weak. Akyab would continue to be an advanced landing ground for refuelling aircraft and to enable our Hudson reconnaissance to reach the Andaman Islands. A small R.D.F. set with a limited range of 20 miles, had been flown in and was operating, but the observer corps warning for Akyab was poor. The posts were few, only the outlines of communication existing owing to the difficult nature of the country.

205. These two actions – at Magwe and at Akyab – in effect terminated the R.A.F. activities based in Burma. The supply of aircraft now became the critical factor. The necessity to build up our defence in North Eastern India and Ceylon brought about a decision by the Commander-in-Chief, India, not to re-equip Burwing. The maintenance of a small force in Burma was uneconomical in view of the lack of warning and increasing weight of attack.

Indeed, such air forces of ours operating in these circumstances would be destroyed piecemeal, giving but small returns for considerable losses.

206. Burwing continued, however, as an organisation, and although bombers were flown in to Lashio and Loiwing to operate for a few days and return to Calcutta, very little could be achieved. Eight Hurricanes that were flown in on 6th April lasted only a few days in the face of Japanese attacks on Loiwing.

207. With the reverse that the Chinese 5th Army sustained on the Southern Shan front on 20th and 21st April which led to the rapid advance of the Japanese to Lashio, Burwing was withdrawn to China to provide British refuelling parties at main Chinese air bases. The personnel of 17 Squadron were withdrawn via Myitkyina to take their part – re-equipped with Hurricane II's – in the Calcutta defence.

208. But using the depth towards India, our bomber operations were continued on a slight but growing scale. Much remained still to be done for the support of the Army and the evacuation of our wounded and civilians.

PART VIII
WITHDRAWAL OF BURMA ARMY TO INDIA.

209. General Alexander's Army moved from the oil field area through the dry zone of Upper Burma to Mandalay with Headquarters at Shwebo, the final withdrawal taking place across the River Chindwin through Kalewa and over the Manipur Road through Tamu. The Army passed through the forward screen of 4th Corps troops on the Lochao pass on the 18th May and General Alexander's force finally reached Imphal on the 20th May.

210. The enemy air force now extended their patrols over a wide area in Northern

Burma and carried out attacks on Lashio, Mandalay, Loiwing and Meiktila. Support was given to their forces operating against our Allies in the Taunggyi and Mawlaik areas whilst flying boats based on the Andaman Islands commenced attacks on shipping in the Bay of Bengal between 28th March and 5th April.

2II. The Japanese reinforcement of Burma took place during the first week in April. Under the cover of a vigorous attack on Ceylon and on our shipping in the Bay of Bengal on 6th April a convoy of ships reached Rangoon. We were powerless to prevent this. Fortress aircraft of the U.S.A.A.C., however, attacked with five and a half tons of bombs an enemy force in the Andamans and straddled a cruiser and a transport. Further night flying attacks were carried out on the enemy convoy at Rangoon with useful results – fires and explosions being seen in the dock area.

2I2. During the eight weeks from 2Ist March,when the Magwe action took place, until May 20th, when the Burma army was finally withdrawn to India, action with bombers and fighters continued against the Japanese in Burma.

2I3. The fighter action was limited to such fighter sorties as could be carried out within the range of the Mohawk Squadron based at Dinjan. Bomber action was exerted either from aerodromes in Assam – Tezpur and Dinjan – or from bases in the Calcutta area, using Chittagong as a forward landing ground. One hundred and three tons of bombs were released on the enemy in these attacks. On arrival in Eastern India Squadrons were reformed and aircraft reconditioned slowly but as quickly as possible.

2I4. On the I2th April the first attack was made in support of General Alexander's right flank, when 9,000 lbs. of bombs were dropped on Japanese troops at Nyaungbintha. The enemy and his transport were also attacked at Singbaungwe, Allanmyo, Magwe, Sandoway and Taungup. In all 15,000 lbs. of bombs were released.

2I5. Attacks, helped by some long range bombers of the U.S.A.A.C., continued on objectives of all kinds. In all 58 raids took place in support of the Army's withdrawal, some to reduce the scale of air attack and the remainder in direct support of the Army. Most of the bombing took place on General Alexander's right flank, although three raids were directed against such places as Mongpawn, Laikha and Kongchaiping on the Chinese front.

2I6. Such airfields as Mingaladon, Akyab and Myitkyina were kept under a harassing scale of attack. Operations against Akyab and Myitkyina were particularly effective and when the enemy attempted to establish himself there on forward bases, bomber action made these untenable by the destruction of his first-line aircraft on the ground.

2I7. Of the 58 raids, I3 were undertaken by aircraft of the U.S.A.A.C. and 45 by the R.A.F. A total of 23I,900 lbs. of bombs in all were dropped, mostly followed by low flying machine gun attacks

2I8. The enemy were using river craft to outflank the Army in Burma. This line of communication was continuously harassed by our aircraft and a total of some 30,000 lbs. of bombs were released on steamers, barges and wharves while the attack on a concentration of river craft at Monywa on the 4th and 5th May was, by its delaying action, largely instrumental in preventing the Japanese encircling movement of the right flank of our forces, then withdrawing from Yu to Kalewa, a movement which if successful would have proved embarrassing to our Army.

2I9. A single Blenheim which had attacked Akyab on the 22nd May was engaged by 4 Army 0.I fighters. The fight lasted 20 minutes and was broken off by the remaining 3 fighters when 70 miles out to sea the aircraft of their leader, the Japanese air ace Lt.-Col. Takeo Kato, was shot down in flames. No other Allied aircraft attacked Akyab on that day.

220. Requests for bombing action and tactical reconnaissance were made by General Alexander to Headquarters in Calcutta. Reconnaissances continued, 55 being completed for Burmarmy.

22I. No. 3I air transport Squadron had been placed at my disposal equipped with D.C.2 and later some D.C.3 aircraft. This Squadron did magnificent work. Their daily effort was about 3 aircraft and considerable air transport requirements had to be met. Food had to be dropped on the 3 routes along which the evacuation of civilians from Burma was taking place. These routes ran from Shwebo – Kalewa – Tamu to Imphal, from Myitkyina – Mainkwan – Shingbwiyang to Ledo and from Katha – Indaw – Homalin/Tonhe to Imphal. Evacuees travelling along these routes required supplies of food and medical stores to maintain them during their march to India. Additionally, many of our wounded were evacuated by air from Magwe, Shwebo and Myitkyina in turn as the battle moved northward. Civilians were also evacuated when there were no wounded to move.

222. In all a total of 8,6I6 persons, which included 2,600 wounded, were flown out to India and I09,652 lbs. of supplies were dropped for victualling refugees and troops. In carrying out this task we had the help of D.C.3aircraft of the American Air Force – I have to record the good work carried out by these crews.

223. About the middle of March a serious situation had risen in the Bay of Bengal. In the Port of Calcutta there was some one-quarter of a million tons of shipping. It was not known how long the enemy naval force would remain within striking distance of our line of sea communication between Calcutta and Ceylon. There were none of H.M. ships available at this time to provide the necessary cover to secure this shipping now also within the range of attack of the enemy long range bombers based at Mingaladon and Magwe.

224. Instructions were issued for the Port to be cleared. There were two courses of action – either to sail convoys close in shore and to provide what fighter protection against bomb attack – and bomber protection against attack by surface units – as was practicable or to use diversional sailing which would spread the ships over a large area in the Bay of Bengal. The latter course was chosen.

225. It seemed possible that the attacks of our coast-wise shipping on the 6th April were an offensive move covering the arrival of the large convoy of troops in Rangoon. Consequently it was likely that if enemy air reconnaissance could be prevented – the sailing of this large tonnage of shipping over a short period might be secured from enemy surface and air attack, since the enemy would be unaware of the operation.

226. We knew where the enemy reconnaissance force was. Nine four-engined and

two-engined reconnaissance flying boats had been located at Port Blair. On the I4th April this figure had risen to I3. Moreover, there were indications that the enemy had developed the aerodrome at Port Blair and that local fighter defence had been put in. Two out of the 3 serviceable Hudsons of I39 (now 62) Squadron, the only aircraft that could (refuelling at Akyab) make the range, were instructed to carry out an attack with the object of destroying and damaging all aircraft of this reconnaissance force. A determined low-flying attack was carried out in which 2 twin-engined boats were left burning, I four-engined flying boat left sinking and all the other flying boats were believed to be damaged. This attack was repeated on the I8th, when 2 Hudsons again attacked I2 four-engined flying boats. Two of these were destroyed and 3 severely damaged. On both occasions the enemy were moored in lines and the Hudsons carried out a number of mast-height runs on them using their turret guns. On the I8th, Navy "O" fighters engaged our 2 aircraft – I failed to return and the second was hit by cannon shell and machine gun fire. After these attacks this enemy force remained inactive. Not only during the critical time when some 70 of our ships made the passage through the Bay of Bengal, but until the end of July no activity by it was recorded.

PART IX.
CONCLUSION.

227. To summarize, during this air action which commenced on the 23rd December, a small Allied air force, consisting of I Squadron of the A.V.G., the equivalent of 2 Hurricane Squadrons, the equivalent of I Bomber Squadron, 2 Army Co-operation Bomber Squadrons and the equivalent of half a G.R. Squadron, engaged the Japanese air force in the defence of Rangoon and in the support of our Army in Tenasserim and Burma. But the early fall of Rangoon, diversion of reinforcements and the shortage of aircraft equipment prevented the air force building up to I6 Squadrons (6 Fighters, 7 Bombers, 2 Army Co-operation and I G.R.) and full maintenance promised on programme. Up to the fall of Rangoon – by which we lost our warning system and our organised airfields, in this vicinity – air superiority over Rangoon had been maintained and after its fall continued until the Magwe action on the 21st March.

228. During this period the enemy, finally unable to subject the base of Rangoon to unrestricted day bombing, which would have given him the best chance of surrounding and destroying the Army, turned his effort to defend his troops and aid their advance. In Tenasserim, enemy day bombing attacks were carried out on our forward troops and Headquarters. Although support was given, our attempts to prevent this bombing were not successful, it being impossible in the circumstances of poor warning and shortage of fighter equipment.

229. It is a remarkable fact that from February 25th – when the enemy's last attack to achieve air superiority over Rangoon failed – he would not face our fighter force until Rangoon was in his hands and considerable reinforcements had been flown into the country after the fall of Singapore. Consequently, this absolute state of air

superiority remained over Rangoon at this critical time – and no "Namsos" here took place.

230. On March 2Ist he began his determined attack to stamp out our now fast dwindling air force at Magwe and Akyab. Having achieved this, although good bombing objectives were constantly present as our Army withdrew to India, he did not follow up his success by attacking our moving columns. Thus the casualties to our Army from enemy air action during withdrawal over great distances with poor cover from air attack were small. This may well have been because the enemy did not know the temporary success that he had achieved. The main weight of the enemy bomber attack was directed on such places as Prome, Mandalay and Maymyo, where great damage resulted with considerable moral effect on the civil population. The bases at Toungoo, Heho, Namsang, Lashio and Loiwing were constantly searched and attacked, though except at the latter there were no aircraft present.

23I. Norgroup was then using the depth to India, and with its base organisation being hurriedly prepared in the Calcutta area and up the Valley of the Brahmaputra, was able with what resources were available, to continue a harassing scale of bombing attack in Burma with some fighter action in the North. By the nature of the campaign and the shortage of warning, of aircraft, of equipment, and of maintenance, we were unable to maintain our 2 mixed Wings in Upper Burma and Akyab.

232. In the Burma campaign the main brunt of the fighting was borne by the P.40 Squadrons of the A.V.G. They were the first in the field with pilots well trained and with good fighting equipment. Their gallantry in action won the admiration of both services.

233. According to the records available in the Intelligence staff of Norgroup, 233 enemy fighters and bombers were claimed destroyed in the air in this campaign, of which the A.V.G. claimed I79 and the R.A.F. 54. Fifty-eight were claimed destroyed on the ground, 38 by the A.V.G. and 20 by the R.A.F. Seventy-six were claimed probably destroyed, 43 by the A.V.G. and 33 by the R.A.F. One hundred and sixteen were claimed damaged, 87 by the A.V G. and 29 by the R.A.F.

234. From January Ist the cost in losses was 38 fighters shot down by the enemy in air combat. Of these 16 were P.40's and 22 Buffaloes and Hurricanes, but the majority of pilots were fortunately saved. I regret to report that there were 2 substantiated incidents when Japanese figher pilots attacked and killed our fighter pilots while descending by parachute.

235. As regards bombers, 8 failed to return from operations.

236. Our losses on the ground due to enemy action were 5I aircraft, I7 fighters, 23 Blenheims, 4 Hudsons. The remainder were transport and communication aircraft.

237. Comparable with the total of 233 enemy fighters and bombers claimed to have been shot down in air combat by the A.V.G. and the R.A.F., the Allies' losses were 46. Thus an average of slightly more than 5 enemy aircraft were claimed shot down for each of our aircraft lost.

238. We destroyed more of the enemy's aircraft on the ground than the enemy destroyed of ours. We made no claim moreover in respect of enemy aircraft destroyed on the ground by bombing attack, the number of which must have been considerable.

239. The bomber action in close support of the Army has been described. Slight as the effort was, valuable results were achieved. Counter-offensive bombing action to reduce the scale of attack made an effective contribution towards the maintenance of air superiority over Rangoon.

240. The evacuation of R.A.F. personnel from Burma by air and sea, with small parties by land, was completed without loss.

24I. As regards stores, much valuable equipment was back loaded at the last moment from Rangoon. The majority of stores remaining in Burma were moved to the Lashio area, whence on the sudden and unexpected Japanese thrust in that region as much as possible was moved into China. The remainder was destroyed except for some large bombs which were rendered useless.

242. The task of supporting General Alexander's Army terminated on May 20th when it was withdrawn to India. Air operations based in Eastern India continue against the Japanese in Burma.

Footnotes

I General Wavell's despatch appears as a supplementary London Gazette *No 38228 of the IIth March, I948.*
2 Photographic Reconnaissance Unit.
3 See covering letter from General Wavell.
4 See covering letter from General Wavell.

2

AIR CHIEF MARSHAL RICHARD PEIRSE'S DESPATCH ON AIR OPERATIONS IN SOUTH EAST ASIA

16TH NOVEMBER, 1943 TO 31 MAY, 1944

The following despatch was submitted to the Secretary of State for Air on 23rd November, 1944, by AIR CHIEF MARSHAL SIR R.E.C. PEIRSE, K.C.B., D.S.O., A.F.C., Allied Air Commander-in-Chief, South East Asia.

PART ONE
INTRODUCTORY

1. As a result of the formation on 16th November, 1943, of South East Asia Command, I assumed operational control of all Air Forces in the South East Asia theatre, with authority to employ them in conformity with the policy of the Supreme Allied Commander, Admiral The Lord Louis Mountbatten, G.C.V.O., C.B., D.S.O., A.D.C. Thus I had at my disposal what had constituted R.A.F. India Command, and those American units in this theatre which comprised the 10th U.S.A.A.F. It was my task to ensure that these forces operated as a coherent body and that the best use was made of the potentialities of each.

2. In addition it was my continued responsibility to develop India as a base for future air operations, as a supply centre, and as a training area for R.A.F. and I.A.F. personnel. Such activities absorb a considerable proportion of the energies of the Command, and constitute a task of which the importance and results are not

immediately apparent. I have therefore devoted Part Four of this Despatch to the progress that has been made in this direction.

3. Responsibility for operations on the North West Frontier and for the Indian Air Force was relinquished to the formation which replaced the Inspectorate-General of the I.A.F. and to which was bequeathed the name Air Headquarters, India.

*

4. To ensure the integrated operational control of Units in Bengal and Assam, a new Headquarters was set up under Major-General G.E. Stratemeyer, U.S.A.A.F., designated Eastern Air Command and located initially at Delhi. This formation, which had previously existed under the title Headquarters, U.S.A.A.F., India-Burma Sector, China-Burma-India Theatre, had administered and controlled the 10th U.S.A.A.F. and provided in addition base facilities for the 14th U.S.A.A.F. The new Headquarters consisted basically of the Operations Section of the old organisation with the addition of an R.A.F. element. This Command, and all those comprising the 10th which had formerly come under Bengal Command and all those comprising the 10th U.S.A.A.F. in the same area. These forces were subdivided into a Tactical Air Force under Air Marshal Sir John Baldwin, and a Strategic Air Force under Brigadier General Howard C. Davidson, U.S.A.A.F. I was authorised to effect such re-grouping of operational units that I considered necessary to achieve maximum operational efficiency, and as a result R.A.F. and U.S.A.A.F. transport units were merged on 15th December into one organisation which was given the title of Troop Carrier Command. This new formation was commanded by Brigadier General D. Old, U.S.A.A.F. Similarly R.A.F. and American photographic reconnaissance units were incorporated into one command which assumed the title of Photographic Reconnaissance Force. Wing Commander S.G. Wise, R.A.F., was appointed Air Commander from the date of formation.

5. In exercising operational control of these forces, the integrity of U.S. Groups and R.A.F. Wings was retained and administrative control and responsibility remained with the respective American and British Commanders. The Chiefs of Staff agreed to the integration with the qualification that in view of American commitments to China, it might become necessary to transfer units from the 10th to the 14th U.S.A.A.F.

6. The chain of command and the conduct of operations by the merged forces almost without exception worked well, and mutual concessions and adjustments were made by each element. In ancillary services, examples of co-operation were most notable in the sphere of maintenance, signals and flying control. Major General G.E. Stratemeyer has said in his report on operations during this period – "The various obstacles which might be expected to arise as a result of combining U.S.A.A.F. and R.A.F. units have been overcome as a result of integration of staffs at Headquarters, Eastern Air Command, Strategic Air Force, Third Tactical Air Force, Troop Carrier Command and Photographic Reconnaissance Force. Such a revolutionary change in staff organisation might well have produced many difficulties and misunderstandings,

but such has not been the case, and we have undoubtedly derived mutual benefit, not only on the staff side, but in the tactical operating of air forces". With these and other evidences of the working of integrated forces I have dealt in detail in the appropriate sections of the narrative.

THE TASKS TO BE ACCOMPLISHED.

7. The tasks which lay before the combined Air Forces were:-

(*a*) To conduct a strategic air offensive in conformity with the general plan to destroy enemy air forces and installations, selected rail, road and river communications, and depots and maintenance facilities.

(*b*) To ensure the air defence of the U.S. Air Transport Command airfields in North-East India and to provide for the defence against air attack of Calcutta and adjacent industrial areas.

(*c*) To provide support for the operations of Fourteenth Army.

(*d*) To provide support for the Chinese-American forces under command of General J.W. Stilwell which were operating from bases in the Ledo area.

(*e*) To support the operations of Long Range Penetration forces, and

(*f*) To conduct photographic reconnaissance and survey.

8. The prosecution of the first of these tasks was not only the best method of maintaining a favourable air situation, which was my principal charge, but would also force the enemy on the defensive and thus provide the best protection for the air route to China, for the Calcutta area and for sea communications in the northern Bay of Bengal.

9. Offensive fighter operations were to be undertaken to the greatest possible extent and it was proposed to use long range fighters in particular in the offensive against enemy airfields and air installations. Moreover, in order to overcome the wide dispersal of my available fighter strength, it was necessary to maintain at the highest pitch of efficiency the early warning system.

10. I planned to employ the strategic bomber force against targets in the following order of priority: enemy occupied airfields and installations, shipping, railways, oil installations in Burma and suitable objectives in Bangkok. The course which the battle took, however, made a readjustment of these priorities necessary and a considerable proportion of the total bomber effort was directed to tactical targets in support of the Army and later, to carry supplies to the garrison at Imphal. Another task which assumed increasing importance during the period was the evacuation of casualties. Much had to be done to build up a successful organisation which could deal with the transhipment of sick and wounded from battle areas and casualty clearing stations to better equipped hospitals in the rear.

THE FORCES AVAILABLE.

11. To accomplish these tasks there was a total of forty-eight R.A.F. and seventeen U.S.A.A.F. squadrons deployed for operations. By May these totals had increased to sixty-four and twenty-eight respectively.

12. The disposition of tactical units in Bengal and Assam was designed to provide defence and support over the three main areas of land operations; in the Arakan, along the line from Tiddim to Homalin, and the Ledo Sector in Northern Burma; they were under the control of 224 Group, 221 Group and the U.S.A.A.F. Northern Air Sector Force respectively. Strategic units continued to be stationed further to the west since the marshy areas of the Sunderbunds and the poor lines of communication in that area made the construction of airfields east of the Brahmaputra up to heavy bomber standards a matter of extreme difficulty which neither the labour, transport nor supply position would allow me to undertake except as a relatively long term plan.

THE SITUATION IN NOVEMBER.

13. Facing the enemy from India there was a more modern, more powerful, and numerically stronger air force than had hitherto been available in this theatre. Moreover, during the monsoon much had been achieved to give the units comprising this force greater striking power. Communications, although overstrained were now better geared to carry war supplies than at any time since the outbreak of hostilities. Advanced landing grounds which had been constructed afforded short-range aircraft a greater radius of action, both offensive and defensive, during the dry weather that was to come and the warning system was now able to give ample notice of the approach of hostile aircraft.

14. The enemy for his part disposed of a force of approximately 250 aircraft concentrated in the airfield groups at Heho, Anisakan, Rangoon and Chiengmai with the remainder at lay-back bases in Siam and the Netherlands East Indies. His ground forces faced ours along a front of 700 miles. In Arakan he held the line from Maungdaw to Buthidaung and was opposed by XV Corps, thence north-west across the inhospitable Chin Hills to Kalemyo and northwards up the Kabaw Valley where IV Corps was deployed. Further north still he was confronted by two Chinese Divisions based on Ledo, and beyond this we held positions as far as the River Salween with a small force based at Fort Hertz. The enemy's bases and lines of communication stretched for 900 miles from Bangkok to Myitkyina, over the whole length of which it was possible to attack him.

15. The security of sea communications meant that General Reconnaissance aircraft had to cover an area ranging from South Africa to Sumatra. The patrol of this vast expanse of sea contributed a problem that could only be met by the careful husbanding and disposition of the small forces available.

*

16. The account of a campaign covering such a wide area and diversity of activities does not admit of chronological treatment. I have therefore dealt separately with each

strand of the pattern of operations, commencing with the primary task, the maintenance of air superiority, and placing air transport operations next in view of the importance they were to assume.

*

PART TWO
OPERATIONS

I. – THE MAINTENANCE OF AIR SUPERIORITY

17. The advent of Spitfires in Bengal early in November had already begun an era of successful interceptions in which the enemy discovered for the first time in this theatre the efficacy of modern fighter aircraft backed by a well developed system of warning and control.

18. The first squadrons (Nos. 615 and 607 A.A.F.) were based on Chittagong in order to protect and cover that vital port and to cover the Arakan front which was to be the scene of the first major battles of the campaign. Within the month the Spitfires destroyed four enemy photographic reconnaissance aircraft of the Dinah type whose excellent performance had hitherto allowed them to range with impunity over our forward bases at a height and speed which Hurricanes could not equal. The enemy reacted by sending out fighter sweeps to test the new arrivals and whittle down our Spitfire strength in order that he could once again range over the Arakan suffering only the minor casualties that Hurricanes could inflict. In both these objects he was unsuccessful, and by the end of December had lost twenty-two aircraft, probably lost seven and had suffered damage to twenty-six against our loss of thirteen. The greatest success scored in these raids was by No. 136 Squadron who, on the last day of the year, scored 12 destroyed, 3 probably destroyed, and 8 damaged against a mixed force of bombers and fighters which were attempting to attack light Naval forces off the Arakan coast. As a result of this victory the Secretary of State for Air signalled his congratulations and commented that the newly arrived Spitfires had come into good hands.

19. The one occasion the enemy could claim as a success at this time was a bold strike aimed at Calcutta with the double object of damaging port installations and demoralising the city. He divined that over a front of 700 miles, defence in depth could not be so uniformly effective and that in the rear areas which included Calcutta, he would probably be met with Hurricanes. On 5th December he sent a mixed force of approximately sixty bombers and fighters in two waves which succeeded in bombing Calcutta for the loss of 2 destroyed, 1 probably destroyed, and 4 damaged, while the three and a half Hurricane squadrons (the half-being night fighters) suffered five destroyed and six damaged. That the enemy put his maximum effort into the attack is evidenced by the fact that the second wave included Naval aircraft.

20. During January the Spitfire squadrons gained valuable experience in air fighting and tactics that was to stand them in good stead in the greater battles to come. The enemy continued to send fighter sweeps over the Arakan, but Spitfires were able to inflict casualties upon them in the ratio of eight to one. By this time two squadrons of Spitfire VIIIs (Nos. 81 and 152) had arrived from Middle East, and I now had at my disposal in the forward areas of Bengal four squadrons of Spitfires and nine of Hurricanes for fighter operations; the stage was thus set for the opening of the battle in Arakan on the 4th February. Anticipating our own ground offensive by four days the enemy launched an attack with the object of annihilating the 5th and 7th Indian Divisions and pressing on to capture Chittagong. This ambitious plan was attended by the most impressive measure of air support afforded by him in this theatre, sweeps by formations of fifty plus aircraft being reported daily. The objects of the J.A.F. appear to have been firstly to intercept our aircraft engaged on close support, secondly to increase the morale of his own troops and thirdly to give some measure of ground support by attacks on our positions and forward bases. As the battle developed, one other task assumed overriding priority for the enemy air forces. The 7th Indian Division, cut off from its supply bases, was being supplied wholly by air. It was of vital importance to the enemy that our supply-dropping aircraft should not succeed in this task, but the air superiority which we had established, the provision of standing patrols – particularly in the Kaladan Valley where, owing to the intervening hills, no radar cover below 10,000 feet was available – and resort to supply dropping by night enabled transport aircraft to maintain the beleaguered forces for the loss of only one Dakota (C.47) to enemy fighters.

21. The tactics which were employed to gain this dominance over the Arakan battle front centred around the three forward squadrons equipped with Spitfire Vs and a few Spitfire VIIIs. Hurricanes were used for airfield cover when Spitfires were re-fuelling and re-arming, and for standing patrols over possible target areas during hostile raids in case of a missed interception. The enemy countered by introducing the Tojo, whose performance exceeded that of the Oscar, adopting the defensive circle and splitting into small groups when the circle was broken. This brought them a relative measure of success inasmuch as their losses decreased whilst those of the Spitfires gradually increased.

22. The advantages of the Spitfire VIII in this battle were not immediately apparent, for the enemy continued to operate at his best performance height, that is 10,000 feet. No.136 Squadron, who re-equipped with these aircraft in February, could not effectively employ their high overtaking speed against an enemy who exploited the manoeuvrability of his aircraft to the full. At first attacks were delivered at too high a speed with a resultant falling off in marksmanship.

23. When the battle switched to the Chindwin front in the second week in March and it became clear that the main Japanese ground effort was to be aimed at Imphal and the railway to the north, 243 Wing and eight squadrons were moved into the area from 224 Group. Spitfires did not immediately repeat their successes of the Arakan campaign for the following reasons. Firstly, although the three Ground Control Interception Stations were excellent and brought off fine interceptions against Dinahs

(No. 81 Squadron scored their first successes in this theatre by destroying two in four days at the beginning of March), the rugged nature of the terrain produced technical difficulties in the way of echoes which left many blank spots in the radar coverage. Secondly, the substitution of Indian Mobile Wireless Observer Companies for R.A.F. Wireless Units resulted in a lower standard of reporting. Thirdly, squadrons which had already lost a number of experienced pilots in action were now losing many more as operational tours were completed. Moreover, the sudden influx of personnel, both Army and R.A.F. could not be met with a similar growth of transport, accommodation and communications. Finally, as the Japanese advanced, more and more of our early warning system was overrun, and the Army Corps Commander decided that he could not employ troops on local protection of airfields and the warning net. Squadron personnel became exhausted through disturbed rest, and guard duties by night combined with operations by day. Certain squadrons were therefore withdrawn from the Imphal Valley whilst others were flown out every night.

24. Once again the problem of protecting transport aircraft operating so near to Japanese bases asserted itself. Deteriorating weather and absence of warning made it increasingly difficult to ensure interception, but that our superiority was never lost is shown by the fact that between the opening of the battle and the end of May, thirty-one enemy aircraft were destroyed, twenty probably destroyed and sixty-six damaged in air combat over the Manipur area, for the loss of seventeen. Of this number, three were destroyed by No. 176 (Beaufighter) Squadron operating at night from advanced airfields near Imphal.

25. Meanwhile the accretion to the Command of long-range American fighter aircraft enabled tactics to be developed which were to have most damaging results for the Japanese Air Force. Already Mustangs (P.51) had proved their worth, notably in a combined victory with Kittyhawks (P.40) against an enemy formation in the Digboi area on 27th March, claiming 26 destroyed and 4 probably destroyed, for the loss of two. The Army reported finding twenty-two crashed enemy aircraft in the area after the interception. At the same time, No. 459 (U.S.) Squadron, equipped with Lightnings (P.38) began to operate under 224 Group. Thus, it was possible to employ Lightnings (P.38) and Mustangs (P.51) to supplement the work of the Spitfires which were still in short supply, and had to be husbanded for purely defensive work. The serious contraction of the warning system around Imphal could now be partly offset by sending the American long range fighters to intercept the enemy on his return to the Central Irrawaddy strips.

26. The first success of the policy of intrusion fell to No. 1 Air Commando Force, which surprised a large concentration of aircraft on the Shwebo group of airfields on 8th March, and destroyed 46 of them. Three days later, the Lightnings (P.38) squadron scored 15 against the enemy at Heho. The primitive nature of the Japanese warning system in the area augured well for the successful continuance of the operations. Pilots became increasingly familiar with the details of those airfields which were within range, and photographs and models aided quick identification of dispersal areas and anti-aircraft posts. In early strikes of this nature the enemy were not airborne

and awaiting attack, and it was possible to make more than one run over the target, the first run being utilised to locate aircraft in their dispersal pens.

27. In May, an improvement in the enemy's warning system became evident, since often fighters were airborne and awaiting the attack. However, losses remained low, since No. 459 Squadron discovered that if they maintained an indicated airspeed of 300 m.p.h. and refused to enter into combat with the slower and more manoeuvrable Oscars and Tojos, they were still able to deliver their attacks at aircraft on the ground, perhaps fire one burst at any fighter which attempted to intercept and make their withdrawal without loss. The prospect of combat during the intrusion therefore proved no deterrent. In this manner No. 459 Squadron destroyed 121 enemy aircraft on the ground or in the air in March, April and May. The enemy was forced in consequence to discontinue the use of the Shwebo group of airfields and even Heho and Meiktila became practically untenable. By the end of May, the J.A.F. had been forced into the humiliating position of providing such support as their army, 600 miles away in the northern mountains, could receive from the comparative safety of airfields around Rangoon.

28. To sum up, the extent of Allied superiority in the air throughout the period can be seen by a comparison of the effort and losses of the opposing forces. The enemy scale of effort amounted to 2,700 sorties sighted or plotted, or less than three per cent. of the Allied effort. To achieve this, the J.A.F. lost 402 aircraft destroyed in the air or on the ground, or some 14 per cent. of their effort, while the comparable total for British and American forces amounted to 230 or less than one-third per cent. of the effort. The air superiority maintained over the period needs no further emphasis.

*

II. – AIR TRANSPORT OPERATIONS

29. Throughout the period under review the number of transport squadrons under my command steadily increased, though their growth was by no means out of proportion to the continually increasing importance of their task in the operational areas. Indeed, it is not too much to say that their services were instrumental in preserving the existence of the Fourteenth Army as a striking force on the Burma frontier. Operations on the Eastern front made calls upon them at an ever increasing rate, so that despite reinforcement, transport squadrons worked at a high rate of effort from the moment they became operational. In consequence, crews underwent a period of considerable strain, for not only does supply dropping in this theatre involve intricate low flying over the dropping zone for as much as an hour in a hot aircraft interior, but the crews were normally responsible for the arduous work of unloading 6,000 to 7,000 lbs. of freight.

Development of Troop Carrier Command.

30. In November, the only R.A.F. transport squadron operating was No. 31, an experienced and pioneer unit, but the 1st and 2nd Troop Carrier Squadrons U.S.A.A.F.

had begun to work over the northern sector of the front and there were other squadrons both British and American, either in training or on their way. Unified operational control of these forces was effected by the institution in December of Troop Carrier Command, Eastern Air Command, under Brigadier General W.D. Old, U.S.A.A.F., administrative control remaining in the usual British or American channels. Headquarters was established at Comilla on 2nd January, 1944, in close proximity to the Headquarters of Fourteenth Army and of the Third Tactical Air Force, as well as to main Army supply bases. Subsequent operations illustrated the dependence of air transport operations upon the tactical air situation, and in order to combine final responsibility for the former with the exercise of our air superiority – as well as to integrate air transport with army policy – Troop Carrier Command was placed under the control of the Air Commander, Third Tactical Air Force, from 1st May. Subsequently Troop Carrier Command was dissolved as from 4th June, by when its component squadrons numbered 8 – 4 R.A.F. and 4 U.S.A.A.F. Moreover, in February the Air Transport Command had loaned to me twenty-two Commandos (C.46) to meet the emergency in the Arakan, and when it became necessary to return these in April, five U.S.A.A.F. Troop Carrier squadrons and the larger part of 216 Squadron R.A.F. were detached to work with my Command from M.A.A.F. Upon their return to the Mediterranean theatre in June, aircraft and crews from the Strategic Air Force were attached to the Third Tactical Air Force to fill the gap until the first of the U.S.A.A.F. Combat Cargo Groups became operational. During its short but eventful life of little over six months, Troop Carrier Command had thus increased more than four-fold in size, and even more in significance.

31. The routine supply dropping missions of No. 31 Squadron over the Chin Hills and Arakan were being continued at the time of the formation of South East Asia Command. The first additional need was that of 81 (West African) Division which already in December received supplies landed for it at Chiringa by U.S.A.A.F. It then moved eastwards over the mountains to the Kaladan Valley at Daletme and began its advance southwards, being dependent throughout for its maintenance upon air supply. From 7th January, 1944, onwards, this became a commitment of No. 62 Squadron R.A.F. At the same time U.S.A.A.F. aircraft came to the help of No. 31 Squadron in building up a large reserve of supplies at Tiddim, while further north, Nos. 1 and 2 Troop Carrier Squadrons U.S.A.A.F. in addition to maintaining the air warning centres screening the Assam Valley, began to supply on a much larger scale the two Chinese Divisions advancing south-east from Ledo down the Hukawng Valley. They also gave help to the Kachin levies waging guerrilla warfare in the Fort Hertz district, as well as to the Gurkha garrison of Fort Hertz itself.

The Arakan Battle – February, 1944.

32. When the Japanese offensive in the Arakan opened on 4th February, the needs of the 14th Army for air supply greatly expanded with only a few days' warning. The land communications of 7th Indian Division were soon cut and those of 5th Indian Division in danger, and it was only by supply dropping that the encircled forces could be expected to stand their ground and turn a potential catastrophe into a decisive

victory. Japanese preparations for an offensive had been observed, however, and the possibility of encirclement envisaged, so that when supply by air was called for on 8th February, there was no delay.

33. On the first day some of our transport aircraft encountered an enemy fighter sweep and one was shot down. Such was our air superiority that throughout the Arakan operations this was the only loss sustained by transport aircraft from enemy fighters, although many aircraft were damaged by fire from the ground. Later, as a measure of protection, much of the supply dropping was done by night with but little falling off in efficiency. The operation while it lasted was of such unexpected magnitude that I was compelled to request the loan of a number of Commandos (C.46) from the India-China Wing of the U.S. Air Transport Command. These aircraft were promptly and unstintingly supplied. The critical period from the 8th February to 6th March inclusive involved the delivery of 2,010 short tons of supplies of all kinds, including rations, animals, ammunition and P.O.L.[1] With such large scale help, ground forces were able to break out of their encirclement and inflict a decisive defeat on the enemy – significant in that it pointed the way towards the neutralisation of the long familiar Japanese offensive tactics. By the end of the month, air supply to the Arakan, though it still continued, was no longer of an emergency nature.

Operation "Thursday".

34. The major offensive action planned and carried out by 14th Army before the onset of the monsoon, was a penetration of enemy occupied territory by columns of Special Force under Major General O.C. Wingate. Its purpose was to disrupt enemy communications and thereby aid the recapture of northern Burma and create a favourable situation for the 14th Army to exploit. The operation as finally planned involved the large scale use of transport aircraft to fly in and supply the brigades, and the energetic employment of close support aircraft to make up the mobile columns' deficiencies in artillery. The First Air Commando Unit under Colonel Cochran, U.S.A.A.F., had been specially created and sent to this theatre to fill these needs, and acted as a task force in support of General Wingate. I have dealt with the activities of this force separately.

35. The long range penetration brigade which was making its way across the Chindwin overland towards Katha received its first airborne supplies on 10th February, and its maintenance thereafter became a continuous commitment. The remaining two brigades were landed on two strips improvised in the jungle during the nights of 5th/6th and 10th/11th March, and a fourth and fifth brigade were flown into another landing ground during the nights of 24th/25th March and 5th/6th April. The successful accomplishment of the air side of this operation was shared directly by the First Air Commando Unit and by the British and American Transport squadrons which participated, although the whole operation was only made possible by the high degree of air superiority gained by the tactical air forces in the preceding months.

36. The initial fly-in was the work of gliders which carried an American airfield engineer company whose task it was to receive Dakotas (C.47) on the following night,

and also a sufficient number of combat troops with equipment to defend the locality meanwhile. Although this preparatory operation was a complete success, it was twice in danger of being compromised. The first occasion was when at the last moment it was discovered by photographic reconnaissance that one of the jungle clearings earmarked for use and called "Piccadilly" had been deliberately obstructed by the enemy. The commanders on the spot decided to continue with the operation and divert the aircraft intended for "Piccadilly" to the other landing zone – "Broadway". Secondly, the towing of gliders in pairs proved impracticable under the difficult flying conditions encountered; tow ropes snapped and a number of gliders failed to reach their destination. Moreover there existed in the clearing a number of undulations not visible on air photographs, so that even on making the best of landings the earlier gliders frequently crashed, and each wrecked glider became a source of danger for its successors. Worse confusion and damage was avoided by the airfield control improvised by Lt.-Col. Allison of the U.S.A.A.F. who was able to stop the arrival of additional gliders. Despite these difficulties, by the next night the American airborne engineer unit and British troops had levelled "Broadway" sufficiently for Dakotas (C.47) to land. The Air Commander 3rd T.A.F. commented particularly on the quality of the airfield control and the excellent flying discipline that were features of the operation, which enabled the strip to be used almost to saturation by a constant stream of transport aircraft in the short hours of darkness available. His report remarks as follows: "Nobody has seen a transport operation until he has . . . watched Dakotas coming in and taking off in opposite directions on a single strip all night long at the rate of one landing or one take-off every three minutes".

37. By D plus 6 day there had been flown in 9,052 personnel, 175 ponies, 1,183 mules and 509,083 pounds of stores.

38. The element of surprise which had accompanied the entry of these forces and which had been aided by diversionary bombing around Bhamo and Indaw was maintained throughout. Even when the enemy divined our intentions, our air superiority was instrumental in rendering his attacks ineffectual. It was not until 11th March and 13th March that the enemy attacked the two landing grounds which had been first extemporised – by which time one had already been evacuated and a detachment of Spitfires of No. 81 Squadron had been installed on the other. Other landing strips were contrived as the occasion arose, though for the most part the thirty columns of the division were supplied by dropping. Much of the effectiveness of this air supply depended upon the standard of training of the Dakota crews. The dropping zones were continually being changed as the columns moved from place to place. Delivery normally took place by night and there was often no other guide than navigational skill supplemented by pre-arranged light signals which became visible only when the aircraft arrived in the vicinity of the dropping zone. Danger from ground fire whilst dropping was a frequent and accepted risk. This was no less true of occasions on which Dakotas were able to utilise a landing ground, for enemy detachments were often in the neighbourhood. The strip opened in the later stages of the operation at Hopin was evacuated because of small arms fire through which our aircraft had unavoidably to pass before landing.

39. Before the advent of the rains made the use of fair weather landing grounds impossible, one Brigade (No. 16) was flown back to its base in India. The others subsequently joined the Chinese-American forces advancing upon Myitkyina under General J.W. Stilwell, and participated in the operations around Myitkyina, to whose success their columns, supplied entirely by air, had contributed.

First Air Commando Unit.

40. This unit came to my command with the specific duty of assisting the fly-in of Special Force, the initial maintenance of its columns and the evacuation of casualties. These functions were extended to include direct support of the ground forces and sustained attacks on installations and communications to hinder the eventual mobilisation of the enemy against these forces. The Bomber-Fighter component was engaged from the 3rd February onwards in attacks on railways and airfields and, as soon as the fly-in had been accomplished, in direct support when called for by the columns. In these tasks the Mustangs (P.51) flew 1,482 sorties and the Mitchells (B.25) 422. Their claims against enemy aircraft destroyed on the ground and in the air amounted to ninety. The glider component of the force carried out fourteen separate operations involving the release of 99 gliders which took into Burma a variety of equipment ranging from bulldozers to river-craft.

41. An important part was played in the operation by the hundred light communication aircraft which the Air Commando possessed. These aircraft (L.1s and L.5s) could land more or less at will even in bad country to convey messages and supplies of small bulk, to carry commanders from one unit to another, evacuate casualties and perform a host of miscellaneous services without the risks attendant upon wireless silence or employing heavy aircraft. I consider their widespread use in future comparable operations essential.

42. The record of the small force of selected personnel with first-class equipment, which constituted the Air Commando, was naturally good, but that record cannot be advanced in support of extending the principle of Air Commando Units. Such a principle gives rise to the danger of tying down fighter and bomber aircraft permanently and exclusively to one particular Army formation with the consequent risks of duplication and lack of flexibility.

43. Such units have a place as spearheads for airborne and air transit operations, but as soon as normal supply can begin, fighter cover and air support, as requisite, should be provided by the tactical air forces as a whole under the direction of the appropriate air force Commander.

*

The Siege of Imphal.

44. Concurrent with the heavy claims on Troop Carrier Command from Special Force and General Stilwell's forces arose an emergency that surpassed in importance all

other transport operations, and on whose successful solution by air supply depended the fate of Imphal and the continuance of support to China.

45. On the 7/8th March the enemy crossed the Chindwin in force with the three-fold object of occupying Indian soil, capturing our main base at Imphal, and cutting the Bengal-Assam railway which fed the airfields from which supplies were flown to China.

46. Before the end of March, the enemy had cut the Tiddim-Imphal and Imphal-Kohima roads, occupied Tiddim and part of Kohima and swept round to the Bishenpur area west of Imphal. From the air point of view, the over-running of our warning system and the loss of advanced landing grounds on the perimeter of the Imphal plain were a serious inconvenience. The encirclement of the IV Corps divisions at Imphal, however, had immediate and heavy repercussions upon the transport situation, since I was forthwith confronted with unprecedented demands for the large scale delivery of reinforcements and supplies, not merely to the beleaguered forces in the Imphal Plain, but also to the garrisons holding out at Kohima and elsewhere. These demands were met, though not without considerable strain upon an already hard-worked force.

47. It was clear that the needs of our ground forces could not long be satisfied by the existing number of transport aircraft under my command. Thus, when the threat of a Japanese offensive westwards from the Chindwin had become apparent, although before it actually materialised, I made strong representations for further reinforcements of transport aircraft. As a result I received on loan from M.A.A.F. the services of the 64th Troop Carrier Group, U.S.A.A.F., consisting of five squadrons and a detachment of No. 216 Squadron, R.A.F. These six squadrons were all operating on the Burma Front by the second week in April. In addition, I was permitted to retain for a further period the Commandos (C.46) temporarily withdrawn from the India-China Wing of the Air Transport Command for supply dropping in Arakan.

48. The needs of our forces in the Manipur area were many and pressing. No. 50 Parachute Brigade was flown from the Punjab to reinforce the garrison at Imphal, and a little later No. 5 Indian Division was moved by air complete from the Arakan in 758 sorties. Between 10th/15th April, an infantry brigade was flown from Amarda Road, south-west of Calcutta to Jorhat in Assam. 99 Commando (C.46) and 189 Dakota (C.47) sorties lifted 3,056 all ranks, 937,000 pounds of stores and the following equipment: 50 motor-cycles, 40 jeeps, 31 jeep trailers, 16 25-pounders and eight 3.7 howitzers. An Army Air Support Control unit was taken by air from Poona to Jorhat for service with 33 Corps. The movement by air of the servicing echelons of tactical squadrons became a matter of routine. In regard to the maintenance of our troops, the most varied articles were delivered to the forces momentarily engulfed within the flood of Japanese infiltration. At Kohima, for instance, owing to the enemy seizure of the wells, it was necessary to drop drinking water as well as routine supplies and medical necessities. Three hundred and seventy tons of bitumenised hessian were delivered by air at Tulihal to make the airfield there all-weather. On the return journeys all transport aircraft brought out with them casualties or troops not needed for active combat.

49. The 79 aircraft borrowed from the Middle East were due to be returned at the beginning of May. If this arrangement had been adhered to the consequences might well have been disastrous. General Stilwell's forces would have been forced to withdraw to their Ledo base, the Imphal Plain would have become untenable, the air route to China threatened, the morale of the Fourteenth Army troops encircled in the Imphal Plain would have been considerably affected and the all-weather airfields and warning system in the Surma and Brahmaputra Valleys would have been lost. Moreover, the major victory the enemy might have won would have had serious repercussions in India.

50. I was compelled to represent that these vital aircraft must stay until the reinforcements envisaged by the Chiefs of Staff arrived and became operational. Agreement was obtained, and I instructed the Air Commander, Eastern Air Command, to employ aircraft of the Strategic Air Force in a transport role should there be any gap between the departure of the M.A.A.F. squadrons and the new reinforcements becoming fully operational.

51. On 15th April my commitment for air supply to the besieged garrison at Imphal was established at the figure of over 400 short tons per day – which even then entailed the occupants going on short rations. The fulfilment of this contract depended upon a modicum of fair weather and upon the speedy loading of aircraft at Army supply bases. Neither of these conditions was entirely fulfilled, and it was only by reorganisation of the ground elements of the air supply system and the unstinted efforts of the U.S.A.A.F. and R.A.F. transport squadrons available that the target figure was reached and surpassed in June. But by the end of May it was clear that the enemy's disregard of air transport as a major factor in the battle was to render his ambitious and costly offensive a failure.

The Advance from Ledo.

52. Throughout the whole period the supply of the Chinese-American forces operating from Ledo under General Stilwell had been proceeding. These troops were advancing down the Hukawng and Mogaung Valleys and thereby gradually bringing the opening of an overland route to China nearer realisation. Each advance took them further from their bases, and consequently their calls for air supply were increasing, necessitating up to 100 sorties per day. Landing grounds were constructed wherever possible along the path of the advance, and light aircraft were employed with good effect. The Dakota (C.47), however, remained as the greatest single factor in maintaining the advance. In April the entire 50th Chinese Division, numbering almost eight thousand men, was flown from Sookerating to Maingkwan, while by then all the combat troops in North Burma, both American and Chinese, had become dependent upon air supply. In May, a fast moving column of American troops, known as Galahad Force and supported entirely by air, made a considerable detour and caught the enemy unawares, seizing the main airfield at Myitkyina on 17th May. All units of Troop Carrier Command in the north had been standing by to carry in those forces which General Stilwell believed adequate to defeat the expected enemy counter attack. Brigadier-General Old was waiting at Shinbuiyang to conduct the initial glider

operation in which troops and engineering equipment were to be conveyed, and himself towed the first glider into Myitkyina. Transport aircraft followed the gliders almost at once. In the course of thirty-six hours of intensive operations by both day and night, during which ground fire was continually encountered, and one enemy air attack was successful in shooting down a Dakota (C.47) and destroying others on the ground, there were landed a complete Chinese Regiment, six light anti-tank batteries, twelve Bofor guns and crews, one airborne engineer company and a Chinese mortar company. Many loads of ammunition, food and stores were also conveyed. Before the end of the month further troops, in numbers equivalent to a division, had been taken by air to Myitkyina, and the first stage of the reconquest of Burma and the reopening of the Burma Road was completed.

Evacuation of Casualties.

53. It would be incomplete to close this account of the operations of transport aircraft under my command without some mention of a further aspect of their work. During the first five months of 1944 the aircraft of Troop Carrier Command flew no less than twenty-three thousand sick and wounded back to safety. It may safely be said that but for the provision of air transport the greater proportion of these would have had little hope of survival. The alternative was many days' journey by sampan, mule and ambulance, and perhaps rail, to the nearest base hospital. Moreover, a proportion of the casualties evacuated were from the columns of Special Force fighting in enemy occupied territory. The 2,126 casualties evacuated from the division by the end of May would have been a total loss had they not been flown out by air.

54. Although evacuation of casualties by air was no new phenomenon in this theatre of war, nevertheless it first assumed considerable proportions during the Arakan battle in February and reached its peak during the struggle for Imphal in April. Transport aircraft, when they landed to deliver supplies frequently received casualties for the return journey. When, however, supplies were dropped, the intervention of light aircraft was necessary for the journey from a small advanced landing ground to a strip further back where a Dakota might land. But since neither heavy nor light aircraft could be spared throughout this period specifically for the evacuation of casualties, the removal of sick and wounded remained an "ad hoc" matter arranged on a basis of expediency and improvisation. R.A.F. medical personnel at airfields were insufficient to deal with the load of casualties which, due to operational exigencies, might be entrusted to them with little or no warning by a flight of transport Dakotas. And so, although the care of all wounded at airfields was officially an R.A.F. responsibility, nevertheless help in this matter was gladly accepted from the Army.

CONCLUSION.

55. Thus air transport played a decisive part in the three great battles of the period. By the end of May the reconquest of portions of northern Burma was in sight, and the garrison of Imphal was still an offensive force. The events related above make a

reiteration of the importance of transport aircraft unnecessary. In connection with the operations, however, certain lessons were learned which I would emphasize. First, it is essential that Army Commanders should not be allowed to regard air transport as an auxiliary arm upon which they can call without reference to the appropriate Air Force Commander. Secondly, the Army must be impressed with the necessity for the quick turn-round of aircraft; during intensive operations loads must be ready for the aircraft as they land. Too often crews wasted valuable hours waiting at an Army Supply Base because their freight had not been assembled ready for loading. Thirdly, when the Army are the main customers of air transport forces, the fullest day-to-day liaison and discussion of problems must be combined with clear statements as far in advance as possible of what they require in the way of air transport, and for what purpose, in order that priorities may be allotted.

56. It is to be noted that the inadequacy of the Army ground organisation for supply by air operations became recognised by the Army as and when these operations became large-scale undertakings. Steps were taken to improve the ground organisation in the light of the experience gained during the operations. The first step was to provide Indian Air Supply companies at supply loading airfields. A further important development was to create Army staff organisations both to control the activities of the Army elements on the airfields, and to organise the flow of Army supplies both from base to airfield and from airfield to aircraft. These developments did not, however, reach completion during the period covered by this despatch.

*

III. – STRATEGIC AIR FORCE

57. Operations by heavy and medium bombers sought to accomplish the following tasks:

(i) Denial and destruction of *the enemy's lines of communication.*
(ii) Destruction of *airfields and other military installations.*
(iii) Destruction of *industrial and stores areas.*

58. In addition to these, the Strategic Air Force was often called upon to furnish direct support to ground forces and to provide aircraft and crews for transport operations.

59. For the transhipment of sea-borne supplies to Burma, there were available to the enemy the ports of Rangoon, Moulmein, Tavoy and Mergui; the three latter are all connected by rail or road to Rangoon. In addition to these, the enemy could use the port of Bangkok and two lesser ports in the Gulf of Siam, Koh Sichang and Sattahib, both with adequate communications to Bangkok. From here the vital Burma-Siam railway, which was completed about the beginning of the period under review, could transport supplies to Moulmein, thence across the Salween by ferry to Martaban, rail again to the Sittang River where the bridge was down, once again a ferry, and so to all points of use by rail. Among the measures designed to deny these facilities to the enemy was the laying of a total of 89 mines in the harbours of

Rangoon, Moulmein, Tavoy and Mergui, and, further afield, at Bangkok and the Gulf of Siam ports. Though the number of mines laid was not large, the results exceeded expectations. Moreover, it must be remembered that the effort involved was considerable, sometimes necessitating flights of 2,300 miles. The enemy's lack of efficient minesweeping equipment caused much delay in the clearance of harbours, and intelligence reports show that considerable dislocation and damage was caused to shipping.

60. Attacks against rail communications accounted for almost 25 per cent. of all operations. Destruction of the larger installations was allotted to the heavy bombers, with particular emphasis on Rangoon, Bangkok and Mandalay. Wellingtons operating by night were directed mainly against railway centres. The Mitchells' (B.25) performance and characteristics made them particularly suitable for railway sweeps and the destruction of bridges. In this connection, the spiked bombs that came into use in March proved invaluable and were used to tear up stretches of the permanent way at intervals over many miles of track. Bridges of strategic importance were attacked continuously and attacks were repeated each time the enemy completed repair work. An excellent example of this was the Sittang Bridge at Mokpalin. Destroyed during the evacuation from Burma, the bridge was repaired after long and arduous work by the enemy. The progress of the work was carefully followed by reconnaissance, and as soon as it was completed the bridge was wrecked once more in a single operation. It has not been repaired since this attack.

61. The overall strategy of rendering each part of the railway system ineffective was exemplified in the spirited low-level attack on the Burma-Siam railway by American Liberators (B.24), the series of attacks on marshalling yards at Bangkok and Moulmein, and the mining of the ferry crossings at Martaban and Mokpalin. At shorter range, the railway from Rangoon to Myitkyina was subject to continuous attacks, with the result that throughout its length there was always one bridge or more out of action. Amongst these bridges which were put out of action were the Mu River, Myittha, Meza, Kyungon, Zawchaung, Budalin, Songon, Natmauk, Tantabin, Swa, Tangon, Ye-u, Sinthe, Pyu, Bawgyo, Pyawbwe, Myingatha, Natkyigon, Daga and Myothit. Whenever intelligence indicated that enemy troops or supplies were moving in quantity, sweeps were undertaken along the stretches of track approaching the battle fronts.

62. Attacks on road facilities and communications began in earnest in April 1944, when the threat to the Imphal Plain assumed serious proportions. One enemy division moving north from the Tiddim area had, as its main line of supply, the motor road leading from Ye-u. Two other divisions attacking from the east across the Chindwin were largely dependent upon the road from Wuntho. Mitchells (B.25) and Wellingtons began on the 18th April an almost daily assault upon these vital arteries and the supplies moving along them. While the former carried out low-level daylight sweeps, the latter took up the role of intruders by night, replacing Beaufighters which Third Tactical Air Force considered could not be usefully or economically employed on moonless nights. The sum of these attacks, other aspects of which I have described

elsewhere in this Despatch, contributed greatly to the constant shortage and slow transit of men and supplies which dogged the enemy throughout his offensive.

63. The effort by strategic bombers to neutralise the Japanese Air Force was directed primarily to the destruction of airfield installations and supplies. At the beginning of February a large-scale operation by night was undertaken against the Heho group of airfields in conjunction with Beaufighters, who were to follow up the attack at dawn. From the Strategic Air Force point of view, the operation was highly successful, photographs revealing many bomb patterns in vulnerable areas. The Beaufighter attacks were hampered, however, by early morning mist.

64. Of industrial targets, oil installations were one of the primary objectives. A concentrated bombing programme was carried out against facilities at Yenangyaung in which American daylight bombers demonstrated their accuracy to such an extent that twice Beaufighters operating in the area the following night reported large fires still burning. In late 1943 this plant was producing 600 barrels of crude oil daily, from which were extracted 5,000 gallons of petrol. By May, 1944, the daily processed yield had been reduced to 1,680 gallons. Installations at Chauk, Lanywa, and Thilawa were dealt with in a like fashion. Attacks against other industrial areas were reserved for the few large towns where targets of a reasonable size presented themselves, notably Rangoon, Moulmein, Bassein, Insein and Prome. The Aircraft Factory and Arsenal at Bangkok received many hits from the 106 tons of bombs aimed at it. When considering the relative lightness of the attack, allowance must be made for the distance involved, which is equivalent to a return flight from London to Tunis.

65. While I had not originally planned to use strategic bombers in close support of ground troops, the Commanders on all three sectors of the front requested their help and were accorded it. I have dealt with these operations in more detail in the section devoted to Army Support, where it will be seen that the greater proportion were in direct support of IV Corps in front of Imphal. Wellingtons were initially employed on this task by daylight, with fighter escort, since the Mitchells (B.25) could more usefully be employed on sweeps along the various Lines of Communication. Subsequently, when Wellington crews had to be withdrawn for air supply duties, the Liberators (B.24) were used in a similar daylight rôle. This method of employment of strategic bombers was all the more acceptable to me since monsoon conditions made night bombing wellnigh impossible. The frequency of these attacks increased, and by the end of May No. 231 Group alone had been able to achieve the creditable total of 646 short tons of bombs dropped on Army Support targets.

66. The above duties of Strategic Air Force involved the dropping, from January onwards, of 6,741 short tons of bombs, of which R.A.F. and U.S.A.A.F. dropped almost equal proportions. The distribution of this effort was as follows:

	Per cent.
Military installations, dumps, etc.	54.7
Railroad communications	22.6
Airfields and landing grounds	10.2
Bridges	5.5
Shipping	3.5

Jettisoned   3.5

67. The Strategic Air Force carried out one more duty during the period, the reinforcement with crews and aircraft of the transport squadrons maintaining the life-line to forces cut off on the Imphal Plain. On 19th May forty Wellington crews were attached to Troop Carrier Command to help the over-worked crews there, and five aircraft and crews were detailed to carry 250-lb. bombs to the tactical squadrons operating at high pressure in the Imphal Plain. Despite bad weather, 544 bombs were delivered by 31st May. In the same period, No. 490 U.S. (Mitchell) Squadron delivered 380 tons of ammunition to the forces defending Imphal. The offensive power which these loads represented contributed to the eventual breaking of the Japanese offensive and enabled the normal transport aircraft to concentrate on delivering other supplies of which the Army was in urgent need.

*

IV. – SUPPORT OF GROUND FORCES

68. Operations on land were renewed and maintained on a large scale during this period, so that there were greatly increased opportunities for giving support to our land forces. The fact that we possessed and held air superiority enabled full advantage to be taken of these opportunities, and throughout the big battles – first in Arakan and then in Manipur and around Myitkyina – ground support reached dimensions which absorbed a large part of the total effort.

69. The successful provision of direct support to our armies in this theatre is faced by two great difficulties. The first of these is the nature of the terrain over which the fighting was taking place. Much of it is close, densely wooded, or covered with thick undergrowth, so that the recognition of targets presents a problem to even the most experienced crews. The second is the nature and characteristics of the enemy as a fighter on the ground. Three things distinguish him: his tenacity and stamina, which enable him to take great punishment from the air and still retain his fighting spirit; his skill in camouflaging his positions and dumps, which makes it very difficult to locate them from the air or the ground; and his beaver-like propensity for digging himself into the ground by excavations that range from a number of shallow foxholes to hold one or two men to an elaborate system of bunkers unharmed by all but direct hits from heavy bombs. By virtue indeed of the nature of each, the terrain and the enemy are strikingly suited to each other.

70. The difficult nature of the terrain and the enemy's complementary skill in camouflage were overcome, to a great extent, by the intimate knowledge that aircrews came to have of the country over which they were operating. Another aid to target recognition was the use of artillery or mortar smoke shells. The enemy, however, on several occasions put down diversionary smoke to mislead our aircraft. One remedy to this ruse is the employment of coloured smoke which has recently arrived in the theatre.

71. The enemy's capacity for absorbing punishment from the air without losing

his will to continue fighting was countered by the application to his positions of a fire-power or a bomb-load of such a magnitude as would seem in a European theatre to be out of all proportion to the objects it was hoped to achieve, having regard to the forces available.

72. Such a concentration of bombs over any area held by the enemy also helped in finding an answer to the gift of the enemy for camouflage and to the fact that the terrain lends itself to concealment. An area was often found to contain more bunkers than even the most careful and thorough reconnaissance had disclosed. If these attacks were confined to pinpoint bombing of those bunkers whose existence was known, then when the bombing ceased and ground troops followed up, other enemy positions were found untouched by the bombardment. For instance, at Kyaukchaw, attacked on 17th January by heavy bombers, it was thought even after bombing had taken place that there were only three bunkers, whereas there were actually eight. Only complete saturation of an area can ensure a chance of all bunkers being hit or the troops in them being at least held down.

73. The problem presented by the strength and depth of many of the enemy's bunker positions was never properly solved. The bombs carried by light bombers and fighter-bombers did little damage unless they made direct hits, and the use of medium and heavy bombers for the task was of necessity restricted. Moreover, when heavy attacks were carried out with the help of the Strategic Air Force no really decisive success was achieved, and as yet the Army has not been able to make an effective assault in conjunction with these attacks. What advantage medium and heavy bombers have in the weight of their blow is offset by their greater margin of bombing error, which makes it necessary to allow a safety margin and so forces troops to start their assault at a greater distance from their objective than is the case with light bombers and fighter-bombers. A good example of the difficulty of co-operation between heavy bombers and ground forces is given in the operation at Razabil, which is described later. Of such attacks, the Air Commander, Third Tactical Air Force, noted in his report for this period: "The Army have not yet been able to carry out an effective assault in conjunction with these attacks. . . . However, the accession of Mitchells in a forward location and under Third Tactical Air Force is expected to be a very considerable help in enabling us to put an adequate and timely weight of attack on ... strongpoints".

74. Another way in which such bombing assisted ground forces was in disclosing the enemy's positions by clearing thick undergrowth from around them. This tactic was of great assistance to our artillery and tanks, but was inclined to be a double-edged weapon in the opinion of the infantry, since not only was the enemy exposed to view, but their own line of advance was also stripped of cover so that they were forced to attack either at night or by a flanking movement.

75. The technique of air attack was determined by the nature of the terrain in which the target lay. Where thick jungle made approach necessary at a height sufficient to locate the target by reference to its surroundings, then dive or shallow-dive-bombing was used. When the location of targets, as for instance on the lines of communication, was not so difficult, then low-level attacks could be carried out. Dive-bombers

therefore and fighter-bombers were used principally against pin-points and specified areas, the ground attack fighters against concentrations of troops and supply dumps immediately to the rear.

76. The results of attacks made in ground support could not always be observed from the air, but an analysis of the reports of Army units that followed up the attacks or watched them as they took place, testifies to their effectiveness in terms of men and animals killed and positions weakened, if not destroyed. Although great destruction of life was not necessarily the primary object of these attacks and was not always achieved, the Army was unanimous in its belief that the air support given helped it to advance when the initiative was ours and to hold out and later counter-attack when the enemy were attacking. Army formations repeatedly expressed their thanks to the air force units that had helped them, and further tribute to the effectiveness of this support is to be found in many reports. One of these may be quoted as being typical of many others: "10th May air strike on Japanese in Lynch position (near Tengnoupal) reported by forward troops to be most successful. Bunkers were seen to be blown in and bodies flying about". This was the work of twelve aircraft of No. 42 Squadron.

77. A more intangible result of direct support was the effect that it had on the morale of our troops. It was the opinion, for instance, of the Commander of the garrison at Kohima in April, that the audible and visible evidence of the arrival of air support on the two critical days, the 15th and 18th April, put new heart into his men towards the end of the siege. The obverse side of the picture is given by prisoners of war who bore complete witness to the effectiveness of our bombing and machine gunning.

*

78. In November and December, squadrons gave the limited scale of support called for by Fourteenth Army, which was then occupied in regrouping for forthcoming operations.

79. In the 4 Corps area the enemy advanced into the Chin Hills and occupied the line Fort White – Falam – Haka. They were held south of Tiddim, and both sides spent the rest of the year consolidating their positions. During this phase Nos. 45 and 110 Vengeance Squadrons did good work in direct support and in destroying supply dumps particularly around the area of Milestone 52 on the Tiddim-Kalemyo road.

80. During the same period in the Arakan, 15 Corps was also regrouping in preparation for an advance, and many attacks were made on enemy positions in order to inflict casualties and disperse enemy troops. Among the targets successfully attacked were the Headquarters of the Japanese 55th Division at Rathedaung.

81. In January the rate of effort increased to support the several intended thrusts forward. 4 Corps took the offensive during this month, and on the 25th occupied Kyaukchaw in the Atwin Yomas, an enemy fortress that blocked their line of advance from Tamu to Yuwa on the Chindwin. From the air point of view this was the most interesting operation of the month, since the first ground assault was preceded by an

air attack in which aircraft of both the Strategic and Tactical Air Forces took part. Eighteen U.S. Liberators (B.24) and nine Mitchells (B.25) escorted by R.A.F. fighters, dropped thirty-five tons of bombs including depth-charges; twenty-four Vengeances and twelve Hurricanes dropped eighteen tons. The bombing was accurate and the whole area of jungle and undergrowth was covered. On the other hand there were no direct hits on bunker positions, and the near misses did little damage to personnel or to positions. The attack took place at 16.30 hours in the afternoon, but the Army did not advance until 08.30 hours the next morning, by which time the effect of the bombing had mainly worn off. The unintended result of the operation, therefore, was that the Army's advance was made more difficult by the lack of cover where blast had laid the undergrowth flat.

82. Meanwhile in Arakan, 15 Corps had begun to move forward shortly before Christmas towards the line Indin – Kyauktaw. At the beginning of January, Maungdaw was taken and the approach towards the Maungdaw – Buthidaung road was continued till the end of the month. The major part of the available direct support effort was now being expended on this front, and our advances at Buthidaung and Maungdaw were both preceded by intensive dive-bombing of enemy strongpoints. More than once the two Vengeance squadrons, Nos. 82 and 8 I.A.F., mounted nearly fifty sorties between them in a day. In the Arakan too this month, the Strategic Air Force took part in direct support bombing to clear a salient in anticipation of the general advance. The target was a position near Razabil, another enemy fortress, three miles east of Maungdaw. The attack was carried out by sixteen American Liberators (B.24) and ten Mitchells (B.25), with an escort of R.A.F. Spitfires and Hurricanes, preceded by twenty-four R.A.F. and I.A.F. Vengeances which indicated the target. The majority of the bombs fell in the area, one 2,000-lb. bomb obliterating the top of a small hill containing enemy positions, but again there was an appreciable time lag before the Army moved to the assault, and the enemy appeared to have suffered no appreciable or lasting damage from the bombardment. The area of attack was 1,000 by 600 yards and the bomb load 145,250 pounds. The target area was too large for the weight of the bombardment, and it is clear that, to be really effective, future attacks will have to be more concentrated.

83. Early in February, the enemy, anticipating our intended offensive by four days, himself attacked in the Arakan. His plan was to separate 5 and 7 Indian Divisions, cut off their overland communications, and then destroy them in detail. 224 Group, therefore, instead of assisting this offensive, found itself involved in a very grim defensive battle. The enemy's move to outflank 7 Indian Division reached as far as Taung Bazaar, harried the whole time by the two Vengeance squadrons. Although there was some difficulty in finding targets in the battle areas, every opportunity was taken to attack reported concentrations, bunkers and lines of communication. Over 600 Vengeance and 800 Hurricane sorties were directed to this end during the month.

84. At the height of the battle, additional weight was lent to the support given the ground troops by the employment of Wellingtons, carrying 4,000-lb. bombs, from Nos. 99 and 215 Squadrons in a tactical role. Targets included enemy headquarters at Godusara and Rathedaung, and enemy-held villages were reported completely

devastated. In addition one operation with R.A.F. fighter escort was carried out, with excellent results, by nine Mitchells (B.25) of No. 490 U.S. Squadron against the entrances to the tunnels on the Maungdaw-Buthidaung road.

85. By the 4th March the battle in Arakan had been brought to a successful conclusion. There is little doubt that our overall air supremacy was largely responsible for this, since it enabled transport aircraft to drop food and ammunition to 7 Indian Division, which could not otherwise have maintained the fight, the Strategic Air Force to lend its weight against tactical targets, and the close-support squadrons to break up many attacks, to maintain a constant harassing of the enemy's line of communication, and to pin him down in his bunkers while our own troops moved in deployment or attack. Air Commander, Third Tactical Air Force, commenting on operations in this area, says "It is interesting to note that in 15 Corps support was allied with artillery rather more than infantry H.Q. This was considered by the Corps to be more satisfactory in that gunners are more used to thinking in terms of supporting fire. . ."

86. In the first few days of March the enemy launched an offensive across the Chindwin on the 4 Corps front. This was not unexpected. During February he had shown increased activity on the east bank of the river, and attacks had been made by Vengeances and fighter-bombers on enemy storage areas along the river as far north as the Uyu river and upon small vessels and concentrations of rafts on the Chindwin. The battle in Arakan had precluded any large reinforcement of the Imphal Plain, although during the preparations for operation "Thursday" it became evident that the enemy's preparations threatened Imphal and the Assam railway. It was indeed a question which only events would resolve, whether the fly-in or the enemy's offensive would start first. As it happened, although the first enemy units crossed the Chindwin on the night of the 7/8th March, the fly-in was begun on the 5/6th, in sufficient time to release important air resources for dealing with the new situation. Had the reverse been the case, the demands of defence and counter-attack against the enemy's thrust and of support for the fly-in could not both have been fully met. The brunt of air support was now switched from the 15 Corps to the 4 Corps front.

87. The Army's intention was, in the event of Long Range Penetration Brigades creating a favourable situation, to push forces across the Chindwin. To give air support to these forces airfields had been developed in forward areas, including one as far forward as Tamu. Now, however, instead of fighting in support of an offensive, direct support squadrons again found themselves taking part in a defensive battle, and Tamu itself was overrun.

88. Having crossed the Chindwin the enemy pushed onwards towards Imphal by the Tamu and Tiddim roads, and towards Kohima through the Somra hill tracts and from Homalin via Ukhrul. Air support to meet the threat was provided to the maximum from the resources available, the two Vengeance squadrons already on this front being joined by No. 82 Squadron from the Arakan and, towards the end of the month, by No. 7 I.A.F. Squadron. There was also at this time a welcome increase in the number of Hurricane squadrons equipped to carry bombs. No. 42 Squadron had

been so equipped since January, No. 34 since the end of February; now, at the end of March, No. 60 and No. 113 Squadrons, too, began to carry out bombing operations.

89. In April Kohima was seriously threatened as well as Imphal, and support was consequently divided between 4 and 33 Corps, although till May the greater part of the effort was centred around Imphal. The four Hurricane fighter-bomber squadrons flew over 2,200 sorties, the majority of which were in the Churachandpur area, on the Imphal-Tiddim road, against the road block set up at Kanglatongbi on the Imphal-Kohima road, against concentrations of enemy troops attempting to open the Tamu-Palel road westwards, and against 31 Division which was operating against Kohima. The four Vengeance squadrons flew over 2,000 sorties during this month. Their bombing was extremely accurate, and in addition to direct support tasks they attacked enemy dumps and camps. On the 5th April No. 82 Squadron carried out its last operations on this front and then rejoined No. 224 Group. Over 750 sorties were flown by Hurricanes in offensive sorties against fleeting targets and troop positions.

90. In May, direct support operations centred around Kohima, where the town itself and the Aradura Spur to the south were eventually cleared of the enemy after intensive attacks by Vengeances and Hurricane fighter-bombers against bunker positions and slit trenches. To the south of Imphal, where the enemy made several attacks on the Tiddim road from the west and also on Bishenpur, fighter-bombers and ground-attack fighters attacked concentrations of enemy troops and vehicles. Further south on the Tiddim road, Moirang was also attacked by fighter-bombers and Vengeances. During this month Vengeances flew over 1,000 sorties on the 4 and 33 Corps fronts and Hurricane fighter-bombers 1,693.

91. In this battle the Strategic Air Force again assisted with its heavier striking power. In May the Wellingtons of Nos. 99 and 215 Squadrons flew 125 sorties against tactical targets, American Liberators (B.24) 12, and Mitchells (B. 25) 106. Apart from one attack on the Mintha-Tamu road, the whole of this effort was made against targets on the Imphal-Tiddim road, especially in the neighbourhood of milestones 120 and 87, two points of great tactical importance in preventing enemy reinforcements from coming up the road. Attacks against enemy strongholds included one against the village of Ningthoukhong, which was accurately bombed by forty-eight Wellingtons and Mitchells (B.25) on the 9th May. Once again, however, the enemy withstood the effects of the bombardment and was able to repulse the subsequent assault by ground troops.

92. The enemy's efforts to deploy in the Imphal Plain during the month were decisively defeated by the Hurricanes and Vengeances which attacked at extremely short intervals any concentrations in the foothills reported by ground troops through the Army Air Support Control operating at a high standard of efficiency. By the end of the month, Fourteenth Army were going over to the offensive and it was possible to predict that the threat to Imphal had been averted. Constant attacks on the tracks through the jungle which served as his Lines of Communication had prevented the enemy bringing his full potential strength up to the perimeter of the plain, and the effectiveness of air attack in thick jungle had impressed on him the futility of advancing over open country without overwhelming forces. The attacker was

becoming the attacked; the period of attrition and defence was over, and the squadrons supporting 4 and 33 Corps could look forward to the prize for which all air forces hope – the annihilation of an enemy in retreat.

93. Positive results in the form of men killed, storage areas devastated, and transport destroyed are hard to achieve against an enemy with such a high standard of camouflage and concealment who, when on the offensive, moves in small groups with little impedimenta. No army can maintain its standard of camouflage in retreat, however, and as this despatch is being written, the air forces in this theatre are proving again what has been and is being demonstrated in every other theatre of war, that an enemy experiencing overwhelming pressure from advancing ground forces provides the best targets for air attack. The experience gained by Army Commanders, who have come to realise the limitations and possibilities of air support during the period of trial, is now paying full dividends, the results of which should form an impressive achievement during the monsoon operations now beginning.

94. During these six and a half months the American squadrons of the Northern Air Sector Force had, as their primary task, the maintenance of the air superiority necessary to guarantee the safety of the air route to China and of the bases of the Air Transport Command. They were also, however, responsible for giving air support to General Stilwell's Chinese-American Forces in their advance down the Ledo Road, which culminated in the assaults on Kamaing, Mogaung, and Myitkyina.

95. By February the ground forces had successfully advanced as far as Maingkwan in the Hukawng Valley, and the Mustangs and Kittyhawks comprising the force had given valuable support in the form of attacks against camps, concentrations of troops, M.T. and stores, both in the valley and along the road from Kamaing to Mogaung. The work of ground attack squadrons in sweeps along the flanks of the road was reported by prisoners of war as particularly effective. Liberators (B.24) and Mitchells (B.25) were also used in attacks on this sector of the front, dropping 155 tons of bombs on Kamaing, 93 on Mogaung and 40 on Myitkyina. This support continued when the Hukawng Valley had been left behind, and by the end of the period covered by this despatch Mogaung was being invested by ground forces and the main strip at Myitkyina, taken on 17th May, was in the hands of the N.A.S.F., forming a potential advanced all-weather base.

*

V. – ATTACKS ON COMMUNICATIONS

96. The comparative lack in Burma of large static targets suitable for heavy bombers has been offset by the extreme vulnerability of the Japanese lines of communication. No. 27 Squadron, R.A.F., has been operating on Beaufighters against these communications since January, 1943, and No. 177 Squadron, R.A.F., similarly equipped, from September of the same year. As a result of their persistent and ubiquitous attacks, both by day and by night, the enemy has been driven to remove the main weight of his transport from road to river and from river to rail. His major

movements have been restricted to the hours of darkness, and for protection during daylight he has been compelled to resort to an ingenious and complex system of camouflage coupled with the establishment of an extensive network of gun posts as a supplement to his more orthodox anti-aircraft defences. The Taungup Pass road, the shipping on the Irrawaddy, the Ye-u and Myitkyina railway lines, as examples, have long afforded daily targets for Beaufighters and, latterly, Lightnings (P.38) and Mustangs (P.51). In November, 1943, there occurred an event of prime importance as regards the supply problem of the enemy troops in Burma – the opening of the Burma-Siam railway. This did not diminish the importance of the routes of Northern and Western Burma, but it did bring into strategical prominence their relationship to these routes from the south and east. New objectives such as the railway junction at Thanbyuzayat, the ferry termini at Moulmein and Martaban, the bridge over the Sittang river at Mokpalin and in general the railway system north, south and east of the all-important junction at Pegu became of cardinal significance.

97. The armament of the Beaufighters of Nos. 27 and 177 Squadrons, consisting of four 20 mm. cannon and six machine guns, proved very suitable weapons for attacking the river-craft, motor transport, rolling stock and locomotives on these routes. They first reached Moulmein on 27th February; thereafter they regularly attacked targets as far south and east as the Burma-Siam railway itself, and the terminus of the main Siamese railway to Bangkok at Chiengmai.

98. In January, 1944, a third squadron of Beaufighters (No. 211) began to operate under my command using rocket projectiles (R.Ps.).The enemy had by this time instituted a system of pens and shelters to protect his locomotives, and although a target thus protected was immune from cannon and machine-gun fire, it was often vulnerable to R.P. attacks. Another development rendered the advent of rocket projectiles even more timely. The opening of the Burma-Siam railway now allowed the Japanese to bring replacement engines into Burma by this quick and easy route. Accordingly, the emphasis of attack was moved to the more permanent installations on Burmese and Siamese railway systems, since the destruction or damaging of locomotives was not now so serious to him. In attacks on stations, watertowers, curved portions of the track which could not easily be replaced, and bridges, the rocket projectile proved a valuable supplement to existing weapons.

99. The delay fuse which was all that was available with which to arm R.P.s was soon found to be unsuitable for attacks on bridges, and their destruction was left more and more to bomb-carrying aircraft of both the Strategic and Tactical Air Forces. I have dealt in more detail with this aspect of strategic bombers' work in the section devoted to their activities. In attacks by tactical aircraft the long range of Mustangs (P.51) and Lightnings (P.38) was exploited to the full. The Shweli suspension bridge for example had often been attacked by bombers but its position rendered bombing from any height difficult. Fighter-bomber attack was not possible until the long-range Mustangs (P.51Bs) of No. 1 Air Commando Unit arrived. Immediately after their arrival the bridge was destroyed by them in April and its emergency replacement a fortnight later. Other attacks on communications by Mustangs (P.51) and Lightnings (P.38) included many against the vital Mandalay-Myitkyina railway particularly on

the section between Shwebo and Wuntho which fed both the divisions attacking Imphal and the forces opposing Special Force.

100. Although not primarily intended for attack on rivercraft, the 40 mm. cannon, with which the Hurricane IIDs of No. 20 Squadron were fitted, did great damage to hundreds of assorted craft with which the enemy supplied his forces dispersed among the waterways of the Arakan coast. This squadron began to operate in December, 1943, using A.P. shells. In February, H.E. ammunition became available and the rate of destruction increased. Craft when holed could no longer be beached, but disintegrated in the water, with the inevitable instead of occasional loss of their cargo. When, finally, aircraft with additional internal tankage arrived, the effective radius of attack was extended south of Akyab, and the rate of destruction, reached a peak which seriously hindered the reinforcement and supply of all Japanese forces occupying the coastal region from Cheduba Island northwards to the front line, a distance of roughly 150 miles.

101. The damage and hindrance that the enemy suffered from these widespread attacks are hard to assess, but one criterion of their effectiveness was the energy with which the Japanese attempted to defend their communications. The statistics show that in 1,276 effective sorties by R.A.F. long-range fighter aircraft, 35 were destroyed by enemy action or did not return from operations, and 29 were seriously damaged by enemy fire, but no statistical summary can adequately record all the damage and delay that the enemy suffered. For example, it was estimated that in April reinforcements travelling from Bangkok to Manipur took six weeks to reach their destination.

*

VI. – GENERAL RECONNAISSANCE

Control and Planning.

102. The vast areas of ocean for which aircraft in this Command were responsible in November precluded the density of patrol that was desirable. Moreover, it was difficult to maintain a sufficiently close liaison with those formations responsible for the security of sea communications in neighbouring areas. In December, however, a new directive from the Chiefs of Staff enabled a more clear-cut policy to be introduced and better defined the system of control and responsibility. The boundaries of the Naval C.-in-C.'s Command were extended to include Aden. This facilitated co-operation with coastal aircraft there, which were, in the interests of consistency, to come under my command. I thus became responsible for all flying boats, G.R. landplane and coastal striking force units allotted for operations in the Indian Ocean, the Mozambique Channel, the Gulf of Aden, the Gulf of Oman and the Bay of Bengal. Day-to-day operational and administrative control remained with the A.O.C. in whose command the aircraft were located. Broad control was normally to be exercised through A.O.C. 222 Group, who was to work in close liaison with the appropriate

Naval authorities and South African Air authorities. Thus A.O.C. 222 Group had a dual responsibility, combining with the command of his own Group the organisation and direction of all G.R. operations in the Indian Ocean. To aid him in this latter task a new body was formed – Indian Ocean G.R. Operations, or "IOGROPS" – with a Deputy A.O.C. and separate staff.

103. In order to make the best use of the relatively few aircraft available to patrol these areas, a new policy was introduced with the object of making G.R. forces as mobile as possible and to concentrate in areas where submarines were known or suspected to be. In addition, the generous allotment of air escort to convoys in areas where no threat existed was reduced to the minimum, and flying hours were thereby conserved for concentrated action where necessary.

104. C.-in-C. Eastern Fleet is in complete agreement with this policy and co-operates to the fullest extent.

105. The concentrations of aircraft needed to implement the policy and carry out intensive patrols when necessary demand considerable shuttling of aircraft between bases. These movements are used to good effect by routeing the aircraft over shipping lanes so that they may carry out traffic patrols while in transit.

106. One of the first tasks carried out by "IOGROPS" was an investigation of the practical application of the system used in the Atlantic, by which air cover is given to shipping in accordance with the degree of risk and the value of the convoy. By the standards of this procedure – known as "Stipple" – the wastage in flying hours during May was assessed as follows:

		Per cent.
(*a*)	Aden area	17
(*b*)	East Africa	59
(*c*)	225 Group	55
(*d*)	222 Group	2½

107. Negotiations are now proceeding with C.-in-C. Eastern Fleet to introduce the procedure, modified to suit local conditions, in this Command.

108. Finally, all operations by Indian Ocean General Reconnaissance aircraft are in process of coming under the control of five Naval Air Operations Rooms at Bombay, Vizagapatam, Kilendini, Aden and Colombo. The resultant cohesion over the areas controlled, and closer liaison with the Navy of which these N.A.O.R.s will permit, promise well for future control of coastal aircraft in this theatre.

Operations.

109. A decrease in enemy submarine activity in November permitted a reduction in air escorts and a subsequent saving in aircraft hours.

110. The lull was utilised to carry out a more intensive training programme as a necessary initiation for No. 203 Wellington Squadron, newly arrived at Santa Cruz; and as a refresher for the other squadrons already operational but in need of training to fit them for their more versatile work in the revised policy of mobility and

aggression then being introduced. Otherwise, traffic patrols and shipping escorts were the main features of G.R. activity.

111. Survivors of a tanker torpedoed in the Seychelles area were located and rescued as a result of continuous sorties flown from the 28th January to 30th January. One Catalina crew flew for forty-two hours on the 29th-30th and was particularly, mentioned in the telegram of congratulation from C.-in-C. Eastern Fleet. The sinking of this tanker was the only one of the month in either 222 or 225 Group areas.

112. December opened with considerable activity and movement of G.R. aircraft in order to protect large shipping movements in the Bay of Bengal. To relieve the congestion on the Bengal communications system, Fourteenth Army were to be reinforced from east coast ports, and extensive patrols were provided to cover the entire eastern approaches to the Bay of Bengal. This involved a large-scale and rapid movement of forces over distances varying from 1,000 to 1,400 miles to concentrate suitable aircraft in strategic positions.

113. Round-the-clock patrols began at first light on the 6th and finished at midday on the 9th as the ships reached Chittagong. The redeployment between Groups, and the conduct of the operation were notable for the high state of efficiency and serviceability maintained. During the operation there was only one sighting of a submarine, thought to be a Japanese of the "I" class. Unfortunately the Catalina was not positioned for an immediate attack and further searches failed to locate the enemy again. Two enemy aircraft were sighted over the Bay of Bengal but were not allowed to come within range of the surface vessels.

114. On the 23rd December the enemy torpedoed the S.S. Peshawar in convoy off the south-east coast of India. The attack was made in perfect weather at midday and while a Catalina was escorting. This was the first example of such an attack while escort was provided. Continuous day and night cover and a hunt to exhaustion was instituted, but apart from a report from the same convoy on the 25th, which caused an extension of the air cover, no other sightings were made.

115. On the 27th, H.M.I.S. BERAR (escort vessel) carried out a submarine attack near the south-west tip of India without any known result. A Catalina of 225 Group witnessed the attacks, and the detailed report and photographs taken by the aircraft's crew were of great value in assessing the results. Further south-west, on the same day, a merchant vessel was torpedoed, and to counter the threat to the many convoys in these waters, Catalinas were moved from Ceylon to Kelai, and Addu Atoll was reinforced.

116. Since commitments in 222 Group were heavy, especially in affording air cover to units of the growing Eastern Fleet, Beauforts were used to escort coastal convoys, and long-range aircraft reserved for the forward island bases and the Australia-Colombo convoys.

117. During this month No. 354 Liberator (B.24) Squadron took over the G.R. patrols previously flown by Wellington medium-bomber squadrons, and extended them to cover the N.E. Bay of Bengal, and the Arakan coastal areas. No sightings of enemy surface or underwater forces were made during these patrols, but this did not

detract from their value as negative reconnaissance. Several small craft off the Arakan coast were attacked and sunk with bombs and gunfire.

118. The early part of January was conspicuous for the dearth of enemy activity in southern and eastern waters, in spite of the increased number of convoy sailings and movements of naval forces. One U-boat was known to be in the Maldives area, and on the 16th another made an attack off Pondicherry, sinking one vessel. A Catalina assisted in the rescue work, but the offensive anti-submarine search which was immediately instituted proved fruitless. What was probably the same submarine was sighted and attacked by a Catalina of No. 240 Squadron returning from a convoy escort on the 22nd. Probable damage was done in spite of the difficult conditions of light and angle of attack, and a hunt to exhaustion was immediately initiated using Catalinas of both 225 and 222 Groups. The enemy was not destroyed, although depth-charges were dropped on a possible sighting, and no further attacks were made on convoys in the area.

119. 225 Group aircraft continued to search for the submarine until after dawn on the 25th, but the 222 Group detachment returned to Ceylon to provide cover for units of Eastern Fleet. Beauforts carried out anti-submarine sweeps in front of Trincomalee harbour, while the Catalinas escorted the arriving ships to port.

120. In spite of defensive air patrols, one independently routed merchant vessel was sunk in the Maldives area, but aircraft again located survivors and guided a cruiser to the spot.

121. Considering the great amount of shipping activity, the month witnessed comparatively few attacks. It is probable, however, that enemy submarines were being employed on reconnaissance, particularly of the growing concentration of naval forces. There is no doubt that the provision of patrols and escorts of the greatest density possible with the forces available was responsible for denying to these enemy reconnaissance submarines much useful information.

122. In February the number of enemy submarines estimated to be in the Indian Ocean rose to ten, and patrol activity was intensified to meet the threat. It became necessary to augment air cover for the threatened areas around Ceylon with Catalinas and Wellingtons from 225 Group. Sinkings were heavy during the month, but one submarine was destroyed by escort vessels with the co-operation of the covering aircraft, and another, after it had sunk H.M.T. KHEDIVE ISMAIL, by H.M. destroyers who were guarding the troopship in such a strength that no air escort was deemed necessary.

123. The sinkings necessitated many rescue operations by aircraft, and the survivors of three ships were located and covered while surface craft were guided to them. The outstanding rescue was that of survivors of a ship torpedoed fourteen days earlier 800 miles from the mainland.

124. The other major operation of the month, which absorbed a considerable number of aircraft hours, was the cover given to a slow-moving floating dock from Bombay to Trincomalee – cover which would probably not have been afforded had the "Stipple" procedure been in force.

125. Towards the end of February there arose a potential threat to the east coast of

India from the move of a considerable portion of the Japanese Fleet to Singapore. Plans were laid for the assembly and despatch of air striking forces including all heavy bomber squadrons should the occasion arise. Bases in Southern India and Ceylon were prepared and stocked for the possible advent of large forces from Bengal, and No. 200 (Liberator G.R.) Squadron from West Africa and No. 47 (Torpedo) Beaufighter Squadron from the Mediterranean arrived as reinforcements. No. 27 (Coastal Fighter) Beaufighter Squadron was detached from Bengal to work with No. 47 Squadron at Madras. The threat did not materialise but the organisation built up has been retained in skeleton form.

126. March witnessed a peak of activity which began on the first of the month with a hunt to exhaustion following the sinking of a merchant vessel twenty-five miles south-west of Galle. In the forty-fourth hour of the search a Catalina sighted and attacked a surfaced submarine by moonlight. The enemy U-boat was not seen after the attack, and although it was probably damaged the search was continued for two more days.

127. Further enemy attacks resulted in two sinkings in the Arabian Sea, four in more southerly waters, and one of a troopship in the northern Bay of Bengal, an area hitherto almost completely immune from submarine attacks. There were regrettable delays in reporting the sinking, and thus the assembling of forces to search for the submarine, but the limited number of aircraft available to 173 Wing which controlled the area, eked out by Beaufighters from 224 Group, carried out a modified search until the arrival of reinforcements. The flying effort and quick turn round of the few aircraft available, however, was particularly creditable, one Liberator of No. 354 Squadron being airborne again forty-seven minutes after landing.

128. No. 230 (Sunderland) Squadron arrived in the Command during March, but it did not begin to operate fully until later, since lack of spares kept its serviceability low.

129. In April the number of submarines operating in the Indian Ocean fell to an estimated two. One was believed to be in the Maldives area and the other to be operating on the trade routes between Freemantle and Colombo, out of range of aircraft operating from the Maldives. Beaufort aircraft were thus employed on coastal convoy escort, and long-range aircraft were held at Ceylon in readiness for a threat further afield. No ships were sunk in the waters around India during the month, and the gradual change-over from the defensive to the offensive was symbolised in this month by the successful escort provided to Eastern Fleet in their strike with carrier-borne aircraft against Sabang in North-West Sumatra.

130. In May, Eastern Fleet was again covered during its journey to and from Sourabaya. During the month, it became possible to discontinue the Arakan coast patrols. No sightings of any importance had been made in the six months that the patrols had been carried out, and the continued absence of a threat in this area now allowed of a diversion of these aircraft to more positive work.

131. The loss of Liberators (B.24) engaged on photographic reconnaissance of the Andamans, Nicobars and North Sumatra led to the investigation of enemy radar by two specially equipped Liberators allotted to my Command. Twenty-six sorties were

flown from Ceylon to the Andaman Islands, Car Nicobar, Simalur, and Northern Sumatra. Conclusive evidence was obtained on these flights that the enemy employ in this theatre beam-swept radar of the type found on Attu and Guadalcanal. At the end of April the aircraft were transferred from Ceylon to Bengal in order to operate along the Burma coastline and in the Bangkok area, but the results of their investigations have not been sufficiently conclusive to be included in this despatch.

132. Searches carried out by coastal aircraft during the period assisted in the location and rescue of a total of 535 survivors from torpedoed vessels in the waters around India.

133. The results of coastal activity are seldom tangible, and an account of the work of forces engaged on this work must of necessity draw attention to those occasions when the enemy's positive attacks overcame the efforts of negative reconnaissance. Such attacks in the area patrolled by India and Ceylon-based aircraft did not and could not meet with sufficient reaction to provide a continual deterrent to the enemy's intrusions, nor was the rate of destruction of submarines high enough to prove a serious obstacle to him, since the maximum forces available in India and Ceylon during the period consisted of ten long-range and three medium-range squadrons.

*

VII. – PHOTOGRAPHIC RECONNAISSANCE

134. In November it was the intention that No. 681 and 684 P.R. Squadrons should eventually come under the control of Strategic Air Force. To this end No. 171 Wing, which had originally been formed as a Tactical Reconnaissance Wing, was moved from Southern India to take over administrative and operational control. The 9th P.R. Squadron, U.S.A.A.F., was still under the control of 10th U.S. Army Air Force.

135. No really long-range reconnaissance had been carried out by this time, since No. 684 Squadron had only recently received Mosquitoes, and there had not been time to explore the potentialities of this aircraft under tropical conditions. The radius of P.R. cover on the 1st December, excluding the Andaman Islands, was only 680 miles. On 15th December the first cover of Bangkok was obtained and provided much valuable information regarding Japanese dispositions and their use of lay-back airfields. Although Bangkok is now a routine target, the sortie was at that time an outstanding achievement, since the range of the Mosquito in this climate was still undetermined.

136. At this time the main rôle of the two squadrons was to provide airfield cover for aircraft counts, to photograph communications and areas indicated by the Army, and to cover potential target areas for attacks in Burma. Twice weekly sorties were flown to Port Blair in the Andamans to secure information on the enemy's anti-shipping activities. In January one of the few Mitchells (B.25) belonging to No. 684 Squadron photographed Mergui on the Tenasserim Coast for the first time, involving a journey of 1,600 miles. Survey photography was also begun during the month to meet a long-felt need for accurate and up-to-date maps of Burma. By the end of May,

not only immediate battle areas had been surveyed, but also approximately 57 per cent. of the whole of the country. The remainder of the effort was absorbed in assessing the extent to which communication facilities were being used and the damage inflicted upon them. The record number of eighty airfields were covered in one day, as was the greater part of the Burma railway system, allowing of an accurate aircraft count and a reliable estimate of the engines and rolling-stock in the country. Another valuable result of the large-scale airfield cover was the issue of target mosaics to long-range fighter squadrons, which proved of great assistance, especially when airfields were attacked.

137. Meanwhile, the American P.R. squadron equipped with Lightnings (F.5) was still working independently. This often resulted in duplication of effort, and closer co-ordination was clearly desirable. Thus on the 1st February, Photographic Reconnaissance Force was formed, incorporating No. 171 Wing Headquarters. This month and March were notable for many sorties to obtain airfield information and to assess the damage to communications by aircraft of Third Tactical Air Force and No. 1 Air Commando Force. Survey work was also carried out, together with regular flights to the Andamans and the vast area bounded by a line joining Kentung, Sittang, Mergui and Koh Si Chang Island (South-East of Bangkok).

138. Small country-craft were now being increasingly used by the enemy, and the waterways of the Arakan and Central Burma were also frequently photographed to assess the density of traffic and staging points. On 27th March the longest flight yet, of 1,860 miles, was achieved by a Mosquito of No. 684 Squadron when a large stretch of the Bangkok-Singapore railway was covered.

139. In April a substantial increase in the number of Army requests entailed numerous sorties over the battle and reinforcement areas. A Mosquito improved upon the record flight of the previous month by photographing many stretches of railway in the Malay Peninsula, flying 2,172 miles to do so.

140. The advent of the monsoon affected photographic reconnaissance work perhaps more than any. In May, instead of concentrating on the programmes laid down, it became a question of finding areas where the weather was best and photographing the highest priority targets in them.

141. The outstanding achievement of the month was the photography of islands in the Great Nicobar group. The flight was intended to discover if it were possible to reach these islands, but on arrival there was sufficient fuel remaining to take photographs before returning. Short-range squadrons during May obtained routine cover wherever possible and were also instructed to bring back as full a weather report as possible, which proved valuable in planning the next day's sorties. Only three of the twenty-three sorties flown on survey photography were wholly successful. An idea of the achievement in the field of survey photography before the bad weather is shown by the following figures, which represent the photographing of an area three times the size of England in four and a half months:

Net area covered	152,000 square miles (approx.)
Made up of:	
6 in. cover	134,000 square miles

12 in. cover	18,000 square miles

In addition:

12 in. cover of areas photographed on a smaller scale

38,000 square miles

142. The foregoing account will give an indication of the great advance in the regularity and extent of the cover obtained. Targets as far away as Rangoon, Bassein and Lashio came to be regarded as routine even by Lightnings (F.5) and Spitfire aircraft, while the ranges achieved by Mosquitoes were little less than phenomenal. A high standard of photography and technical work was maintained.

*

PART THREE
SURVEY OF RESULTS AND LESSONS LEARNED

143. Although territorial gains in the campaign until the end of May were small, the ground won back from the enemy in Northern Burma marked the first step towards the re-opening of overland communications with China. The advance of the Chinese-American forces, and the disruption of enemy communications by Special Force which aided it, would have been impossible without the air superiority which had been gained, allowing the free use of transport support aircraft and of fighters and bombers in close support. The same is true of both the less positive achievements of the campaign, the breaking of two large-scale enemy offensives – one aimed at Chittagong and the other at Imphal. Of the attack on Imphal, C.-in-C. 11 Army Group stated: "There is absolutely no doubt that had we not had air supply we should have lost the Imphal Plain, and the position on the eastern frontier of India would have been very grave". He might with equal truth have said "Had we not had air superiority".

144. The campaign established that the employment of air transport in this theatre is capable of indefinite expansion, and yields dividends that could not be gained by any other agency. Moreover, there is scope for a wider range of transport aircraft than obtains in Europe, where thick jungle and high mountain barriers do not impede swift communication. Light aircraft which can land in a space too small for Dakotas are able to carry out a multitude of tasks for commanders, and, by eliminating the feeling of isolation brought on when fighting so far from established bases, have a beneficial effect on the morale of the forces engaged.

145. Close support of ground troops in such terrain has proved the value of accurate bomb and gun attacks in a locality where pin-points are few and targets difficult to identify, requiring a thorough knowledge of the sector. Such knowledge is clearly of special significance in this theatre. Air liaison officers when briefing crews can give targets that would often be refused in other theatres as too difficult for identification. The same is true of dropping zones for supply-dropping aircraft.

Crews and staff officers from the European theatre of operations state that the dropping points given here would be considered impossible there. Thus, complete familiarity with the area over which they have to operate has been found essential for crews engaged in ground or transport support work.

146. I have discussed the complexities of close support in Burma in the section dealing with that type of operation. Certain conclusions follow that are worthy of note. First, unless used in overwhelming strength, the heavy bomber is no more the answer against an entrenched enemy than has been found in other theatres. Secondly, if air bombardment on a heavy scale is used, the infantry must follow the attack immediately in order that the limited effect on the enemy is not lost before the attack goes in. Thirdly, specialised trials are necessary to determine the best types of bombs for use against jungle targets. These are now being carried out in this Command. Finally, the fighter-bomber and the dive-bomber, with their extreme accuracy, proved excellent aircraft in close support in difficult terrain. The Hurricane, for example, could be employed against targets in valleys hemmed in by cloud, conditions that demanded high manoeuvrability if the target was to be reached at all. Comparable aircraft of higher performance and with the ability to carry a greater weight of bombs should prove an even more decisive weapon.

147. In combating the Japanese Air Force, the lack of long-range fighters was acutely felt until Mustangs (P.51) and Lightnings (P.38) of the U.S.A.A.F. became available. Once our air superiority was established in the forward areas the enemy utilised bases too far away for normal-range aircraft to reach them. I have recounted later how it was that pressurised long-range tanks were not yet ready for the Spitfires, which could not therefore be used in the rôle of long-range counter air offensive. In this theatre, where distances are so great and the enemy so widely dispersed, long-range fighters are essential both for escort and offensive operations.

148. Finally, it has been proved in this theatre as in others that air power is co-equal with land power, and that Army and Air Commanders should work from a Joint Headquarters if they are effectively to implement the principles of command required by a combined Army/Air Plan. It is according to this broad principle, which has been agreed with the General Officer Commanding-in-Chief 11 Army Group and approved by the Supreme Allied Commander, that future air operations in South-East Asia will be conducted.

*

PART FOUR
EXPANSION AND DEVELOPMENT

I. – ORGANISATION, REINFORCEMENTS AND BASES

149. The remoteness of this theatre of war from centres of control at home, together

with the obligation of developing so economically backward a country as India as a supply base, has inevitably led to the assumption by my Headquarters Staff of functions which rightly belong to an Air Ministry, a Ministry of Aircraft Production, a Ministry of Labour, a Ministry of Economic Warfare, and perhaps even a Board of Trade. Estimated at its lowest, Air Command, South-East Asia, exercises the powers at least of Deputies to such bodies.

150. The formation of South-East Asia Command resulted in extensive developments in organisation, and a whole hierarchy of Headquarters has been called into being. Headquarters, Supreme Allied Commander, South-East Asia, moved from Delhi to Kandy in March, 1944. It was not possible to move my Headquarters to Kandy at this time, as the expansion and development of my Command necessitated maintaining the closest contact with G.H.Q. India, and so it was necessary to form an Advanced Headquarters, A.C.S.E.A., consisting of a Planning and Liaison Staff, to accompany H.Q. S.A.C.S.E.A. in its move to Kandy. Air Headquarters, India, was set up as an autonomous unit to control operations on the North-West Frontier and assume responsibility for the I.A.F., directly responsible under its own A.O.C. to C.-in-C. India. Eastern Air Command was established to co-ordinate air operations on the Burmese frontier. Its Headquarters moved on 15th April to Calcutta in order to maintain closer touch with its subordinate units – the Strategic Air Force, Third Tactical Air Force, Troop Carrier Command and Photographic Reconnaissance Force. Thus administrative control of American units also gravitated to Calcutta, since this remained the responsibility of Major-General G.E. Stratemeyer in his other capacity, that of Commanding-General of the U.S.A.A.F. in the India-Burma Sector of the China-Burma-India Theatre.

151. In December, 1943, three new R.A.F. Groups were formed – Nos. 229 (Transport) Group, 230 (Maintenance) and 231 (Bomber). Within the period covered by this despatch eleven R.A.F. and I.A.F. squadrons were added to my command either by formation or on transfer from another theatre. In addition, a second flight has been added to Nos. 681 and 684 P.R. Squadrons, whilst at the height of the defence of Imphal, No. 216 Transport Squadron was operating under my command on detachment from the Mediterranean. A further eight squadrons were held in back areas for re-equipment, and seven others changed their battle rôle. The conversion programme has been mainly bound up with the further infusion of Mosquitoes and Spitfires into the Command, while Thunderbolts are also arriving, and plans to re-equip the Hurricane squadrons with them have been formulated. The flow of aircraft in support of this modernization has been steady, though the R.A.F. in South-East Asia remains, as far as aircraft types are concerned, at least a year behind other theatres. Parallel to this expansion and re-equipment has been the rationalisation of the areas for which Groups in India are responsible to correspond with the boundaries of Army Commands.

152. The large programme of airfield development has been continued, with the ultimate purpose of providing accommodation for the approved number of squadrons included in my long-term target. Save for certain new sites in the forward areas and in Ceylon, all development has been of existing airfields. Five airfields west of

Calcutta have been developed for the U.SA.A.F. as bases for V.H.B. aircraft. The need for pressing forward our offensive and air transport operations has been responsible for the expansion of a number of airfields in the Fourteenth Army area east of the Brahmaputra. In Ceylon, work has begun on the development of two new airfields at Kankesanturai and Negombo for heavy aircraft, while, for special operations, runway extension and strengthening of taxi-tracks has been undertaken at China Bay. Work is being started on a plan for reinforcement route development. In this field of development effective use has been made of bitumenised hessian – "bithess" – for both runways and apron hard standings. The serviceability of this experimental material under monsoon conditions is being closely observed.

153. The procedure of implementing works projects was altered slightly in January, 1944, though the difficulties and delays remained as before. In the Fourteenth Army area, priorities awarded to the R.A.F. services have been liable to alteration by Army commanders without any reference being made to the Air Commander concerned, and without any appreciation of the effect of such alterations on the future of the air offensive. Labour and material has been diverted and moved without giving any notification to the R.A.F. authorities concerned; frequently the first intimation that they receive of such action is the complete cessation of work upon some R.A.F. project.

154. The expansion of establishments connected with the formation of new Headquarters units and the preparation of cadres for the reception of future reinforcements has aggravated the manpower shortage. The overall Command deficiency of effective strength against current establishments has throughout the period been approximately 12 per cent.; but although this deficiency may not appear unduly in excess of the global R.A.F. shortage, nevertheless there has been very severe lack of personnel in individual trades. Since reinforcements in the period reached this Command in only negligible quantity, various alternative sources of supply to meet the deficiencies have been tried. An extensive scheme has been inaugurated for remustering British other ranks from lower trade groups into the more severely deficient higher trade groups, but this, besides merely transferring the shortage from one trade to another, has also meant a loss to effective strength of the airmen undergoing conversion training. The recruitment of Indians both as officers and men to fill the vacancies has also offered some solution, but this has continued only at a diminished rate and it has been very difficult to find suitable officer candidates. Further, some months must elapse even after the period of formal training before such reinforcements can be counted on as fully effective. The question of substitution by women has also been given special attention. The W.A.A.F. mission from the Air Ministry led by Air Chief Commandant Dame Trefusis J. Forbes arrived in February. As a result of her investigations discussions have been begun with the Government of India. Meanwhile W.A.C. (I) recruiting for the Air Forces in India has been at a standstill. It may be added that with the advent of the decentralised system of establishment control introduced at the end of 1943 manning has been placed on an entirely new basis. Personnel are now demanded against ceiling

establishment figures as fixed by the Asian Establishments Committee after consultation with my Headquarters.

*

II. – MAINTENANCE AND REPAIR

155. I referred in my last despatch to the uphill task confronting the maintenance organisation in this Command. Without actual knowledge of the conditions, however, many of the inherent difficulties cannot be fully appreciated and deserve further emphasis.

156. The low standard of industrialisation in India throws a heavy burden on the shoulders of Service maintenance personnel, who receive none of the assistance from contractors' working parties that is available at home establishments. Even when it is possible to sub-contract work to civilian firms, the quality of the products leaves much to be desired. Secondly, the vast distances involved call for a wide dispersal of existing stocks and make A.O.G. procedure extremely slow. Thirdly, there is a case for stating that it is not sufficiently realised that more manpower is needed per unit of output than in other theatres of war where spares are more readily available, the sickness rate lower, and base repair not rendered so difficult by the distances between depots and the operational areas, with the inevitable deterioration of damaged aircraft in transit. It is in the light of these and similar difficulties that the work of maintenance and repair should be considered.

157. Expansion during the period was directed mainly to preparations for dealing eventually with the load of 156 squadrons envisaged under the Long Term Target for the Command. Additional civilian capacity has been mobilised; one unit – No. 2 Command Maintenance Unit Trichinopoly – is in process of being doubled in size, and three new C.M.U.s have been formed. No. 322 M.U. at Cawnpore is now in operation, constituting the largest service base repair depot in India. When it reaches full capacity it will be able to deal with major repairs to about 55 large aircraft and with the overhaul of nearly 500 engines per month.

158. A comprehensive organisation has been built for holding reserve aircraft at Aircraft Storage Units and Reserve Aircraft Pools so disposed as to cover the whole of India in three zones. The A.S.U.s hold a two-months' reserve, while the R.A.P.s hold a fortnight's reserve of aircraft ready for immediate issue. This organisation has contributed in no small measure to the high rate of serviceability in squadrons, since it is generally possible to replace aircraft within twenty-four hours.

159. Lack of storage accommodation for holding main stocks has been due to poor progress in the erection of new buildings planned long since, and is a most serious problem at the present time, when approximately 30,000 cases of R.A.F. stores have had to be stored in the open.

160. Often in this Command an aircraft which has crashed or force-landed away from an airfield has to be written off because of the fundamental and ineradicable shortcomings of the transport system. Even if a damaged aircraft can be taken to the nearest railway, the journey thence to a repair depot generally causes so much further

damage that a machine that was capable of repair is fit only for write-off when it reaches its destination. One remedy, which is having encouraging results, was the formation of an Airborne Salvage Section in November 1943 to fly to the scene of a crash in a specially fitted transport aircraft which can carry spares, tools and engines. On reaching the site, patch repairs are effected and the damaged aircraft nursed to the nearest depot. The Airborne Salvage Section was given one of the first Dakotas it salvaged, and in that aircraft mainplanes of large aircraft and complete Spitfires have been carried. Up to date, the Section has salvaged eighteen aircraft; the possibility of forming further similar sections is under consideration.

161. An example of the shortage of manpower to meet emergencies arose in April when transport operations necessitated the maximum output of Dakotas both from major inspections and repair. By diverting all available resources, the time taken on the floor was progressively reduced until it became half of what it had been at the end of 1943. This rapid turnover was only achieved, however, by concentrating maintenance personnel on Dakotas at every stage of their travel, with a consequent reduction of work on other types. The output of Dakotas from repair rose from two in December to ten in April and eleven in May. The later figures would have been higher still but for the complete lack of certain spares in this Command which had to be demanded from America.

162. Attempts to produce locally jettison tanks exemplify the difficulties and delays experienced in indigenous production. The tanks were requested in October/November 1943 to implement the long-range fighter policy. The most suitable firm for their manufacture was chosen, but found that it could not work to the required limits laid down in the standard Vickers' drawings, and more generous tolerances had to be permitted. In spite of this, one difficulty after another arose, and metal tanks are still not available for issue. I have already indicated the urgency with which they were needed in the Third Tactical Air Force. As an alternative, a plywood tank was developed and successfully flight tested in December 1943. There were, however, the inevitable delays in getting it into production, and they were not actually available for operational use until May.

163. Simple types of equipment more suited to the manufacturing resources of the country have been produced to the fullest extent, and British production thereby relieved of a considerable burden. The monthly output of supply-dropping parachutes increased from 35,000 to 144,000, and it is anticipated that this figure will be increased to 250,000 by the end of the year.

164. Very close liaison has been maintained with the U.S. Air Service Command. There is a free and complete exchange of technical information and liaison officers are established at both Headquarters. At the time when the Dakota position was acute, the Air Service Command released to the R.A.F. one-third of their total stocks of Dakota spares in the country.

165. Despite the increased operational effort, the serviceability of squadrons has been well maintained. To some extent the higher wastage of aircraft has had to be met from reserve stocks, whilst the number of airframes and engines under or awaiting repair has increased. It is not certain that this back-log will be fully

eliminated during the monsoon, because of shortage of personnel in the various trades and the inherent shortcomings of an organisation of rapid growth working with inadequate local resources.

*

III. – SIGNALS, COMMUNICATIONS AND RADAR

166. One of the major problems of the Command has always been the provision of efficient communication facilities over long distances. Trunk telephone and telegraph systems give poor and unreliable service, nor can any appreciable improvement be expected until the Indian Posts and Telegraphs Department is reinforced by Military signals units. Meanwhile the construction of long-distance overhead carrier systems is proceeding, although the maintenance problems that will arise when they are complete cannot be solved without additions to personnel. The six Air Formation Signals units within the Command have worked well in view of their deficiency of seven Officers and 270 British Other Ranks on the 1943 target. Indeed, shortage of personnel has been the greatest single limiting factor in the expansion of signals facilities. The situation was further aggravated by the need to supply to Special Force 185 Wireless Operators and Mechanics and eight Officers. These personnel are still with the Division.

167. The formation of Eastern Air Command resulted in a high degree of co-operation and exchange of technical information between American and British forces, particularly in the sphere of radar. Two G.C.I. stations were sited to cover American bases in the Brahmaputra Valley and another was sited at Shinbuiyang in May to provide early warning for the Chinese-American forces advancing down the Hukawng Valley. Further British and American Light Warning sets were also deployed in the area. Another G.C.I. set has been modified in order that it may be carried by air and made available to U.S. forces. New American Light Warning sets have been tested jointly by R.A.F. and U.S.A.A.F. officers. Moreover, with the prospect of Loran stations for the use of A.T.C. aircraft proceeding to and from China being installed, the operational use of this device by the R.A.F. in the Command has come nearer to realisation. Information on Radio Counter Measures has been provided to XXth Bomber Command and to other American units. Finally, all American units in this theatre have adopted the R.A.F. call-sign procedure.

168. All signals planning for future operations has been undertaken with mobility as the keynote. Specialist signals vehicles have been produced within the Command and are designed to meet needs peculiar to this theatre. Moreover, static establishments in operational units in the Third Tactical Air Force have been replaced by mobile units with the result that Group and Wing Headquarters will in future be self-contained and fully mobile as regards signals requirements. The formation of No. 5 Base Signals Unit provided the cadre for operational training under field conditions. Personnel thrown up by the substitution of Wireless Observer Units by Indian Mobile Wireless Observer Companies were among the first to use these

training facilities. It has thus been possible to establish No. 4 Group Control Centre and 104 Mobile Air Reporting Unit which will replace the existing organisation in the Tactical Air Force of Group Operations Rooms, Filter Rooms, etc. The installation of Radar units in barges has been used to good effect already. In November, the most advanced units were those along the Cox's Bazaar-Ramu Road and the terrain in front of these was unsuitable for more extended siting. As soon as the Army had advanced to Maungdaw, an Air Ministry Experimental Station (A.M.E.S.) was anchored off St. Martin's Island. This station, together with a G.C.I. and Mobile Radar Unit (M.R.U.) sited at Maungdaw, provided most useful cover and assisted in successful interceptions off the Arakan coast. G.C.I. sets have also been installed in a jeep, amphibious jeep and an amphibious DUKW.

169. There has been an overall increase of 30 per cent. in navigational aids since November. The installation of static H.F. D/F[2] stations is practically completed and the delivery of V.H.F. D/F[3] equipment permitted a start to be made on its erection at all airfields along the main transport and reinforcement routes within India. An up-to-date map is issued quarterly giving details of all aids to navigation, and the combining of R.A.F. and U.S.A.A.F. facilities has been of great value.

170. Details of the airborne investigations of enemy Radar have been given in Part Two of this Despatch.

171. Signals traffic saw a large increase with the creation of Advanced Headquarters, Air Command, South East Asia, in Ceylon, and of Eastern Air Command, Strategic Air Force, No. 230 and 231 Groups in Bengal. Cypher traffic increased from 11¼ to 15½ million groups per month, and a High Speed Automatic W/T channel was installed to handle the increased traffic between Delhi and Colombo arising from the move of the Supreme Allied Commander's Headquarters to Ceylon. To offset the increase rendered inevitable by the creation of many new Headquarters, an airgram service has been started within the Command. That such a step was necessary is an apt comment on the vast distances over which messages have to travel in this theatre.

*

IV. – FLYING CONTROL

172. Although the value of Flying Control facilities has always been recognised in the Command, development has been hampered by the continued shortage of trained personnel and necessary equipment. An efficient Flying Control organisation has become more and more essential in this theatre where bad weather, a lack of land-line communications, and widely dispersed landing grounds make diversion a complicated task. Moreover, air transport operations into the Imphal Valley could have been intensified but for the low standard of proficiency among the inexperienced controllers on the few airfields available. Within these limitations, however, much has been done, and its value is evidenced by the fact that at the only two airfields in 221 Group which could be provided with proper flying control, there were in

February no avoidable accidents among the four squadrons accommodated there.

173. In November there were only thirty trained British Flying Control Officers in the Command. This small body was reinforced by forty resting aircrew and thirty I.A.F. officers. There were forty main airfields along the reinforcement routes and in Ceylon, with no airfield controllers, no trained airmen and very little equipment, among which these personnel were distributed.

174. In anticipation of the arrival of trained controllers from England, plans were made to institute a full Flying Control organisation in the operational areas and along the reinforcement routes by February. Unfortunately the flow from U.K. was stopped in January and the plan could not be implemented. The urgent needs of operational airfields had to be met by stripping other areas below the safety margin and diluting their establishment with too high a proportion of I.A.F. officers. At the end of May deficiencies on current establishments amounted to 150 officers and 100 airfield controllers.

175. One of the most encouraging features of the development is the progress made towards complete integration with the U.S.A.A.F. Liaison has been pursued since September 1943, and in March of this year a joint conference proposed the setting up of one system of Air Traffic Control throughout the Command. A committee was set up to examine the technical problems involved and make recommendations. These included a Joint Flying Control Board which will meet at intervals and, it is hoped, maintain the unanimity achieved by the initial committee. Application was made to U.S.A.A.F. H.Q. to send to the Command officers trained in the joint system now working in U.K.

176. I therefore anticipate that a unified system of Flying Control will soon be operating throughout the Command, and that every crew will receive standard briefing and standard aids on all flights.

*

V. – ARMAMENT

177. The slow receipt and dissemination of up-to-date information on armament matters, as indeed in all technical branches, has hindered the work of making the best use of weapons and developing the striking power of the Command. New publications take two months to arrive and an even longer period to reprint and distribute. One remedy has been an extensive use of the microgram service to hasten the process of keeping technical personnel informed on all current developments.

178. Operational failures have been reduced in spite of the fact that fighter squadrons do not possess Armament Officers. It has been found that the stoppage rates on squadrons more than twenty miles from their Wing Armament Officer are from 1.5 to 2.5 times those on squadrons less than twenty miles from the wing. In spite of the fact that there are established posts for only ten squadron Armament Officers in the Command, which are naturally allotted to the bomber squadrons, and that there are many establishment vacancies which have not been filled because of

the serious shortage of armament officers, .303 gun failures have fallen from 0.11 to 0.08 and 20 mm. from 2.07 to 1.48 per thousand rounds. Bomb failures have similarly fallen from 0.47 to 0.25 per hundred bombs. The measures which contributed to this improvement were a decentralisation of the training and maintenance branches, a better system of check on failures, and careful distribution of available manpower. To aid in this distribution a certain dilution of I.A.F. personnel has been accepted. These have proved suitable and efficient tradesmen at certain tasks and have enabled the following dilution to be effected:

	per cent.
(i) I.A.F. Squadrons	100
(ii) M.U.s	50
(iii) Other non-operational units	25
(iv) Operational R.A.F. Squadrons	25

(provided British Other Ranks are substituted when available.)

179. A number of new weapons have arrived in the Command and come into use, operationally, during the period. Hurricane IID aircraft armed with 40 mm. cannon first operated in No. 20 Squadron in December, 1943. The initial A.P. ammunition was supplemented in February by H.E. which has proved very effective against rivercraft. R.P. has been used by No. 211 Squadron since January. It was at first employed against bridge targets, but the delay fuse was found to be unsatisfactory for this type of attack and no proper facilities were available for modifying it. In view of this, R.P. attacks have been directed against rolling stock, transport convoys, oil installations, factories and rivercraft with good effect. 500 lb. M.C. bombs came into use early in the new year, and in addition to the supply to Bengal, stocks have been built up at selected stations in Southern India and Ceylon should action become necessary against a Japanese Naval Task Force. 2,000 lb. A.P. bombs have been distributed for the same purpose.

180. A 4,000 lb. bomb was dropped on Burma for the first time in November, 1943, against railway targets at Sagaing; its employment since then has been extended both by day and night. Among American weapons which have been introduced since November are parachute fragmentation bombs, 300 lb. spike bombs for use against railway lines, the noses being of indigenous manufacture, and the rocket-gun employed in the same manner as the R.A.F. rocket-projectile.

181. Close liaison between British and American Armament Staffs resulted in much inter-change of information and resources. American aircraft used R.A.F. flares and the R.A.F. used American mines, incendiaries and drift lights.

*

VI. – TRAINING

182. The re-orientation of the training organisation early in the period allocated responsibility on a geographical basis, and No. 227 Group was no longer regarded

primarily as the training group. From January onwards, each group supervised and administered training within its own area.

183. Much of the available resources have been absorbed by the need to convert crews to the latest types of aircraft, since reinforcements arriving in the Command have not been familiarised with these types, and many existing squadrons are re-equipping. The change-over from Vengeances to Mosquitoes, from Wellingtons to Liberators and from Hurricanes to Thunderbolts are the outstanding examples. As a result, it is hoped that there will be five trained Liberator and nine Thunderbolt squadrons by November, and two Mosquito squadrons by October. Wastage replacement crews are trained concurrently and provide a valuable reserve without calling upon outside assistance.

184. Refresher flying training was provided at Poona for 614 aircrew either newly arrived in the Command or returning to operations after a period of rest. Air Gunner Instructor courses, I.A.F. ab initio W/Op. A.G. courses and R.A.F. Pilot Refresher courses have been carried out continuously at Bairagarh in Bhopal where two I.A.F. squadrons (Nos. 3 and 9) also completed armament and gunnery training. The Air Fighting Training Unit gave advanced courses on tactics and gunnery control, through which 71 pilots and 83 gunnery leaders passed, and which were attended by many U.S.A.A.F. personnel. No. 22 Armament Practice Camp carried out six bomber and fighter refresher courses, one of which was attended by No. 459 Squadron U.S.A.A.F. whose results improved markedly during the course. No. 231 Group Navigation School passed 420 aircrew through its courses.

185. I.A.F. G.D. recruiting did not come up to expectations. The following table of output during the period indicates the scale of I.A.F. production and wastage:

From I.T.W.	224
From E.F.T.S	101
From S.F.T.S	80
From O.T.U	113

186. Ground training was mainly of I.A.F. personnel, of whom 8,049 were admitted to Recruit Training Centres. A fraction over 9,000 I.O.R.s were under training of all kinds at the end of the period. One important task, the training of flight mechanics, was taken over from the Director of Civil Aviation, and as a result the civilian schools were closed or taken over as Schools of Technical Training.

*

VII. – INTERNAL AIR ROUTES

187. The formation early in December of No. 229 Group of Transport Command enabled me to introduce a stricter supervision of internal transport flying, passenger and freight services, and of the movement of aircraft in India and Ceylon. The need for this had long been apparent but the means had been lacking. One of the more positive results of the decentralisation of control I was able to make was a reduction

in the accident rate for the aircraft which came under No. 229 Group's control from 46 per 10,000 in December, 1943, to 13 in May, 1944.

188. The number of aircraft available for internal services continued to be small in comparison with requirements and the distances involved. Since it was necessary to earmark nearly all Dakotas for the replacement of wastages in squadrons operating at pressure on the Eastern frontier, the formation of another transport squadron (the sixth) had to be continually postponed, and the conversion of No. 353 Squadron from Hudsons to Dakotas delayed. This squadron, based on Palam at Delhi, together with the B.O.A.C. and the few aircraft belonging to Indian civil air lines, was all I could make available for the Air Routes. No. 229 Group's task was thus no easy one. In the six months from December to May, Hudson aircraft of No. 353 Squadron flew 7,570 hours on transport work. The age of the Hudsons makes this a creditable figure. It was only achieved by a high standard of maintenance and by using as engine spares such parts from obsolete Mohawks as were available. Six Dakotas were also made available to the squadron in April and May as a detached flight based on Dum Dum. They flew 860 hours in these two months on services between Calcutta, Colombo and Bombay. This flight was given concurrently two Dakotas to maintain a service to China which had formerly been carried out by No. 31 Squadron. Thus this one squadron was operating services extending from Ceylon to Kunming and Calcutta to Bombay.

189. Ferrying and the movement of reinforcing aircraft accounted for an average of over 1,300 aircraft deliveries a month within the Command. These flights were used to the fullest extent to supplement the internal air services. By this means, over 1,060 passengers and 500,000 pounds of freight were flown from Karachi alone.

190. I am glad to say that trunk routes to the United Kingdom have been vastly increased. The weekly R.A.F. Liberator service from Karachi has been doubled and a weekly service by R.A.F. Dakota from Colombo has been started. In May a B.O.A.C. Sunderland began to ply twice weekly from Calcutta. For communications with the Mediterranean there has been since March a B.O.A.C. Ensign service three times a week between Cairo and Calcutta. The establishment of No. 229 Group in my Command, followed by a personal visit of the A.O.C.-in-C. Transport Command and many representatives of his staff has been amongst the happiest auguries for the future that I have to record in this Despatch.

*

VIII. – R.A.F. REGIMENT

191. The strength of the R.A.F. Regiment throughout has been insufficient to justify the acceptance of full responsibility for the local defence of Royal Air Force Stations and to meet the threat of infiltration by enemy ground raiding parties to airfields and Radar stations. A remedy was sought in November, 1943, whereby the Army agreed to withdraw all static garrisons from R.A.F. stations in areas remote from enemy action, and to provide them at stations where attack was possible. The R.A.F. was to have made a contribution to the defence of its stations within the limit of available resources.

192. By December, 1943, R.A.F. Regiment personnel had been organised into units with independent establishments. It was possible to form only five field squadrons, the remaining personnel being organised into A.A. flights armed with light machine-guns, since there were not enough officers nor the requisite equipment to allow larger units to be formed. These units functioned with considerable efficiency and, in addition, station personnel instructors drawn from the Regiment trained in defence a large percentage of all personnel in threatened areas.

193. By January, 1944, Army garrisons west of the Brahmaputra had been withdrawn, but no static garrisons had been provided for the more vulnerable stations in either the 4 or 15 Corps areas. The local defence of these stations depended entirely upon the few R.A.F. Regiment Units and the station personnel. Despite repeated representations, the reduction of the Regiment to nearly half its initial strength was insisted upon by Air Ministry, and in February action to remuster personnel to other trades was initiated. The results were seen when in April the Air Commander, Third Tactical Air Force, was obliged to withdraw a number of operational squadrons from the Imphal Valley. I had no alternative but to direct that further reduction of the Regiment, already down to 3,434 all ranks, should be suspended. My Command Defence Officer was sent to England in May to explain the circumstances and to request, not only that the suspension of the Regiment reduction should be confirmed, but that a force adequate for the task of defending airfields and ancillary stations in the battle areas should be provided.

194. I append a comment by the Air Commander, Third Tactical Air Force, upon the Regiment units under his control:-

"Units of the R.A.F. Regiment have proved themselves of the greatest value in this campaign, of which the insecurity of airfields and warning establishments in forward areas has been a feature. When Radar Stations were established at St. Martin's Island and later in the Maungdaw area, the unusual situation existed of Radar Stations being actually well in advance of the frontline and within range of the enemy's guns and night patrols. It says much for the R.A.F. Regiment personnel that the Radar crews enjoyed undisturbed conditions in which to carry on their work under such trying conditions. It has proved to be quite unsound to rely on the Army maintaining troops for local defence in times of crisis when the land situation deteriorates. This is the time when they are really needed by us, but this is the time when they are invariably withdrawn to take part in the land battle".

*

IX. – AIR SEA RESCUE

195. The Air Sea Rescue organisation in this Command has been based on that of the United Kingdom, with the necessary adaptations for local conditions and the scale of equipment that is available. The responsibility for operations has been delegated

to the A.Os.C. of Groups, to whom in turn the Group Controllers of Naval Air Operations Rooms, keeping constant watch, are responsible for initiating such operations.

196. Officers responsible to their respective A.Os.C. for the efficient arrangement of Air Sea Rescue and for keeping squadrons informed of any new developments in methods of search and ancillary equipment have been established in Commands and Groups as follows:-

Eastern Air Command – One Squadron Leader.

Third T.A.F. – One Flight Lieutenant.

No. 225 Group – One Squadron Leader; One Flight
Lieutenant.

No. 222 Group – One Squadron Leader.

197. Twelve Warwicks have now after some delay arrived in India and are undergoing major overhaul at Karachi, Allahabad and Jessore. Seven Sea Otters are being off-loaded at Karachi and crews have been detailed to take a conversion course as soon as the aircraft become serviceable. When they are ready for operational flying, these aircraft will join No. 292 Squadron, the Headquarters of which will be at Jessore.

198. Meanwhile searches have been carried out by the four Walruses already in the Command, and by operational aircraft, which, whenever possible, carry the Lindholme Dinghy Gear. Experiments are being made to fit this gear to Liberators.

199. Little progress has been made in the formation of A.S.R. marine craft and Units. This is chiefly due to the slow rate at which launches have been delivered. By July, 1943, there were nine in the Command. Between this date and January 1944 no more arrived, and as a consequence no additional units could be formed. With the improvement, however, in the shipping position, four launches have recently arrived from the United Kingdom and four from the U.S.A. There has also been notification of another seventeen being shipped to this Command.

200. Air Sea Rescue Units have been formed or are now in the process of forming at the following places: Chittagong, Maiakhal Island, Calcutta, Dhamra River, Vizagapatam, Madras, Cochin, Bombay, Karachi, China Bay, Colombo, Galle, Kayts (Jaffna), Jiwani and Jask (Iraq). The craft, however, allocated to most of these units have not yet arrived in the Command, or are still being fitted out and so are not yet operational.

201. The maintenance of these craft has been a difficult problem owing to the limited supply of spares and special tools, to the great distances between operational areas and the overhaul workshops, and to the lack of transport that prevails. The problem has been met by using naval facilities where possible for shipping and engine overhauls and by locating rescue craft by types, so that they are within as easy reach as possible of the workshops capable of doing the overhaul of their respective types of engines.

202. Thirty-seven aircraft in all were searched for. The number of aircrew personnel in these aircraft was 168, of which 102 were saved. An American

amphibious Catalina, based on Calcutta, was responsible for two ocean landings and the saving of twenty-one aircrew, both R.A.F. and U.S.A.A.F., in the Bay of Bengal.

203. The demand made upon the marine craft has on the whole been light, except in the Chittagong area where some lone sorties have been made off enemy-controlled coasts, and where an advanced rendezvous position off Katabdia Island was manned day and night for several months. This position has now been superseded by an advanced base established on Maiakhal Island.

*

X. – BALLOONS

204. Balloons were flown subject to weather conditions at six sites: at Calcutta for the protection of the docks and Howrah Bridge; at Jamshedpur, defending the vital iron and steel works; at Colombo and Trincomalee to protect harbour installations and naval anchorages; at Chittagong to protect dock facilities and the Janali Hat Bridge; and, since 12th May, at Kharagpur airfield to protect the Very Heavy Bomber base established there.

205. There were no impacts with balloon cables by enemy aircraft, but two by Allied aircraft. During the enemy attack on Calcutta in December, many bombs were dropped in the area occupied by No. 978 Squadron, killing two and wounding ten other ranks. Some equipment was destroyed and buildings damaged, but the efficiency of the unit was unimpaired.

206. Indianisation of Balloon Squadrons has continued and by the beginning of May there were 1,246 I.A.F. other ranks compared with 971 B.O.R.s. There are now no surplus R.A.F. Balloon Operators in the Command, and all those rendered redundant by the Indianisation are being absorbed into other trades. When the process is carried further it should be possible to release another 400 to 450 British airmen.

*

XI. – PHOTOGRAPHY

207. Photographic reconnaissance and survey commitments in India have produced a high quality of photographs, and the speed of reproduction has been good considering the many technical difficulties involved. The construction of mobile photographic processing vehicles is progressing, and a plan to construct two self-sufficient photographic units each comprising eleven vehicles will be begun in the near future.

208. Experiments in night photographic reconnaissance by Ceylon-based Liberators of 160 Squadron are proving satisfactory. Cameras and storage for 28 flashes have been installed in aircraft, together with the means of releasing the flashes at variable intervals to obtain line-overlaps. Other trials have proved the practicability of obtaining stereo pairs at night using two F.24 cameras installed in tandem. Plans

to use carrier-borne aircraft for long-range reconnaissance have been implemented to the extent of installing and testing equipment in Hellcat aircraft. Experiments now wait upon the provision of American and British cameras.

209. R.A.F. and U.S.A.A.F. processing and interpretation in Eastern Air Command have been integrated at Photographic Reconnaissance Force Headquarters at Bally Seaplane Base, Calcutta, where British and American staffs work together and have achieved a high degree of co-ordination.

*

XII. – MEDICAL: WELFARE

210. The health of the Command as a whole shows only a slight improvement compared with the analogous period for the preceding year. The sickness rate for malaria and dysentery, although lower than that for 1943, has since February maintained the seasonal rise; that for venereal disease alone has steadily declined. The rate of invaliding in the Command has risen gradually. In 1943 the incidence was 1.44 per thousand, whilst in 1944 the rate has increased steadily from 2.00 in January to 2.50 per thousand in May; these figures are doubtless connected with the increasing average length of the sojourn spent by personnel in the Command. Malaria has continued to be the most important single cause of lost service days through sickness, and measures have been actively taken in hand further to combat it. A Deputy P.M.O. (Malariology) has been appointed to re-organise the plan for malaria control and to give the necessary technical directions. Action has been initiated to raise, by propaganda and instruction, the standard of personal anti-malaria discipline, and plans have been prepared for forming anti-malaria units. A further step has been the experimental spraying from aircraft of areas where malaria-carrying mosquitoes are known to breed, and a flight of No. 134 Squadron has been detailed for this purpose.

211. It is hoped to increase the liaison with the Army and the U.S.A.A.F., which has hitherto not been as close as desirable. Arrangements are being made to increase hospital accommodation to meet the potential needs of the eighty-five squadrons accepted as the short-term target. Work is now proceeding on the conversion of the buildings of La Martiniere School, Calcutta, to serve as the 500-bedded General Hospital, the first R.A.F. Hospital in the Command, for whose opening sanction was given in April. When open, the existence of this hospital should not only obviate to a very large extent the present necessity for sending R.A.F. casualties in the forward areas to army hospitals, with all the consequent administrative difficulties, but should also put the four R.A.F. Mobile Field Hospitals in a much stronger position with regard to the supply of stores and equipment. They have been frequently overcrowded, and on occasion it has been found that essential equipment for which they had vainly been asking was nevertheless being made available to neighbouring Army hospitals.

212. At the beginning of the year a representative of the R.A.F. Physiological

Laboratory, Farnborough, toured the Command and investigated flying conditions, including such matters as oxygen needs, flying clothes, flying rations and length of operational tour. A report on his visit has since been received and action is being taken where necessary.

WELFARE

213. The provision of amenities for airmen has continued to be a pressing and difficult problem. The greater proportion of R.A.F. personnel live in scattered communities on the eastern marches of India, housed in bamboo huts or tents, often widely dispersed in small groups of less than a hundred, and generally at least a day's journey from the nearest centre of what to them represents civilisation, and perhaps even from the nearest R.A.F. unit. To ameliorate as far as possible the drab and lonely life inevitable under these circumstances, 170 gramophones and 363 wireless sets have been made available during the period and distributed at special rates to units. It is the aim ultimately to provide a wireless set for every hundred men. Special arrangements have also been made for the distribution of books and the supply of sports gear. Correspondence courses which have been made accessible for airmen at a specially low fee have been meeting a heavy demand. Six mobile cinemas have been set up in Bengal to which the average attendance is 15,000 weekly, and touring concert parties have visited many units.

214. No single factor has conduced more to ill-feeling between the airman and the people of the country in which he is living than the uncontrolled operation of the laws of supply and demand at a time when so many men whose standards of self-respect and personal cleanliness are high were arriving, and stocks of tooth-paste, shoe polish and razor blades were short. The rise in the price of such essential goods was aggravated by the fact that there is in India no N.A.A.F.I. to cater for the essential needs of the serviceman, the Government of India preferring to retain the contractor system. Thus the only possible obstacle to the exploitation of the airman by bazaar store-keepers has been a progressively more rigid supervision of local canteen contractors. The problem has been made easier during the last few months by the provision from abroad of large stocks of essential articles which are disseminated through service channels and sold at controlled prices in canteens. The problem is now one of distribution rather than supply and in general it may be said that the airman can buy essential commodities at fair prices in his canteen – though not yet at all times or in all units.

215. Without the services of N.A.A.F.I., the provision of entertainment parties from England proved impossible for a long period. The Government of India have finally been prevailed upon to allow E.N.S.A. parties to perform in this country, and G.H.Q., India, has partly defrayed the cost from excess canteen profits.

216. Other advances which may be mentioned include the improved scales of accommodation and furnishings which have been sanctioned for Hill Depots, and the development of airmen's clubs. The number of beds available for personnel on leave has practically doubled during the past year, and Hill Depots have been made as informal as possible with no parades at all and a minimum of restrictions. In spite of

this, approximately 70 per cent. of airmen still prefer to spend their leave in towns. I cannot see any alteration in this proportion until travelling facilities on Indian railways vastly improve, and proceeding to distant leave centres becomes less of an ordeal. The unhealthy nature of most large Indian towns makes this improvement even more desirable.

217. Assistance has been given by my Welfare Staff to 915 airmen in need of advice or undergoing avoidable hardship, in addition to the many cases handled by the welfare officers in subordinate formations. The provision of amenities has continued with grants from the Amenities, Comforts and Entertainments for the Forces Fund, while the Royal Air Force Welfare Grant has been received from 1st April onwards. To deal with the growing scope of welfare duties, six selected airmen have been commissioned in the A. & S.D. (Welfare) Branch and five welfare officers with the rank of Squadron Leader have arrived from the United Kingdom.

XIII. – INDIAN OBSERVER CORPS

218. In November, 1943, the Indian Observer Corps consisted of three control units, six mobile companies in Bengal, static units in four main areas, Calcutta, Chittagong, Vizagapatam and Madras, and fourteen other mobile companies under training. These together with Care & Maintenance companies and training centres made up a total strength of 10,851 personnel. In December it was decided to breakdown the static organisation and certain Care and Maintenance formations, and form from them seven additional mobile companies. By May, 1944, the number of control units had increased to four, and that of operational mobile companies to seventeen with ten others under training or in process of formation.

219. During the battle in Arakan, four companies were involved, and re-deployment of a number of posts was necessary. Such posts as were forced to retire succeeded in destroying their equipment before retreating. Similarly, when the enemy advanced towards Imphal, nearly 50 posts had to be evacuated or redeployed. The posts east and south of Imphal naturally lost much equipment, but a high percentage was saved and all abandoned equipment was denied to the enemy. Casualties, too, were light in view of the little or no warning provided, consisting of some six missing and six others wounded.

220. Experience gained during the period led at the end of April to the substitution of Mobile Control Units for the Base and Forward Control Units, with resultant closer supervision and greater flexibility. Ultimately there will be seven of these to control the seventeen companies, and each of the latter will control fifteen observer posts.

R.E.C. PEIRSE,
Air Chief Marshal,
Allied Air Commander-in-Chief.
23rd November, 1944.
Air Command, South East Asia.

Footnotes:

1 Petrol, Oil, Lubricants.
2 H.F. D/F – High Frequency Direction Finding.
3 V.H.F. D/F – Very High Frequency Direction Finding.

3

AIR CHIEF MARSHAL SIR KEITH PARK'S DESPATCH ON AIR OPERATIONS IN SOUTH EAST ASIA

FROM 1ST JUNE, 1944, TO THE OCCUPATION OF RANGOON, 2ND MAY, 1945

The following despatch was submitted to the Secretary of State for Air on 16th November,

1945, *by AIR CHIEF MARSHAL SIR KEITH PARK, K.C.B., K.B.E., M.C., D.F.C., Allied Air Commander-in-Chief, Air Command, South East Asia.*

PART ONE.
FOREWORD.

1. This Despatch is a review primarily of air operations in Burma during the last year beginning in June, 1944. During this period a fanatical and over-confident enemy has been driven back from his foothold in India at Imphal over 800 miles, which included the complete rout of the enemy's field army in the open plains of Burma and culminated in the occupation of Rangoon by our forces on 3rd May, 1945.

2. The primary cause was the defeat of the Japanese Army. This achievement has been made possible by air power, which not merely took an intimate share in the ground attack, but also isolated the enemy's forces in the field. Confronted by overwhelming air power, the enemy's air forces withered away, and this same air power helped to undermine the stability of his land forces, so that after their decisive defeat at Imphal, although they made a tenacious stand on a number of occasions, they were no match for our well-equipped field army – well equipped in large

measure by the unstinted effort of air supply to provide their daily needs. Though air supply did not and could not supplant all other means which themselves involved a great effort to maintain, without it the campaign could not have been successfully fought. Regardless of weather, climate, and distance, the air supply line was maintained unhindered by enemy air opposition, which had been driven from the skies.

3. The Burma campaign should make its mark in the annals of history as a triumph of air power and air supply and as a feat of endurance of Allied land forces.

COMMAND.

4. In June, 1944, the Allied Air Forces in South East Asia were under the command of Air Chief Marshal Sir Richard Peirse, K.C.B., D.S.O., A.F.C. Upon his relinquishment of the appointment on 26th November, temporary command was assumed by Air Marshal Sir Guy Garrod, K.C.B., O.B.E., M.C., D.F.C., until my arrival on 23rd February, 1945.

The Position in June, **1944.**

5. Two events mark the beginning of the period. The major Japanese offensive against Imphal had been blunted and was in process of being broken by means of air supply on a hitherto unprecedented scale to the forces cut off from land communications with their base; and second, the south-west monsoon was reaching its full intensity over the operational areas. It remained to be seen whether air forces could materially influence the land battle in weather which had in preceding years prohibited their effective employment, and whether the enemy defeat in Manipur was to prove the turning point in South East Asia strategy which would enable the primary tasks of the Command, the re-opening of the land route to China and the clearance of Burma, to be accomplished.

6. The dry-weather campaign which was drawing to a close had brought few positive results. Only in the north-east had any territorial gains been made, and here General Stilwell's forces had cleared the Hukawng Valley and were in possession of Myitkyina airfield. In the Fourteenth Army sector, Imphal was still invested, though 33 Corps was driving the Japanese from the Kohima-Imphal road, and 4 Corps was attacking the Japanese in the Imphal plain. In Arakan, although one enemy offensive had been frustrated, the Japanese still held the Mayu peninsula and the rice port of Akyab. The other British forces operating on the offensive were the long-range penetration groups of Special Force.

7. The Air Forces, having just completed a period of intensive operations, were envisaging some retrenchment, a "reculer pour mieux sauter". An extensive programme of re-equipment was in train which would convert nine squadrons of Hurricanes to Thunderbolts, the two Wellington squadrons to Liberators, and four squadrons of Vengeances to Mosquitos. The relative sparsity of all-weather airfields in the forward areas entailed a withdrawal of these squadrons to bases in India for

their conversion, and the monsoon campaign was undertaken with a total of 17 squadrons out of the line, re-equipping, resting or training. Having regard to the nature of monsoon conditions and of the fighting in progress, the forces remaining in the line were ample, nor indeed could any more be deployed. The net result was that the air component conducting tactical operations that culminated on all three sectors in the capture of springboards for a dry-weather assault, was a moderate, well-balanced force of experienced squadrons, versed in the ready identification of jungle targets and trained in close co-operation with the formations whom they were supporting.

*

Plans for **1944-5** *Operations.*

8. The broad mission of S.E.A.C. was formulated at the Octagon conferences as . . . "the destruction or expulsion of all Japanese forces in Burma at the earliest date. Operations to achieve this object must not however prejudice the security of the existing air supply to China, including the air staging post at Myitkyina and the opening of overland communications with China".

9. The plans that were prepared to this end during the monsoon of 1944 envisaged an elaborate series of airborne assaults that did not appreciate the reliability and self-sufficiency of an army supplied unstintingly from the air. Indeed, had it then been suggested that Rangoon could be reached by an army travelling overland and supplied largely by air, the proposal would not have received serious consideration. The overall strategy can best be judged from the four main plans which were formulated during the 1944 monsoon:-

(i) *Plan "X"* involved an overland advance from the Mogaung-Myitkyina area to Katha and Bhamo, co-ordinated with another advance from Imphal to the Chindwin and an airborne operation in the vicinity of Wuntho. The furthest penetration that was envisaged was the occupation of territory north of a line stretching between Kalewa and Lashio.

(ii) *Plan "Y"* intended to employ airborne troops in the seizure of Kalewa, and a second air landing at the point of debouchment into the Mandalay plain to exploit the confusion that would be caused.

(iii) *Plan "Z"* entailed an airborne assault in strength with all transport aircraft in the theatre immediately north of Rangoon, to capture the city.

(iv) *General Stilwell's plan* was for British forces to press forward towards Shwebo – Mandalay, while N.C.A.C.[1] profited by the diversion to occupy Bhamo, whence they could mount an airborne operation to capture Lashio.

10. The part that the Air Forces were to play in these operations was given in an

Operational Directive in which the order of priorities was interesting, putting as it did close support and transport operations very low in the scale. In the event, a reorientation of tasks took place which gave greater emphasis to the work of close support and air supply. The results of such a shift in the centre of gravity to a machine geared to the classical form of air warfare involved changes in organisation, control, supply and maintenance which are discussed at more length in the appropriate context.

11. Plans "Y" and "Z" were approved in principle by the Chiefs of Staff in July and August, and called "Capital" and "Dracula" respectively. In point of fact, however, operations in Central Burma progressed more quickly than anticipated. Continually outflanked by Allied forces, to whom the manna of air supply gave an unprecedented degree of mobility, and continually harried by our close support aircraft, the enemy was never allowed to consolidate the new positions that he occupied along the line of his retreat. Thus by January, the airborne aspect of "Capital" had been rendered unnecessary, a fact which caused great relief to the Allied Commanders, for it was increasingly evident that the transport aircraft to train for and launch the operation, scheduled for mid-February, would be difficult to find from existing resources.

12. Operation "Dracula" was to be the greatest airborne operation yet conceived, involving a fly-in over a distance of 480 miles by some 900 transport aircraft and 650 gliders. The necessity for retaining these forces in Europe, and their high attrition rate in operations there, precluded their re-deployment in this theatre as planned, and in October "Dracula" was postponed with the prospect of not being mounted until the winter of 1945-46.

13. The emphasis now lay on Central Burma operations. An advance to the Monywa – Mandalay area was considered to be the furthest point that could be reached before the 1945 monsoon. Exploitation further south was not thought to be practicable in view of the difficulties of supply. In the event, the advances made exceeded all planned expectations. This can be attributed to the following main causes:-

(i) The magnitude of the Japanese defeat at Imphal, which was not realised until much later.

(ii) The virtual elimination of enemy air opposition resulting in complete predominance and liberty of action of our offensive and air transport forces.

(iii) The steady growth of air supply resources and improvements in their organisation.

(iv) The occupation of Akyab and Ramree, which had been decided upon to provide advanced air supply bases. This enabled us to reorient and shorten the supply lines in relation to the advance southward of Fourteenth Army.

14. By February, 1945, the possibilities of a more ambitious plan were becoming

evident, and Fourteenth Army and 221 Group submitted a plan for vigorous exploitation of the favourable set of circumstances then obtaining. G.O.C. Fourteenth Army considered that if the enemy elected to stand and fight around Mandalay, there was every hope of destroying the Japanese Army in the open plains of Central Burma, thereby opening the route for a swift advance upon Rangoon by highly mobile columns. The plan aimed at encirclement of the enemy forces on the Mandalay Plain to be completed by air attack on such lines of communication as remained open to him. In conjunction with a direct thrust by 33 Corps towards Mandalay, 4 Corps were to carry out a wide encircling movement directed towards Meiktila which would cut the main line of communication southwards. Meiktila itself was to be secured by a small air transported force who would consolidate our position athwart this vital route.

15. This bold plan was highly successful, and as a result the Japanese Army in Burma suffered heavy casualties in a costly and bloody killing match to which the Air Forces contributed in large measure. Notwithstanding its success, the battle of extermination took longer than had been contemplated, and the time-table for the dash to Rangoon by 4 Corps was in jeopardy. The prospect of a race against a reduced time limit caused considerable anxiety in the mind of C.-in-C. Allied Land Forces, South East Asia (A.L.F.S.E.A.). In his opinion the overland advance by highly mobile forces might not have the necessary impetus to overcome opposition en route, together with the final opposition estimated from the defenders of Rangoon, reinforced by the remnants of field formations extricated from Central Burma. Upon his urgent recommendations, the capture of Rangoon before the monsoon was made more certain by the mounting of a modified "Dracula" by sea and air.

16. To carry out this operation, it would be necessary to utilise forces which were earmarked to seize concurrently with the capture of Rangoon a springboard on the Malay Peninsula. In the event, this modified "Dracula" proved to have been unnecessary, as the following pages will show. Nevertheless the capture of Rangoon entailed such a large expenditure of effort and resources that planning has had to be conducted since then on the premise that large-scale refitting, redeployment and marshalling of forces is necessary before the next step is undertaken. The occupation of Rangoon therefore constitutes a milestone in the history of South East Asia, marking the end of a well-defined period.

*

PART TWO.
THE OPERATIONAL BACKGROUND,
JUNE, 1944 – MAY, 1945.

17. When, on 22nd June, 1944, an overland junction was effected on the Imphal-Kohima road between the garrison of the Imphal plain and the relieving ground forces which had advanced from the north, a major crisis had been resolved, and our land

forces, despite the monsoon, were able gradually to turn more and more both tactically and strategically to the offensive.

18. The Fourteenth Army, with its headquarters beside those of the Third Tactical Air Force at Comilla, controlled the Allied units on the southern two-thirds of the front. On its coastal section, 15 Corps held the port of Maungdaw and a monsoon line along the Maungdaw-Buthidaung road; its left flank was thinly covered by the Lushai Brigade which operated in guerilla fashion over the desolate hill country as far north as Haka and the valley of the Manipur River. In the Imphal Valley, although 4 Corps had linked up with 33 Corps advancing from Assam, the Japanese were still holding tenaciously to their positions among the hills east of Palel overlooking the plain; further to the north-east, however, the position was more favourable, and elements of 33 Corps were pressing forward towards Ukhrul.

19. Beyond the operational area of the Fourteenth Army, Special Force, which had been boldly launched into the heart of enemy held territory in March, was fighting both the weather and the enemy in the general area of the railway corridor east and south-east of Lake Indawgyi. It was controlled by the Northern Combat Area Command under General Stilwell, and had effected a junction with the Chinese and American forces now investing the Japanese garrison of Myitkyina, where the main airfield had passed into their hands. Further still to the north-east, a Chinese army based on Yunnan was fighting in the upper Salween valley.

20. The front remained static, during the period of the monsoon, only in the coastal area. On the Imphal sector, 33 Corps – which took over from 4 Corps when the latter was withdrawn from the line for four months – remained on the offensive. In the course of July the enemy was finally driven by combined air and ground bombardment from his tenaciously held positions, on the perimeter of the Imphal plain, and with the capture of Tamu in early August the Allied forces had re-established a foothold in the Kabaw Valley and were ready to push southwards towards Yazagyo and Kalemyo and eastwards to the Chindwin.

21. On the right flank, a series of Japanese delaying positions on what was euphemistically called the Tiddim Road, was overcome during August and September, the "Hurribomber" again proving itself a most effective weapon for close support in jungle country, as the wreckage along the Tiddim Road testified. Tiddim itself fell on 18th October, and the way was now open for a double thrust towards Kalemyo from the west and north. Japanese resistance in the Kennedy Peak area, albeit grim, proved no match for the experienced Allied troops and the accompanying air bombardment, and Kalemyo fell on 15th November. With the capture of Kalewa on 2nd December the chapter of mountain warfare was closed and the Fourteenth Army was ready to debouch upon the plains of Central Burma.

22. Comparable progress had also been made in the Northern Combat Area Command sector, where the enemy garrison at Myitkyina had been reduced early in August. In the railway corridor, 36 Division, which had replaced Special Force, made steady progress; it captured Hopin on 7th September and by 10th December had reached the junction at Indaw. A drive southwards from Myitkyina carried Chinese units to Bhamo at approximately the same time. Thus by the end of the monsoon

period the forces of the Northern Combat Area Command were in a position seriously to threaten the right flank of the enemy elements facing the Fourteenth Army.

23. Before the opening of the campaigning season proper, a certain number of changes had been made in the organisation of the ground forces facing the Japanese in Burma. Since with the converging advances of both the Fourteenth Army and the Northern Combat Area Command the opening of a continuous front in Central Burma seemed probable in the near future, Lieut.-General Sir Oliver Leese, Bart., K.C.B., C.B.E., D.S.O., was allotted command of all the Allied Land Forces in Burma. This Headquarters absorbed that of 11 Army Corps, and was set up at Barrackpore outside Calcutta, while an off-shoot was maintained at Kandy. 15 Corps, operating in Arakan, was removed from the control of Fourteenth Army and placed directly under his command – a step which enabled Headquarters, Fourteenth Army, to move forward and establish itself beside 221 Group on the Imphal plain. With the return of 4 Corps to the field in early November it thus retained command of two army corps, for 33 Corps remained in control of the operations developing against Kalemyo. Such was the general organisation of the ground forces when the new campaign fairly opened in November, 1944.

24. In the coastal sector, 15 Corps had begun the preliminaries to its offensive at an early hour and before the end of October, 81 (West African) Division, supplied entirely by air, had crossed into the Kaladan valley from its monsoon quarters at Chiringa and was beginning to advance southwards against some opposition. The main offensive was opened west of the Mayu Hills in mid-December; its purpose was to secure air bases on Akyab and Ramree Islands, from which support could be mounted for future operations in southern Burma, and also by driving the Japanese from the coastal strip west of the Arakan Yomas to liberate the considerable Allied forces they had contained there. It met with even less resistance than had been anticipated. Forward units of 15 Corps reached Foul Point before Christmas, and an Allied landing on Akyab Island on 3rd January was unopposed. A further landing on Ramree Island on the 21st met with only slight opposition. The core of Japanese resistance was, however, met along the coastal road from Myohaung to Taungup, and a number of amphibious landings which were effected in January and February at various points along the coast provoked fierce fighting (whose issue was beyond doubt due to the heavy and accurate air support that was given), and gradually the enemy was driven towards the two routes leading eastwards from An and Taungup towards the Irrawaddy valley. With the capture of Taungup in the middle of April the coastal campaign was virtually over.

25. The climax of the main battle in central Burma was meanwhile not long delayed. During December the Fourteenth Army struck eastwards, and with the occupation of Wuntho by 4 Corps on the 20th, secured its left flank by laying the basis for a continuous front with the Northern Combat Area Command. The railhead at Ye-U was occupied by 33 Corps on New Year's Day, and the Japanese stronghold at Monywa was finally reduced on the 21st, by when 33 Corps had reached the general line of the Irrawaddy, on which it was evident that the enemy had resolved to make a stand. Bridgeheads had however been secured by 20 Division on the left

bank of the river at Thabeikkyin and Singu, and in the great bend of the Irrawaddy the Japanese stoutly defended the approaches to Sagaing on the right bank. In these two sectors, where the contending forces were not separated by the river, bitter fighting continued throughout the second half of January and the first half of February. To the northeast, the Northern Combat Area Command forces were moving southwards across the Shweli valley and towards Lashio; Hsenwi was taken on 19th February, and Namtu on the 23rd.

26. While these events were taking place in the Irrawaddy valley and to the northeast, the main strategy of the campaign was beginning to take shape. 4 Corps was removed from the left flank of the Fourteenth Army as soon as the junction with the Northern Combat Area Command was assured, and with two divisions was given the task of pushing southwards from Kalemyo along the Gangaw valley towards Tilin and Pauk. The natural obstacles on this wild route were every bit as great as those prepared by the enemy, who did not appreciate the threat to his left flank that was thus being unfolded. His ignorance of the situation was due to the fact that his reconnaissance aircraft dared not cover the area, and to his tardy realisation of the new mobility of the Allied armies with which air supply endowed them. His defences at Gangaw were overwhelmed on 10th January after an air bombardment to which the Army paid full tribute, and by the 27th the forward units of 4 Corps had reached Pauk. Early in February they established themselves on the right bank of the Irrawaddy below Pakokku. The stage was now set for the crowning blow of the campaign.

27. After a few days' pause, a series of concerted crossings at various points of the Irrawaddy below Mandalay began on the night of 12th-13th February. A new bridgehead was established by 33 Corps opposite Myinmu, in the teeth of determined opposition on the part of the Japanese, who took it to be part of a major encircling movement against Mandalay in conjunction with the forces in the Singu bridgehead to the north. They accordingly threw in most of their available reserves to combat it. A feint crossing was made far to the south, opposite Seikpyu, while the main thrust was made a little upstream, opposite Myitche, where 4 Corps was able to establish a foothold against comparatively light opposition from the enemy, who still underestimated the threat to his left flank. When this bridgehead had been consolidated, a motorised brigade was concentrated behind its lines.

28. On the 23rd, this Brigade moved swiftly eastwards, reaching the railway at Taungtha the next day. It then turned south-east along the line towards the junction of Meiktila, a nodal centre in the communications of central Burma, in the neighbourhood of which there were also several good airfields. The enemy was completely taken aback by this thrust into his rear areas, and although his line of communication troops fought hard, they were unable to do more than delay slightly our advance. By the afternoon of 3rd March, the garrison of Meiktila had been annihilated and 4 Corps had thus placed a brigade, which our air transport speedily built up into a division, squarely athwart the main enemy line of communication from his base at Rangoon to the fighting zone.

29. It was in March that the battle which was to decide the fate of most of Burma

north of the Gulf of Martaban was fought. The Japanese reacted speedily to the major strategic thrust whose significance they had grasped too late, and hastily moved southwards all their available forces, in an effort, first, to break our stranglehold on their communications, and, when this failed, to withdraw to safety as many as they could of their troops in the Mandalay – Meiktila noose. Mandalay itself fell to our troops advancing from the north by the middle of the month.

30. Meanwhile the whole area Mandalay – Myingyan – Meiktila had been transformed into a vast battlefield, in which the Fourteenth Army and No. 221 Group attacked from three directions the disorganized forces of the enemy, whose casualties were heavy. A number of scattered units made their escape, but by the beginning of April it might fairly be estimated that Japanese military power in Burma had been shattered. In the Northern Combat Area Command sector, the course of events in central Burma had helped to quicken the pace of the Japanese withdrawal; Lashio was captured by a Chinese division on 8th March, and the enemy soon broke contact, retreating southwards into the Shan States.

31. The Fourteenth Army resumed its large-scale offensive on 12th April, after a short period for regrouping its forces. 4 Corps, supplied by air, struck along the main Mandalay – Rangoon axis; by the end of the month it had covered some 250 miles and had reached the outskirts of Pegu, less than 50 miles from Rangoon, which the Japanese were known to have evacuated two or three days; earlier. 33 Corps had moved south-west to Magwe, which was captured on the 18th, and thence advanced down the Irrawaddy valley; its forward elements reached the railhead at Prome on 1st May. Nowhere was the enemy able to bar the advance by a frontal stand. Such were the circumstances when the combined operation for the capture of Rangoon from the south was put into execution at the express wish of C.-in-C. A.L.F.S.E.A.

32. As already explained, Operation "Dracula" met with little or no opposition. It was a copy-book operation, and the troops advancing into the city from the south partook more of the nature of a triumphal procession than an assault force. They were met by the commanding officer of No. 110 Squadron R.A.F., Wing Commander Saunders, who on the previous day, perceiving no signs of the enemy at Mingaladon airfield, had decided to land and reconnoitre the city. He took formal possession of Rangoon on behalf of the Allied forces. It was fitting that the vital part the Air Forces had played in the campaign should be symbolically rounded off by the occupation of Rangoon by the Royal Air Force.

*

PART THREE.
ALLIED AIR DOMINANCE.

33. Until October, 1944, when the enemy began to withdraw aircraft from this theatre to reinforce his garrison in the Philippines, the overall strength of the Japanese Air

Force in this theatre remained at some 450 aircraft in operational units. Normally about 150 aircraft, 70 per cent. of which were fighters, were disposed in Burma and Thailand for immediate use. The majority of the remainder were retained in Malaya and Sumatra, and comprised bombers and floatplanes for shipping escorts and anti-submarine duties, fighters for the defence of the Sumatra oilfields, and operational echelons refitting or training. With General MacArthur's invasion of the Philippines, when up to 100 aircraft left S.E.A.C., a steady decline in strength set in, aggravated by the constant attrition caused by our fighters, for which full replacement was not forthcoming, until in May, 1945, the enemy could muster but 250 aircraft in the S.E.A.C. area, of which over 100, stationed in Malaya and Sumatra, were for most purposes ineffective by reason of their distance from the battle areas.

34. Following the sharp lessons he received between March and May, 1944, the enemy's warning system became somewhat less embryonic, so that it was difficult to achieve complete surprise in any part of the theatre. By listening to Allied W/T and R/T, and by supplementing a skimpy radar system with observation posts and sound locators, a comprehensive albeit somewhat thin warning-system had been established around the whole of the Western Perimeter, and it was only a question of time before growing technical proficiency rendered the task of Allied aircraft in search of all too rare targets, even more difficult.

35. By comparison, the strength and composition of the Allied fighter force was most satisfactory. Spitfires, Lightnings, and latterly Thunderbolts and Mustangs, completely transformed the situation which had obtained until November, 1943, when our Hurricanes were outclassed and out-manoeuvred by the enemy. Backed by a warning and control system of high standard, Allied fighters had without fail rendered the enemy's incursions into our defended areas costly and ineffectual. During the eleven months covered by this despatch 165 enemy aircraft were destroyed on the ground or in the air, together with 47 probables and 152 damaged. This destruction was achieved against a total enemy effort, offensive and defensive, of 1,845 sorties. One enemy aircraft was destroyed for every eleven sighted; that the air superiority established before the period of this narrative was well maintained over the year, needs no further proof.

36. This virtual dominance of the air over Burma was the result of hard work with small dividends upon the part of our fighter organisation. Freed from the necessity of establishing superiority, the major problems remaining to Allied fighters by the time this despatch opens were the interception of sneak raids, usually undertaken by the Japanese Air Force under the protection of cloud-cover, and the searching-out and destruction of a meagre enemy air force dispersed upon a generous network of rear airfields. Initially, the greatest danger was to the stream of transports hauling supplies to the Imphal Plain, which offered the best prey ever presented to any air force. Some one hundred unarmed aircraft flew daily in and out of the area, and fighter patrols laboured under the handicaps of extensive cloud conditions and a shortage of P.O.L.[2] at their bases.

37. Moreover, the mountainous terrain to the east precluded efficient early air raid warning, and the enemy could at will come unannounced through the valleys. To

minimise the danger, traffic was routed along a corridor from the Khopum Valley to Palel under a fighter umbrella. Ground signs were displayed en route to indicate the presence of enemy aircraft which was also broadcast by R/T. The sight of a stream of transports flying into the Imphal Valley with a screen of Spitfires circling overhead was a most heartening sight to the garrison, who thereby received constant assurance that their aerial life-line was unbroken. The precautions taken and the impotence of the enemy resulted in only two transports being destroyed by enemy action during the whole of the siege, a remarkable achievement.

38. The danger to transport aircraft persisted during the whole of the advance, since they were continually operating in front of the warning screen, and fighter bases were not always established as far forward as was tactically desirable. For this there were two main reasons; in the early stages of the advance through hilly jungle no airstrips could be constructed near the front, and second, having debouched on to the plains, the Army were not willing to devote supplies and resources to establish fighter bases in the area of dropping operations.

39. On two occasions, therefore, our transport aircraft were victims of enemy sneak raids; on one day in November while dropping along the Tiddim Road, five aircraft were destroyed by the enemy, and on the 12th January four were shot down while supply dropping near Onbauk, an airfield recently recaptured from the enemy which, however, had not by that time been prepared for defensive fighters. Even when during the temporary halt around Mandalay, and Spitfires were able to occupy the Shwebo and Monywa airfield groups, air supply was proceeding over a hundred and thirty mile front which the four available squadrons of Spitfires were hard pressed to cover in conjunction with their other defensive commitments. It is a lesson of the campaign that the air supply of ground forces depends on the immediate deployment as far forward as possible of fighter squadrons to patrol the Lines of Communication. Had the enemy used his fighters effectively instead of frittering away their effort on infrequent low-level attacks against forward troops, he would have been able to do great execution among our Dakotas and Commandos, thus seriously impeding the advance.

*

40. Since it was not always possible to engage the enemy in the air, it was necessary to search out his aircraft on the ground. To this end, intruder raids were undertaken at frequent intervals, and paid a dividend of 80 destroyed, 25 probably destroyed and 78 damaged aircraft on enemy airfields. In October, a series of raids were undertaken against the Rangoon airfields with the additional motive of hindering the transfer of units to the Philippines. In this operation, many types of aircraft were employed, including Beaufighters, but, as aircraft resources became more suited to operational requirements, intrusion was progressively left to the Mustang squadrons of the Air Commandos, who on more than one occasion in the spring of 1945, made the 1,500 mile round trip to the Japanese base airfields in Siam with good results totalling 38 destroyed, 10 probably destroyed and 21 damaged aircraft.

41. The problem of destroying an enemy intent on conserving his forces and

possessing a wide choice of airfields containing many revetments (Meiktila airfield disposes of over a hundred) is not an easy one. In addition, the enemy's skill with light anti-aircraft and machine-gun fire is well-known, and low-level "strafing" runs are apt to be costly. It was found uneconomical to make a preliminary reconnaissance run to discover which revetments were occupied, and often only a quick snap-shot at a target seen late in the "strafe" was possible. In view of these factors it will be seen that the result achieved is more than creditable.

42. Early attempts to ground or destroy the enemy by bombing his airfields were ineffective and were discontinued in favour of more worthwhile targets.

*

43. The enemy's offensive effort was so ineffectual as to be hardly worth mentioning except to recount the losses he sustained. In late September the Japanese Air Force began a series of reconnaissances with disastrous results. Cover was attempted of the Manipur Road, Silchar, Chittagong and battle areas. Four Dinahs were destroyed during this brief spell and since then no reconnaissance over the India border has been attempted. On Christmas night three bombers attempted to penetrate to the Calcutta area; of these, two were destroyed by Beaufighters and the third returned in a damaged condition. Enemy attempts to interfere with shipping off Akyab in January were decisively dealt with by the Spitfire squadrons who moved in five days after its occupation, No. 67 Squadron destroying five out of six attacking Oscars in one day.

44. Thereafter, the enemy effort degenerated into a series of sporadic and infrequent attempts to disrupt our forward columns. The ineffectual nature of these attacks was evident to all who flew over the battlefield and noted, on the enemy side no signs of activity, but, behind the British lines, long lines of transport moving in uncamouflaged safety, supply-dropping parachutes in use as tents, and all the apparatus of war left in full view by troops whose immunity from air attack was scarcely ever violated even by fast-flying fighters, for the enemy dared not send a bomber over the Allied lines by daylight.

*

45. It is unnecessary to recount in detail the enormous advantages accruing to both ground and air forces when the enemy air arm is small and misemployed, and when our own squadrons are superior in performance, training and control. It is, however, worth pausing to consider the results had enemy aircraft been allowed unrestricted use of the sky. The air supply on which the whole land campaign hinged would have been impossible, the attrition rate of our close support squadrons, which worked with accuracy and effect, would have been prohibitive, and the disuption caused by our strategic bombers to the enemy's communications far to the rear could not have been such as to have materially influenced the battle.

*

PART FOUR.
TRANSPORT SUPPORT OPERATIONS AND DEVELOPMENT.

46. The Burma campaign has proved beyond all doubt that once air superiority has been achieved, the air maintenance and supply of forces in the field is governed primarily by the availability of airfields and of transport aircraft. The supply and maintenance of the Army, in the field and engaged in intensive operations together with a tactical air force in support, is a major problem under most favourable conditions. It should be borne in mind, however, that supply bases were some 250 miles distant, and that the intervening country comprised vast stretches of impenetrable jungle and a formidable mountain barrier rising up to 10,000 feet. In addition, weather conditions were by no means favourable, and experience has shown that monsoon cloud develops a degree of turbulence which has been the cause of a number of fatal accidents.

47. Despite these many difficulties, the success of the air supply operations in the Burma campaign has been fully testified. It is fair to say that without air supply the Burma campaign could never have been fought on its present lines. It was in fact a decisive factor of the land campaign. Admittedly mistakes occurred, sometimes due to miscalculation but more often due to unforeseen contingencies. Even so the air supply operations in Burma will probably rank as one of the greatest, if not the greatest, of air supply achievements in this war.

48. The organisation and operation of air supply is a problem which calls for mutual understanding of each other's difficulties by the respective Services. In this respect it cannot be too strongly emphasised that it is the operators and not the consumers who determine the most efficient method of delivering the goods. Moreover, it is up to the consumers to state precisely what is required, in a given order of priority. It is their responsibility also to deliver these goods in the required quantities and at the right time to the air supply heads. The swift and unco-ordinated growth of the air transport organization did not allow of a full appreciation, by either the Army or the Air Force, of the importance of the ancillary services necessary to promote the full effectiveness of the machine. As the campaign advanced, this tendency has been progressively eliminated, and the situation is now that only a lack of resources prevents the air transport organisation from incorporating all the lessons that have been learnt, and giving it the full effectiveness with which experience can endow it. From this observation, the air supply organization that has developed within the area of Northern Combat Area Command and Tenth Air Force is excepted. There, a realisation of the importance of firm backing to the supply system was evident from the outset, and resulted in a very high standard of operating efficiency.

*

49. In June, 1944, there were in Air Command eleven transport squadrons engaged on air supply, four British and seven American. By May, 1945, these figures had risen

to nine and sixteen respectively, an increase which still left the air supply force with little or no margin of reserve. The growth of air supply during the period can well be imagined.

50. At the beginning of the period, attention was still centred upon the critical position of 4 Corps besieged in and around the ancient capital of Manipur. There were still twenty-three days of June to go before the road to Imphal was to be re-opened. Working to supply the garrison and to build a stockpile to exploit the anticipated Japanese retreat, as much as 700 tons were being flown in on a single day under monsoon conditions. When the road was re-opened, effort was not allowed to drop and for the remaining days of June the squadrons flew at maximum effort in order to build up stocks and ascertain the peak air lift that could be achieved. The wisdom of this was doubtful; all concerned were already exhausted, and experience has illustrated the value of retaining a margin of effort in reserve, and of not over-straining a complicated machine without urgent necessity.

51. However, by the end of the month, the enemy was in retreat, and food and munitions were available to speed his withdrawal. The threat to India and to the China life-line had been removed, and a grim defence, sustained solely by air supply, was becoming a vigorous offensive, whose progress was also fed from the air. From July until November, 33 Corps fought its way eastwards to the Chindwin, southwards along the Kabaw valley and down the Tiddim Road, provided entirely with munitions and food by our transport squadrons. Until the end of the monsoon, supply was carried out under conditions of unbelievable difficulty. In July the commander of 33 Corps sent the following signal to No. 194 Squadron: "Your unflagging efforts and determination to complete your task in spite of appalling flying conditions are worthy of the highest praise." In August, another squadron summarised its efforts as follows:- "It has taken on occasion six to seven days of battling through torrential rain, strong winds and 10/10ths cloud down to 200 feet to achieve one mission, but it has been done."

52. In August and September it was becoming clear that the planning and day-to-day control of air supply operations required an organisation separate from Third Tactical Air Force, whose responsibility air supply operations had been since the dissolution of Troop Carrier Command. This was rendered all the more necessary by the large part that it was proposed airborne operations should play in the coming dry season. Thus, in October, Combat Cargo Task Force (C.C.T.F.), an integrated U.S. A./British Headquarters, was formed and became responsible for the day-to-day control and the planning of air transport operations in support of Fourteenth Army and 15 Corps.

53. One of the first measures undertaken by H.Q.C.C.T.F. was the reorganisation of the allocation of tasks, whose importance when demand is always outrunning supply cannot be stressed too strongly. The original procedure had been that, prior to the beginning of each month, Fourteenth Army submitted to Third Tactical Air Force its planned air supply requirements, which were based on the assumption that the Army's advance in the various sectors would invariably be strongly opposed. Consequently, demands were always high and supplies were occasionally fifty per

cent. below the planned figure but withal more than sufficient for current requirements. The Rear Airfield Maintenance Organisation (R.A.M.O.) received its day's tasks direct from the headquarters of the Corps which it was supplying, and at the same time asked the Air Forces for the requisite number of aircraft. If, as often happened, the Army's daily requirements exceeded the air resources available, considerable confusion resulted, since no proper system of allocating priorities had been evolved.

54. This problem was solved by forming, alongside C.C.T.F., the Combined Army-Air Transport Organisation (C.A.A.T.O.) which received and collated daily requests, assessed their urgency and, having a full knowledge of aircraft states, allotted the tasks accordingly. The organisation was thus more in line with current European practice, with two notable exceptions, the lack of signals and telephone communications was such as to clog any air supply machinery no matter how well-planned, and second, there were crippling deficiencies of personnel in such ancillary bodies as Staging Posts and Casualty Air Evacuation Units.

55. On December 20th, the first strip for landing-on of supplies was opened at Indainggale. Others followed in quick succession, Taukkyan near Kalemyo, Kawlin and Indaw trans-Chindwin as soon as the river had been crossed, and Kan in the Myittha Valley where 4 Corps had returned to the line, replacing the Lushai Brigade and representing another and growing commitment to our transport forces.

56. Thus, by January, the increasing demands of mobile warfare, which did not accord with the plans on which resources had been allotted and organisation developed, and the engagement of larger forces, witnessed a gradual and sustained rise in the demands of Fourteenth Army for air supply. Many unforeseen difficulties were now coming to light, and when the Supreme Commander visited the forward areas he was informed that the Air Forces were not carrying enough supplies. C.-in-C. A.L.F.S.E.A. circulated a memorandum calling for more resources in transport aircraft, without which, he stated, not only would the advance to Mandalay and beyond be arrested, but due to the impossibility of supplying forces in front of the roadhead he might be forced to withdraw beyond the Chindwin for the monsoon. This view of the situation (which in my opinion was unduly pessimistic) caused an urgent request to the Chiefs of Staff for additional transport squadrons, and as a result Nos. 238 and 267 Squadrons arrived in March. Actually a better organisation of existing ground transport resources would have met every commitment, and for this reason Air Marshal Garrod undertook a tour to investigate the working of the system.

57. It is as well here to outline, for the sake of comparison, the working of air supply in the N.C.A.C. area, to which but little reference has so far been made.

Air Supply in the Northern Combat Area Command.

58. The most striking feature of this organisation was the high standard of co-operation achieved by all agencies concerned – N.C.A.C., Service of Supply, Tenth Air Force, Air Service Command and all ancillary formations. Collective responsibility for the task of aid supply was rated higher than service allegiance; each body trusted the ability of the others to carry out their part of the work and did not

attempt to dictate on matters outside its own sphere. The second great advantage was the abundance of good signal communications; every link in the chain, organisational, supply, squadrons, co-ordinators, being linked by a teletype and telephone network which allowed of a quick dissemination of the next day's tasks and priorities as allotted by the collating agency in N.C.A.C., and of speedy re-adjustment if necessary. A last-minute change in location of a Dropping Zone could be signalled back by a Division and retransmitted to an aircraft already airborne for another objective. Moreover, the packing and loading processes were organised on a moving-belt principle whose efficiency eliminated a multitude of small delays; these ancillary organisations worked with the industrial efficiency of a large commercial factory.

59. A comparison between the American packing loading agencies at Dinjan and the R.I.A.S.C. Air Supply Companies at Hathazari reflected no credit on the British ground organisation. Here it should be emphasised that no reflection is intended on the personnel involved; British Officers and Indian Other Ranks were strained to breaking-point, and often had to work seventy-two hours at a stretch to complete their tasks; the fault lay in the fact that the importance and nature of the work demanded a much more generous scale of personnel, facilities, and organising ability than could be allotted by the Army.

*

60. An examination of the data gathered on Air Marshal Garrod's tour brought to light the differences of organisation and procedure between the two air supply systems, and revealed a crying need for improvement in the organisation operated by C.A.A.T.O. and C.C.T.F. Too numerous to recount here, these points did have the effect of initiating action to improve the operating procedure. Meanwhile, Air Command was pressing for the speedy development of the recaptured bases along the Arakan Coast at Akyab and Ramree whose employment would shorten the haul into Central Burma. Journeys from the established bases at Chittagong, Comilla and Tulihal were now becoming so long that in order to complete three trips in a day, aircraft had to take off at first light and perhaps not finish until after dark. The strain on technical maintenance, flying and loading personnel can well be imagined.

61. It was in February that an overland advance to Rangoon supplied entirely by air was first put forward as a serious proposal. Fourteenth Army prepared a plan which envisaged two parallel drives southwards along the axes of the River Irrawaddy and of the Mandalay-Rangoon railway, while a large force from 33 Corps, of up to three and a half divisions, struck east to Takaw with the object of containing and destroying all enemy forces cut off north of Meiktila.

62. Air Command reactions to the plan were:

(i) A re-orientation of supply lines, using Akyab and Ramree as advanced air supply heads which would result in substantial reduction in length of the air supply line as the force advanced south of Mandalay.

(ii) We doubted the soundness of the plan which aimed at a total destruction of the enemy in addition to the capture of Rangoon if the former necessitated a drive eastwards to cut off and destroy the enemy in the hills. This would inevitably involve a supply problem in that direction in addition to sustaining a main advance southwards.

63. A study of the situation after the fall of Rangoon shows that these reactions were fully justified. Apart from this, the plan had many advantages, and at a major conference in Calcutta on 23rd February which heralded my arrival as Allied Air Commander-in-Chief, it was approved in principle and the target for tonnage to be hauled in its execution decided. The maximum lift was assessed at 1,887 tons per day between 20th March and 1st April and 2,075 tons per day between 1st May and 15th May. I emphasised that these figures would entail a very high rate of effort from the squadrons involved, and would entail considerable retrenchment during the monsoon to pay off the mortgage in maintenance and overstrain we would have contracted in its achievement.

64. Meanwhile, the air lift was still increasing. In February, C.C.T.F. hauled 51,210 short tons of supplies into the operational area. In addition, at the end of the month, a small though vital airborne operation took place to consolidate the capture of Meiktila, which had been seized following an armoured dash from their bridgehead on the Irrawaddy by 17 Division.

65. Troops were landed to reinforce the flying column which had seized the airfield and was now being fiercely attacked on all sides by the enemy. Transport aircraft landed and discharged their loads under fire, many suffering damage while so doing. One aircraft taking on wounded for its return journey had a shell explode inside it, causing further injuries to the casualties who were already emplaned. Thus, within very few days, landing became impossible, and it was necessary to resort to the less economical practice of dropping, which still further increased the load on our transport squadrons.

66. The Meiktila operation was a success, and a captured Japanese Staff officer assessed it as the turning point in the battle for Burma. It was not accomplished without mistakes, however, which rendered it far more hazardous than it might otherwise have been. It should be established that aircraft will not land until the possibility of the airfield being subjected to heavy fire is ruled out. Planning should be carried out on this premise. Secondly, the R.A.M.O. that was established on the airfield was pitifully inadequate, the officer in charge having to guide aircraft to unloading points instead of being free to organise their quick turn-around under fire. In a critical operation, such points might make all the difference between success and dismal failure. They merit much greater consideration in combined planning than has hitherto been accorded them.

*

67. By the beginning of April, Meiktila was again safe for landing, although shells were still bursting less than 200 yards from the strips. Preparations were immediately commenced to build up stocks to maintain Fourteenth Army in the final dash which

was to carry them 250 miles southward in the second half of the month. On the 20th, the main airfield at Lewe was captured and speedily prepared for light aircraft and gliders, which began landing on the morning of the 21st. Toungoo, 50 miles further south, was occupied on the 22nd and, in spite of bad weather, over 100 Dakotas and Commandos landed on the 24th. Within five days, Pyuntaza, another airstrip 70 miles further south, was also receiving supplies, and a battalion group was flown in to cut the enemy escape route eastwards from Pegu. The enemy was still active on both sides of the narrow strip along the Mandalay-Pegu railway which had formed our corridor, and while the capture of Rangoon was left to an assault from the south, transport squadrons continued with unabated activity the supply of Fourteenth Army, who but for these outstanding efforts would not have been able to hold the ground they had won.

*

Casualty Evacuation.

68. Throughout the period, the saving of lives, the morale of the fighting troops and the mobility of our ground forces has been materially assisted by the work of light aircraft and Dakotas flying out sick and wounded from the battle areas. The total of men thus saved from avoidable pain and suffering, from many days' journey by sampan, mule and ambulance, and from dying for lack of hospital facilities was formidable.

69. The flexibility of air power, by no means lessened when used in the interests of humanity, was well illustrated by a unique operation carried out by Sunderlands of No. 230 Squadron, which landed on Lake Indawgyi behind the enemy lines and flew out 537 wounded men of Special Force, whom General Wingate's columns would otherwise have been forced to abandon to the mercy of the Japanese.

70. This operation was, however, exceptional. The normal procedure was for light aircraft of the R.A.F. Communication squadrons and the U.S.A.A.F. Liaison squadrons to bring in the sick and wounded from extemporised landing strips to grounds where Dakotas and Commandos were discharging their cargo, and whence they would take them to base hospitals on return journeys. It was proposed at one time to attach light aircraft to the transport squadrons, and form one co-ordinated flying unit to undertake the whole process of casualty evacuation, but such a scheme would either have impaired the mobility of the light aircraft components or would have left them continually detached from their parent squadrons with no administrative or domestic backing for the difficult conditions under which they live and operate. Accordingly, as the American light aircraft are withdrawn from this theatre and the R.A.F. take on the whole of the work, it is proposed to form independent self-sufficient flying units to reinforce the Group Communication Squadrons in casualty evacuation. The resultant organisation will be sufficiently elastic to cover the whole front and yet be capable of concentration where casualties are heavy.

71. Casualty evacuation has been a regular part of the Air Forces' work in this theatre since the middle of 1943. It is unfortunate that with the increase in traffic which intensified operations have caused, there has been insufficient parallel growth of resources. Nursing Orderlies are 11 per cent. below establishment, and the buildings and accommodation for the reception of wounded at base airfields are not of the standard which good hygiene and humanity demand. If the Royal Air Force is to maintain the high reputation it has built in this sphere, far more generous scales of equipment and personnel must be authorised.

*

Conclusions on Air Transport.

72. The first essential for air supply is good ground organisation. One weak link in the chain can vitiate the work of the aircrews and maintenance personnel, the estimates of the planners and the efforts of the fighting troops. It is worth outlining some of the faults that have occurred in order that they may be avoided in the future:

(i) Dropping Zones should always be located where a drop is feasible. This might sound a platitude to anyone who has not flown on supply-dropping operations in Burma and found dropping areas continually located in narrow valleys whose negotiation after each run is a major hazard.

(ii) The system of communicating information on dropping areas, on the composition of loads, on changes of location, on enemy interference and all other aspects of air supply must be such that the one small and vital item of knowledge which might make the difference between a successful or an abortive sortie is available at all links in the chain.

(iii) The British Army-Air supply system in South-East Asia has been continually marred by the failure to provide for meticulous organisation in a sphere where great efforts can be rendered nugatory by inaccuracy in minor details.

The following are some of the lessons learnt:-

(*a*) Adequate distributing facilities must be made available by the land forces at landing grounds to ensure that perishable goods are quickly distributed when unloaded from aircraft.

(*b*) Aircraft should not be detailed to convey food to areas in which the same commodities can easily be obtained by local purchase.

(*c*) Packing of goods must be strong enough to ensure that containers do not burst in transit.

(*d*) Adequate facilities must be provided for feeding and resting aircrews engaged on this arduous flying, as they are often absent from their bases for as long as ten hours at a time.

(*e*) An efficient supply of re-fuellers and facilities for night maintenance must be arranged, otherwise aircraft which could otherwise be making an effective contribution to the battle will be grounded.

(iv) Forward airfield commanders and flying control personnel took a long time to realise that air supply traffic is as vital as any other, Cargo aircraft should not be kept circling an airfield while tactical aircraft take off on a routine operation whose delay by half an hour is immaterial.

(v) Each part of the planning and assessment of air lift must be carried out by the Service in whose province it lies. Much confusion has been caused here by the Army attempting to quote and work on flying hours per aircraft with no knowledge of the implications of U.E. and I.E.[3], aircraft serviceable or aircraft on strength. Moreover it was consistent practice for the Army to require full data on the performance of our aircraft and explanations for any short-fall that might occur, while never giving equivalent information upon their own short-fall in overland or inland water transport.

73. Air supply depends on so many agencies, and is affected by so many imponderables, that the allocation of resources and good brains to ensure efficiency, speed and good liaison can never be too generous. The campaign in Burma would have been rendered easier had the engineering resources that were poured into less profitable projects been directed towards timely building of forward airfields, more efficient supply depots and stronger lines of communication to the air haulage centres. The Ledo Road, for example, is surely the longest white elephant in the world. Had the wealth of ability and material that went to its building been employed in strengthening the air supply system, the recapture of Burma could probably have been advanced by an appreciable period.

*

PART FIVE.
TACTICAL SUPPORT OF THE GROUND FORCES.

The Organisation of Tactical Support.

74. Air forces operating in tactical support of the Allied Land Forces in Burma comprised Nos. 221 and 224 Groups R.A.F. and 10th U.S.A.A.F. all under the command of Headquarters, Eastern Air Command. Each worked in close association with a corresponding army headquarters – the Tenth U.S.A.A.F. with the Northern Combat Area Command, 224 Group with 15 Corps and 221 Group with 33 Corps and 4 Corps, and finally from the beginning of December onwards with the Fourteenth Army. 221 Group and Fourteenth Army remained together at Imphal only until the end of December, when the latter moved forward to Kalemyo, being accompanied by the A.O.C. and his air staff. The two headquarters were again united fully at Monywa from 9th February until the middle of April, when they moved to Meiktila, their final staging post before Rangoon. The mobility of 221 Group headquarters had a less active counterpart in that of 224 Group, which remained with the headquarters of 15 Corps first at Cox's Bazar and later at Akyab. In both cases the close relationship of the headquarters of the two Services was an essential element in their successful co-operation.

75. In the campaign in central Burma, just as all the ground forces came under the Fourteenth Army, so all the aircraft engaged in close, as distinct from tactical, support of the former were controlled by Headquarters, 221 Group. There were however two exceptions. The two Air Commando Groups operated directly under Eastern Air Command, and the Mustangs of the Second Air Commando Group, which played so important a role in the operations of 4 Corps which led to the seizure of Meiktila, were for the crucial period of these operations controlled by an advanced headquarters of the Combat Cargo Task Force located with 4 Corps headquarters. The second exception was provided by the Thunderbolt squadrons of 905 Wing, for which, owing to administrative reasons, there was no room east of the Lushai Hills and which were therefore located in Arakan under 224 Group.

76. In this connection the very difficult problems of administration confronting 221 Group must be recalled. Its wings and squadrons operated from bases covering a front of some two hundred miles, and a depth which at the beginning of the campaigning season in November was no less, and which by the end of April had expanded to some six hundred miles, from the Mosquito wing at Khumbigram to the fighter squadrons on forward strips near Toungoo. Most were on a highly mobile basis, with personnel reduced to the minimum; the separation of squadrons from servicing echelons which was generally effected towards the end of 1944 contributed materially to the mobility of units in the group. Fighter squadrons moved forward in

pace with the advancing front as quickly as the army were able to prepare landing grounds and forego air transport for them; the squadrons of 906 Wing, for instance, were operating from airfields near Ye-U by the middle of January, a fortnight after the occupation of the district by 33 Corps, and before the end of April no less than nine fighter squadrons were located at Toungoo, which had not been captured until the 22nd, and another four at Magwe, which fell on the 18th, in preparation for the assault upon Rangoon. These moves were effected with the aid of transport aircraft, overland communications being almost non-existent. There was, however, some feeling among the squadrons that in the matter of motor transport and indeed of supplies generally the army was at a distinct advantage.

77. The enormous area over which the squadrons of 221 Group were scattered, together with the meagreness of communications by land and telephone, also precluded the wholesale adoption, for the operational control of fighter aircraft in close support, of the organization which had been evolved in the European theatre of war for army-air co-operation. The former system of Army Air Support Units was replaced in the closing months of 1944 by the establishment of Air Support Signals Units with Visual Control Posts (V.C.Ps.), Air Advisers being also provided for both corps and divisional headquarters. A Combined Army/Air School for training V.C.P. personnel was set up at Ranchi, and it was soon found that the greatest difficulty in the establishment of Visual Control Posts was the provision of personnel, particularly of Controllers, who it was agreed must be chosen from experienced junior officers of the General Duties branch. Ten teams were however operating by the end of 1944 and by the beginning of May, 1945, their number had risen to thirty-four. The special value of the V.C.Ps. lay in the extra flexibility and accuracy which they lent to air operations planned in conjunction with the ground situation; the former device of indicating targets by smoke shells, always liable to inaccuracies in both place and time as well as to counterfeiting by the enemy, was now needed only when the target lay in flat jungle country, invisible from the air and not determinable in relation to any obvious feature of the landscape.

78. Of the general success of the V.C.P. system there can be no doubt, from both air and ground points of view. It contributed materially to that close and efficient co-operation of ground and air forces which was so marked a feature of the campaign of 1944-45. It led however to a tactic of less unquestionable value in the employment of the "cabrank" method, by which aircraft patrolled continuously over selected areas, maintaining touch all the time with the V.C.P., who as opportunity offered would call them down to attack any fresh target revealed by the progress of the battle. This tactic was very popular with our own troops, as the continued presence overhead of our own air support had excellent morale effect. Furthermore, air support was available to engage any target at a moment's notice. It was however wasteful of flying hours and reduced petrol stocks, in that the aircraft were liable to be kept waiting and targets could not always be provided, while it diminished the weight of air attack, since in order to maintain a continuous patrol the aircraft could seldom operate in more than pairs. If the army requires direct air support to be available at such short notice, it is considered that their desires could more economically be satisfied by providing the

A Hawker Hurricane Mk.IIC of 42 Squadron RAF based at Kangla, Burma, piloted by Flying Officer "Chowringhee" Campbell, is pictured diving to attack a bridge near a small Burmese settlement on the Tiddim Road during May 1944. The bombs of the previous aircraft can be seen exploding on the target. (HMP)

The immediate aftermath of an attack by Beaufighters on a pipe line carrying oil from Yenangyaung to Syriam refineries on 28 February 1944. The cannon shells have severed the pipe line and the oil has burst into flames. (HMP)

High explosive and sticks of incendiary bombs explode on a Japanese supply dump in a wooded area at Taungup, on the coast of western Burma, during a heavy daylight attack by Consolidated Liberators of No.231 Group during December 1944. (HMP)

A Japanese train alight after an attack by Beaufighters, ten miles north of Kokkogon, on 15 December 1943. As this image shows, a number of the wagons were set on fire; the dense black smoke and the rapidity with which this happened suggests that the vans were carrying oil drums. (HMP)

Sticks of bombs from Consolidated Liberators explode on the marshalling yards at Mandalay, Burma, during a daylight raid by aircraft of No.231 Group, again during December 1944. (HMP)

A low-level oblique photograph showing the extent of the damage caused by Allied air attacks on the town and railway junction of Pyinmana in central Burma. Much wreckage of rolling stock can be seen throughout the sidings. (HMP)

A post-raid aerial photograph of the damage caused to the railway facilities at Kanbalu, Burma, following an RAF attack in July 1944. Note the stacks of wood fuel stacked for use as blast shelters for locomotives by the Japanese. (HMP)

Water gushing from a tank at the Kume Road railway station after an attack by Beaufighters. (HMP)

A Bristol Blenheim attacks a Japanese column on the lower Chindwin river, March 1943. Note the aircraft's tail wheel at the top of the shot. (HMP)

A low-level oblique aerial photograph taken by an attacking Bristol Beaufighter Mk.VIF of 27 Squadron RAF, showing Japanese goods wagons under fire on the railway line between Monywa and Sagaing in central Burma on 18 July 1943. (HMP)

Chindwin air drop: The crew of a 40mm Bofors anti-aircraft gun of the 11th East African Division watch as an RAF Dakota drops supplies on the western side of the Chindwin River, 8-11 December 1944. (James Luto Collection)

The 2,760 ton Japanese transport *Angthong Goo* on fire after an attack by Liberators of 159 Squadron in the Gulf of Siam, 4 June 1945. (HMP)

Paddle steamers and similar low draught vessels were often used by the Japanese as headquarters or accommodation on some of the Burmese rivers; they were moored to the river bank and camouflaged. It is once such vessel that is pictured here under attack between Kyaukpadaung and Muale during November 1943. (HMP)

The aftermath of a Beaufighter attack in the Minhlayathaya area on 16 December 1943, with four or more native craft left burning on the shoreline. The original caption states that "they burst into flames immediately and emitted dense smoke showing them to be carrying an inflammable cargo, probably petrol or oil", for the Japanese. (HMP)

A series of images which illustrate the dangers of the "minimum altitude bombing" often undertaken by the Allied air forces in the Far East. They were taken by a RAAF aircraft during an attack on camouflaged Japanese ships in Hansa Bay, New Guinea, on 28 August 1943, and show the consequences of following the preceding bombing aircraft too closely, without allowing sufficient time for its bombs to explode.

The top left picture shows bombs from a preceding B25 dropped but not exploded. A second 'plane is coming in low from over the land, with smoke from gunfire. In the top right picture, a bomb dropped amidships from the first attacker is exploding under the second. The violence of the bomb's explosion, see bottom left, blasts the wing and tail off the second B25, catapulting it into the sea. The image bottom right shows the moment that the stricken bomber hits the water. (HMP)

air forces with airfields as close behind the front line as the reasonable security of the ground installations will warrant.

*

Close support of the Fourteenth Army.

79. The aircraft employed in close support operations were of various types. In June, 1944, there were still four squadrons of Vengeances operating, two on the Imphal and two on the Arakan front; they had done excellent work in the 1943-44 campaign, but had soon to be withdrawn. In September, the first R.A.F. Thunderbolts began operations; Thunderbolts had already been in use for some time with the Tenth U.S.A.A.F. which had also occasionally employed its Lightnings (P.38) in close support work. As the new campaign developed, and it became clear that the enemy was in no position seriously to challenge the Allied air superiority, Spitfires were increasingly diverted to the ground-attack role, particularly in the Arakan sector.

80. But the backbone of direct air support was always provided by the Hurricane, with or without bombs. The "Hurribomber" had well proved its worth in the 1943-4 campaign, and some in particular of the "Hurribomber" squadrons enjoyed an immense reputation for their accurate pin-pointing of targets within a comparatively few yards of our own positions. Their value in this was particularly evident during the period of mountain warfare that ended at the beginning of December, 1944, and subsequently in the interval of semi-static fighting that was marked by the battle of the bridgeheads in late January and February, 1945. In conjunction with fighter-bombers as well as independently, ground-attack fighters also frequently operated in close support, doing particularly effective work in attacks upon gun sites and patrols over areas in which enemy artillery was suspected to be located.

81. Heavier aircraft were also taken into service in support of ground attacks. Mitchells (B.25) had already been employed for this purpose in the 1943-4 campaign, but the four squadrons of the Twelfth Bombardment Group were now withdrawn from the Strategic Air Force and placed under the operational control of first 224 Group and later 221 Group, so that their work might more simply be dovetailed into the general tactical pattern. They operated sometimes independently, but in close support more frequently in conjunction with fighter-bombers, and added greatly to the weight and effectiveness of large-scale close support operations; the term "Earthquake" which was ultimately taken into official use to describe these concerted attacks upon Japanese bunker positions originated among these Mitchell squadrons, who earned for themselves the name of "the Earthquakers."

82. An outstanding "earthquake" operation, for instance, was the air contribution to the combined army and air attack directed on 10th January against the enemy stronghold at Gangaw in the Kabaw Valley, where an extensive and well-defended system of bunkers and gun emplacements was holding up the advance of 4 Corps southwards in its vital thrust against the Japanese left flank. Four Mitchell squadrons participated in this operation, as did some thirty-four "Hurribombers," defensive

cover being supplied by Spitfires and Thunderbolts. It turned out to be a highly successful day; the bombs were dropped at approximately 1430 hours and within ninety minutes five out of the six main Japanese positions were in Allied hands. The subsequent withdrawal of the enemy from the whole neighbourhood during the next few days was attributed by 4 Corps to be due in great measure to a lowering of his morale as a result of this air attack. But the participation of so large a number of aircraft in a single operation was not usual, and as the campaign wore on it was realised that Mitchells operating in numbers as low as two or three could do effective work in accurately winkling out small enemy parties from their lairs.

83. Heavy bombers of the Strategic Air Force were also employed on "earthquake" operations from time to time, mainly in support of the Fourteenth Army during the battle for the bridgeheads in January and February, 1944, though they also intervened effectively in support of 15 Corps during the struggle for the possession of the coastal road at Kangaw at the end of January. But well-marked targets suitable for their employment in direct co-operation with the ground forces were of necessity few, owing to the Japanese skill in camouflage, and the heavy bombers were therefore of most assistance to land operations in their attacks upon targets not in the immediate battle-zone.

*

Indirect Support of the Fourteenth Army.

84. On numerous occasions the ground forces requested the help of the Strategic Air Force, and nominated targets some distance behind the battle area though still in the tactical zone of land operations. These targets were, in the main, supply centres or nodal communication points or built-up areas in which the enemy was believed to be living. A notable attack of this type was mounted on 13th January against Mandalay, the keystone of the whole Japanese defensive system in central Burma and directly threatened in two directions by the advance of the Fourteenth Army. Fifty-four aircraft attacked the Japanese-occupied district and a further 12 the suburb of Sagaing on the opposite side of the river, the operation being preceded by attacks by Thunderbolts upon anti-aircraft gun sites in the neighbourhood, and accompanied by fighter sweeps over the airfields at Aungban and Meiktila. Photographic evidence confirmed the destruction of some 70 major buildings in the Japanese quarters, while intelligence reports variously estimated Japanese casualties alone at 600 and a 1,000, in addition to those inflicted upon Burmese puppet troops.

85. Such operations undertaken at the request of the Allied land forces reached their zenith in February, during which month nearly two thirds of the total number of sorties flown by Liberators of the Strategic Air Force were directed against targets in or near the battle-front as requested by the Fourteenth Army. These included, for instance, the stores dumps near the railhead at Madaya, from which the enemy forces fighting to contain the Singu bridgehead were supplied, which was attacked by forty-five heavy bomber aircraft, and the garrison districts at Yenangyaung, which were

attacked by 50. Later in the month, heavy bomber targets included objectives designated by the Army at Myittha, Mahlaing and Myingyan – all towns lying on or close to the path being followed by the armoured columns of 4 Corps in their thrust towards Meiktila. To take a final example, the climax of the air attacks upon the potential stronghold of Toungoo, where the enemy was expected to make a serious effort to stop the drive of 4 Corps southwards towards Rangoon in the second half of April, was supplied by over 40 Liberators, which bombed the garrison area there on the 21st, when the nearest Allied troops were already within striking distance, and indeed entered the town the following day.

86. Very effective operations against targets in the immediate rear of the enemy were carried out by ground-attack fighters throughout the period; their most vulnerable objectives were to be found along the lines of communication, where animal and motor transport units were carrying to his troops in the field, and also along the waterways where miscellaneous rivercraft served the same purpose. In these operations varied aircraft were employed, from Hurricanes and Spitfires to Beaufighters, Lightnings, Thunderbolts and Mosquitos, while Mitchells also participated, particularly by night. Armament included rocket projectiles and bombs, as well as 40 mm. cannon, also guns of lesser calibre.

87. Some small foretaste of the weight and pattern of this tactical support of the army was given in July, when the enemy was endeavouring to withdraw from the perimeter of the Imphal plain, and good toll was taken of his transport forced to brave the open road to Tiddim and the other routes eastward to the Chindwin. Direct attacks upon vehicles, mainly by Hurricanes, were varied by successful efforts to block the Tiddim road by causing landslides, and to break the bridges both along it and in the Kabaw Valley – achievements for which Lightnings and Vengeances were responsible. In all, over 75 motor transport units were successfully attacked in this area during the month. These operations, though invisible to the army, were controlled with the military situation always in view, and evidence was subsequently forthcoming in plenty from captured diaries of enemy officers and men of their effectiveness in hindering the passage of supplies and the movement of personnel, and in aggravating the conditions of disease and undernourishment under which the Japanese ground forces laboured.

88. In August the tactical picture on the Fourteenth Army front came to centre round the Chindwin river, which for two or three weeks became of considerably enhanced importance as a supply route. It had long been in use by the Japanese as a line of communication, and the riverine ports, particularly Monywa and Kalewa, were active points of supply. The still worsening military situation continued to impose upon the enemy the necessity for emergency movements of men and supplies behind the Manipur sector of the front. Since the capacity of the Sagaing-Ye-U railway had been greatly reduced by air action, and the other overland routes were more or less unusable owing to the monsoon, they were forced to have increased resort to the Chindwin as a line of communication.

89. Early in the month the toll of rivercraft successfully attacked began to increase and it became apparent that something was afoot. The Spitfires and Hurricanes which

had hitherto been covering the river were reinforced by a detachment of Beaufighters from 224 Group. "Hurribombers" were joined by Wellingtons, and later by Mitchells, in a series of attacks upon riverside targets. In addition, mines, both magnetic and ordinary, were laid in the Chindwin by Mitchells so as to catch traffic attempting to move under cover either of cloud or darkness. The total number of rivercraft successfully attacked on the Chindwin during the month was not far short of five hundred, and included seven launches; of this total the Beaufighters accounted for slightly over half, together with five of the launches.

90. Attacks upon road transport vehicles continued throughout the campaign, their effectiveness being increased with the advent of better weather at the close of the monsoon. In particular, the periods during which a major Allied advance was in progress and the battlefront was therefore fluid, were marked by the presence of transport targets in otherwise unusual quantity. This was so during the advance to the Irrawaddy in December, the thrust towards Meiktila during late February and early in March, and above all during the final advance of 4 Corps towards Rangoon in the second half of April. Ox-carts belonging to the local population had long been habitually pressed into service by the Japanese, and were attacked at all times. But lorries moved mainly under cover of darkness, and the Beaufighters which lit upon a convoy of forty to fifty vehicles travelling westwards along the road from Meiktila to Kyaukpadaung on the afternoon of February 5th and successfully strafed them made an exceptional discovery. But it was probably no coincidence that on the night of February 15th/16th, just after the Fourteenth Army had made its decisive crossing of the Irrawaddy below Mandalay, another Beaufighter located some fifty vehicles all moving eastwards along the Chauk-Meiktila highway.

91. A little later, on the night of the 27th/28th, a Mitchell on intruder patrol discovered a convoy of over a hundred vehicles, together with some armoured cars and six tanks, travelling northwards along the road from Taungdwingyi to Myothit, doubtless to be thrown into the attempt to stem the advance of the Fourteenth Army. The aircraft delivered attacks by both bombing and strafing for the space of an hour. It then attacked another smaller group of vehicles some distance to the south-east, after which it returned to the large convoy and was able to observe that some forty units had been knocked out by its previous attacks; finally it delivered one more strafing attack, setting three more vehicles on fire.

92. In the second half of April, with the final stages of the advance southwards in progress, such targets became unprecedentedly plentiful. A Hurricane squadron, for instance, caught over forty vehicles on the 19th standing nose to tail, heavily loaded and camouflaged, off the road a little south of Pyinmana, and was subsequently able to count seventeen in flames and many more severely damaged. The same squadron located an even larger number near the site of the bridge over the Sittang at Mokpalin on the 30th, when a total of forty-three lorries finally was counted in flames. Both Mustangs of the Second Air Commando Group and Beaufighters of 224 Group had each already made a haul similar in size and nature in this escape corridor on the 26th. In all, during this second half of the month, approximately three hundred and fifty motor vehicles were successfully attacked behind the enemy's lines throughout

Burma. The analogous figures for the whole period covered by this despatch may conservatively be assessed, on the basis of visible evidence, at 3846 M.T. vehicles.

93. One operation in tactical support of the Fourteenth Army is worthy of special mention, namely the achievement of a Hurricane IID squadron, firing rocket projectiles, which on February 19th – in the course of a single day – put out of action twelve tanks which the Japanese were about to throw into the battle for the bridgehead opposite Myinmu. These belonged to the single tank regiment of which the Japanese forces in Burma were known to dispose, and it was a measure of the importance attached by the enemy to the outcome of the struggle in the Myinmu bridgehead that he now sought to commit them in the field for the first time since they had been withdrawn from the Imphal front in the previous June. They were, however, destroyed before they came within range of infantry weapons, their destruction being shortly afterwards verified by advancing Allied troops who inspected their remains.

94. Somewhat different in character from the harassing of Japanese road communication was the interdiction of the railways used by the enemy in supplying his troops in Burma. Already, before the opening of the period covered by this despatch, the operation of ground attack fighter aircraft over these lines had become a difficult and expensive undertaking. Trains had practically ceased to run by day, their component parts generally being camouflaged and dispersed until sunset with the locomotives hidden in specially constructed shelters, often at the end of long sidings deep in the jungle. All obvious railway targets were guarded by efficient anti-aircraft defences, dummy or derelict locomotives being placed to decoy the aircraft into traps or at least to draw their fire. Nevertheless, some three hundred and ten locomotives were successfully attacked by day, Beaufighters accounting for one hundred and eighty-seven. Most of the remainder were claimed by Mosquitos, Mustangs, Lightnings and Thunderbolts.

95. Of the number of rolling stock destroyed it would be unsafe to give any estimate, but in any case there were always more than enough waggons available in Burma to satisfy Japanese military needs – in contrast to the position in regard to locomotives, which, as a result of past Allied air attacks were always in short supply, the Japanese going so far as to import them from Siam and to use petrol driven cars to haul railway waggons. Water-towers always presented a vulnerable target, difficult to hide, and thirty-nine were holed during the period. It should be noted that these day attacks by ground-attack fighters reached as far as the northern extremities of both the Burma-Siam and the Bangkok-Chiengmai railways.

96. A further one hundred and twenty-two locomotives were put out of commission as a result of night attacks, thirty-seven being contributed by Mosquitos and thirty-seven by Mitchells. These attacks were of course delivered upon trains in full employment, and were not infrequently accompanied by spectacular results, with engine boilers exploding, trucks aflame and a series of secondary explosions. They may be reckoned as having inflicted greater material injury upon the enemy than a numerical comparison between the numbers of locomotives damaged by day and by night would suggest.

97. Concurrently with attacks upon locomotives, key points in the Burmese railway

system, such as the junctions at Thazi and Pyinmana, were bombed, mainly by Mitchells and Lightnings. But the main weight of attack continued to be directed upon bridges, which were so numerous that it was impossible to provide anti-aircraft defences for more than the most important. The enemy pursued his established policy of erecting by-pass trestle bridges to serve as temporary substitutes for the permanent structures wrecked or menaced by air attack.

98. In all, about three hundred bridges were put out of commission by medium, light and fighter bombers; of this total, one hundred and twelve were railway bridges. So great, however, was the success of the bridge destruction policy, that in connection with the unexpectedly rapid advance of the Fourteenth Army it provoked the query whether we were not destroying our own future land line of communication in advance, and agreement was reached by which, from February onwards, the indiscriminate destruction of bridges was abandoned in favour of a policy of keeping specified major bridges unserviceable. When, in course of time, the sites were occupied by Allied troops, Bailey bridge sections flown in by transport aircraft were available to mend the broken thoroughfare.

99. Attacks on watercraft in Burma were pressed home by ground-attack fighters of all types throughout the campaign, particularly along the Irrawaddy, always an important Japanese line of communication, and also on the Arakan coast and the waterways of southwest Burma, though, as along the land routes so on the waterways, the enemy moved mainly by night. A rough estimate of the total number of inland or coastal watercraft in enemy use successfully attacked is 11,822 of which 302 were power-driven units. Towards the end of the campaign, the Irrawaddy tended to become less a line of communication for the Japanese than a hindrance to their lateral mobility, so that boats collected for ferrying rather than supply craft provided the main targets. At the same time, air reconnaissance and attack was maintained at a high rate over the Bassein – Henzada district in order to discourage the enemy division located there from moving eastwards to reinforce the main battlefront in central Burma. In the course of April, the motor launches supplying this garrison formation were successfully attacked on a number of occasions, notably on the 25th, when their hiding-place south-west of Rangoon was located and bombed and strafed with rocket projectiles by a mixed force of twenty-seven Beaufighters and Mosquitos.

100. A word must be added in connexion with the patrols flown by Beaufighters to intercept enemy shipping in the Gulf of Martaban. Owing to the reduction through air attack of the carrying capacity of the overland routes of entry into Burma, the Japanese had increasing resort during 1944 to the shipment of goods northwards along the Tenasserim coast and thence westwards across the Gulf of Martaban to Rangoon, employing for this a number of coasters of wooden construction eighty to one hundred and twenty feet in length. A daily patrol was maintained by Beaufighters, whose base at Chiringa lay not far short of five hundred miles distant from the Gulf at its nearest point, and resulted in the sinking of twenty-eight coasters, many of which were destroyed at dawn or dusk soon before ships reached or after they had left the nooks in which they hid during the day.

101. Attacks by all types of aircraft likewise continued, throughout the campaign,

to be directed against enemy bivouac and barrack areas and against storage points from small stacks of petrol drums near the front line to the great dumps north of Rangoon mentioned elsewhere in this despatch. Despite the undoubted accuracy of operations against this type of target, more particularly by Lightnings, Mosquitos and Mitchells, difficulties of terrain often forbade the assessment of results, even with the aid of photographs, and in default of the subsequent occupation of the target area by our own troops it has often only been a reference in a Japanese diary or an intelligence report which has arrived weeks or even months later which served to clinch the evidence of success. To take one instance out of many, it was not until several weeks after the event that the full success of the heavy raids of 8th February on targets at Yenangyaung was confirmed, when two prisoners of war agreed that they had been most terrifying, and stated that one bomb had destroyed thirty-four motor vehicles parked under shelter, and that another had landed in a trench in which some thirty Japanese were sheltering, killing all the occupants.

*

Tactical Support of 15 Corps.

102. Tactical support of 15 Corps followed lines closely parallel to those on which air support was furnished to the Fourteenth Army. There were, however, certain special characteristics which deserve mention. After the initial advance down the Kaladan Valley, the major forward moves of the ground forces were marked not by overland offensives leading to a break-through by mechanised formations, but by a series of amphibious landings at half-a-dozen points on the coast. Of the three island landings, those on Akyab and Cheduba were completely unopposed, while that on Ramree met only with slight opposition; few or no targets presented themselves and the air support on these occasions was therefore akin to a peace-time exercise. The mainland landings each achieved tactical surprise, but were all followed shortly by bitter fighting when the enemy entrenched himself in characteristic fashion and attempted to prevent the exploitation of the initial landing. Fierce battles then developed on the same general pattern as those for the Irrawaddy bridgeheads.

103. Two developments confined to operations by 224 Group deserve mention. The first was the use of Spitfires in the fighter-bomber role. The second was the employment from February onwards, of airborne Visual Control Posts, whose success was undoubted. From a light aircraft they were able to discern targets in the coastal jungle that were well concealed from ground observation, and so to pass directions to the aircraft waiting to attack. Two of these teams were operating by the end of the campaign.

104. Indirect support of 15 Corps centred largely around the maintenance of air attacks upon the long supply line on which the Japanese depended for the existence of their troops in Arakan. Its forward end among the coastal waterways and along the parallel road southwards to Taungup was covered by ground-attack fighters of all types, while the eastward track from An to Minbu – whose existence had been

established by Beaufighters on reconnaissance – and the mountain road from Taungup to the railhead at Prome, also yielded valuable targets. Stress was laid by the army in March and April, 1945, upon the need for maintaining a continuous interdiction of the latter road by cratering its surface or precipitating landslides by bombing, even at the cost of denying ourselves the future use of a much needed supplementary land line of communication to the Irrawaddy valley, and fighter-bombers and also heavy bombers of the Strategic Air Force were accordingly diverted to this purpose. Targets along the Prome-Rangoon railway were attacked as elsewhere in central Burma; in this, the destruction of its bridges by Lightnings of the 459th Squadron in February was especially notable. The stores areas at Taungup and Prome were watched and bombed from time to time.

*

Tactical Support of the Northern Combat Area Command.

105. On the north-eastern sector of the front, direct air support to Special Force and later to Thirty-six Division together with the Chinese divisions and the American Mars Task Force further to the east, was provided by the P.47s., P.38s. and also by the B.25s. of the Tenth U.S.A.A.F. The general principles of army/air force co-operation were as on other sectors of the front, the Visual Control Post being known as the "air party". There were, however, two directions in which the technique of close air support as practised by the Tenth U.S.A.A.F. was more advanced than on the 221 and 224 Group sectors. The first was in the more highly developed signals methods used in R/T communications between the "air party" on the one hand and the attacking aircraft and also the light aircraft – L.5s. – used for observation on the other.

106. The second lay in the special use made in the N.C.A.C. area of photography for tactical operations. Photographs of all sorts were used – low level verticals, reconnaissance strips, obliques and pin point shots. A simple method was worked out by which a common photograph grid was accepted by both ground and air forces for marking photographs; this was all the more necessary in that the country through which the N.C.A.C. forces were advancing consisted of an expanse of jungle-clad hills with few natural features by reference to which a target could be simply identified. The effectiveness of close air support was acknowledged by the ground forces in this sector no less than elsewhere, despite the considerable obstacles offered by the wild terrain to an exact collaboration.

107. It was no doubt in part the very success of air support operations in the N.C.A.C. area that led to their comparatively early cessation. The country through which the land forces advanced with a continually growing momentum offered few or no sites for the construction of forward landing-grounds, and the leading army units tended more and more to draw away from the available air bases as a consequence. Enemy opposition also dwindled, and, from the end of March onwards, contact was lost with the Japanese. Thenceforward, the air effort was thus inevitably

restricted to long-range attacks upon the transport routes, supply centres and bivouac points along the enemy line of retreat through the Shan States southwards into Siam.

*

PART SIX.
STRATEGIC AIR FORCE.

108. Operations by heavy bombers in this theatre were conditioned by the restricted nature of the targets available and by the vulnerability of the all-important Japanese lines of communication. To understand the pattern of attack, and to assess its results, demands some knowledge of these circumstances, which are discussed in some detail hereunder.

109. The factors of climate, topography and the occupation of large areas of China combined to make the Japanese grip on Burma one which, it was early realised, the Allies would have great difficulty in prising loose. Notwithstanding his seemingly inviolable front, the enemy possessed an Achilles' heel in his poverty of natural resources and his consequent dependence on seas that he has never actually controlled. A high percentage of everything upon which his industry thrives must cross the sea in crude form to be processed in the homeland; thence it must recross the seas to arrive at the fighting line. From Japan to Burma the sea lanes stretch for some 4,000 miles, of which more and more were open to attack by Allied bombers as strength, experience and airbases developed. The railways which carried his supplies thence to the front were at the mercy of Allied bombers to an even greater degree.

110. Communications by sea were not disputed during 1942 and much of 1943. It was simple to follow the normal channels of commerce to the ports of Siam and Malaya in the east, Singapore in the south, and Mergui, Tavoy, Ye, Moulmein and Rangoon in the west. But Japan herself had proved by the sinking of the "Prince of Wales" and "Repulse" that control of the sea demands control of the air above the sea. In her early victory lay the seeds of her own defeat, for Allied aircraft disputed with her, and won, control of the air over all her lines of communication in Burma and Siam.

111. From the nodal ports, the railways of Burma and Siam constitute a system of strategically connected lines with a total length of approximately 5,000 miles. From Phnom Penh, north-west of Saigon, the railway goes west and north-west through Bangkok, Pegu and Mandalay, where it forks into two lines terminating at Lashio and Myitkyina with branches to Rangoon, Bassein, Kyaukpadaung, Myingyan and Ye-U. The tactical importance of all these railheads was reinforced by their strategic positioning on the lines of supply. Their function was not only to feed forward material from Japan, but to shuttle within the occupied territories the natural resources whose employment would ease the load on Japanese shipping – rice, tungsten, oil,

tin and rubber. It has been estimated that at least 50 per cent. of the Japanese Army's requirements in Burma were produced locally.

*

112. In June, 1944, the Strategic Air Force underwent changes in organisation and composition that materially reduced its strength and effectiveness during the monsoon months. The Twelfth Bombardment Group, comprising four squadrons of Mitchells, was transferred to Third Tactical Air Force, a step for which Air Marshal Baldwin had long pressed, and the Seventh Bombardment Group of four squadrons of Liberators was diverted to haul petrol to China. This was considered more remunerative employment for them than the conduct of bomber operations under active monsoon conditions. Strategic Air Force therefore retained only its British component, totalling three Liberator and two Wellington squadrons, excluding the Special Duty and Air Sea Rescue element. In consequence of the reduction in strength, and with the monsoon at its height, a change in policy was necessary, and a new Operational Directive (No. 10) declared that objectives would be tactical targets best calculated to assist Fourteenth Army; communications, shipping and railways, with particular attention to the Martaban – Pegu, Pegu – Mandalay and Bangkok – Nampang sections.

113. In October, the Seventh Bombardment Group returned to Strategic Air Force, and in the following month, Nos. 99 and 215 Squadrons returned to the line having been re-equipped from Wellingtons to Liberators. With one more accession to its strength (No. 358 Squadron formed within the Command and operating by January), Strategic Air Force reached its full power for the vital six months to follow. Its operational function was accordingly expanded from October onwards to include all the duties of strategic bombers, including mining, and the Force was ready for the decisive campaign which lay ahead.

*

114. Operations fell into well-defined categories, the first of which was the effort against shipping and harbour installations; the second, and most important, was the interdiction of the overland supply routes into Southern Burma; and the third the destruction of the enemy's powers of resistance in Burma by disorganising his internal communications, razing his dumps, and denying him the use of his airfields and military installations.

(I) *Attacks against Shipping and Harbours.*

115. Although the main weight of attack fell upon railways, some effort was directed towards the furtive and well-camouflaged shipping which plied the coasts, seldom moving by day and never venturing far within the radius of action of strike aircraft. Such operations were carried out with the purpose of deterring the enemy from committing his supplies to the perils of the sea rather than of sinking the ships en

route. It was a policy of denial rather than of destruction. This choice was necessary since shipping was never frequent enough to justify intensive search for it, and the most remunerative targets were therefore harbours, docks and port facilities. Of these Mergui, Martaban, the new port of Khao Huagang, and Bangkok were most often attacked, and considerable destruction achieved. A typical intelligence report on a raid against Bangkok in March, for example, was- "Concentrated and successful attack causing destruction of forty per cent. of the storage units; sixty Japs killed".

116. Accepting that enemy shipping was hard to search out, Strategic Air Force had resort to the policy of hindering what it could not destroy. Mining was already proved by photographic reconnaissance as being a profitable method of delaying the passage of supplies, for in harbours already mined there had been a serious curtailment of Japanese shipping, and such craft as continued to approach the harbours anchored outside so that cargoes had to be lightered ashore.

117. Thus from August onwards plans and technique for very long-range mining were developed and soon bore fruit. In September the Pakchan river, housing the newly constructed port of Khao Huagang, was heavily mined and the flow of coastal traffic seriously disrupted. Similar operations against Bangkok, Goh Sichang and Tavoy followed. In October a remarkably successful flight was carried out to the inner approaches of Penang harbour. Fifteen Liberators each laid four 1,000 lb. mines "precisely in the positions ordered", with no mishap or failure although the round trip was over three thousand miles. Such operations continued throughout the campaign against all ports and anchorages along the Tenasserim Coast and from March onwards against those in the Gulf of Siam. Mining was the special and exclusive province of No. 159 Squadron R.A.F. who throughout the period laid the impressive total of 1,953 mines at ranges which a year before would have been considered impossible. The following results were observed from reconnaissance:

(i) Jap launch and passenger steamer sunk near Victoria Point (February).

(ii) 3,000 ton tanker Kuisho Maru sunk at Bangkok (January).

(iii) 200 ft. M.V. sunk at Bangkok (March).

118. If the anti-shipping effort was intangible in effect, that against railways was spectacular, and its results immediately apparent. By far the greatest attention was paid to the Bangkok-Moulmein railway on which an overall total of 2,700 tons of bombs were dropped. With the interdiction of nearly all alternative routes, this railway was of paramount importance to the Japanese to supply and maintain their forces in Burma. Approximately two-thirds of the railway pursues a winding course in jungle hill-covered country, and it is not suitable for low-level attack, in addition to providing first-rate concealment. But as the strength and efficacy of the bomber force grew and the Burma-Siam railway became more vital, techniques were developed for its neutralisation. No precise date can be given for the introduction of these methods. A modus operandi was hammered out and in use before it became a doctrine, but its broad principles were as follows:-

(i) Bridges were the best targets because they were the most vulnerable and the most difficult to repair.

(ii) The underlying motive was to isolate segments of the line, and then to destroy at greater leisure the rolling stock and locomotives stranded thereon.

(iii) Diversity of attack was necessary to confuse the enemy.

(iv) Close photographic reconnaissance was maintained to detect any abnormal build-up at sidings or stations which would repay attack.

119. These principles were followed to such good effect that between January and April the average number of bridges unserviceable at one time was 9.2 over the stretch of railway from Pegu to Bangkok. It has been estimated that this reduced the traffic from 700-800 tons to 100-200 tons a day. The value of the attacks needs no further emphasis.

120. Operations similar in concept but less in intensity were maintained against the Bangkok-Chiengmai line, the Kra Isthmus railway, and the Bangkok-Singapore line. In all cases, the enemy reacted by placing the strongest A.A. defences he could muster along such a dispersed network of lines, by rebuilding and repairing bridges with beaver-like zeal, and by constructing as many as four by-pass structures at one crossing to counter or anticipate our attack.

(III) *Destruction of the Enemy's Powers of Resistance within Burma.*

121. To sever the external supply routes was not enough, for the enemy held at least six months' reserves of supplies that were contained in vast dumps, mainly dispersed in the Rangoon area. Therefore, during March and April, systematic destruction was initiated on the Rangoon Dumps in conjunction with XXth Bomber Command. Their destruction was vital, since with the stores contained therein the enemy might have been able to delay our advance and even halt it above Toungoo. The Dumps contained about 1,700 storage units well dispersed in revetments, and of these, photographic evidence alone showed 524 destroyed, and ground observers reported that well over 50 per cent. destruction was achieved.

122. The attacks on Japanese Headquarters and concentration areas can be illustrated by a strike on 29th March against the Japanese Burma Area Army Headquarters located in Rangoon. Reports indicate that four hundred Japanese, with a high proportion of officers, were killed. News of the attack spread to the Allied prisoners in Rangoon, and was the cause of considerable encouragement to them. The enemy's evacuation of the city a month later is much more understandable in the light of these attacks, which made Rangoon such a dangerous area even before ground forces were within striking distance. Mandalay had already suffered such attacks, notably one in January when it was reported by agents that six hundred Japanese were killed. The part played by such air blows in persuading the enemy to abandon his strategic positions earlier than anticipated must surely have been great.

*

"Special Operations."

123. Air operations in connection with intelligence and guerilla raising activities in this theatre have increased greatly during the past year. From a strength of two squadrons totalling 15 U.E. aircraft in June, 1944, resources were increased by the end of April, 1945, to three squadrons and one flight totalling 61 U.E. aircraft. The dividend that has been paid definitely justified the effort involved. From a handful of informants supplying skimpy information at great risk, the organisations grew, by the end of the campaign, into a powerful force capable of exerting a considerable influence on the course of the battle, and the air effort to support them reached a total of 372 sorties in the lunar month 18th April to 17th May. Between November, 1944, and May, 1945, over 1,350 sorties were flown, in which 2,100 tons of stores and 1,000 liaison officers were dropped behind the enemy lines. The effort for the preceding comparable period resulted in 34 tons of stores and 35 bodies being parachuted in.

124. One of the major results of the great effort involved was the prevention of the Japanese Fifteenth Army from taking any part in the defence of Toungoo during our advance, and rendering unnecessary the major battle which Fourteenth Army anticipated in front of the town. Other guerillas killed up to seven hundred Japanese, including a General, in the Toungoo-Rangoon area alone.

125. From the Air Force point of view, the great value of the Special Duty effort flown by Strategic Air Force was the provision of targets for the tactical Groups. During the final fortnight of April almost the whole of the long-range Fighter-Bomber resources of No. 224 Group were employed on Force 136 targets. Troop trains were caught at rest and a pagoda reported as a petrol/ammunition dump blew up with a huge explosion.

126. Special Duty operations in this theatre are of vital interest to the Air Forces in view of the difficulty of locating targets without the help of informants. Thus the diversion of effort to secret work has not been grudged, and current developments, foreshadowed in the R.A.F. Airborne Commando, will make the information supplied by operators behind the lines of even greater value. It is emphasised that parties should be thoroughly briefed in the limitations and potentialities of air strikes and that they should develop a speedy and accurate method of reporting if a full harvest is to be reaped from the information whose garnering depends so much upon the operations of our S.D. squadrons.

*

PART SEVEN.
PHOTOGRAPHIC RECONNAISSANCE.

127. At the opening of the period, photographic reconnaissance was carried out mainly by the aircraft of the Photographic Reconnaissance Force commanded by

Group Captain S.G. Wise, D.F.C. These included the Spitfires, Mosquitos and Mitchells of 681 and 684 Squadrons, R.A.F., operating from Alipore, and the Mustangs, Mitchells and Liberators of three U.S.A.A.F. squadrons, the last of which specialised in mapping. A fourth U.S.A.A.F. squadron flying Lightnings, began to operate in September.

128. The dense cloud banks habitually shrouding the operational area of South East Asia during the period of the monsoon interfered greatly with photographic reconnaissance, but advantage was taken of the northward passage of the monsoon in August to procure the first large-scale and survey cover of northern Sumatra by Mosquitos detached to operate from Ceylon. Other detachments were later sent eastwards to operate with the forward tactical air force headquarters from Tingawk Sakan (where at the beginning of September an American tactical reconnaissance squadron was placed under the P.R. Force), Imphal, Comilla and Chittagong in preparation for the forthcoming campaign, and these were later reinforced and moved forward in step with the ground forces. From the beginning of September onwards, a considerable measure of decentralisation in the planning and conduct of operations was introduced, with the purpose of giving squadron commanders more latitude in the allotment of sorties.

129. With the return of fair-weather conditions in October, the effort of the photographic reconnaissance squadrons rose to its former level, and during this month the daily average of sorties represented over a third of the total aircraft available in the whole force. The methodical cover of enemy airfields, communications and other targets was resumed, survey photographs being supplied as required by Headquarters Air Command, and Headquarters Allied Land Forces, South East Asia. In proportion with the increased flying, the photographic work of the photo sections of the P.R. Force was expanded, nearly 354,000 prints being produced during January, 1945, the peak month. Technical photographic developments included the introduction of the moving film camera on operational sorties, and the fitting into Mosquito aircraft of forward facing oblique cameras. The latter were first used on 14th February, when a set of stereoscopic pairs covering the Burma-Siam railway was thereby secured.

130. An exceptionally valuable photographic reconnaissance of the Burma rice areas was carried out by Squadron Leader C. Fox during 1944. The results shown by an analysis of the pictures were subsequently checked up on the ground, and were found to be correct within 5 per cent.

131. The main hindrances to the operations of the P.R. Force continued, even in the campaigning season, to be factors inseparable from flying in the tropics rather than the opposition of the enemy, which remained slighter than was usual in other theatres of war.

Successful cover of the waterfront at Akyab, for instance, was secured in November, 1944, by two Spitfires flying at from 50 to 200 feet, at neither of which a shot was fired. But the lengthening range of Mosquito sorties month by month bore witness to the mastery of climate and terrain. It was in December, 1944, that the first cover of Puket Island was obtained, in the course of a flight involving a round trip of 2,100 miles, which marked the furthest penetration to be made in this area. This record was, however, eclipsed by another aircraft which in January flew 2,431 air miles in eight hours and 20 minutes to cover Moulmein and the railway from Bangkok to Phnom Penh. Finally on 22nd March a Mosquito XVI broke the long distance record for this type of aircraft in any theatre of war with a flight of 2,493 air miles in eight hours forty-five minutes, covering the Bangkok-Singapore railway to a point south of the Malayan frontier. It was thus that the Mosquito made amends for the structural defect which had seriously curtailed its use during November and December, 1944.

132. The work of the P.R. Force was co-ordinated at one end with the short-range photography of the tactical reconnaissance squadrons, while at the other end, long distance survey work over Malaya was undertaken by the Superfortresses of XXth Bomber Command, U.S.A.A.F. The P.R. Force was responsible, for instance, for all the workaday survey and mapping required by the Fourteenth Army. As the Officer Commanding, No. 11 Indian Air Survey Liaison Section, R.E., reported in February, 1945, 684 Squadron, R.A.F. alone had achieved, in twelve months, three-quarters of the basic cover for the whole campaign and 1/30,000 cover for maps, photomaps and artillery block plots over the battle lines from Dimapur nearly to Rangoon and Moulmein. The work of photographic reconnaissance in general in this theatre has, of course, been of all the greater importance owing to the comparatively meagre intelligence available from ground sources; for air force purposes alone it provided an indispensable factor in the maintenance of Allied air superiority by providing speedy evidence of the location of enemy aircraft, while the work of the Strategic Air Force would have been unprofitable without the coverage of targets it furnished.

*

PART EIGHT.
GENERAL RECONNAISSANCE.

133. As the period under review opened, a deal of uncertainty existed as to whether the Indian Ocean U-boat warfare would be intensified by the arrival of long-range German U-boats. Such a possibility was not improbable, and had the contemplated threat materialised then, all General Reconnaissance air power in this theatre would have been harnessed under the co-ordinating and supervising control of IOGROPS.[4]

134. The period from June to August witnessed a decided increase in enemy U-boat warfare, although at no time can it be said that the threat reached alarming proportions. During these three months the enemy (operating with considerable wariness) sank thirteen ships of the medium-sized merchant vessel class, and, in turn, suffered the loss of one submarine as a result of a combined attack by aircraft and Naval Force 66.

135. In July, a concentration of enemy units in and around the shipping lanes to the east of the Maldives – resulting in the loss of five ships – portended a possible

menace. In this connection it is worthy of comment that Catalina aircraft employed on rescue searches co-operated in the location and eventual rescue of 244 survivors.

136. Having regard to the amount of shipping in the Indian Ocean, and the fact that during August there were possibly five German units operating in these waters, the enemy's achievements might be considered singularly paltry. This is a tribute to the constant vigilance of General Reconnaissance aircraft in the flying of anti-U-boat sweeps and patrols. Such a policy might not have produced many sightings and kills – a consideration of the immense expanses of ocean to be guarded will clearly show the difficulty of locating enemy units – but it kept U-boats submerged and out of range of our shipping.

137. With September came a falling-off in U-boat operations, and this was continued during October and November. A slight increase during November was considered as a parting shot of little weight and trifling importance. As an explanation of this it is reasonable to assume that American aggressiveness in the China Seas and the Pacific was absorbing the attention of Japan, as was the European war the attention of Germany. Thus the expected threat did not develop but rather declined, and as a consequence the need for an over-all centralised control as vested in the organisation of IOGROPS diminished with the declining U-boat threat.

*

Offensive General Reconnaissance.

138. The second half of the twelve months under review opened with No. 222 Group still being primarily concerned in supplementing the hunting and striking powers of the East Indies Fleet in anti-U-boat warfare. But it was becoming apparent that the U-boat threat no longer existed. Therefore, in the due consideration of alternative employment was conceived the undertaking of an offensive role. The mining of enemy waters in the Malacca Straits and the Chumphorn, Singora, Padang, Singapore areas; anti-shipping operations to deny the waters of the Andaman Sea to enemy shipping – this was to be the future employment of General Reconnaissance aircraft.

139. Mining operations were the first to commence, on the 21st January. From that date until 3rd May, 1945, 833 mines have been carried to enemy waters by No. 160 Squadron, the high percentage of 86.9 being successfully laid. The success of these operations, although not immediately apparent, will be revealed with the broadening of the operational scene in this theatre.

140. Only a short period of training was necessary to prepare No. 354 Squadron for its new assignment of low-level anti-shipping strikes, which were commenced early in February.

A second Liberator squadron – No. 203 – began to augment the anti-shipping effort in March. A statistical summary of the material damage inflicted as a result of these operations proves that these two squadrons played no small part in complicating the enemy's acute problem of shipping shortage.

*

The Development and Control of Offensive General Reconnaissance.

141. The last four months had seen General Reconnaissance changing the nature of its operational function with deftness and adaptability. The reinforcement and development of this new offensive role was envisaged during March, when No. 346 Wing was formed at Akyab, to provide escort for "forward area" convoys and to make easily available a striking force against enemy shipping off the Arakan and Burmese Coasts.

142. One squadron of Sunderland aircraft based on the depot ship S.S. "Manela" constituted a significant part of 346 Wing. This vessel ultimately proceeded from Colombo to Rangoon via Akyab, and her advent to these waters was an important milestone in offensive General Reconnaissance. Should a situation develop wherein it was necessary to conduct anti-shipping and similar operations in a theatre where the scene of operations might be constantly and rapidly changing (with a consequent paucity of adequate land-bases) then a mobile flying boat base would be an invaluable asset. If this situation did not develop, then the inherent mobility of such a unit could be usefully adapted to the requirements of Air Sea Rescue and Transport operations, where, as always, the lack of immediate land-bases establishes a major problem.

143. The period closed on an encouraging note. General Reconnaissance had already struck a worthwhile blow at enemy shipping, and plans were in hand for an intensifying of these operations in the months to come. In considering the strategic plan of anti-shipping sorties, mention should be made of the invaluable contribution of those General Reconnaissance Liberator and Mosquito aircraft based on Ceylon, in their day and night photographic reconnaissance over the Andamans, Nicobar Islands, Northern Sumatra and parts of Malaya. Meteorological flights were also flown regularly, and materially assisted weather forecasts for aircraft flying over vast expanses of water.

*

PART NINE.
ADMINISTRATIVE AND OTHER ASPECTS.

(I) *Administration.*

144. Administrative development of Air Command, South East Asia, during the year was dictated by the following factors:-

    (i) The move of Command Headquarters to Kandy.

    (ii) The need for identifying group administrative areas inside India with the geographical boundaries of the Indian Army Command.

(iii) The traditional problem of administering units spread over vast areas with insufficient resources.

(iv) The desirability of removing from operational formations extraneous administrative burdens.

(v) The necessity for providing operational units with greater mobility.

(vi) The planning of the administrative network to sustain and control units advancing into Burma.

(vii) The formation of new units in anticipation of future operations, while hardly meeting present commitments with existing resources in manpower and material.

(viii) The development on an unprecedented scale of air supply for the Allied forces advancing into Burma.

145. The primary British interests in South East Asia were the re-conquest of Burma, the Federated Malay States and Singapore, the Netherland East Indies, Thailand and French Indo-China. British air responsibilities in South East Asia also included the air defence of India and of Allied shipping in the Indian Ocean, the Arabian Sea and the Bay of Bengal. With these somewhat diverse objectives and geographical vagaries in mind it was essential to evolve an administration covering Royal Air Force commitments which would effectively meet the situation in South East Asia.

146. The extensive re-organizations which took place during 1944-45 were effected against a background of strict and cumbrous control of expenditure by the Government of India, and of dependence upon India through the organization known as the War Projects Co-ordination and Administrative Committee for the provision of resources. There was, too, a crippling shortage of manpower in precisely those trades which make for good administration – non-flying officers (notably signals and maintenance staffs), clerks G/D., equipment assistants, cooks and the like. Moreover, the growing body of Air Command continually bumped its head against the Command manpower ceiling. It is not intended to infer that the R.A.F. in South East Asia was badly served in relation to other commands, for it was well understood that the allocation of manpower had to be assessed in relation to theatre requirements. Nevertheless, it was considered that perhaps the incidence of and the remedies for the growing pains experienced were not fully recognised at home.

*

The Move of Headquarters, Air Command, to Ceylon.

147. The move of the Command Headquarters to Kandy was compelled by the insistence of the Supreme Allied Commander that his Commanders-in-Chief should work beside him. It was, however, rendered the more acceptable to Air Command on account of the growing need for divorcing operational and higher administrative

control from the extensive and complicated negotiations necessary with the Government of India and with G.H.Q., India, relative to administrative services, which had tended to hamper the primary tasks of the Allied Air Commander-in-Chief.

148. The institution of H.Q. Base Air Forces at New Delhi, had, therefore, many advantages. It liberated the Air Commander-in-Chief and his staff from direct day to day responsibilities for developing India as a base, and thus enabled him to address his attention more closely to the general problems of planning and policy control.

149. Before Base Air Forces was established and re-organisation was under consideration, it was generally supposed that a vertical split between the Air Staff and Administrative Branches offered the best solution to a complex problem. This meant that operations sections of the staff would move with the Air Commander-in-Chief to Kandy while the administrative sections remained at New Delhi. It was intended that administrative representation at Kandy should be effected by the provision of small cells or projections of the administrative branches concerned, which would work in an advisory and liaison capacity. This at the time was broadly the view of Air Chief Marshal Sir Richard Peirse.

150. Difficulties ahead if such an administrative set-up was adopted at New Delhi as suggested, were foreseen by Air Vice-Marshal Goddard. The reins of higher administrative control and policy, he considered, must in the first instance, be held firmly at Air Command in order to effect perfect co-ordination with the Air Commander-in-Chief and the operational branches at Kandy. Beside, the geographic factor was an important consideration, for Delhi was fifteen hundred miles from Kandy.

151. A new scheme which would more effectively meet the situation once re-organisation was established and yet ensure the retention of higher administrative control at Air Command, was brought up for consideration during the visit of Air Vice-Marshal Goddard to London in July, 1944. This revised project was, in the main, largely adopted when, at the beginning of October, Headquarters Air Command moved to Kandy and Headquarters Base Air Forces was formed at New Delhi.

152. The essence of the new arrangement lay in the retention at New Delhi of an administrative staff competent to deal with all questions, save the important policy matters, direct with the analogous departments of General Headquarters, India, and the Government of India. This ensured adequate Air Force representation at the centre of political power in India and, at the same time, avoided the creation of a duplicate headquarters under Air Command for which neither the men nor the means were to hand. The administrative services, whose heads remained in Delhi were, nevertheless, represented at Kandy by responsible and independent skeleton staffs under a senior officer competent to inform and advise on his own specialist topic as required, so that broad policy might properly be formulated at the Headquarters of Air Command.

153. During October and November, 1944, there persisted a considerable amount of uncertainty as to the basis on which the administrative machinery would ultimately rest. For instance, as matters of high policy were decided at Kandy, it was decided by the Air Commander-in-Chief that he must have by his side the head of the service primarily concerned. This applied successively to the Principal Medical Officer, the

Command Accountant, the Command Welfare Officer and the Command Catering Officer, and finally to the Air Officer in charge of Training.

154. The situation was finally crystallised and clarified in October, when a revised directive was issued to the Air Marshal Commanding Base Air Forces. For all day to day matters affecting administrative services, the heads of those services were solely responsible to the Air Marshal Commanding Base Air Forces. But when matters of administrative policy affecting the Command as a whole arose, then the heads of the administrative services were responsible to the Allied Air Commander-in-Chief through the Air Officer (Administration) (A.O.A.), Headquarters, Air Command. Similarly, when matters of new Command policy came under discussion and the agreement of the Government of India was required, the heads of the administrative services concerned were empowered by the Air Commander-in-Chief, through the A.O.A. Air Command, to deal with their opposite numbers in G.H.Q. India, on behalf of the Air C.-in-C.

155. As a corollary to this arrangement, the staff officers under the A.O.A., Air Command at Kandy were not established as mere liaison officers. Their allegiance and responsibility was towards the A.O.A. Air Command, who looked to them for staff work, for records and for facts. They were not, however, his advisers in the formulation of new policy – these continued to be the heads of the services in New Delhi, who might if they wished send their own staff officers from Delhi or come themselves to make representations to the A.O.A., Air Command, on matters of Command policy external to the responsibility of the Air Marshal Commanding, Base Air Forces. This was not a normal system. But the separation of the Supreme Allied Commander and the Headquarters of his Commanders-in-Chief from the seat of the Government of India and duality of channels to the United Kingdom Government – either through the Government of India or direct – constituted an abnormal situation.

156. The value and effectiveness of the base organisation thus created was endorsed by the Air Member for Supply and Organisation (A.M.S.O.) during his visit in February, 1945. Air Chief Marshal Sir Christopher Courtney was impressed by the extent of the negotiations which were necessary in New Delhi with the numerous organisations concerned with the conduct of the war from India. He counselled a progressive decentralisation of functions to Base Air Forces and its gradual endowment with a greater measure of autonomy; this was of course in keeping with the original scheme and was accordingly pursued.

*

Disbandment of Third Tactical Air Force and Formation of H.Q., R.A.F., Bengal-Burma.

157. Eastern Air Command, from its formation in December, 1943, onwards, was an exclusively operational Headquarters with no administrative responsibilities. When its Headquarters moved to Calcutta in March, 1944, administrative services for the area of Eastern (Army) Command were being provided by Headquarters No. 231

Group, and this Headquarters also administered the R.A.F. element of Eastern Air Command. But it was clearly anomalous that a Bomber Group engaged in active operations should continue to be saddled with the wide responsibilities for administration which were of no concern to the Strategic Air Force.

158. This, and other considerations pointing towards a re-organisation of the groups in India, was discussed with the A.M.S.O. in August, 1944. The logical course would have been to confer administrative responsibilities upon the R.A.F. Element of Eastern Air Command and to form a new Group Headquarters under it to exercise them. But owing to the manpower shortage it was impossible to create a new headquarters altogether distinct from Headquarters, Eastern Air Command, and it was therefore agreed that H.Q. No. 231 Group should give up its extraneous administrative responsibilities, and that the administrative staff so released should be reconstituted as Air Headquarters, Bengal. At the same time, the Deputy Air Commander, Eastern Air Command, was to become Air Officer Commanding, Bengal, with administrative responsibilities extending eastwards as far as the Brahmaputra.

They could not be further extended, since this would have meant that the Air Marshal Commanding, Third Tactical Air Force, would have been administratively subordinated to the the Air Vice-Marshal, A.O.C. Bengal.

159. It was therefore decided to propose the disbandment of Headquarters, Third Tactical Air Force. For such a course there were other good reasons outside the administrative sphere – operationally, the title was now a misnomer, since in June, 1944, the Tenth U.S.A.A.F. had been reconstituted as an independent formation under Eastern Air Command, and the Headquarters of the Fourteenth Army was due after the opening of the new campaign to move forward to Imphal, where Headquarters, No. 221 Group had long been established, leaving XV Corps in the Arakan to operate independently under the G.O.C.-in-C., Allied Land Forces. Authority for the disbandment of Headquarters, Third Tactical Air Force was given in October, 1944.

160. The disbandment of Third T.A.F. involved also the expansion of Headquarters, No. 221 Group and the allotment to Eastern Air Command of direct operational control of all its subordinate operational formations. The date of this further re-organisation was timed to synchronize with the move of Headquarters, Fourteenth Army to Imphal beside Headquarters, No. 221 Group, and the establishment of Advanced Headquarters, Allied Land Forces, alongside Eastern Air Command at Calcutta. This move took place on 4th December when the Air Marshal Commanding, Third Tactical Air Force, became Deputy Air Commander, Eastern Air Command and Air Marshal Commanding, R.A.F., Bengal-Burma.

161. Headquarters, R.A.F., Bengal-Burma was the name given to the administrative formation now brought into existence to combine the functions of R.A.F. Bengal and the administrative responsibilities previously wielded by Third T.A.F. Geographically, its responsibilities covered both the base area of Bengal and the more easterly marches, bit by bit being extended into Burma with the advance of the Fourteenth Army. The military suzerain of the former was G.H.Q., India, and of the latter, Headquarters Allied Land Forces. Headquarters, Bengal-Burma was

accordingly built up on a dual basis commensurate with the existence of two sets of army authorities with which it would have to deal, and also with an eye to future development whenever the reconquest of Burma should compel it. This stage was reached in February, 1945, when it became possible to carry out the anticipated divorce between Bengal and Burma components of the Air Marshal Commanding's province. R.A.F. Bengal was then expanded into Headquarters, No. 228 Group and returned to Base Air Forces, though the filling of its establishments proved a slow process.

*

Administrative and Training Groups.

162. In order to ensure better co-ordination of administrative services, to facilitate combined training, and to ensure close liaison on internal security measures, the groups in India underwent a rationalization of their areas to coincide with those of the army formations.

This measure was brought to its logical conclusion by the formation of No. 228 Group in February, 1945, to provide functional and/or administrative control of all units of Base Air Forces within the area of Eastern (Army) Command, and to provide R.A.F. administrative services within that area. As Eastern, (Army) Command extends its boundaries to the Burma frontier, the area of responsibility of No. 228 Group will expand. R.A.F. India is thus split up between four administrative and training groups.

Introduction of Wing H.Q. and Servicing Echelon Organisation.

163. In the Far East more than in the metropolitan air force, the administrative problems confronting junior operational commanders are such as to hinder them in the performance of their primary tasks. In recognition of this and to improve the mobility and flexibility of the wing organisation, it was decided to introduce the principle of wing headquarters and servicing echelons for single-engined and light twin-engined aircraft. The scheme came into effect by the end of September, 1944, with the wing headquarters based on certain major airfields, and the servicing echelons became responsible for the upkeep of the squadron aircraft. The squadrons were thereby relieved of the responsibility for their own administration and most of their first-line maintenance.

164. In anticipation of a more mobile kind of warfare, it became necessary in December, 1944, to remove the geographical restriction implied by naming the wing according to its current location. The wings were accordingly given numbers, and their attitude to mobility thus greatly enhanced, as evidenced by the advance of No. 906 Wing from Imphal to Rangoon in six months, in a series of well-organized moves. The scheme has been successful, and its principle has been extended to other squadrons in order to centralize control of resources and administration and to economise in overheads.

165. Perhaps one factor has marred full advantage being taken of the inherent mobility and flexibility which the organisation would afford. The provision of more servicing echelons than squadrons would allow of peak periods of operational effort at very short notice from advance airfields, for an additional servicing echelon could be flown in to supplement the existing maintenance personnel. This lesson was learned at Akyab where the providential presence of a servicing commando allowed of a much higher rate of effort from the island during the early days of the occupation than would otherwise have been possible.

*

The Manpower Situation.

166. The Command has been continually hampered by an ill-balanced allotment of manpower, whereby shortages have been concentrated in certain vital trades, rendering the administrative machine extremely difficult to operate efficiently.

167. In June, 1944, the establishment and strength of the Command for ground British personnel were as follows:-

	Establishment	*Strength*	*Shortage*
Officers	6,277	5,170	1,107
Other ranks	88,636	80,967	7,669
	94,913	86,137	8,776

The deficiency of 18 per cent. in ground officers was concentrated principally in such important branches as Admin. G., Tech. (E), Code and Cypher and the like. The airman deficiency of 9 per cent. more seriously affected the clerical trades.

168. By May, 1945, the position had changed, but not improved, as the following figures and illustrations will show:-

	Establishment	*Strength*	*Shortage or Surplus*
Officers	8,103	7,573	530 Shortage
Other ranks	105,470	110,459	4,989 Surplus
Total	**113,573**	**118,032**	**4,459 Surplus**

169. The 6½ per cent. deficiency in ground officers affects principally the following branches, Admin., Code and Cyphers, Tech. (E), Catering, etc. The shortages in the Technical Branch have caused particular difficulty. The overall 5 per cent. surplus in airmen does not give a true picture of the situation, for there are very serious deficiencies in clerical and domestic personnel which are hampering the development of the Command. Clerks G/D are below establishment by no less than 36 per cent., Equipment Assistants by 29 per cent. and Cooks by 28 per cent. The surplus was concentrated in the technical trades and amounted to 7,100. Such a surplus was more of a liability than an asset, since it created additional work for the already overburdened administrative and domestic personnel and could not be used to offset the shortages elsewhere.

170. Since February, 1945, very strenuous efforts have been made to disband redundant units and prune such establishments as can conceivably be reduced. The diminishing air threat to the east coast of India and Ceylon has made it possible to thin out the early warning Radar system, and considerable economies have been effected. Much has been done to distribute the shortages where they could more easily be borne, and it was Command policy to make the strongest where it was most effective, that was nearest to the enemy.

*

Conclusion.

171. The administrative network covering the vastness of India is now as complete and rational as present resources allow. It cannot be said, however, that the administrative problems of the Command are now solved. As the armies advance, the area to be controlled grows, and the net is in many places thin. This is particularly so in those areas vacated by the advancing tactical groups, and extra provision must continually be made to administer those formations left in the backwash of the advance. It has even been necessary to graft additional administrative responsibilities on to the air supply group in the forward areas (No. 232), for lack of personnel to set up the requisite administrative framework. The conflicting factors of function and distance have called for an organization far more complex than would be the case in a more compact theatre. For this the only solution is a realization at home that additional personnel and transport facilities to maintain India as a base, and conduct an energetic campaign in Malaya and beyond, must be allotted on a more generous scale than previously.

*

(II) *Maintenance.*

172. The maintenance organisation in South East Asia embraces supply, servicing, repair and salvage of all air force material in India, Ceylon and Burma; an area approximately the size of Europe. It was realised at an early stage that it was impossible to have the same maintenance system operating throughout the Command, since the extensive topographical diversities encountered necessitated that the ultimate systems adopted be dictated by the geography of the country. Broadly speaking, therefore, one system applies in Ceylon and India as far eastwards as the Brahmaputra, and an entirely different one was evolved to operate throughout Assam and Burma. In the former area conditions are more or less static, the ground communications, although greatly inferior to those of Europe, are reasonably good with no considerable land or water barriers. Here, a large and efficient base maintenance organisation has been built up which provides adequate backing for the air forces far beyond the Brahmaputra; it is in this base area that the Base Repair

Depots, Equipment Depots and Aircraft Storage Units are to be found. In Assam and Burma, however, the situation bears a vastly different appearance, parsimonious communications from Calcutta to the railhead at Dimapur and thence by road over the Naga and Chin Hills to Central Burma prohibited the use of a maintenance organisation which was possible in England and which, to a limited degree, has also been found possible in India.

173. From the time of the siege of Imphal to the capture of Rangoon, air lift, the principal means of supply to our combat Army and Air Force formations, was restricted to essential needs and could not be provided to support avoidable maintenance at forward airfields. As a result, a policy was agreed of flying aircraft back to India for comparatively simple servicing requirements such as periodical inspections and engine changes. This obviated the necessity for flying spare engines and to some extent, equipment and spares, into the forward areas; at the same time it increased the mobility of squadrons and reduced their maintenance personnel requirements. Aircraft which crashed away from airfields had normally to be written off charge, while those which crashed on airfields, provided the damage was not too great, were repaired on the site. Surface movement back to India was restricted to a minimum, since damage to an aircraft during transit in this part of the world is normally so great that it is beyond economical repair on arrival at its destination. On occasions, damaged fighter aircraft were dismantled and flown back to India, the servicing personnel becoming so expert that they were able to pack the whole of a fighter aircraft and its components into one Dakota fuselage.

174. Owing to the speed and intensity at which the campaign was being fought, and the vital need to capture the strategic base of Rangoon before the onset of the monsoon, I decided that all the normal rates of effort must be exceeded, and all our Air Force resources were thrown into the battle. During one month of 1945, no less than 700 aircraft passed through the Aircraft Storage Units and Reserve Aircraft Pools in order to provide replacements for the 75 squadrons operating east of Calcutta. During the early stages of the campaign, the small number of combat losses introduced a major maintenance complication, since low wastage rates, giving aircraft a long life, placed upon the repair organisation a storage commitment which had not been foreseen. A further strain was caused by severe deterioration owing to climatic conditions, such as to subject aircraft to monsoon rains accompanied by sudden bursts of sunshine. This had an adverse effect upon the timber, fabric, rubber and electrical parts of aircraft. In the autumn of 1944, for instance, Mosquito aircraft had to be grounded as a result of such defects, until extensive repairs had been effected.

175. The maintenance organisation in the forward areas consisted of the Repair and Salvage Units (R. and S.U.) supporting squadrons at their airfields, and taking on all work which the flying units could not complete within forty-eight hours. Air Stores Parks held sufficient stocks of spares and equipment for three months supply, and the Forward Repair Depots which were located far enough forward to undertake major inspections and repairs beyond R. & S.U. capacity. In addition Motor Transport Light Repair Depots were deployed in the forward areas, and the importance of their work can be measured by the fact that in traversing the tortuous line of

communication from Calcutta through Dimapur and Imphal to central Burma, mechanical transport vehicles had expended the major part of their useful lives before reaching their destination. Thus a great deal of ingenuity and inventiveness on the part of M/T servicing personnel was necessary in order to keep vehicles running, vehicles which in base areas would have been scrapped.

176. The maintenance effort in Burma can best be summarized as a triumph of improvisation to overcome bad climate and worse terrain, the paucity of spares, tools and equipment which was designed for the European theatre of war and not designed to be flown over, driven through or manhandled in the cruel country of Assam and Burma. The overloading of home production, and the overriding need to finish off the western war first, were adequate reasons for this situation, and the maintenance effort during the period which culminated in the capture of Rangoon was very largely dissipated in a desperate struggle to keep the units of the maintenance organisation abreast of the operational flying units. That this was achieved speaks volumes for the tenacity, skill and loyalty of the maintenance personnel.

*

(III) *Internal Air Lines.*

177. The growth of air routes during the past year is best illustrated by the following figures:-

	Passengers	*Freight*	*Mail*
May, 1944	2,103	166,313 lbs.	99,435 lbs.
April, 1945	11,514	1,579,119 lbs.	777,944 lbs.

178. This rapid increase was attributable to a greater intensity of operations, and better planning followed somewhat tardily by a growth of resources. At the beginning of the campaign, one squadron (No. 353) shouldered the whole burden while still largely equipped with Hudsons. In July, 1944, No. 52 Squadron was formed, and by flying 19,000 hours without an accident, speedily gained an excellent reputation for its high standard of operating and freedom from accidents over routes that include the hazardous flight over the Hump to China. In April, 1945, a flight of No. 232 Squadron, equipped with Liberator C-87 aircraft, began to operate on the longer routes, forming the most recent addition to a force the strength of which has grown to two and a half squadrons.

179. Parallel action to build up a ground organisation to handle greater traffic and more complex problems was necessary. To this end, static transport wings have been established at Delhi, Karachi and Calcutta; that at Delhi was intended eventually to move to Rangoon. Located at nodal points on the trunk routes, these wings also gave advice on all matters affecting air transport and ferrying to the group in whose area they were located. When their establishments were fully implemented, 229 Group Headquarters was relieved of a great deal of day to day work in administering some sixty units spread over India.

180. Even now, internal air communications within the theatre are not adequate. This fact cannot be fully realised by anyone who has not appreciated the vastness of

India from a railway carriage or travelled over roads on which the twentieth century has barely left its mark. Moreover, in a sub-continent whose urban centres are so distant from one another, it is often necessary to plan an operation eight hundred miles from its mounting base, while the allocation of resources may be effected from another centre which may be fifteen hundred miles from the controlling headquarters. Furthermore, the major base for the prosecution of a campaign in southern Burma, Malaya or Java, is still India, and the need for swift communication between base and combat area is another continually growing commitment for squadrons who serve an area ranging from Karachi to Kunming and from Peshawar to Ceylon.

181. At times, local operational tasks have made the diversion of aircraft from internal routes to air supply a tempting solution to a pressing problem. This temptation has always been resisted, and it is a first principle that the vital arteries of South-East Asia Command shall remain open. The mobility of the staffs, the despatch of urgent freight, close contact with the battle areas, and the building up of India as a base, must always be a prime consideration when assessing priorities for air transport resources in this theatre. Not only is the work of all three services dependent upon speedy communication over long distances ; it is on the air routes that the Air Force can reap a dividend from the transport aircraft which are so frequently operated for the benefit of others. The R.A.F. should also use the speed and flexibility of its transport squadrons to improve the efficiency of its own organisation.

182. Air Command has derived great benefit from the Transport Groups allotted to this theatre, which has made possible a closer study of transport problems and a more effective supervision of this specialised type of flying. The improvement in operating standards is well illustrated by the accident rate. In October, 1943, there were 49 accidents per 10,000 hours of transport and ferry flights. By April, 1945, the rate had been reduced to 9 per 10,000 hours. Such an improvement reflects the greatest credit on all concerned and demonstrates the close co-operation which has been achieved between South-East Asia and Transport Command.

*

(IV) *The R.A.F. Regiment.*

183. Until mid-1944 the strength of the R.A.F. Regiment was deployed to the extent of rather more than two-thirds in machine gun anti-aircraft units, and the remainder in field squadrons designed for an infantry role. Events then forced a fundamental revision of the part for which the R.A.F. Regiment in South East Asia was cast. It had become apparent that advanced airfields, radar sites and other air force installations would not necessarily be guarded if their locations did not happen to fit into the tactical schemes adopted by the local army formations, and that unless the air forces were to withdraw everything to a safe distance behind the front lines they would themselves have to provide the necessary defence force. For this purpose the R.A.F. Regiment during the later months of 1944 was expanded and re-organised into ten wing headquarters, twenty field squadrons, three armoured (holding) squadrons and ten anti-aircraft squadrons, so as to provide tactical defence for air

force units as required. The balance of functions in the Regiment as between air and ground defence was thus completely reversed.

184. The wisdom of this re-organisation was abundantly proved in the course of the 1944-45 campaign. As has already been explained, the essence of the tactics by which the re-conquest of Burma was achieved lay in the rapid advance of mechanised units thrusting through or around enemy positions, the strength of which had been weakened by air bombardment. The fighter bombers which provided the backbone of the latter, and also the fighters required for air defence could only operate effectively from airfields close behind the advanced army units. The supplies on whose delivery the maintenance of the Army's advance depended were likewise landed at airstrips as close as possible to troops in the line. Allied transport aircraft were often being unloaded on captured airfields within a few hours of their being seized. But as the army units advanced, it frequently proved impossible, despite the presence of enemy troops lurking in the neighbourhood, to leave garrisons behind to protect the airfields they had overrun. The defence of the latter thus fell to the squadrons of the R.A.F. Regiment. On their shoulders there thus rested the defence of the army lifeline and also of the air bases indispensable for air support and defence, and they were accordingly moved forward step by step with the progress of the campaign, sometimes by air.

185. The main airfield at Meiktila for instance, was occupied early in March, 1944, and was speedily transformed into a forward base for the supply of the Fourteenth Army, whose units had forged ahead both southwards and eastwards, leaving numerous organised parties of the enemy in their rear. The defence of the airfield thus fell mainly upon two field squadrons of the R.A.F. Regiment, which went into action on a number of occasions against Japanese parties attempting to dig themselves in within the airfield perimeter. For a short period indeed, the landing strip used to change hands twice daily, the enemy infiltrating by night only to be expelled the next morning when, as soon as all was clear, the transport aircraft would begin to land. The Regiment casualties in the course of these engagements included two officers and twelve other ranks killed.

*

PART TEN.
CONCLUSIONS, RESULTS, AND LESSONS LEARNED.

I. *Operations.*

186. One of the major difficulties under which an Air Force works, is the impracticability of ever drawing up a full balance-sheet which will give in detail the full results of air action. Unless a detailed examination of enemy records is made, air forces must rely upon the disjointed accounts of the ground forces, the reports of informants, and photographic reconnaissance, for an assessment of their results. This

has been particularly the case in Burma, where so much of the effort has been expended upon fleeting targets, reported troop concentrations, or objectives obscured by thick jungle. Notwithstanding the vagueness of the information, it is certain that the number of casualties inflicted upon the enemy as a direct result of air action has undoubtedly been large, the isolation of the battlefield by the interdiction of the supply lines has been almost complete, and prevented the enemy from deploying his full strength in every major engagement that has taken place, while the new mobility given to armies by the unstinting use of air transport has undoubtedly been the major factor in the expulsion of the enemy from Burma.

187. There have at times been grounds for a belief that the effort of our close support squadrons has not been used to full advantage because of a lack of experience on the part of Army commanders of the relative efficacy of certain types of air attack against the varied objectives. A more scientific application of the fire-power afforded by ground-attack aircraft might have led to an economy of effort thus made available to apply to other targets. Whether the attack by twelve fighter-bombers against a well-camouflaged single machine-gun is justifiable, must always be a moot point until machinery is devised to assess the debit and credit side of the picture. It is not difficult in a staff study to deduce that the effort is unprofitable, but the same point of view may not be held by the troops making the actual assault. The results of the air bombardment may be just what was needed to make the action successful. It is certain that the high standard of accuracy developed in our tactical squadrons during 1944-45 has had an enormous effect upon enemy resistance.

188. The low incidence of casualties during assaults by our own troops also bears this out, as do the unvarying tributes paid by battalions and divisions to the work of the squadrons who supported them. Recently, further evidence has come to light from informants on the efficacy of attacks. With the co-ordination of Visual Control Post teams and other sources, an even more efficient direction of fire-power on to targets and better observation of results will be possible. If analysed, the plans compiled from these sources would provide valuable proof of the decisive part that can be played by close support squadrons properly trained and handled.

II. *Planning.*

189. The amount of planning that has been necessary to bring the campaign to a close has been large, due in part to some misappreciation of Japanese intentions and to frustration imposed by non-arrival of resources. There was a tendency also on the part of ground forces to formulate a plan of operations without consulting the Air Commander in the early stages of planning. In consequence, much effort was expended in the recasting of operational plans to take advantage of the striking power of air forces.

190. Much of this could have been avoided had the Army Commander been able to remain alongside the Supreme Commander and the Allied Air Commander-in-Chief instead of having to base himself at an Advanced Headquarters in Calcutta. Not only was proper liaison at C.-in-C. level impossible, but the full flow of information and views between the staffs was rendered difficult. The Burma

campaign proved that no plan of operations is complete unless it represents the views of the air as well as of the ground forces at all stages.

III. *Maintenance.*

191. South East Asia Air Forces have a background of three years' development under trying conditions with insufficient resources. The organisation became vast and was spread over a wide area. The first phase for which this organisation was designed is now completed; the flow of supplies has become secure, and the necessity for tying down large numbers of men and stocks of essential equipment in India has decreased. A more fluid and economical base organisation should be possible as the war progresses.

192. Energetic action has been taken, now that the pipe line is secure, to reduce the reserve holdings of aircraft and equipment which clog the machinery of supply and absorb so much of the Command resources in manpower and storage space in India. An extensive reorganisation to undertake more maintenance in the field is contemplated, and, it is hoped, will do much to avoid the bottlenecks to which centralised maintenance is prone. Such a reorganisation is only possible if the scales of ground equipment, hand tools and other servicing facilities are adequate and fully maintained. For an Air Force working in the field a generous scale of equipment is essential, and the lack of it was largely responsible for the uneconomical base maintenance organisation which events forced upon South East Asia in its early stages. The saving in man-hours that results from a generous scale of ground equipment is vast. This should always be taken into account in campaigns in tropical countries where sickness and lack of communications militate against units possessing their full establishment.

*

IV. *Administration.*

193. The standard of unit administration in the operational areas was not high. With formations spread over wide areas, and deficiencies in ground officers also in the majority of vital trades, notably among clerical and signals personnel, much of this has been inevitable. Nevertheless a very real need exists for the indoctrination of service personnel in overseas theatres of war with the principles of self-reliance and better improvisation.

194. The principles of mobility and self-help have only resulted from the perception of those on the spot to train personnel in the rudiments of active campaigning. In so doing they have made the best use of local resources to achieve that standard of morale and wellbeing which are the prerequisite of good discipline. The posting of a squadron commander from a well-established bomber base at home to an overseas appointment with no preliminary training in his changed circumstances cannot but have an adverse effect upon the well-being of the Unit. The setting-up of Junior Commanders' Courses within the theatre is the best immediate remedy, but

the problems of accommodation, and the time absent from units, rendered it little more than a palliative in this theatre.

V. *Air Transport.*

195. Finally, the Air Forces, having given a new-found mobility to land warfare, must also take advantage of it. When assessing bids for air transport and air supply, the highest priority should be given to the rapid movement of spares, personnel, and indeed whole R.A.F. units, in order to keep the force working at maximum efficiency. It is bad economy to keep the 15 serviceable out of 20 available aircraft supplying the ground forces when the diversion of one aeroplane to collect A.O.G.[5] spares would raise the serviceability rate to 18. If full advantage is taken of air transport, the striking radius of the Air Force can be still further extended, and the application of air power to any situation made more rapid and more decisive than hitherto.

K.R. PARK,
Air Chief Marshal.
Allied Air Commander-in-Chief,
South East Asia.
Kandy, Ceylon.
October, 1945.

Footnotes

a1* Northern Combat Area Command.
2 Petrol, Oil, Lubricants.
3 U.E. = Unit Equipment.
 I.E. = Initial Equipment.
4 Indian Ocean G.R. Operations.
5 Aircraft on Ground.

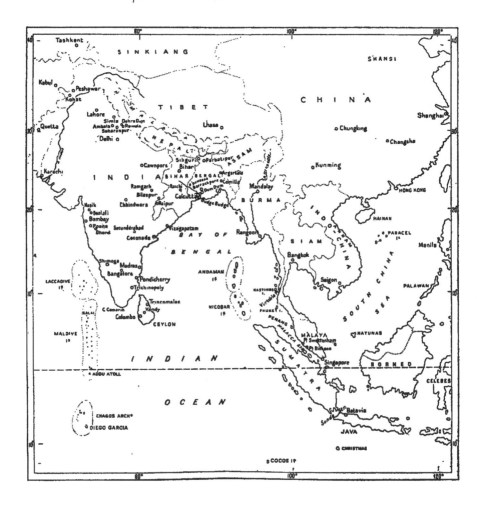

4

AIR CHIEF MARSHAL SIR KEITH PARK'S DESPATCH ON AIR OPERATIONS IN SOUTH EAST ASIA

3RD MAY, 1945 TO 12TH SEPTEMBER, 1945

The following despatch was submitted to the Secretary of State for Air in August,
1946, by AIR CHIEF MARSHAL SIR KEITH PARK, G.C.B., K.B.E., M.C., D.F.C.,
Allied Air Commander-in-Chief, South East Asia.

FOREWORD.

1. Air Power's contribution to the overthrow of Japanese land forces during the closing stages of the war in South East Asia, is reviewed in this Despatch, which opens with the period following the Allied Forces' victorious entry into Rangoon on 3rd May, 1945, and culminates in the official surrender of the Japanese Southern Army to Admiral The Lord Louis Mountbatten, at Singapore, on 12th September, 1945.

2. During this period, squadrons of the Royal Air Force played a conspicuous rôle in the last battle against the enemy land forces on Burmese soil. More than ten thousand Japanese troops, ill-equipped, sick and demoralised, were annihilated by our air and ground forces while attempting a mass escape from the Pegu Yomas across the Sittang River and south to Moulmein. Their Air Force had already been eliminated from Burma.

3. August 1945 brought with it Japan's realisation of defeat and her decision to

surrender. It forestalled by only a few weeks the planned invasion of Malaya in which over 500 aircraft of the Royal Air Force and about 200 carrier-borne aircraft of the Royal Navy would have demonstrated again the power of air superiority.

4. Instead, squadrons of the Royal Air Force re-directed their energies to the most extensive mission of mercy by bringing relief and liberation, in the initial stages, to tens of thousands of Allied prisoners-of-war and internees in the many Japanese prison camps scattered throughout the vast territories of South East Asia.

5. The successful accomplishment of this task made a fitting conclusion to Air Power's participation in a war against a ruthless and fanatical enemy whose years of aggression in these territories ended with crushing and complete defeat.

PART I.
RANGOON AND AFTER.

THE SITUATION IN MAY, 1945, AFTER THE
FALL OF RANGOON.

1. With unconditional surrender of Germany on 8th May, 1945, the conflict in South East Asia and in the Far East against the last remaining of the Axis Powers took on a new significance, with the balance weighted heavily in favour of the Allies against Japan.

2. The only outcome of the war in the East, like the one prescribed for Germany, could be complete and unconditional surrender of Japan.

3. Decisively beaten in Burma, and with Rangoon recaptured only five days before the surrender of Germany in Europe, Japan, fighting alone, faced almost certain invasion of her homeland in the coming months. The systematic loss of territories throughout South East Asia which she had invaded during her orgy of conquest some three years before, was now inevitable.

4. A redeployment of manpower and material resources from Europe for the war against Japan was scheduled to begin, which would thus quicken the tempo of operations. But long before the collapse of Germany had taken place in Europe, the plans for the re-conquest of Malaya and Singapore had been prepared. With the other Commanders-in-Chief in this Theatre, I shared the conviction that the second half of 1945 would bring the reinforcements promised by London.

5. On the entry into Rangoon on 3rd May, 1945, theatre strategy was directed to the liberation of Singapore at the earliest possible date with a view to opening up the sea-route to Indo-China and the East Indies, and to liberating enemy-occupied countries. Thereafter, strategy subsequent to the re-occupation of Singapore would depend upon the march of events in the Western Pacific Theatre.

6. It had been the contention, hitherto, that the capture of Singapore would involve at least two intermediate operations before the final goal could be achieved. Firstly, it was considered that an initial operation would be necessary to establish an advanced

air and naval base. Through this base, aircraft and assault craft could be staged and operated in support of the next operation for the seizure and occupation of a bridgehead on the Malayan Peninsula. Occupation and development of this bridgehead on the mainland was considered an essential prelude to the final overland advance on Singapore itself.

7. Hastings Harbour was originally selected as the initial objective, but this was postponed to take place after the Monsoon. Further examination by the Joint Planning Staff at Headquarters, S.A.C.S.E.A., however, indicated that a stepping-stone still further south than Hastings Harbour was not only desirable in relation to the time margin, but also a practicable proposition as regards the fly-in of single-engined fighters and close support aircraft. It was essential, however, from the aspect of resources available, that such an operation should be a limited commitment as a military operation and also as regards the shipping lift. These limitations, therefore, narrowed down the selection of this objective to a lightly defended island. Puket Island fulfilled this requirement. Its occupation was therefore planned for June, 1945.

Puket Operation or "Roger".

8. The Puket operation – ("Roger") – was approved in principle by the Chiefs of Staff in February, 1945, but they reserved judgment as to its timing in relation to the fall of Rangoon. A plan for the operation was nevertheless prepared by the Joint Planning Staff and Force Commanders' Staffs were appointed.

9. Force Planning began in Delhi on February 2nd, but it became apparent that the occupation of an island so close to the mainland would involve a greater military commitment than had been envisaged earlier. The Army concept of this operation demanded one Division for the assault and initial occupation of the island, including a small bridgehead on the mainland, and one follow-up Division to consolidate the position. The Japanese garrison of this island was reported to be approximately one battalion, but other land forces could have been assembled on the mainland once the attack was disclosed.

10. Owing to the distance from our own mainland bases, air cover and support would have to be given by carrier-borne aircraft initially until the capture of the first airstrip, when the Air Forces would accept full responsibility for all air operational requirements. I suggested that the Army demands, both in manpower and material, were excessive for so small an operation (the same opinion being expressed by the Supreme Allied Commander and the Naval C. in C.). I felt that if such demands were persisted in, it might mean that the operation (which would have given vital air bases to support a major operation) would have to be dropped. These fears were well-founded, as the proposed operation was subsequently abandoned, mainly for this reason.

11. Development of the air base at Puket envisaged the completion of three runways to all-weather standard, with an initial force of three Single Engine Fighter Squadrons and an ultimate build-up to:-

3 S.E.F. Squadrons.
1 Fighter/Recce Squadron.
3 Light Bomber Squadrons.
2 Heavy Bomber Squadrons.
Detachments of Air Sea Rescue and Photographic Reconnaissance Unit.
Staging facilities for air transport and other types of air traffic.

12. In addition to this, the base would also require to be capable of staging airborne operations in relation to future requirements of the campaign in Malaya. The air base, too, would require to be fully operational by D plus 100 days, while its development to full capacity was so timed as to provide the necessary air support and cover for the next stage of operations comprising re-occupation of the Ports Swettenham and Dickson areas, and a bridgehead for the final overland advance on Singapore. The occupation of this bridgehead was planned to take place some four months after the initial occupation of Puket with a view to the final assault for the capture of Singapore.

13. Events in Burma, however, had forced a change of plan, which envisaged the necessity to capture Rangoon from the sea before the monsoon broke, and open it as a port to relieve the other overworked supply routes.

14. In this connection, it can now be put on record that a R.A.F. Mosquito aircraft, carrying Wing Commander Saunders, made a low reconnaissance of Rangoon the day before the British Armada disembarked. Finding the city empty of Japanese, and Allied flags flying over P.O.W. camps, he landed at the nearest airfield, hitchhiked into Rangoon and released some of our P.O.W.'s. Wing Commander Saunders then borrowed a native boat and rowed down the river to tell the British Commander that Rangoon was unoccupied by the enemy, and offered his services as guide to the Expedition. This unusual incident revealed that the enemy forces in Rangoon itself had departed between the times of departure and arrival of the sea convoy. It was later revealed that the Japanese Commander of the Burma Area Army had been ordered to hold Rangoon to the end, but on his own initiative decided to withdraw in the face of the Fourteenth Army's pressure.

15. It was realised after Rangoon's capture that to postpone the Puket operation later than mid-June, 1945, would inevitably retard the progress of subsequent operations timed progressively for the capture of Singapore by the end of the year. The Puket operation was therefore abandoned. With it, there vanished a stepping-stone to Singapore which the British Air Forces could well have utilised to great advantage.

Effect of Delay upon Future Strategy.

16. The importance of accelerating the Allied Malayan offensive had been emphasised. In the first instance, it necessitated planning for the occupation and development of Puket approximately one month after the Monsoon had set in. Any further delay than this incurred a steady deterioration in weather conditions and a heavy swell on exposed beaches. The cumulative effect of rain was also calculated

to cause a steady increase in the saturation of the ground and proportionately greater difficulty in airfield and road construction.

17. It was estimated that the closing stages of the campaign in Burma, involving at the eleventh hour a mounting of the amphibious operation "Dracula" to make doubly certain Rangoon's capture, had imposed a minimum of nine weeks delay in the initiation of the operation to capture the weakly held Puket. It followed, therefore, if Malayan strategy was to be implemented to meet the proposed time schedule for the capture of Singapore that this initial delay must be made good quickly.

18. To achieve this there were three courses open for consideration, each of which involved much planning:-

(1) To select an alternative objective where airfield development was an easier proposition in relation to weather conditions and time available, or where airfields already existed.

(2) To retain the existing objective but on a less ambitious scale of airfield development and military occupation, thereby speeding up development.

(3) To abandon any project for development of a stepping-stone, and to embark upon the second phase of our overall strategy which envisaged a bridgehead on the Malayan Peninsula as a prelude to the final advance on Singapore.

19. Course 1, on examination, revealed that areas more suitable for airfield development did not fulfil the operational requirements, while the occupation of existing airfields in suitable areas was likely to require a major military operation.

20. As regards Course 2, if some reduction in the scale of effort was acceptable, particularly as regards the requirements of heavy bombers, then a substantial reduction in runway development could be achieved. This, however, would reduce the overall period of development to the extent by which the base could be fully operational to provide the necessary air support and softening up operations on a lighter scale in relation to the next phase of Malayan operations as timed. Furthermore, if reduction in base development were accompanied by a decrease in the scale of military effort required to occupy the island, this would result not only in saving time, but also in a general economy in resources and shipping. The Army, however, would not agree to any reduction in strength of assault and garrison forces.

21. Course 3, when considered, had the great advantage of making up the total time lost, which, for reasons which have already, been stated, was of paramount importance.

22. It was obvious, however, that without intermediate air bases, close support by land based aircraft could not be provided either as a prelude to or during the initial occupation of the bridgehead.

23. For this purpose, complete reliance had therefore to be placed upon air support and air cover by carrier-borne aircraft until suitable airstrips could be prepared within the bridgehead. Furthermore, the degree of heavy bomber support would be severely

limited by distance and weather. Even on the most optimistic assumption that one or more heavy bomber airfields would be available in Burma by September, air bombing involved a distance to targets of 1,000 miles with a consequent reduction in bomb load and intensity of effort.

24. It was obvious, therefore, that operations at such a range could not afford the required support for the initial occupation of the bridgehead. The lack of an advanced air base also introduced difficulties as regards the fly-in of aircraft for the build-up, and a routine service for aircraft replacement.

25. When the problem was examined, the Joint Planning Staff recommended Course 3, provided that carrier-borne air forces could be assured.

26. Course 3 was therefore adopted, and the operation which, in planning, became known as "Zipper", envisaged the occupation of a bridgehead in the Port Dickson – Swettenham area. The assault, it was intended, should be carried out by two Divisions of No. 34 Indian Corps, with 15 Corps in the following-up rôle. The amphibious operation would be undertaken by a naval task force.

27. It was planned that air cover and support would be provided initially by carrier-borne air forces, presupposing that at least three light fleet carriers would be available for the operation in addition to the escort carriers already in the Theatre. The R.A.F. Squadrons of 224 Group, which had given outstanding service in Burma, were to be flown into the bridgehead as soon as strips were available.

28. As complementary to operation "Zipper", planning was also initiated for the occupation of Singapore Island under planning code word "Mailfist".

29. The initial assault for "Zipper" was timed to take place in early September, 1945, and subsequent exploitation southwards in Malaya was so timed as to permit of the final assault on Singapore by the end of December.

30. From the air point of view I consider the "Zipper" plan for the assault on Malaya possessed one distinct disadvantage – its great range from established air bases, principally in Burma. Had it not been for the diversion of considerable military resources to the capture of undefended Rangoon, I would have preferred an intermediate step to Singapore which would have permitted adequate air support and staging of aircraft. Time, however, was not on our side. In view of the Army's commitments at Rangoon, and of the naval disinclination to make an assault without a suitable anchorage nearby, the prospects of any intermediate operation completely faded away.

31. The "Zipper" plan, on the other hand, gave the recently occupied Cocos Islands a new and important rôle as an offensive air base in addition to its primary function as a staging post to the South West Pacific. Originally, it was intended that the garrisoning Air Forces to be based in the Cocos should comprise one Single-Engined Fighter and one Coastal Torpedo Fighter Squadron. The inclusion of the Coastal T.F. Squadron was mainly on account of a possible threat of enemy sea-borne attack. This threat, however, had steadily declined. In consequence, the operational role of the T.F. Squadron virtually disappeared, while the limited range of T.F. aircraft precluded them from employment offensively against targets within and beyond the Netherlands East Indies barrier. Therefore, I decided to substitute one Long Range General

Reconnaissance squadron in the Cocos in place of the T.F. Squadron, thus enabling General Reconnaissance Liberator aircraft to carry out strikes from the Cocos on targets along the coast of Malaya and N.E.I. An additional advantage of the Cocos was the certainty of more favourable weather conditions during the monsoon.

32. In short, the R.A.F. developed the Cocos Islands into a most valuable offensive air base, and air staging post.

THE AIR BUILD-UP IN BURMA FOR FUTURE OPERATIONS.

33. From the review of strategy and planning for the impending assault of Malaya, it was evident that the air forces would be called upon to fulfil commitments extending over a vast area from Central Burma southwards to Southern Malaya and around N.E.I., until the defeat of the enemy in the South East Asia Theatre.

34. As the result of this trend in future operations, the problem of command and control of the Air Forces became far wider in responsibility than that which had obtained hitherto. Accordingly, it was decided that operational command and control of all R.A.F. Groups other than those serving in Burma should be exercised directly by Headquarters, Air Command, South East Asia, through the respective Group Commanders. Air power, it was realised, would soon embark upon a large scale intensification of operations against the Japanese, not only in South East Asia, but also in the South West Pacific Theatre.

35. While the tempo of air operations had eased off considerably after the capture of Rangoon, the immediate task nevertheless facing the Air Forces was to secure bases and all weather airfields for the future redeployment and reinforcements of the squadrons in Burma and Malaya in the quickest possible time.

36. The decrease in air operations which coincided also with the arrival of the monsoon, was, in every respect, a welcome relief for squadrons. The task of the preceding six months in supporting and supplying the Allied land forces in the non-stop advance to Rangoon had exhausted R.A.F. personnel to a degree never experienced in the Middle East or North West Africa or the Central Mediterranean during 1942-1945. Headquarters S.E.A.C. required our squadrons to operate at maximum effort for a longer period than called for in other Theatres. Aircraft, too, had withstood the gruelling test of climate and semi-developed airfields. In the race through Burma to beat the Jap and the monsoon, No. 221 Group Headquarters had moved four times; moves of Wing Headquarters totalled twenty-five, and squadrons made no less than 112 movements. These moves by the Air Forces in Burma through a tortuous country whose roads and communications were notoriously bad, had meant some disorganisation and much discomfort, but hardly an operational sortie had been lost owing to any forward movement. Neither the men, nor the aircraft, however, could go on indefinitely. For the former a period of rest was necessary; for the latter, re-equipment was in many instances, already long overdue.

37. It was during this lull in operations that certain of these squadrons in Burma were rested and re-equipped before the next phase in the campaign in South East Asia was due to begin. The "Battle of the Break Through" by thousands of Japanese forces

trapped in the Pegu Yomas of Southern Burma had still to come – a battle in which the Air Forces had conspicuous success.

38. At this time there were ominous signs that the Japanese Empire was beginning to reel under the fury of American air attack, which was now directed upon it without pause.

39. With the next blows in South East Asia about to descend upon Malaya, the trend of the Air Forces was a movement to the south – as far south as possible with Southern Burma as the springboard for the major operation which was to come.

40. The plan required a gradual movement of squadrons of fighter bombers, light and medium bombers and indeed, heavy bombers, to Southern Burma. It was hoped that by August, 1945, Mingaladon Airfield, Rangoon, would be capable of providing facilities for 100 aircraft, Toungoo with a capacity for 70 aircraft; Pegu 70 aircraft; Zayatkwin 48 aircraft; Pabst 50 aircraft; Myingyan 70 aircraft; and Meiktila 70 aircraft.

41. This phased build-up was by no means firm, for there was a decided lack of engineers' information on the eventual ability of certain of the more important and vital airfields. In face of Army representations that the original plan for the net of airfields in Southern Burma could not be met without diverting Army engineers from other tasks in Rangoon, I had to agree, most reluctantly, to a much reduced constructional programme in the Rangoon area.

42. On entry into Rangoon, speed in airfield construction was absolutely essential. Delivery of bithess, for servicing the only airstrip, was, however, retarded owing to the land communication difficulties within the area, and I had to give orders that No. 96 (Dakota) Squadron should be given the task of flying-in bithess from Bengal to Mingaladon. The task was completed to scheduled time.

43. I regret that the Air Forces should have had to call upon the Army for airfield construction in Burma owing to the absence of R.A.F. airfield construction units and Air Ministry Works Supervisory personnel in this Theatre. There is no doubt that the American system of providing aviation engineer battalions in Burma proved better and more satisfactory. It might also be noted that some fifteen thousand R.A.F. constructional personnel were allocated by Air Ministry to the Tiger Force Operation in the Pacific, although South East Asia Command was deplorably short of engineers, and it must have been evident that this new Air Force was most unlikely to operate before the defeat of the Japanese.

Hastening Construction of Burma Airfields.

44. Early in June, my Air Marshal Administration visited Rangoon to obtain first-hand details of the problems being encountered, and to hasten construction of airfields as much as possible. On my own visit to Rangoon on June 15th, 1 was assured by Major General Administration, Headquarters, A.L.F.S.E.A., that all points brought up by my Air Officer Administration were receiving attention.

45. The enormous increase in the Air Forces' radius of action which the new airfields under construction would afford was foreshadowed in June, when R.A.F. heavy bombers, operating from bases in Bengal, attacked and sank a 10,000-ton

Japanese tanker in the Gulf of Siam. One aircraft damaged by flak was forced to land at Mingaladon Airfield, Rangoon, which was not yet completed, and over-ran the available length of the runway, killing the crew.

46. The continued pressure by Air Command on the Army for more speedy construction brought better results, and it was a little more heartening, on June 28th, to be given dates estimated for the various stages in the completion of the following airfields in the Rangoon area:-

Zayatkwin – 1,750 yards. A/W runway by July 20th.
Zayatkwin – 2,000 yards. A/W runway by July 31st.
Mingaladon – 1,750 yards. A/W runway by July 31st.
Mingaladon – 2,000 yards. A/W runway by August 15th.

47. By October 1st, it was estimated that Mingaladon Airfield would be capable of accommodating a total of 150 aircraft for operational purposes. The airfield at Zayatkwin was expected to handle 130 Thunderbolts or Mosquitos, and would be staging through the Squadrons for "Zipper" by 1st October. Pegu was also being developed as quickly as possible as a heavy bomber airfield.

48. While it was expected that squadrons would be able to move into the new airfields by the end of July, No. 224 Group, which had been linked with Lieutenant-General Sir Philip Christison's 15 Corps in some of the fiercest fighting in Burma, was preparing to leave the Arakan with its units and to proceed to India for training and re-equipment in preparation for the mounting of "Zipper".

49. The move of 224 Group squadrons was greatly delayed and handicapped on account of the shortage of shipping and the inadequate land transport facilities in Burma. The fact that Army units were also leaving Burma at the same time did not make the position easier for the movement of Air Force personnel and their equipment. June, indeed, ended with the move of 224 Group far from complete, and it soon became apparent that units would not succeed in clearing from the Arakan before the third week in July.

Withdrawal of U.S.A.A.F. from Air Command, South East Asia.

50. On June 1st, 1945, because of our air dominance, the narrowing front, and the fact that the tactical situation after Rangoon, permitted no offensive action by the 10th U.S.A.A.F., the British and American Air Forces reached the parting of the ways in South East Asia Command. The American commitment in Burma had ended with the capture of Northern Burma and removal of the enemy threat to the supply line to China.

51. Each Air Force was now to prosecute the air war against the Japanese in neighbouring Theatres. For the Royal Air Force, the offensive now headed down the Malay Peninsula to Singapore. For the U.S.A.A.F., however, the route lay across the Himalayas to China, since the sphere of the American Command was designated the China – Burma – India Theatre. Yet another reason for the withdrawal of the 10th U.S.A.A.F. was the critical air supply situation in the Northern Combat Area Command, due mainly to the high rate of effort at which the 10th Air Force Transport

Squadrons had been operating and which was now beginning to tell on personnel and aircraft alike. At the same time, the American squadrons required refitting and rest before their impending move to China.

52. The withdrawal of American Squadrons for service in another Theatre did not affect the strategic situation in South East Asia Command. The only aircraft which could have been retained with advantage were (*a*) the transports which were being phased out gradually to bridge the gap until the arrival of our Stage 2 aircraft, and whose withdrawal could not be further delayed on account of the urgent need in China, and (*b*) the photographic Liberators of the 24th Combat Mapping Squadron.

53. The period of integration between British and American Forces in South East Asia had shown a very real spirit of close co-operation – a fact which I emphasised in a special Order of the Day published on June 1st, announcing the withdrawal from Air Command, South East Asia, of the United States Army Air Forces under Major General George E. Stratemeyer, Eastern Air Command, Calcutta.

54. In my Order of the Day, which I sent to General Stratemeyer, I revealed how air power had followed the basic principle in modern warfare – that the air battle had first been won before embarking on the land battle. Once the air battle was decided, air power was then able to provide the ground forces with direct forms of assistance.

55. "Having taken a vital part in the defeat of the Japanese in Burma", I said, "the U.S.A.A.F. units are being withdrawn from Eastern Air Command to fight the Jap in another Theatre. The closing down of the fully integrated Eastern Air Command Headquarters is, therefore, an important milestone in the war against Japan.

"Eastern Air Command was formed on 15th December, 1943, at a critical time in the Battle of Burma, in order to weld into one Command the British and American Air Forces on this front.

"The British Army was hanging on to the western fringes of Burma, having stemmed the Japanese advance into Bengal.

"When the British Army was besieged in Imphal due to Japanese infiltration resulting from their superior mobility, the first task of the newly formed Eastern Air Command was to obtain air superiority in order to enable our close support squadrons to assist the land forces.

"Within a short time air superiority was obtained, due in no small measure to the long range fighter squadrons of the U.S.A.A.F. It enabled the Allied Transport Squadrons to supply and reinforce the beleaguered Army; also, it gave them the mobility which previously the Japanese had monopolised. From this time, until the capture of Rangoon in May, 1945, the Allied Land Forces enjoyed all the benefits of air supremacy which, in turn, kept inviolate the air supply lines and endowed the Allied Army with the mobility and striking power to forge ahead to Mandalay, followed shortly by Rangoon. It made possible the isolation of the Japanese Army in Burma by Allied aircraft, thus preventing the arrival of reinforcements and supplies from Siam and Malaya.

"In Northern Burma, the Tactical and Transport Squadrons of the 10th U.S.A.A.F. played a decisive part in the repulse of the enemy from the Chinese border and in the reopening of the overland route to China.

"A Japanese officer who was captured in Burma attributed the defeat of the Japanese Army to the superior mobility of the Allied Army. This mobility was almost entirely due to the air supply provided by the Allied Air Forces, whose record tonnage exceeded 2,900 tons per day in April, 1945. Due mainly to their superior numbers and operating at maximum effort, the American Transport Squadrons carried the greater portion of the air lift in support of the land forces in Burma.

"In conclusion, it is fair to say that without the support of the American Air Forces in Burma, we could not have defeated the Japanese Army as rapidly and as decisively in 1945. All British Forces, both land and air, are deeply grateful for the whole hearted support and complete harmony that existed between the American and British Air Force units in this Theatre.

"I am exceedingly proud to have had these American Air Force units in my Command, and, together with all members of the British Air Force in South East Asia, wish them good luck, and good hunting."

56. In my Order of the Day announcing disintegration of Eastern Air Command, I did not make especial mention of units of the Air Service Command, but, instead I wrote to Lieutenant General D.I. Sultan, Commanding General, India-Burma Theatre, U.S. Army, and expressed the valuable and splendid work which the Air Service Command had performed under Major General T.J. Handley, Jnr. Without this help, we should have failed to carry through the intensive operations of the previous 12 months.

57. While it was necessary to sever the British and American Combat units of Eastern Air Command, and Air Command, South East Asia, there was, however, no break as yet with the Air Service Command.

58. With disintegration of Eastern Air Command, the air offensive in South East Asia now passed in its entirety to the Royal Air Force, and an exceedingly active period in the deployment of squadrons in Burma began. Thus, the integration ordered by the Supreme Commander in December, 1943, had been fulfilled in so far as it concerned the integration of British and American Air Forces employed in the defeat of the Japanese in Burma.

The Impact of "Tiger Force" on Air Command.

59. For some time after the capture of Rangoon in May, there were indications that Tiger Force was going to be favoured by London in men and material resources previously promised to South East Asia Command.

60. The Supreme Allied Commander, Admiral Mountbatten, showed his reliance on the Air Force in this Theatre, by a strong signal to the Chiefs of Staff expressing his intense disappointment at the contemplated step since he considered it would delay his carrying out their directive to open up the Straits of Malacca and to recapture Singapore at the earliest possible date.

61. I also communicated the concern felt by the Supreme Allied Commander to the Chief of Air Staff, emphasising that future strategy and operations in this Theatre had been based on the agreed rate of build-up of the British Air Forces and especially of British Transport and Heavy Bomber squadrons. Moreover, the withdrawal

programme of the U.S.A.A.F. forces for China which had now begun, had been agreed and phased in with the rate of build-up of the British Air Forces.

62. The question of airfields in South East Asia for staging Tiger Force through to the Far East also presented some difficulties, since the most suitable area was Rangoon where insufficient bases for our own aircraft were available. In the United Kingdom it was thought that Chittagong and Cox's Bazaar were too far from Manila, and they were not accepted as alternatives.

63. It became clear that Air Command, South East Asia, must accept the situation wherein the air war in the Pacific against Japan received higher priority than ourselves. This was finally confirmed by a signal from the Chief of Staff in London on June 22nd, part of which read:-

"In case you are in doubt, 'Zipper' and 'Mailfist' have been approved by the Combined Chiefs of Staff with the proviso that these operations are conducted without prejudice to the preparation and execution of operations for the invasion of Japan and other operations directly connected therewith."

64. At the beginning of July, Air Vice-Marshals Sharp and Satterly arrived at Air Command on their return from the West Pacific where they had been making preliminary arrangements for air bases of Tiger Force.

65. I then learned that, owing to the lack of airfields, operations by the V.H.Bs. (Very Heavy Bombers) were not expected to begin until the end of 1945. This delay greatly simplified the problem of providing staging posts for Tiger Force aircraft through India and Burma since, by the time Tiger Force could be in transit, both the monsoon and "Zipper" would have finished, leaving fair-weather airfields available for Tiger Force in the Rangoon area.

66. It was indicated by the visiting Air Vice-Marshals that A.C.S.E.A. were expected to provide staging facilities, not only for the initial aircraft, but also for the reinforcement flow and for a daily transport service of three aircraft each way. They further expressed the hope that the maintenance of their reserve aircraft would be accepted by this Command.

67. I consider it worthy of note that while Air Command South East Asia was barely making do with transport resources of Dakotas which still constituted the major life-line of the 12th Army, engaged with the Japanese at bay in the Sittang area of Southern Burma during July, the representatives of Tiger Force assumed that Yorks and C.87s would be forthcoming as a matter of course, for their transport requirements.

68. Other examples of this clash in priorities were not lacking, for it was disappointing to learn from Air Ministry by signal on July 21st that, owing to prior needs of Tiger Force, no Lancasters or Lincolns could be expected save for Air/Sea Rescue before mid-1946.

69. My appeal to Air Ministry for Lancasters and Lincolns had been for no other reason that I was concerned about the future heavy bomber supply situation in the Command. I took the long view that we could not expect to rely upon U.S. supplies

of Liberators and, as the result of the difficulties which were already arising over spares and maintenance backing, I was, therefore, anxious to start the re-equipment of the heavy bomber squadrons and to introduce Lancasters vice Liberators into Air/Sea Rescue, Meteorological and several training units.

PART II.
THE AIR WAR IN BURMA AND BEYOND.

AIR SUPERIORITY.

Won and Maintained after Air Battles over Arakan in **1943-44.**

70. Allied air superiority in South East Asia was won and maintained in the Theatre after the air battles over Bengal and Burma late in 1943 and the Spring of 1944, and remained almost unchallenged until the final surrender of the Japanese.

71. This air superiority is not always given its full value when the fortunes of war in Burma are weighed. Without it, the history of the indomitable 14th Army might well have centred around a fighting force, justly capable of defence, but not capable of sustained offence. Air superiority too, meant a "safe conduct" for the air transport fleets engaged upon air supply and reinforcing of the advancing troops. At one time no single Dakota in Burma could with safety have taken the air on any supply mission had not the air lanes been protected by our short range fighters,

72. Air superiority, whether used for the close support of the ground forces, or the interdiction of lines of communication far beyond the battle area, or in air supply or in casualty evacuation, was indisputably ours, a fact which Japanese Army Commanders themselves confirmed after their surrender in August, 1945.

73. In the Japanese Army, one Commander had said, there had never been any real plan to develop the Military Air Forces. The air weapons he said, had been neglected from the beginning in favour of ground weapons. Ever since the China Incident, however, there had been a growing feeling that Japanese air power must be developed at all costs, but this realisation had come too late, and even then, the Army's claims had over-ridden the long term policy which recognised the absolute necessity of a wide expansion of air power and the production of aircraft.

74. Another Japanese officer, after fighting against us in South East Asia, said that almost always the Japanese Army had left the construction of airfields until the last, having concentrated firstly upon its own ground defences.

Few Airfields left to J.A.F. in Burma.

75. While the main Japanese Army had retreated to Moulmein after the fall of Rangoon in May, it still preserved enough strength to make a spirited stand during July at what came to be known as "The Battle of the Sittang Bend".

76. The Japanese Air Force, on the other hand, had been driven out of Burma

completely broken. No attempt, indeed, was made to alleviate the distress in which the thousands of trapped Japanese forces in Burma found themselves during July.

77. Only twelve months earlier, the Japanese Air Force in South East Asia had made 333 sorties in May of 1944 in their last bid to tip the scales in their favour at the siege of Imphal, but had failed. For them, this air effort was a record for the Japanese Air Force for any single month when the targets were Allied airfields and troop concentrations in the Manipur Valley.

78. The enemy had behind them at that time the important air bases at Shwebo, north of Mandalay, and, in Central Burma, they possessed the airfields at Meiktila, Magwe, Pyinmana, Prome and Toungoo. Their most southerly bases were those which comprised the Rangoon group of airfields.

79. The Allies' sweep through Burma and the capture of Rangoon however, had taken all these airfields from the Japanese. All that remained to them in Southern Burma were three serviceable airfields located at Tavoy, Mergui and Victoria Point, on the Tenasserim Coast, and these soon became the regular targets for our aircraft based at Rangoon.

80. In June, 1945, yet another indication of the weakness of the Japanese air power in South East Asia in face of air superiority was the withdrawal of R.A.F. fighter protection for the air transports – a protection which had been maintained consistently from the beginning of the Allied advance through Burma after Imphal in 1944, and had involved fighter cover over a front extending many hundreds of miles.

81. When Fourteenth Army marched a thousand miles through Burma in six months they achieved a great military feat in a country which had been deemed hitherto to be almost physically impassable and medically disastrous for the mass movement of men. With that Army, the Air Forces went every mile of the way – scouting, supporting, reinforcing, supplying, evacuating wounded and striking ahead of the advancing troops, to disrupt Japanese lines of communication and supply bases.

82. The same air-ground co-operation which brought about the fall of Rangoon and the re-conquest of Burma would have been repeated on a grand scale for the assault planned on Malaya – forestalled only by Japanese surrender. Even then the flexibility of Air Power was such that, in the emergency which followed the cessation of hostilities, it was able to re-direct its energies in one of the greatest relief and liberation operations of World War II.

83. In any final analysis of the war in South East Asia, air superiority is of paramount importance, and an indispensable factor upon which maintenance and supply of all our Forces in the Theatre depended.

TACTICAL AIR OPERATIONS.

After Rangoon.

84. When the Japanese pulled out of Rangoon, and the remnants of the main army succeeded in reaching Moulmein after the disastrous retreat down the Central Corridor in April, hostilities in Burma were by no means over.

85. There was no question of the enemy's capacity to stage a serious comeback;

his supply lines were no longer reliable and the Japanese Air Force was out of the race.

86. But there was one aspect of the campaign which was not yet complete and one which began to assume greater importance now that the Allied Forces had established themselves firmly in Southern Burma and Rangoon. It was the presence of the large isolated forces of Japanese troops in Central and North Burma, estimated at over 50,000 men. While the Allied advance down the Central Corridor during March and April had driven a wedge through a crumbling enemy defence, it had, at the same time, forced a considerable strength of Japanese troops into the hill regions of Eastern, and Western Burma, isolating them from the main Japanese army as it retreated on Moulmein.

87. The Air Forces, principally those of No. 221 Group, and the Allied ground forces deployed in Southern Burma, swung round to face these large concentrations of Japanese troops in the north between the Irrawaddy and the Mandalay railway corridor in Central Burma and the railway corridor and the Sittang and Salween Rivers to the east. Their object was to close the principal escape routes which these Japanese forces must pass through to get out of Burma.

88. Few factors sustain the morale of fighting men more than the knowledge that supplies of provisions and equipment are assured. The isolated Japanese forces in Burma, however, as the result of disruption and disorganisation of their rear lines of communication, were ill-equipped, and certainly denied any possibility of supply by air. They suffered considerably through shortages of food, also medical supplies, and took to eating attractive looking but dangerous fruits.

89. So long as these trapped Japanese forces remained on Burmese soil, however, they required considerable effort from the air to watch their movement and to destroy them as opportunity arose.

The Competitive Spirit of Squadrons.

90. The task of hunting and destroying these isolated pockets of Japanese forces, in co-operation with the Allied ground troops, fell largely upon the squadrons of No. 221 Group, since No. 224 Group, after its fine record of achievement in Burma, was now in the process of pulling out for training and re-equipment in Southern India prior to the assault on Malaya.

91. The competitive spirit among squadrons soon produced keen offensive patrols in seeking out the enemy with Mosquitos, Beaufighters, Hurricanes, Spitfires and Thunderbolts covering wide areas of country – in spite of Monsoon weather – and succeeding in driving parties of Japanese troops off the main escape routes and forcing them to seek the cover of jungle or scrub.

92. In this offensive drive by the squadrons during May and June, a total of 4,813 sorties was flown by our aircraft in monsoon weather to bomb and strafe the enemy.

93. It was during this period that a return was made to jungle warfare in Burma, as grim and fierce as anything experienced by the air and ground forces during previous months. The air forces faced the considerable hazards of monsoon flying

conditions as they attacked enemy troop concentrations attempting to regroup and reach appointed regrouping areas.

94. The effectiveness of these R.A.F. jungle strikes was not only substantiated in appreciative messages by the Army, but also by Japanese officer prisoners-of-war captured at this period. Of the air forces operating against them, a Japanese officer, a L/Cpl., and a Superior Private had said during interrogation:-

> "Dawn found us heading towards a village on the opposite shore. Later, we found that it was near Mumbu. We cooked some rice and afterwards all went to sleep in a bamboo clump on the bend of the river. Sleep, however, was not so easy, for the enemy planes were roaring overhead, and we would awake in a cold sweat in the midst of a horrible nightmare."

95. There could be no doubt that the enemy had a healthy respect for our British Air Force and sought the cover of undergrowth when surprised by our fighters, which strafed them incessantly. A Japanese Private of the 82nd Air Field Battalion, captured in Burma, when shown a collection of silhouettes of Allied aircraft, picked out the Spitfire as the aircraft most feared by the Japanese.

Closing the Net around the Enemy in Burma.

96. By the end of June, the net was gradually tightened around the isolated Japanese land forces holding out in the Pegu Yomas in Central Burma. The monsoon continued. The heavy rains made the movement of Allied troops and their supporting arms exceedingly difficult on the fringes of the Pegu Yomas and along the Mawchi Road east of Toungoo.

97. The Japanese, however, got no nearer to escape. Whenever weather permitted, the squadrons of 221 Group were overhead endeavouring to locate the enemy in the most difficult of wooded country, and bombing on every occasion whatever targets presented themselves. For days, aircraft continued to search for heavily laden animal transports which the enemy were pressing into service to carry accoutrement of every description. Even lumber elephants, taken from their work in the famous Teak Forests of Burma, were employed in carrying light guns and other heavy equipment for the enemy. If the monsoon proved a handicap to the Allied Forces it was worse for the Japanese, who were completely cut off from sources of supply. In the Pegu Yomas, the plight of the enemy, as a result of the vigilance of air power and the movement of Allied ground troops, became desperate as they struggled against malaria and starvation, or suffered foot-rot and stomach and skin troubles.

Some, indeed, were like skeletons when captured, while the remainder, still imbued with fanaticism of glory and death, rather than disgrace in surrender, struggled on.

98. In their jungle strikes and "hunting" expeditions, the squadrons obtained a large number of good results in spite of the difficulties of weather and thick ground cover. If the enemy looked for a lull in operations as a result of the monsoon, thus giving them an opportunity to regroup, they got none from the R.A.F. squadrons and ground forces.

99. In the Mokpalin area, where No. 20 Squadron had damaged much enemy transport, a message sent by Headquarters, 4 Corps, after the strike, said:-

"Thanks for the magnificent efforts yesterday on the Mokpalin road."

100. When Mosquitos of 47 Squadron went out on a strike, they bombed a village north east of Nyaunglobin, where it was reported that the Japanese, moving south, had taken cover during the day. The Mosquitos dispersed their bombs well among the bashas and on dumps of packing cases seen on either side of the roadway, while many low flying attacks made across the area did extensive damage.

101. An Army report which reached 221 Group Headquarters stated that during an air attack in the Meprawse area, some 30 to 40 bullock carts carrying food were accounted for, two petrol dumps destroyed and 50 to 70 Japanese troops killed.

102. Up the Mawchi Road, Hurricanes went after a number of guns or tanks stated to be moving in the district. Two attacks which they made on heavily camouflaged objects, revealed large guns with limbers or tractors. They left the targets in flames.

103. The plight of the enemy as a result of these jungle strikes worsened. A report brought in, following an air strike by No. 11 Squadron, said that "the villagers reported that they carried away 30 Japanese corpses after the strike."

104. Some time earlier, a strike by Nos. 79 and 261 Squadrons brought the following message from Headquarters, 20 Indian Infantry Division:-

"One 75 mm gun, one 70 mm gun, one 77 mm A/T gun, one 20 mm A/T rifle, six pistols, six swords, approximately 100 rifles, three stacks of ammunition and much artillery ammunition," were found by ground forces after a successful air attack.

105. In the last week of June, the main concentration of Japanese forces in Central Burma, was opposite Nyaunglobin, with protective forces north west of Pegu and south west of Pyu, which gave R.A.F. Thunderbolts opportunities for attacks. During one raid, six aircraft of 79 Squadron bombed the village of Thaingon. Some days later it was learned that 170 Japanese and 40 mules had been killed.

106. On the Sittang river too, where movement by the enemy became more active, Spitfire aircraft undertook patrols down the river, damaging and sinking small river craft of every description almost daily, thus helping our ground forces to interrupt enemy efforts in that area to escape across the river.

"Force 136" *and Sittang River Air Patrol.*

107. There were other major difficulties which stood in the way of the trapped Japanese forces in escaping from Burma. The guerrilla tactics of "Force 136", which later played a conspicuous part in the slaughter of the enemy on the Sittang River, helped to seal this stretch of water against any large scale enemy crossing.

108. The forces of Burmese guerillas, which began to assume considerable importance at this time in Burma, had caused the utmost concern to small parties of Japanese stragglers, who suffered severe losses at their hands. These guerillas had been operating with success during the latter weeks of March, and throughout April, but they were even more active during June and July, as the Japanese casualty figures testified.

109. Organising the Burmese patriots was the work of the British Organisation in Burma known as "Force 136". It was an independent body which operated both with the Air Forces and the Army. The Force consisted of trained and specially picked officers who were dropped by parachute into enemy-occupied areas to organise Burmese levies and to wage surprise attacks against the Japanese. This guerilla warfare demanded the closest liaison with the Air Forces. Supplies, including arms and ammunition, were air dropped once the parties of levies had been organised.

110. It was through the machinery of "Force 136" too, that much valuable information on enemy dumps, troop movements, headquarters, and concentrations of transport carrying food, stocks and equipment, was passed by W/T to Army Headquarters, and special air-strikes quickly organised for the squadrons of 221 Group, R.A.F. These tasks were carried out eagerly by pilots, and many profitable and successful strikes were made against the enemy. The Japanese casualties showed a sharp rise as a result of these sudden air attacks.

111. The air patrol on the Sittang River, on the other hand, consisted of three standing patrols daily – dawn, midday and dusk. The duration of the patrols up and down the river was so varied that the Japanese could never be certain of escape.

112. During one such patrol in June, two Hurricanes of 28 Squadron came upon 50 river craft of all types in the Suppanu Chaung and, after damaging them by strafing, went on to Letpan and there strafed several boats drawn up on the bank of the river near some villages.

113. There could be no doubt that the vigilance maintained by aircrews engaged on offensive patrols over the Sittang River was a contributory factor to holding up any river crossing in strength, which the Japanese may have contemplated during June.

Disaster overtakes the Japanese in Burma.

114. Disaster overtook the Japanese during July, when their final bid to break through the Allied net and escape from Burma ended in a debacle.

115. It was one of the blackest periods for the enemy throughout their ill-fated campaign. More than 10,000 men were killed in the month's operations. Those who succeeded in getting away and joining the main Japanese forces at Moulmein, took with them a picture of the punishing they had faced from the British air forces, the warring guerillas, and the newly-formed 12th Army under Lieutenant General Sir Montague Stopford.

116. Operations by the air and ground forces in this last major battle in Burma took on an entirely new character from the mobility and speed which had so characterised the pursuit of the enemy down the central railway corridor during April and May. Instead, the lull period in June had given the squadrons and ground forces a better opportunity to deploy at strategic points in Southern Burma, so that the enemy break-through from the Pegu Yomas, when it ultimately took place, developed into a wholesale killing. The monsoon forced R.A.F. Squadrons to base themselves at airstrips other than they would have preferred, but, even so, the operations were maintained.

117. The squadrons of 221 Group, R.A.F., accounted for at least 2,000 Japanese casualties.

Throughout the campaign it was always difficult to assess with accuracy the number of actual casualties inflicted by the air forces and our own artillery.

118. Four separate phases characterised the July battle.

(*a*) There was a sudden flare-up of enemy activity on the Sittang Bend at the opening of the month where the Japanese, firmly established at Mokpalin, succeeded in making a bridgehead across the river and, after some grim fighting, succeeded in holding on the right bank, an area of approximately one square mile of country, encompassing the villages of Nyaungkashe, Abya, and Myitkye.

(*b*) Up country, on the Sittang, taking in an area between Shwegyin and Kyaukkye, parties of Japanese troops, as they endeavoured to escape by crossing to the left bank of the Sittang, continued to fall into the hands of organised guerillas.

(*c*) Yet further to the north 19 Indian Division and Patriot Burmese Forces in the worst of monsoon weather, were struggling along the Mawchi Road from Toungoo in an effort to reach Mawchi, and cut the main escape route of large Japanese forces retreating southwards down the road from Loikaw, and Kemapyu, on the Salween River, and then south by valley tracks which led to Papun and Kamamaung. From Papun, one escape route continued southwest to Bilin with easy access by road and rail to Moulmein. The second escape route from Papun went south-east to Kamamaung, thence by ferry down the Salween to Shwegun, and there joined a track leading through Pa-An to Moulmein.

(*d*) The final, and major phase, was the large scale attempted break-through across the railway corridor from the Pegu Yomas, starting on July 21st, by Japanese troops whose strength had now been estimated to be about 18,000, of which about 1,000 were left behind sick in the Yomas and could not take part in the breakout operations.

119. Squadrons which played such a conspicuous part in these operations were deployed as follows:-

(*a*) When the sudden flare up at the Sittang Bend began, No. 906 Wing with Nos. 273 and 607 Squadrons; one detachment of night Beaufighters, and the H.Q. and one flight of No. 28 Fighter Recce Squadron, were based at Mingaladon, Rangoon, thus within easy reach of this enemy force.

(*b*) Based at Kinmagon was No. 908 Wing with Nos. 47 and 110 Mosquito Squadrons, which were able, weather permitting, to afford valuable support to the parties of guerillas in their successful attacks on the Japanese in the Sittang river area.

(*c*) No. 910 Wing was based at Meiktila with four Thunderbolt squadrons, Nos. 34, 42, 79 and 113, ready for action at the first sign of the break-through from the Pegu Yomas.

(*d*) Assisting 19 Indian Infantry Division on the Mawchi road, was 909 Wing at Toungoo, with No. 155 Spitfire Squadron, and later strengthened by No. 152 Spitfire Squadron which moved down to Thedaw for a short period, and, at other times, staged through Toungoo.

120. When the break-through by the Japanese from the Pegu Yomas started on July 21st, the whole of the air support was switched over to this area and, for eight or nine days, the bewildered enemy was strenuously harassed by the squadrons supporting the 12th Army.

Battle of the Sittang Bend.

121. In an attempt to create a large scale diversion of the Allied ground forces, the Japanese, at the opening of July, launched an offensive at the Sittang from the bridgehead which they tenaciously held on the right bank opposite Mokpalin.

122. It was flat, open country with scattered scrub, and some very fierce fighting took place in appalling weather at Nyaungkashe, Abya, and Myikye. The village of Nyaungkashe, indeed, changed hands several times.

123. Air support thrown in by 221 Group, included the Spitfire and Thunderbolt squadrons operating continuous patrols or "Cabranks" in the Nyaungkashe area. The enemy took exceedingly heavy punishment. His determination to hold this area, at all costs, however, until the large Japanese forces to the north got down past Bilin, with the strategic town of Mokpalin on their right, safeguarded by the Sittang troops, was obvious.

124. Day after day, gun positions, troop concentrations, and river craft of all descriptions were subjected to intensive attacks by the air forces, bringing sincere thanks from the Army. On July 4th, No. 42 Squadron's Thunderbolts had a most successful day, when a 105mm gun was wrecked and two other guns silenced at Nyaungkashe.

125. It was at this time that some forces of 7 Indian Infantry Division found themselves in a precarious position as a result of the determined Japanese thrust, but, assisted by air attack, succeeded in extricating themselves.

126. "With the help of excellent air support quickly given," wrote Lieutenant General Messervy to Air Vice-Marshal Bouchier, A.O.C. 221 Group, "I have been able to extricate some four hundred men, including sixty wounded, from a difficult situation with good knocks to the Japs at the same time."

127. It was noted throughout these air operations, and further substantiated by ground reports, that a considerable number of Japanese troops were killed as a result of air attacks.

128. By July 11th, the Japanese offensive at the Sittang Bend had been contained,

though the enemy still retained their foothold on the right bank of the Sittang, opposite Mokpalin.

Air Power Assists the Guerillas.

129. As the month advanced, a notable movement of enemy troops endeavouring to cross the Sittang River in parties at various points between Shwegyin and Kyaukke, kept the Spitfire squadrons on continuous patrol over the Sittang River exceedingly active. Thunderbolt squadrons, too, came down from the Meiktila area to attack forces of Japanese numbering, in some instances, one thousand strong, as they made their way eastwards. The large scale break-through from the Pegu Yomas had not yet started.

130. It was in this area of the Sittang, and also in the east, on the right bank of the Salween, that the organised guerillas, which had been brought under the control of 12th Army, ambushed hundreds of escaping Japanese troops moving down from Loikaw to Papun, and literally massacred them. No enemy party was safe from these guerrillas under Force 136 who, with portable W/T, kept base informed of the enemy's movements and as a result provided the Mosquitos and Spitfires with definite targets, which they bombed and strafed untiringly.

131. The guerillas' flag was seen regularly by pilots heading for their targets. They were assisted by large indicator arrows on the ground, and even cryptic messages which the levies had conceived. On one occasion, pilots, correctly interpreting a message, "In M", located a Japanese force in a marsh.

132. Following a heavy raid on Pa-An, one of the principal staging villages used by the Japanese while moving down the Salween valley, a message sent from our land forces to 273 and 607 Squadrons on July 1st said:-

"More than five hundred Japs killed in last heavy raid on Pa-An. Did not tell you before as awaiting confirmation. Congrats to pilots."

133. An earlier report had described this whole area after the raids as covered in dust and smoke, with Japanese soldiers seen running about in panic and rushing for shelter as aircraft came down to strafe them. The Mosquito Squadrons got equally effective results for, during a strike at Kawludo, an enemy staging post in the Salween valley, north of Papun, a ground report stated that over one hundred Japanese troops had been killed.

134. Thunderbolts and Spitfires carried out a very successful attack on July 15th and 16th, in the Shwegyin Chaung area of the Sittang, and a message from Kyadwin to 113 Squadron and 607 Squadron said:- "Tell R.A.F. strike great success."

135. North East of Kyadwin, at Paungzeik, Mosquitos of 47 Squadron, on July 16th, made a bombing and strafing attack in the Paungzeik valley and 51 dead Japanese were counted after the attack. Yet another attack by aircraft on the 19th, at Shanywathit, resulted in two direct hits being made on a house which was full of Japanese troops, and over eighty are believed to have been killed.

136. The reports of successful air strikes against the escaping enemy were many and varied. In the credit for their success the guerillas of Force 136 must equally

share. Their daring in approaching large enemy parties and making sudden furious assaults on them with gunfire and grenades before retiring to their hideouts to plan further surprise raids, was outstanding in this final killing of the Japanese in Burma. The risks, too, which they ran, while blatantly guiding aircraft on to enemy concentrations, frequently involved them in hazardous escapes. Many escapes were only made possible indeed, by aircraft swooping in between the levies and the enemy, strafing the Japanese pursuers. If caught, guerillas were tortured cruelly by the enemy.

Tribute to R.A.F. from Guerilla Leader.

137. A tribute paid to the Royal Air Force in Burma came from the leader of one of these courageous parties operating in the Okpyat area of the Sittang:

> "Both I and every guerilla would like to make it known to every pilot who took part in the battle of the Okpyat area just how much all the brilliant offensive action of the R.A.F. fighter-bomber pilots was appreciated," wrote Captain J. Waller, British Officer in charge of Force 136 Guerillas, Okpyat. "From our point of view on the ground, we wished that we had more air ground strips so that we could write in full – 'Hats off to the R.A.F. pilots. You are killing hundreds of Japs and your perfect co-ordination and patience in reading our crude signals is saving the lives of many thousands of defenceless civilians.' "

138. Whilst these exploits revealed the magnificent work of aircrews, they illustrated at the same time the confidence and daring of the British-led irregular, for whom the pilots of Group squadrons felt most strongly that it was a case of "Hats right off" to the guerillas.

139. "From Letpangon we were attacked by two hundred Japs at 23.30 hours. We only killed fifteen of them, but we kept them there for you to attack next day when you put in two good strikes. They cleared out after dark, and went on to Yindaikaein where you were able to attack them again," said Captain Waller.

140. The combined attacks on the Japanese aircraft and guerilla parties constituted a war of attrition on the enemy. They could never be sure of safety in any village they passed through, and roads, planked with thick scrub, were a perpetual nightmare. The guerrillas were masters in the art of ambush. With the air forces to supply and assist them they seemed to be everywhere, and to know the enemy's next move. This was evident from the casualties they inflicted against the Japanese.

141. It was after an attack by air forces on a large concentration of Japanese troops at Letpangon, that the Okpyat Guerilla party, which had been pinning down the enemy until the aircraft arrived, went out in a most successful mopping-up task.

142. Captain Waller reported to the R.A.F., "We only killed 15 of them but you killed 105 in three cracking good air strikes. You also saved the lives of almost three thousand occupants and evacuees in Okpyat who were completely cut off."

Japanese Break-through from Pegu Yomas Fails.

143. The desperate and last bid by the 28th Japanese Army to escape across the

Sittang began on July 21st, when some 15,000 to 18,000 enemy troops, sick and demoralised, moved out of the jungle and scrub shelter of the Pegu Yomas.

144. The moment for which the squadrons and Allied ground forces had been awaiting had now come. The ground forces of 17 Indian Infantry Division, ranged in groups along the 100 miles stretch of roadway between Toungoo and Pegu, which formed part of the railway corridor, engaged the enemy, bursting over the road at several points simultaneously, and slaughtered them.

145. The squadrons of 221 Group were switched over to this battle area in support of 17 Division, and for almost nine days air assault was directed on the wretched Japanese as they made desperate attempts to reach the Sittang River.

146. From a captured enemy document it was revealed that the main break-through from the Pegu Yomas had been delayed by the enemy to allow the move of the Japanese 28th Army to co-ordinate. The greater part of the Mayazaki Group (Lt.-Gen. G.O.C. 54 Division) had planned to attempt to cross the Sittang between Nyaungbentha and Pyu. Coinciding with this move, Koba Group (Major-General Koba) had planned another major break out, and while the area of the move was not determined, it was anticipated that it would take place north of Toungoo in 19 Division area where troops were deploying along the Toungoo-Mawchi Road.

147. The enemy's plan was to form road blocks at selected points and to pass through them assisted by "Jitter Squads" to create diversions. All movements were to be made by night and the keynote of the break-through was to be "speed" so that the maximum time would be available for the collection of boats and rafts from the Sittang river in order to complete the crossing before daylight. The enemy had planned, on reaching the Sittang to cross on a wide front using barges, rafts, logs, bamboo poles and even petrol tins to assist the buoyancy of escapees in the water.

148. It would be invidious to state that one squadron, more than another, inflicted the greatest punishment on the escaping enemy. All squadrons thrown into the "Battle of the Break-through," overcoming monsoon with low clouds and heavy rain for long periods, did what was expected of them with credit. The keenness of squadron ground personnel was equal to the occasion. They worked hard and ungrudgingly. All, indeed, in the air, as well as on the ground, felt that something substantial was being accomplished in this last show-down with the Japanese in Burma.

149. The July killing lasted until the 29th. The Thunderbolt squadrons, carrying three 500 lb. bombs on each aircraft, played havoc among concentrations of moving Japanese troops. The Spitfires too, carrying one 500 lb. bomb on each aircraft, pursued the enemy relentlessly, strafing them as they ran for cover. As many as 62 sorties were flown on July 23rd by Nos. 152 and 155 Squadrons.

150. The extent of the full air effort by the R.A.F. squadrons in this battle cannot be adequately measured in the many squadron reports which told of the effectiveness and killings made during their strikes. The confusion and disruption caused among the Japanese forces, amounted to almost chaos. More convincing, perhaps, were the reports sent by 12th Army Divisional Commanders to H.Q. 221 Group, who were not slow to express their gratitude for the support given to their troops.

151. After almost nine days of intense fighting, the attempted break out by the Japanese from the Pegu Yomas ended in utter and complete failure. More than 10,000

men were killed, as against only three hundred odd casualties sustained by the Allied forces. Out of approximately 1,300 Japanese troops who succeeded in crossing the Sittang between Meikthalin and Wegyi, it was estimated that 500 of their number had been killed during air strikes by Spitfires and Thunderbolts.

152. The whole Japanese plan for organised escape petered out in the closing days of July, and the air and ground attacks were then transferred once more to the Sittang Bend, where the other Japanese forces, to their credit, had held out bravely in their struggle to keep open the last doorway leading out of Burma. In the July battle, R.A.F. squadrons had flown a total of 3,045 sorties – 92 per cent. of which were offensive strikes in support of ground troops, while a total weight of 1,490,000 lb. of bombs had been dropped.

153. As the last few hundreds of exhausted Japanese were making their escape to Moulmein with bitter recollections of the ordeal they had passed through, Lieutenant-General Sir Montague Stopford, G.O.C. 12th Army, when recalling the severity of the weather, its flooding, rains and cloud, showed his appreciation of the RA.F. in these words:-

> "Grateful if you would accept and pass on to all ranks under your command my most grateful thanks for the admirable support given during break-out battle and my congratulations on splendid results achieved. Flying conditions must have been most difficult but on all sides I hear nothing but praise of the keenness and determination of pilots to get through. You have all played a great part in the Twelfth Army's first big operation."

154. Over and above the R.A.F. contribution, our victory was won by our superiority over the Japanese in training, fighting ability and weapons; the accurate intelligence which was obtained before the battle began; the fine work of the guerillas, and above all the high morale and fighting efficiency of the troops.

STRATEGIC AIR OPERATIONS.

A Well Sustained Offensive against Enemy Supply and Communications.

155. With the capture of Rangoon and the disbandment of the integrated Anglo-American Strategic Air Force on June 1st, the R.A.F. heavy bombers of 231 Group were left to carry out the next phase of the battle against the enemy's communications leading to Singapore, and on other important targets.

156. The partnership which had been forged between heavy bomber units of No. 231 Group, R.A.F., and the 7th Bombardment Group, U.S.A.A.F. had, over a period, produced a striking force so effective that it brought about a serious disruption to Japanese strategic communications in this Theatre, with a critical decline in the quantity of supplies intended for their ground forces in Burma.

157. The departure of the 7th Bombardment Group had one important significance. The Group had operated twelve aircraft fitted with "Azon" equipment, consisting of a radio transmitter in the aircraft and a radio receiver on the bomb which, once

released, could be guided in such a way that line errors could be eliminated. Throughout the series of "bridge-busting" missions on the Burma-Siam railway, which, on account of anti-aircraft defences could not be attacked from low level by Liberators, the Azon equipment was used with great success.

158. The destruction of bridges in Burma and Siam, notably on the Bangkok-Pegu railway, which was one of the principal tasks of the Strategic Air Force, was a vital factor in crippling the enemy's land communications.

159. In a six-month period between December 1944 and May 1945, there was photographic confirmation of bridge destruction as shown hereunder:-

	Destroyed	*Damaged*
Rail	96	36
Road	13	4
Total	**109**	**40**

160. Feverish efforts made by the Japanese engineers, who worked with great energy repairing and rebuilding bridges, failed to keep open many of the vital communications upon which the Japanese in Southern Burma depended.

Greater Distances Flown to Target Areas.

161. On the Allied occupation of Rangoon, R.A.F. Liberators carried the heavy bomber offensive much further afield into the enemy occupied territories of South East Asia, involving frequent flights of over 1,000 miles radius from their Indian bases in Bengal. This was inevitable, as the newly occupied airfields in Southern Burma, after the capture of Rangoon, were not yet big enough to take heavy bombers. The long distance flights undertaken by these aircraft across the Bay of Bengal in difficult monsoon, weather were most hazardous.

162. From Moulmein, at the mouth of the Salween River, to Victoria Point, the southernmost tip in Burma, is nearly 500 miles. This coastal tip, known as the Tenasserim, together with Japanese bases in the Andaman Islands, came in for attention by the heavy bombers after our entry into Rangoon. Nearly 1,000 tons of bombs were dropped by the R.A.F. squadrons during May, which reflected the determination of the crews to carry on their heavy bombing work in the disruption of the enemy's communication system. Indeed, what was to have been a V.E.-Day celebration in May, was spent by crews of the squadrons standing by for an attack on shipping in the Andamans. This culminated in a bombing raid on May 17th against the most westerly Japanese base in the Bay of Bengal – Port Blair. The bombing force on this occasion concentrated on important harbour installations, including marine workshops at Phoenix Bay, while buildings at Hope Town, the main coaling point, were destroyed. A large orange red explosion, with flames rising up to 1,500 feet, was seen by the crews after they had hit their target. The enemy had fortified the whole area of Port Blair with shore batteries and A.A. guns, which succeeded in shooting down one of our aircraft.

163. But the main battle against the enemy's communications – notably those affecting Singapore – was now on. The same air strategy which had disrupted the

Japanese supply line between Bangkok and Rangoon was applied in the succeeding months with equal effectiveness to the line linking Bangkok with Singapore.

164. Communications on this mountainous peninsula, embracing territory of three States – Burma, Siam and Malaya – had, for the most part, been seaborne, though, as the Japanese advance in 1941 showed, Singapore still had a backdoor by means of the rail route to the north.

165. With the sea lanes in the Strait of Malacca made more and more hazardous for Japanese shipping through the effectiveness of our mine-laying from the air and the vigilance shown by R.N. submarines, the enemy was forced to fall back steadily on the use of the Bangkok-Singapore railway for the movement of supplies. This line snaked for a thousand miles up the narrow neck of land between the Gulf of Siam and the Andaman Sea.

166. Not all the stretch of railroad was within range of the R.A.F. Liberators. With persistence, however, they succeeded in getting as far south from their bases in India as the Bay of Bandon at the Isthmus of Kra, to inflict heavy damage on the important railway junction of Jumbhorn at the narrowest part of the Isthmus.

Enemy's concern over Systematic Damage.

167. I must express most sincere admiration for the aircrews who flew these Liberators such abnormally long distances, frequently through atrocious monsoon weather, to bomb their targets in Siam and Malaya.

168. Crews of Bomber Command in Europe flew 1,200 mile round trips to Berlin when attacking targets in the capital of the Reich, but the R.A.F. Liberators in South East Asia flew from their bases in India round trips well over 2,000 miles to bomb objectives at Bangkok, and other targets on the Isthmus of Kra. This is equal to a flight from London to Naples or well to the east of Warsaw – flights, it should be noted, which the R.A.F Liberators in my Command carried out regularly against the Japanese.

169. The concern of the enemy over the systematic damage to, and destruction of, their lines of communication in Siam and Malaya was revealed in a document which came into our hands entitled "Protection of Communications". This document called upon Japanese Unit Commanders to overhaul their A.A. defence methods as "enemy aircraft are carrying out continuous and unceasing attacks on our rear communications and planning to cut our rear lines altogether. We must perfect our counter-measures."

170. The enemy's increased vigilance, however, appeared to make no material difference to the preservation of their rail bridges, dumps, water towers, locomotives, rolling stock and shipping.

171. On June 5th, seven Liberators attacked railyards at Surasdhani on the Bangkok-Singapore line. Surasdhani was an important supply post for the Japanese and, to reach it, our bomber crews flew for 17 hours, mostly across the Bay of Bengal, and through some of the worst weather which the monsoon during 1945 had produced. This flight of 2,400 miles was one of the longest undertaken, up to that time, on a heavy bombing mission in this Theatre. The bombing was well

concentrated, and the results were good. Subsequent reconnaissance confirmed all claims made by the crews.

Liberators sink 10,000-ton *Japanese Tanker.*

172. A shipping strike in Siamese waters on June 15th, when a 10,000-ton Japanese tanker was set on fire and left sinking by the stern, was one of the most noteworthy operations of its kind during the closing stages of the war against Japan in South East Asia.

173. To effect this strike, aircraft had to make a round trip of approximately 2,500 miles to the expected anchorage, the route being almost entirely over the Bay of Bengal and the Andaman Sea.

174. The tanker was the largest enemy vessel reported in Siamese waters for many months, and was believed to be one of the last of its size remaining to the Japanese in the Southern Area. It was sighted by a Sunderland aircraft of 222 Group when it was apparently trying to make a northbound run through the Gulf of Siam and along the east coast of the Malay Peninsula. The tanker had an escort.

175. The Air Forces at the disposal of 231 Group for this strike were four heavy bomber squadrons – Nos. 99, 159, 355 and 356, equipped with Liberator Mark V aircraft. A detachment of six aircraft from No. 159 Squadron, based in India, moved down temporarily to Akyab, on the Arakan, for the operation. This enabled the aircraft of the detachment to load up during the night and to take off at 0900 hours on the day of the strike. They were, therefore, the last squadron in to attack.

176. Due to exceedingly bad weather encountered by all aircraft on the route to the target, a number of the aircraft were forced to abandon the operation and returned to base. The master bomber and deputy master bomber were, unfortunately, included in this number. The remaining aircraft, which pressed on, came upon their target in the early afternoon as the tanker was moving past Samui Island. An escort was some distance away.

177. Three aircraft of 99 Squadron attacked the tanker at low level but did not succeed in securing hits. All three aircraft were damaged by A.A. fire from the escort vessel and the tanker itself. One aircraft had a fin shot off. After delivering its attack, it eventually reached Mingaladon Airfield, Rangoon, where it crash-landed. The second aircraft, also damaged, by A.A. fire, crash-landed at Akyab.

178. The battle against the tanker was continued later with three aircraft of 356 Squadron attacking at low level, and a direct hit produced fire and a series of explosions. The tanker still fought back fiercely, and all three aircraft were damaged by A.A. fire, one of which crashed when landing at Salbani in Bengal. The fight continued with the arrival of three further aircraft from 159 Squadron which pressed home the attack, claiming four and possibly six hits. With smoke billowing to 7,000 feet, the tanker was left burning from stem to stern and sinking. The tanker's escort succeeded in making its escape.

179. Subsequent reconnaissance showed that the tanker was sunk, the funnel and mast were seen showing above the sea.

180. Loss of so vital a supply vessel as an oil tanker of 10,000 tons, particularly

at a time when supply meant everything to the enemy in South East Asia, added further to the embarrassment of the Japanese.

181. For this outstanding success I sent a message of congratulation to Major-General J.T. Durrant, S.A.A.F., who, on June 15th, had assumed Command of 231 Group, vice Air Commodore F.J.W. Mellersh, C.B.E., A.F.C., repatriated to the United Kingdom.

182. The attack on the Japanese tanker ended a month of most successful shipping strikes by the air forces of 231 Group during June, for, on June 1st, Liberators had surprised enemy vessels at Satahib in the Gulf of Siam, when a 335-foot submarine depot ship – "Angthong" – was sunk.

183. The stranglehold on the Japanese supply and communications system was further tightened on June 24th, when Liberators destroyed two important bridges at Kanchanaburi, eighty miles west of Bangkok. The raid on these bridges across the Meklong River at Kanchanaburi was a disruption of serious consequence on the Burma-Siam railway. The ultimate result of this attack was that three spans were demolished and one span displaced.

184. Strategic bombing by the air forces of this Command drastically cut down the use of the enemy's railroads, compelling the transfer of more and more supplies to road and sea transport, which inevitably slowed up the enemy's war supply machine.

185. When the A.C.S.E.A. Command formed in December, 1943, our heavy bomber effort was only 449 tons dropped by Liberator aircraft. In 1944 the figure had risen to 3,846 tons, and by August, 1945, it had again risen to a total of 9,441 tons.

186. Behind these tonnages is evidence of the contribution by the heavy bomber aircraft of this Command to the overall strategy of the Supreme Allied Commander, South East Asia, in bringing about the disruption of Japanese supply and road, rail and sea communications.

AIR SUPPLY

A Testing Period for Squadrons During Monsoon.

187. Although the capture of Rangoon brought an end to the more intensive Army-Air co-operation in Burma, the day by day air supply for ground troops concentrated in Southern Burma, and still engaging large isolated forces of the enemy, was still maintained.

188. There was no alternative. Air supply, it was realised, would have to meet the Army's demands until seaborne supplies began to function, and road and rail communication inland from Rangoon were re-established.

189. Much was being done to hurry forward rehabilitation in Rangoon generally and to get port facilities working, but this was no easy task. Looting of property and bomb damage to those essential services which are the mainspring of a busy commercial port were extensive. Entry of larger ships into the harbour was also delayed until dredging of the river channel was completed, while there was the

additional task of repairing docks, wharves, and badly disrupted road and rail communications. All these were vital factors which indirectly affected supply to a vast Allied ground force which had pushed its way into Rangoon.

190. The period May to August, 1945 – covering the re-entry of the Allied forces into Rangoon, and later the surrender of Japan – cannot be termed spectacular in air supply operations, when reckoned against such efforts as persisted during the Allied advance down through Burma earlier in the year, and the supply tonnage record was broken in April, 1945, with 2,900 tons on one day. But it was, nevertheless, an exacting period for squadrons and personnel alike, for the following reasons:-

(a) The period of the monsoon had set in, making flying exceedingly hazardous in so mountainous a country as Burma.

(b) With the disintegration of the British and American Air Forces after 1st June, 1945, American Transports were withdrawn, leaving R.A.F. squadrons of No. 232 Group to continue air supply operations unaided.

(c) Supply demands made by H.Q. Allied Land Farces were not immediately reduced after entry into Rangoon. On the contrary, the Army persisted in a continuance of air supply on a scale which it was not always practicable to meet in face of atrocious weather and fewer available aircraft.

191. The departure of the American transport squadrons towards the end of May, 1945, resulted in a corresponding reduction in air supply to the ground forces. With hostilities in Burma virtually over, this was only to be expected. What air supply did not anticipate was the enormous concentration of Allied ground forces which had pushed into Rangoon at the last minute to ensure its speedy capture. These troops had still to be fed and supplied, as had the Allied ground forces engaging the remnants of the Japanese main Army trapped in the Pegu Yomas of Southern Burma as the result of the rapid Allied drive to Rangoon.

192. Throughout the campaign in Burma it had been the practice to pool the air resources for the mutual benefit of the British and American elements of Eastern Air Command. The result had been a building up of a balanced organisation known as Combat Cargo Task Force, capable of operating at an intensive rate of air supply.

193. The operational achievement of Combat Cargo Task Force, covering the period October,1944 (the date of its inception) to the end of May, 1945, when disintegration took place, is best indicated by the following figures:-

Total hours flown	386,283
Supplies carried (short tons)	332,136
Number of persons carried	339,137
Number of casualties carried	94,243
Total tonnage carried, including weight of persons and casualties	379,707

Forecast for Air Lift after Rangoon.

194. From the examination of results achieved during the advance through Burma, and the lessons learned, it was possible, in the middle of May, to agree that each transport squadron's effort as from 1st June, 1945 to 31st July, could be 125 hours per aircraft for the month. This demanded an effort of 156 hours per aircraft on the squadron strength.

195. A better flow of reinforcement aircraft was expected, which would thus greatly help towards making the new transport effort possible, also a stepping-up and increase in efficiency of maintenance organisation, with consequent increased monthly output and quicker turn-round of aircraft undergoing repair, was taking place.

196. On the assumption that two R.A.F. squadrons were made available for airborne training by 1st June, that internal airlines requirements were met, and that U.S.A.A.F. transport squadrons were all out of the Theatre from 10th June, it was calculated that the following transport aircraft would be available:-

1 – 10 June –
   8 R.A.F. Squadrons – 240 C-47
   4th C.C. Group   100 C-46
11 June – 31 July –
   8 R.A.F. Squadrons – 240 C-47

197. On such a basis, the capacity for the daily lift on long tons of squadrons was estimated as under:-

1 – 10 June –
   1,474 long tons
11 June – 31 July –
   800 long tons

198. This capacity measured against the Army's requirements of 14th May, 1945, showed the following situation in tons:-

	ALFSEA requirement	*Capacity to Deliver*
Period	tons	tons
1 – 8 June	1,310	1,474
9 – 10 June	1,070	1,474
11 – 18 June	1,070	880
19 June – 8 July	840	880
9 – 31 July	600	880

199. On calculation, therefore, a total surplus capacity of 2,120 tons existed from 1 – 10 June, and a deficiency of 1,520 tons from 11 – 18 June, giving a surplus airlift. The surplus airlift from 1 – 10 June, it was calculated, could be stock-piled to offset the deficiency from 11 – 18 June. From these calculations, therefore, it was considered that the transfer of the U.S.A.A.F. squadrons could be accepted without detriment to any foreseen operations. Unfortunately, a variety of factors militated against this target which had been so carefully planned.

Some Difficulties with the Army over Supply.

200. On 11th June, Advanced H.Q. A.L.F.S.E.A. signalled direct to the Supreme Allied Commander that the short fall in air transport for the first nine days in June totalled 955 long tons, and asked, therefore, for the retention of No. 238 Squadron already overdue to go to the Pacific.

201. I proceeded to Rangoon to discuss this matter more fully with Lieutenant General Sir Oliver Leese, C.-in-C, A.L.F.S.E.A. and Major-General Bastyan (Major-General Administration), A.L.F.S.E.A.

202. The Army had come fully briefed, and it was obvious that any detailed discussion in Rangoon without a full knowledge of all factors would place the Air Force at a disadvantage. Accordingly, I signalled Air Command to take all possible measures to lessen the short fall and, for this purpose, to allocate 22 additional Dakotas at once. Upon my return to Command, at Kandy, I held a full discussion on the problem.

203. The varied aspects of the problem are worth detailing since they illustrate the many links upon which air transport depended at the time, and also the strong disinclination of the Army to accept responsibility for breakdowns in air supply. Factors which had upset the air supply target planned in the middle of May included the following:-

    (*a*) The reinforcement flow had not been sufficient to equip the squadron up to a Unit Equipment of 24 plus 6 as planned and, in consequence, aircraft strength was 12 per cent. deficient.

    (*b*) Ramree airfield, which had been built by the Army for the express purpose of monsoon air supply operations, was often so waterlogged that aircraft could not get off.

    (*c*) There had been an epidemic of main bearing failures in Dakota aircraft engines which had caused an appreciable drop in serviceability; one squadron needed 26 new engines.

    (*d*) Although we had a margin of surplus lift available in May, the Army could not take advantage of it in June, owing to shortage of transport.

    (*e*) Army demands remained high because they could not withdraw sufficient troops through Rangoon due to shipping and communication difficulties.

204. It was decided to take the following steps:-

    (i) Inform B.A.F.S.E.A. that the allotment of 24 aircraft to each squadron was of the greatest urgency.

    (ii) Press the Army for better drainage of Ramree airfield.

    (iii) Transfer as soon as possible one or two transport squadrons from Ramree to Akyab.

(iv) Give the squadrons a target of 100 short tons per day. This was desirable, for it provided a goal that could be reached, and prevented the frustration that had so often been felt in the past at being given a target impossible of achievement. Any margin above the stated figure would be in the nature of a bonus and have a stimulating moral effect.

(v) Withdraw one of the two squadrons engaged from airborne training and employ it on transport. This would give a total of 810 long tons a day against the Army requirements of 880. The difference was so small that it could surely be made up by inland water transport or other means and would certainly entail no drastic cut in rations or amenities.

205. Even then, air transport problems were not solved. There were still in Burma tactical squadrons whose speedy withdrawal for refit and training in preparation for "Zipper/Mailfist" Operation could not be effected through the overloaded land and sea lines of communication. The only method of withdrawing these units in sufficient time was to fly them out. I decided, therefore, that such a task held priority over the airborne training 96 Squadron was accomplishing at that time, and accordingly I received the Supreme Allied Commander's agreement to 96 Squadron's temporary withdrawal to enable air lift to be provided for R.A.F. personnel and equipment of the units already mentioned.

Transport Preparations for "Zipper/Mailfist".

206. An important step was taken in July when I directed that Air Force representation should be made available for Army planning bodies in order to prevent the Army supply authorities from budgeting for airlift which could not possibly be met. By means of closer liaison it was hoped that the Army would make bids for air transport which would be practicable, so that there would be no need for the Air Forces to overwork their squadrons in order to make good the backlog. In addition, it was possible, in planning, to leave some airlift for domestic requirements such as the carriage of A.O.G. spares, etc.

207. For the coming months air transport commitments could be divided into the following categories:-

(i) The requirements of "Zipper/Mailfist" Operation.

(ii) The supply of 12th Army fighting in Burma.

(iii) The maintenance and expansion of internal airlines.

(iv) Continuance at a higher rate than hitherto of airborne training.

208. In order to meet requirement (i) it had been anticipated that there would be a sharp diminution in the supply of 12th Army in Burma as the port of Rangoon became cleared. It became apparent in the first week of July, however, that the requirements

of the Army in Burma were going to be very considerably in excess of the figures that had been estimated at the time when aircraft had been allocated for "Zipper/Mailfist."

209. A complete review of air transport plans was thus once again necessary. The Army suggestions for meeting the new situation were given in a signal from H.Q., A.L.F.S.E.A., which, however, could not be agreed. The Army was accordingly asked to await recommendations which would be available with all data at the next meeting of the Supreme Allied Commander, when the whole question of air transport requirements would be reviewed and priorities adjusted.

Hazards of Weather in Monsoon.

210. Weather was the one dominant factor which affected air supply operations throughout Burma after the breaking of the monsoon. It is no exaggeration to state that the transport aircraft, probably more than any other aircraft employed in the Burma Theatre, had to wage a day to day battle against the elements.

211. During the crucial months, while the Allied advance down through Central Burma was in progress, transport aircraft had been able to fly long hours, often in good weather, which greatly contributed to the successful completion of their commitment.

212. The proposition, however, was different in May, after the arrival of the monsoon. Not only did weather make flying hazardous and difficult, but it was frequently impossible for meteorological staffs to determine in advance what weather the transport aircraft were likely to encounter en route to their destination.

213. The monsoon in Burma is at its worst during June and July, when cumulo nimbus cloud, the greatest enemy of aircraft flying over Burma, builds up frequently from low level to above aircraft ceiling.

214. Comparing aircraft effectiveness in the monsoon months of June and July with that of February and March, 1945, it appeared that the effectiveness dropped to 70 per cent. As the average length of trip was less during June and July, however, the cargo tonnage carried per aircraft dropped only to 76.5 per cent. of the fine weather standard.

215. An indication of the monsoon's toll on aircraft and crews may be seen from the study of figures of losses for the month of June, 1945. During this period No. 232 Group lost 12 aircraft due to bad weather; casualties to crews and passengers inclusive of those killed, injured and missing totalling 72. This was a high price paid in men and material for the continued success of air supply in Burma.

216. It is on record that one Dakota aircraft flying over Burma actually found itself turned upside down in a storm, and it was only the skill and presence of mind of the pilot which averted disaster.

217. Yet another example of the hazards which faced transport supply crews in Burma during that monsoon was the experience of a pilot who found himself completely closed in with cumulo nimbus cloud during a return journey from Meiktila to Akyab. After three attempts, a break in the cloud was found which brought the aircraft out on to the coast opposite Ramree Island. The aircraft descended to 300

feet but cumulo nimbus again closed in behind, and the pilot, after making several unsuccessful attempts to climb out of the cloud, was eventually forced down to sea level. For almost an hour the aircraft circled around until the pilot finally succeeded in climbing to 7,000 feet where more cumulo nimbus was encountered and the radio compass was rendered unserviceable. The aircraft then turned on a reciprocal course and found a small gap in the cloud which again closed in. In the face of this predicament, the pilot decided there was no alternative but to descend and to risk a blind forced landing. The pilot succeeded in bringing the aircraft to a standstill in a paddy field without injury to any of the crew.

Stocking Rear Airfields with Supplies.

218. Most of the supplies carried by the R.A.F. Transport Squadrons in Burma after the departure of the American units were for the purpose of stocking rear airfields, where the Army organisations distributed the supply to various Army and R.A.F. units. Civil commitments also continued to be fulfilled in Northern Burma.

219. With the experience gained in June regarding the consumption of petrol required by C-47 aircraft for each trip during average monsoon flying conditions, squadrons located at Ramree, Akyab, and Chittagong were instructed to increase their load from 5,500 lb. to 6,000 lb.

220. In preparation for the final showdown with the trapped Japanese forces in Burma, during July, special instructions for supply dropping in the Toungoo area were issued. Weather, however, was again the big handicap, and as dropping operations were frequently impossible in this area, arrangements had to be made to land loads in Central Burma so as to form a stock-pile near the source of ground operations and later take advantage of periods of fine weather in which to deliver the backlog. This system made it unnecessary for aircraft to carry undropped supplies back to base, with a consequent increase in the number of hours required to deliver them. In the event of abortive trips producing a back log at Toungoo, aircrews were briefed to proceed to that area on supply dropping operations, after which the aircraft landed at Toungoo or Magwe and carried out second and possibly third trips before returning to base.

221. During the flare up in ground operations in the third week in July, when the break-through from the Pegu Yomas by the trapped Japanese forces began, air supply to the Allied ground forces engaging the Japanese assumed considerable importance until the battle had ended. Rainfall was widespread over the whole area of operations, and difficulties under which aircraft had to operate were acute. With exceedingly bitter fighting taking place, and thousands of Japanese troops pressing forward in their anxiety to escape, the state of the ground situation was ever fluid, and made the accurate dropping of supplies no easy task. Many of the dropping zones used, indeed, were less than 100 yards from local enemy forces and there were occasions when a dropping zone was surrounded by Japanese troops and some of the containers overshot the mark and fell into enemy hands. It speaks well for the aircrews trained in dropping supplies that more containers did not fall into the hands of the Japanese,

whose desperate plight during the previous two months was due to lack of air supply and to the fact that the enemy were cut off from their Headquarters and bases in Southern Burma and Siam by our land forces. Even in this last and major battle with the Japanese in Burma it was significant that air supply – of which the enemy had none – was one of the cardinal factors in assuring triumph for the Allied ground forces and disaster for the enemy. Air supply in Burma made history which outdistanced in merit and achievement the more publicised air supply operations of the war in Europe such as that of Arnhem, or the food dropping to the Dutch in Holland. These, without doubt, were important and commendable efforts in themselves, but they bore no comparison to the enormous and sustained efforts of transport aircrews who faced the hazards of monsoon weather.

End of the War Affects Air Supply Operations.

222. With the Japanese surrender in South East Asia in August, air supply operations to the Allied ground forces in Burma took on a new aspect in keeping with the new situation.

223. This did not mean that the commitment of the air supply squadrons would cease, or indeed, that fighting in Burma was entirely over. On the contrary, it was expected that in certain respects air supply commitments would increase. There could be no doubt, however, that the nature and the location of loads which would be carried, would greatly change. Evacuation of prisoners-of-war and internees, the "fly-in" of Allied ground forces to occupy large and vast territories held by the Japanese, were all commitments which faced the transport squadrons in South East Asia on the cessation of hostilities. Materiel of war, on the other hand – so important a cargo throughout the campaign in Burma – ceased to have a first priority. Movement of personnel, carriage of rations and civilian supplies replaced the transport of military supplies.

224. Operations of the transport squadrons during August fell into two distinct categories. The first half of the month, when Japan was still at war, supply operations continued much the same as on previous months. After 15th August, when surrender was announced, the situation became somewhat confused.

225. The supply tasks by aircraft during the first half of August were confined principally to the carrying of ammunition and petrol for the two most active areas of fighting in Burma – the Mawchi Road and the lower Sittang – where the remnants of the Japanese forces who had survived the July "Killing" were still holding out. There were, of course, other numerous and important supply tasks, the biggest of which was the stocking of airfields in Southern and Central Burma in preparation for the sustained effort which would be required once the assault on Malaya, under operation "Zipper", began.

226. One squadron during the first half of August had the sole task of taking food supplies to the civilian population of Northern Burma. This was an important commitment owing to the lack of other means of transport.

Operations to relieve Allied Prisoners of War.

227. With the Japanese surrender in the second half of August, there came orders for the move of six R.A.F. Transport squadrons to the Rangoon area to transport stores, and to evacuate Ps.O.W. from Siam, French Indo-China, Malaya and the Netherlands East Indies. As the result of these squadron moves, and the military situation at the time, the number of normal transport operations fell away very considerably. The majority of the trips, indeed, were concerned with moves by squadrons and the stocking up of the Rangoon airfields with provisions for the liberated territories and the P.O.W. Camps.

228. August 28th – the historic date on which Operation "Mastiff" was launched to bring relief to the thousands of Allied Ps.O.W. in the prison camps throughout the vast territories of South East Asia – saw the transport squadrons, as well as other aircraft of the Command, including those of the R.A.A.F., take part in what was described as "one of the greatest mercy missions of the war".

229. Many of the flights undertaken in these operations were equivalent to a Transatlantic flight, and yet 75 per cent. of the crews succeeded in reaching their targets and dropping their messages as well as parachuting medical supplies, Red Cross parcels and teams of medical and signalling personnel provided mainly by airborne formations. Later, many thousands of Ps.O.W. and internees were evacuated from these territories by air.

230. It is not difficult to visualise the plight, in which our Allied Ps.O.W. would certainly have found themselves after the official Japanese surrender, had not all resources, including Air Power, been used, and organised quickly, to bring relief, comfort and sustenance to these unfortunate men, many of them too weak to stand on their own legs. Only Air Power could have penetrated these vast territories throughout South East Asia with the speed required to initiate that essential relief. The pin-pointing of many Japanese P.O.W. camps, in addition to the great distances flown by aircraft and the hazards of weather encountered in these tropical regions, speaks magnificently for the navigational and flying skill of our aircrews.

231. The period, May to August, 1945 – covering the re-entry of the Allied Forces into Rangoon and later the surrender of Japan – cannot be termed spectacular in air supply operations when reckoned against such efforts during the Allied advance down through Burma earlier in the year, when the mobility of Fourteenth Army was almost entirely provided by the Allied Air Forces whose record supply tonnage averaged 2,900 tons per day in April, 1945.

232. The period, May to August, was not only the monsoon period but the period, with the exception of the July battle in Burma, during which the Allied Forces on ground, sea and in the air were building up their organisation and strength to deliver the next blow which would have fallen upon the Japanese in Malaya in early September. Nevertheless, the R.A.F. Transport supply squadrons met the demands required of them, and the supply effort for that period may be summarised as follows:-

	May	*June*	*July*	*August*	*Total*
Tactical Trips	7,998	7,211	8,258	3,779	27,246
Personnel Carried	7,795	2,321	3,017	4,651	17,784
Casualties Evacuated	3,899	2,515	2,044	1,514	9,972
Supplies Delivered (Short Tons)	23,172	19,978	22,170	9,418	74,738
Estimated Total (Short Tons)	23,951	20,210	22,472	9,883	76,516

CASUALTY EVACUATION

A Prominent Lesson which Emerged from the Campaign in Burma.

233. The great saving of lives and raising of morale due to air casualty evacuation was one of the main lessons which emerged from the Campaign in Burma.

234. This service was easily one of the best morale builders among Allied front-line troops. It inspired the fighting man's confidence and allayed any fears he may have had about being wounded, with the possibility of falling into the hands of the Japanese as a prisoner.

235. Air casualty evacuation, once it became known as the recognised method for dealing with serious cases by flying them out of the forward areas in Burma, was a triumph both for the Allied medical staffs and the aircrews alike. The Japanese had no air organisation for similar evacuation of their troops, and the low condition in which many enemy prisoners were found as a result of acute sickness in the jungle areas was, in itself, a contributory factor to their defeat.

236. The general policy was for supply aircraft to deliver supplies and take back from forward airfields on their return trips loads of casualties to the base hospitals, and the special centres established at Comilla, but when adverse landing conditions compelled supply by dropping, there were temporary difficulties in clearing casualties from Corps and Army medical centres. Austers and L.5 aircraft (Sentinels) were used in the Theatre with conspicuous success in the forward areas.

237. For the purpose of handling casualties from forward medical units and forward transport landing grounds, R.A.F. Casualty Air Evacuation Units were set up. These units were situated on the transport air strip covering a particular area. Emplaning of the casualties on to the aircraft was effected according to their degree of urgency for base hospital medical treatment. The average strength of a Casualty Air Evacuation Unit was 40 British other ranks, with a varied number of Indian personnel. Approximately 100 wounded could be staged at these C.A.E.U.s. for as long as was necessary. As many seriously wounded and sick personnel required medical attention whilst travelling in aircraft to base, an air ambulance orderly pool was established at base. This was composed of specially trained nursing orderlies who flew in all aircraft. It is noteworthy to record that these nursing orderlies flew as much as 200 hours a month. They carried with them complete first-aid equipment, including oxygen-giving apparatus. In the Burma Theatre, due to the mountainous

nature of the country, portable oxygen equipment proved to be essential in air casualty evacuation work, and its employment actually saved many lives.

238. The Casualty Air Evacuation Units in the forward areas were also responsible for the off-loading, treatment and conveyance of casualties received direct from the battle line in light aircraft such as the L.5. These aircraft proved invaluable in evacuating casualties from jungle clearances and small strips in the forward areas.

239. Air evacuation of casualties began in Burma in the opening months of 1944, when the Allied ground forces found themselves encircled in the Arakan, and later during the period of the Siege of Imphal. By September of that year, some 48,789 casualties had been evacuated by air, and as the months passed, and the campaign developed in intensity, the casualty evacuation figures steadily increased.

240. By the end of April, 1945 – three days before the fall of Rangoon – the total casualties evacuated by British and American aircraft in Burma was 110,761, of which 50,285 were evacuated by R.A.F. aircraft.

241. In the period May to August, 1945, the closing stages of the war against the Japanese, R.A.F. aircraft evacuated a total of 9,972 casualties.

242. That air casualty evacuation proved itself a triumph both from the point of view of morale and the lives saved, is undisputed. Perhaps more convincing is the fact that, throughout the campaign, only one death in the air among ground personnel evacuated was recorded, and only one aircraft, carrying 24 casualties, was lost due to weather.

243. H.Q. A.L.F.S.E.A. stated that air evacuation reduced mortality of wounded by 60 per cent.

American Experience in Casualty Evacuation.

244. Since American aircraft operated as part of the Allied Air Forces in the Theatre until integration in the Command ceased on 1st June, 1945, it is not inappropriate to mention something of the interesting experience of American L.5. aircraft employed in Burma in casualty evacuation and in other secondary important tasks associated with supply to the ground forces.

245. A special research report on evacuation of casualties from the forward areas in Burma which was produced in July, 1945 by Air/12G (Research) Headquarters, Allied Land Forces, South East Asia, described the work of two American squadrons operating L.5. aircraft with Fourteenth Army in the campaign.

The purpose of the report was:-

(*a*) To consider the best method of using L.5. aircraft for casualty evacuation in the light of the American experience.

(*b*) To estimate the number of aircraft required to evacuate the casualties from a Corps in action with varying degrees of battle activity.

246. Throughout the period considered in the report – November, 1944 to April, 1945 – the squadrons worked with 4 Corps and 33 Corps from a rear strip close to the Casualty Clearing Station. The squadrons of light aircraft were allotted on the basis

of one for each Corps of three Divisions. The C.C.S. was sited at the edge of the strip. Forward strips were made by the troops, and the location of the strips was signalled to the squadrons. A reconnaissance plane would fly over the site in the early morning and photograph the strip. If it was considered satisfactory for landing and take-off, the required number of aircraft flew out immediately.

247. During the Meiktila-Rangoon advance of 4 Corps, the number of strips constructed was greater than that during a corresponding period at any other time, yet none of the strips was refused by the squadrons. When the strips could be built more than 500 yards long, it was possible to evacuate two sitting cases in one sortie, but there were few opportunities for this.

248. All the squadron commanders understood their primary role to be casualty evacuation. But important secondary tasks were also performed. Except in the case of the fly-in of important medical supplies, these secondary tasks were never allowed to interfere with the evacuation of casualties.

249. The secondary tasks undertaken were:-

(*a*) The emergency flying-in of medical supplies, especially whole blood.

(*b*) Flying-in reinforcements, mail, food, ammunition and items of personal kit. These trips were always part of an evacuation sortie.

(*c*) Transporting V.I.Ps. within the Corps area.

(*d*) Spotting for artillery.

(*e*) Dropping and picking up messages.

(*f*) Reconnaissance flights.

250. The importance of the evacuation of casualties relative to other duties was, indeed, interesting. The total trips by one squadron over a given period of one month, when activity was intense, was 12,017 of which 9,238 were casualty evacuation flights, or 77 per cent. of the total, as against 2,779 secondary missions.

251. In an analysis of the secondary tasks undertaken by these aircraft, the flying-in of reinforcements proved exceedingly valuable, since these missions could be combined readily with the collection of a casualty, while most of the other missions could not. In various ten-day periods, for example, the total number of casualties evacuated was 7,705 as against 3,345 reinforcements flown in. The percentage of evacuated casualties which were replaced by reinforcements was therefore 43.

Evacuating Casualties from a Corps in Action.

252. For the peak period March, 1945, a squadron of 32 American light aircraft operated under 33 Corps.

253. During this period, all the cases required to be evacuated were taken out by air. No cases were evacuated by road or rail. The aircraft were based at Shwebo during the first half of the month and flew as far as Ondaw, 35 miles away. In the second half of the month, the aircraft were based at Ondaw and flew as far as Wundwin, 65

miles away. The numbers of ground forces evacuated and the hours flown in three ten-day periods were as follows:-

Date	Number Evacuated	Hours Flown
1 – 11 March	1,793	1,604
11 – 22 March	1,464	1,431
21 – 31 March	1,362	1,688
Total	4,619	4,723

Maximum distance between base and forward strip (miles)	65
Minimum distance between base and forward strip (miles)	35
Average per cent. aircraft in commission daily	96·7
Average number of aircraft in commission daily	30·6
Average number of hours flown per plane per day	5·2
Average number of hours flown per plane per month	153
Average number of cases evacuated per plane per day	5
Average number of hours flown per day	157
Average number of cases evacuated per day	154
Maximum number of flying hours a pilot a day	9

254. The above achievement by this squadron was a record for the American squadrons in the Group. The effort was believed to be near the maximum which any squadron could reach in similar circumstances.

255. During the period some of the pilots flew for nine hours a day for five consecutive days, and made up seven sorties in one day on several occasions. This intensification of activity for short periods could not have been achieved without the very high level of maintenance attained, nor could it have been exceeded without putting too great a strain on the pilots or replacing some of the aircraft. Three of the pilots had to be replaced before the end of the operation owing to exhaustion, and 14 aircraft had to be replaced when the squadron came out. The deterioration of the engines, however, cannot be ascribed simply to this operation, as the aircraft had had three months of operations before operating with 33 Corps. The Squadron Commander, it was interesting to note, considered that the factor limiting the monthly carrying capacity of a squadron was the ability of the pilots, rather than that of aircraft, to withstand the strain of intense activity. Few of the pilots in question could have remained efficient if the squadron had attempted to carry on for longer than six weeks at the same level of activity.

Maximum Monthly Carrying Capacity of L.5 Aircraft.

256. While the average daily number of cases evacuated per aircraft was 5, some of the aircraft actually exceeded this number, while some failed to reach it. On the other hand, had all aircraft been used to the same extent as those which flew more than the average for the whole squadron, the average daily number evacuated would have been six, or 180 for the squadron of 30 aircraft. This figure was agreed upon by the Squadron Commander, who estimated that the maximum daily carrying capacity of

a single squadron of light aircraft was 180 and the maximum monthly capacity 6,000. This, of course, was based on the maximum distance of 65 miles between the rear and forward strips.

257. The situation was somewhat altered in the instance of 4 Corps' advance down the Meiktila-Rangoon road in April, 1945, when an American light aircraft squadron was evacuating cases from Toungoo to Meiktila for a short period. The distance involved was 330 miles for a whole sortie, and the flight lasting approximately four and a half hours. This meant that it was not possible to evacuate more than two cases per plane per day for more than a total of 60 casualties per day for the whole squadron. It was interesting to note in this connection, however, that 4 Corps' rate of advance in April was approximately 14 miles per day. While the distances flown by light aircraft engaged on casualty evacuation were correspondingly great, the squadron was nevertheless well able to handle all cases, because ground casualties were very light.

258. Altogether the data derived as a result of the operational experience of these light aircraft in Burma suggests that one squadron of 32 L.5 aircraft is sufficient to evacuate all the cases requiring evacuation from the forward areas of a Corps of three Divisions, provided the average daily number of cases does not exceed 180 and the average distance flown is not greater than 60 miles per trip (120 miles per round sortie). One other important proviso, of course, is that we have air superiority and that there is no prolonged heavy fighting with an exceedingly high sickness rate.

GENERAL RECONNAISSANCE.

A Period of Great Versatility for G.R. Aircraft.

259. When the period under review opened, offensive general reconnaissance had become effectively established as the primary operational function of air-sea power in this Theatre. The opening weeks of 1945 had incontestably indicated an entire absence of enemy U-boats throughout the vast expanses of the Indian Ocean, and pointed to the urgent need for alternative employment. Thus evolved the plan for an intensive anti-shipping campaign to disrupt the enemy's sea transport in and around the waters of the Andaman Sea. Four months of vigorous anti-shipping strikes and carefully planned air-sea mining operations revealed that these tactics were greatly harassing the enemy, and an intensification of offensive general reconnaissance was rightly considered a remunerative policy to pursue.

260. Although the primary operational role of 222 Group in May 1945 was that of sinking and immobilising the enemy's shipping, it must be borne in mind that there were continued and increasing commitments in the spheres of photographic reconnaissance, meteorological flights and air-sea rescue. I had, in fact, delegated the responsibility for the organisation and control of air-sea rescue operations and units to Air Marshal Commanding 222 Group as from 1st April, 1945, for the whole of South East Asia Command. Moreover, there was always the possibility that the enemy might recommence his U-boat warfare with renewed vigour, and the G.R. forces under my control had always to be prepared for such a contingency.

Developing the Anti-Shipping Campaign.

261. With the re-occupation of Rangoon on May 3rd, 1945, it became possible to establish a new and invaluable base from which to develop the anti-shipping campaign in more easterly waters. Sunderland aircraft of 230 Squadron (relieved in July by a detachment of 209 Squadron, similarly equipped) operating from the depot ship S.S. "Manela" under the operational control of 346 Wing were able to spread their tentacles over the areas of the Tenasserim Coast, Kra Isthmus, Gulf of Siam and South China Seas, adding confusion and perplexity to the enemy with their constant armed reconnaissance and timely attacks wherever suitable targets presented themselves.

262. As a counterpart to this newly established base of Rangoon in the north, the development of Cocos Island in the south constituted an equally important strategic base

for similar operations off the west coast of Sumatra, the south coast of Java and the Sunda Straits. No. 321 Squadron, equipped with Liberators (Mark VI), commenced operating a detachment of six aircraft from Cocos Island on July 22nd, 1945.

263. No. 354 Liberator Squadron, which had initiated the offensive anti-shipping strike aspect of the campaign in early February, disbanded on 15th May, 1945. No. 203 Liberator Squadron, however, which had commenced strike operations on 20th March, 1945, continued its programme of incessant and forceful attack over the Andaman Sea, Straits of Malacca, Gulf of Siam, Java Sea, Bangka Strait and off the west coast of Sumatra until the cessation of hostilities. This squadron was based at Kankesanturai (North Ceylon) but frequently operated detachments from Akyab, Ramree and Cocos Island under adverse conditions.

264. The paramount problem of the shipping strike operations was the lack of forward bases. Liberator aircraft had been operating from bases far removed from this scene of operations, and the period of patrol in the operational area was inevitably curtailed, thus detracting from the efficacy of the sorties. Furthermore, flying-boat facilities at Rangoon were inadequate, and prevented the Sunderlands from being used to the fullest operational capacity. For example, there were no slipway or beaching facilities, so that it was impossible for flying-boats to undertake operations likely to cause severe damage to their hulls. Neither the Sunderland nor the Liberator aircraft is ideal for low-level shipping attacks, but the nature of the operation and existing conditions demanded long-range aircraft and these were the only types available.

265. It is interesting to note that Liberator aircraft of Nos. 203 and 354 Squadrons carried out a series of long-range sea reconnaissance patrols during May 13th-19th which proved invaluable in the location and eventual destruction on May 16th of the Japanese heavy cruiser "HAGURO" in the Straits of Malacca by H.M. Naval forces. (26th Destroyer Flotilla – Captain M.L. Power, C.B.E., D.S.O., in H.M.S. "SAUMAREZ".)

266. Having regard to the many and varied complexities of conducting strike operations within this vast theatre of operations, such as the unfortunate paucity of

air bases, the irremediable problem of distance and the unsuitability of aircraft, my G.R. Air Forces achieved results both impressive and commendable. The enemy's shipping sustained considerable blows at a time when every ship in his possession was of vital importance. When the war came to an abrupt conclusion, offensive general reconnaissance was getting into its stride. Had hostilities continued, past experience permits an optimistic speculation in connection with the heavy toll general reconnaissance would have taken of Japanese sea transport, particularly on the shipping routes between Batavia and Singapore.

Air-Sea Mining as Part of the Campaign.

267. Mine-laying operations were planned as an essential part of the anti-shipping campaign, to be executed concurrently with the more directly offensive anti-shipping strikes programme. Initially, it was planned to lay mines during the hours of darkness in the shipping lanes of Northern Sumatra and Northern Malaya, and 160 Squadron (Liberators Mk.V.) underwent an intensive period of training in long range flying and the technique of mine-laying to implement these plans. They commenced these operations on 21st January, 1945 and continued until 24th May – a period of 124 days during which 196 sorties were flown. After operational experience had been gained, the mining commitments were increased to include drops in the areas of Sonchkla, Chumborn, Port Swettenham and Singapore. Mine-laying operations were discontinued after 24th May, 1945, because the stage was then being finally set for Operation "Zipper", and to have continued mine-laying beyond that date might have had serious repercussions when Allied landings took place on the west coast of Malaya.

268. It is difficult, if not impossible, to assess accurately and fully, the damage and inconvenience caused to the enemy by these particular operations. The strategy employed was to mine a number of different and well separated targets at frequent intervals so as to cause the enemy the greatest possible inconvenience in constantly deploying his inadequate force of mine sweeping craft over a large area. It is reasonable to assume that many thousands of tons of enemy shipping were immobilised at a time when they could ill be spared, and the task of constant mine-sweeping must have been heart-breaking if not overwhelming. Whatever the material achievements of these operations, it must be added that the programme was extremely well-conceived and well executed.

Employment of General Reconnaissance Aircraft on Special Duty Operations.

269. The year of final and complete victory in South East Asia Command was a period of strenuous re-orientation for G.R. Air Forces. With the Indian Ocean no longer a hunting ground for enemy U-boats, the days of vigilant defensive warfare had passed, and it became essential to re-model the defensive Air Forces into a strong and penetrating arm of offence with which to sever the enemy's sea communications. (The broad strategy of general reconnaissance in the Indian Ocean had always been concerned with the passive protection of shipping rather than the hunting of U-boats

– a strategy rendered inevitable by the enormous expanse of water to be reconnoitered and the inadequate number of aircraft and few advance bases at our disposal.)

270. Unfortunately, it was impossible to devote our entire G.R. resources to the execution of this offensive plan, for there were more urgent operational demands to be satisfied, and general reconnaissance aircraft could be quickly and satisfactorily diverted to the rescue. When mine-laying operations ceased, it was envisaged that 160 Squadron, together with Nos. 8 and 356 Squadrons, would reinforce the shipping strike campaign, but the growing requirements of the S.D. organisation absorbed these squadrons to the detriment of offensive general reconnaissance. The effort of G.R. aircraft operating in the S.D. role does not properly belong to this chapter, but rather to that of S.D. operations as a whole. Suffice it is to say here that these squadrons acquitted themselves in a creditable fashion, and manifested once again the comparative ease with which Air Power can be moulded into different forms or styles to meet the changing requirements.

271. Towards the end of the war, No. 222 Group had become responsible for the operational control of some six squadrons engaged on S.D. operations, with the result that the functional and administrative experience gained therefrom provided the Command with a competent and well-versed organisation for the vital and intricate operations immediately following the end of the war. No. 222 Group also played a large and important part in Operations "Birdcage" and "Mastiff", for the requirements of these operations were in many ways similar to those of S.D.

272. The achievements of general reconnaissance aircraft engaged upon the relief and liberation of Allied prisoners-of-war, are recorded in the appropriate chapter. It was a satisfying conclusion to the history of general reconnaissance in the Indian Ocean – a history of dexterous and highly competent adaptation to the many and varied exigencies of an immense and complicated theatre of war.

SPECIAL DUTY OPERATIONS.

An Integral Part in the War Strategy of South East Asia.

273. Operations by S.D. aircraft of my Command contributed very materially to the success of the highly organised guerilla forces of this Theatre which, themselves, were an integral part of the strategy of the Supreme Allied Commander, South East Asia.

274. In the initial stages, S.D. operations were primarily in support of our own forces operating in the enemy-occupied territories, concerning which our Intelligence from ground sources was exceedingly scarce. In the closing stages of the war, however, operations by aircraft in introducing personnel to the Japanese occupied areas of Burma, Siam, French Indo-China, Malaya, Sumatra and Singapore Island, and supplying them as well as the guerilla formations under their control, grew to proportions which called for the maximum effort of aircraft and crews engaged on this special work. Indeed the true picture was that our Liberator position in the Command was exceedingly tight, since the S.D. effort was carried out largely by this type of aircraft.

275. By May, 1945, guerilla organisations in the Theatre had become firmly established, so much so, that the Burmese Guerillas played a prominent part with our Air and Ground Forces in the killing of ten thousand Japanese troops during an attempted mass escape from the Pegu Yomas in July.

276. A brief account of their activities in co-operation with the Tactical Air Forces is covered in another chapter.

Control of the Guerilla Organisations.

277. The control of the Guerilla Organisations in this Theatre was vested in the Supreme Allied Commander, South East Asia, with a branch, known as "P" Division, which delegated part of its functions to special staff officers at various lower formations.

278. Guerilla operations in South East Asia took on an entirely different character from the work of the underground forces in Europe, where patriots speedily organised themselves as a resistance movement. In South East Asia the sympathies of Asiatics had first to be won over to our cause by special agents and leaders, and parties of guerillas organised among the local inhabitants and often fanatical hill tribesmen. Aircraft made flights of 2,000 and 3,000 miles regularly on these expeditions for on aircraft almost entirely did the build-up of these secret forces depend.

279. Briefly, the Guerilla Organisations operating in the Theatre were as follows:-

   (*a*) *Force* 136. This was a British Organisation mainly responsible for raising, training, arming and controlling guerilla forces and sabotage teams. It also had a tactical intelligence role and operational control of "Z" Force which had a more limited but similar function.

   (*b*) *O.S.S.* The American Officers of Strategic Services had a similar object to that of Force 136, and also collected and distributed strategic intelligence.

   (*c*) *I.S.L.D.* The Inter-Service Liaison Department was a British Organisation and was concerned mainly with the collection and distribution of strategic intelligence from many sources.

280. In addition to the above, there were also miscellaneous organisations which had guerilla functions, and sometimes called upon Special Duty aircraft to assist them.

Allied Air Force Units Involved.

281. Liberators, Dakotas, Catalinas, Lysanders and L.5 (Sentinels) were used for the S.D. operations. The principal units employed were:-

   (i) *No. 357 Squadron.* This squadron was the one permanent complete S.D. squadron in this Theatre. It consisted of 10 Liberators, 10 Dakotas and a detached flight of up to 10 Lysanders. The role of the Lysanders was the infiltration and withdrawal of men and mail by landing in enemy territory. The Dakotas were also available for similar landings, as well as for parachute operations.

(ii) *No. 240 Squadron.* This G.R. Catalina squadron included three Catalinas for Special Duty Operations in alighting in enemy waters. These Catalinas were also capable of minor parachute operations.

(iii) *No. 358 Squadron.* This heavy bomber squadron was transferred indefinitely from 231 Group to the S.D. role, and consisted of 16 Liberators which were modified to S.D. standards.

(iv) 10*th U.S.A.A.F.* Until the withdrawal by the American Army Air Forces from the Command on 1st June, 1945, a proportion of the effort of the 10th U.S.A.A.F., by arrangement with the O.S.S., was allocated to S.D. operations.

(v) *Tactical Groups.* By local arrangements between the Guerilla Organisations and No. 221 Group, Tactical squadrons sometimes carried out S.D. operations authorised by the Group Headquarters.

(vi) *S.D. Air/Sea Rescue Operations.* Special Duty Air/Sea Rescue operations were carried out from time to time by A.S.R. Catalinas under the control of No. 222 Group. These operations were concerned with installing dumps of foodstuffs and equipment for missing aircrews on coasts in enemy waters, and were arranged by "E" Group.

282. As the S.D. squadrons during the closing stages of the war in South East Asia were operating regularly at an intensive rate of effort on these missions, other units were also brought in to supplement the S.D. work.

Planning of S.D. Air Operations.

283. The training of aircrews and army personnel to the R.A.F. standards took as high priority as the operations themselves. Where practicable, and when the Guerilla Organisations agreed, the training of army personnel and aircrews was combined. This was particularly essential during training for night landing operations on enemy territory, and for ground-to-air special radar and signals equipment.

284. It was estimated that a sustained rate of five successful sorties per aircraft per month could be maintained by an S.D. squadron of twelve aircraft, giving a total of sixty sorties per month. Generally, planning did not exceed more than fifty sorties per month, in view of the maintenance difficulties, the extremely long sorties which had to be flown, and the fact that the Guerilla Organisations might not have continuous operations in hand. While it was possible to carry out the majority of the operations over Malaya with safety during daytime, or under last light conditions, it was not considered wise to make these flights in daylight in the immediate vicinity of Singapore.

285. The three principal home bases for the S.D. operations were at Jessore in Bengal, Minneriya in Ceylon, and later the Cocos Islands. The operations from the Cocos did not begin until mid-July, when sorties were flown to all parts of Malaya.

From Bengal, the S.D. operations were principally over Burma and French Indo-China, but flights were also made deep into Malaya, one aircraft logging twenty hours thirty-nine minutes for one of its sorties.

Operations Increased for Malaya.

286. The strategic plan for the assault on Malaya called for an even greater effort by the S.D. squadrons based in Ceylon. By July, the underground forces had been so organised by our personnel, and supplied with arms and equipment to such proportions, that they constituted a very real threat to isolated garrisons of Japanese troops. The time was considered opportune to foster and galvanise these organisations into a formidable, fighting force to harass the enemy at the time of our own landings in Malaya. For this purpose, therefore, it was decided to use heavy bomber aircraft, based on the Cocos Islands, to supplement the S.D. operations into Southern Malaya, and to employ these aircraft on the first ten nights of the July and August moon periods. These operations were controlled by Headquarters, No. 222 Group. Aircraft airborne from the Cocos Islands were routed in daylight through the gap in the Sumatra mountain range between 1° North and 2° North, and carrying a payload of 5,000 lbs. In this way, approximately 75 per cent. of the Malayan dropping zones was covered.

287. In order to carry out very long range S.D. operations within the Command with worthwhile payloads, Liberators at one time were operating with an all-up-weight (a.u.w.) of 66,000 lbs. This had paid a great dividend in establishing links with the underground forces in Malaya.

288. To keep the a.u.w. within the margin of safety, however, and at the same time carry the maximum payloads, it was necessary, on occasion, to cut the amount of extra petrol carried to the irreducible minimum; to strip aircraft of non-essential equipment, and to carry only essential crews.

289. In the weeks immediately preceding the Allied landings on Malaya, a considerable weight of weapons, ammunition and concentrated food was dropped to thousands of organised guerillas, together with trained guerilla leaders.

290. The operational records of the aircraft engaged on S.D. operations in the Command show that aircraft of No. 222 Group alone flew nearly 11,000 hours between May and September, 1945. The Cocos squadrons, although not altogether fully experienced in S.D. work, speedily established an enviable reputation for accurate dropping. When it is realised, too, that the sorties carried out by Catalina aircraft entailed, for the most part, night landings on enemy waters in varying conditions of sea, without benefit of flare-path, some idea is gained of the high skill required from these R.A.F. pilots.

291. The sudden end of the war in South East Asia did not conclude the tasks of the S.D. squadrons, but brought instead a new series of commitments under Operation "Mastiff" for the relief and liberation of Allied prisoners-of-war, an aspect which is dealt with in a later chapter of this despatch.

Outstanding Operations by Lysander Aircraft.

292. Any report or narrative on S.D. operations would be far short of completeness without mention of the magnificent work done by light aircraft, notably Lysanders. The untiring efforts of Lysander pilots, indeed, greatly assisted Force 136 to carry on their activities behind the enemy lines during the drive through Burma, and I feel justified in singling them out for especial mention.

293. Particularly outstanding work was done by the Lysander Flight of 357 Squadron. Not only were personnel infiltrated, but seriously wounded personnel were evacuated from the field. In addition to the urgent operational stores flown in, commitments had included transport of Staff Officers to Party Commanders in the field, and the evacuation of enemy prisoners-of-war and documents.

294. The versatility of the flight had increased with each operation. Sorties often necessitated flying in foul monsoon weather and landing on very small strips. On one occasion a landing was attempted at Ntilawathihta, near the Papun-Momaung Road, on a very short strip and on wet and slippery grass. The aircraft slid into a deep ditch at the end of the strip, but escaped with negligible damage. In attempts to extricate the aircraft, lumber elephants would not go near, but the combined efforts of fifty local inhabitants eventually succeeded in hauling the plane back on to the strip; the pilot then flew back to base.

295. On many occasions Lysander sorties came near to failure owing to the presence of Japanese troops in the area. Force 136 nearly always had to cover the landing area for fear of surprise by Japanese patrols.

296. On another occasion, a pilot was involved in a skirmish between Japanese troops and Force 136 Guerillas at Lipyekhi, when his aircraft failed to start for the return journey to Rangoon. Firing took place across the strip, but the aircraft escaped damage. It was rendered serviceable next day by a rescue sortie, and was able to return to base.

297. Another escapade was accomplished when Squadron Leader Turner, Flight Commander, damaged his Lysander in an attempt to pick up personnel at Ngapyawdaw, near Kinmun. Shortly after he had landed, the neighbourhood was compromised by Japanese forces and repair of the aircraft was impossible. Attempts to rescue Squadron Leader Turner were abortive until ten days later when a rescue aircraft made a well-timed evacuation. In the meantime, the Flight Commander stayed with Force 136 Guerillas.

The Advantages of the Lysander Aircraft.

298. The advantages of the Lysander for the unique type of work it was called upon to carry out were as follows:-

    (i) Weight lifting capacity.

    (ii) Automatic flap action, meeting all the conditions of flight, e.g. a sudden loss of lift in a sudden violent turn or in conditions of turbulence over the hills.

(iii) Capability of cruising at low speed in conditions of bad visibility.

(iv) High rate of turn, of great value in confined spaces.

(v) Fixed undercarriage, strong and able to stand the shocks of heavy landings.

(vi) High engine power and light wing loading, facilitating quick take-off from waterlogged strips, and an immediate high rate of climb.

(vii) Reasonable flying endurance of aircraft, the pilot never being embarrassed in a difficult operation by shortage of fuel.

299. But even with these advantages, the technique required of the Lysander pilots was one of skill, particularly when landing on very small strips. On such occasions the normal approach speed of 85 m.p.h. had to be reduced to 70 m.p.h., and a precision touchdown at the very beginning of the strip, with throttle promptly closed, had to be accomplished.

300. From May, 1945, to October, 1945, 357 Squadron Lysanders flew no less than 1,310 hours. 405 sorties were attempted and 363 of these were successful. Personnel infiltrated had numbered 214, and evacuations.

330. In addition, some 104,580 lbs. of stores were landed behind the enemy lines.

301. A fitting tribute to the Lysander operations was paid by Headquarters, Group "A" of Force 136 on 23rd June, 1945.

PHOTOGRAPHIC RECONNAISSANCE

A Record of Achievement Built on Perseverance of Crews.

302. Photographic reconnaissance has come out of the South East Asia Theatre with a record of achievement built upon the perseverance of its air crews to master the difficulties of climate and terrain. A flight of 2,600 miles in nine hours five minutes was one of the longest flights ever done in P.R.

303. The radius of P.R. cover in December, 1943, when the Command was formed, was not more than 680 miles, since long range reconnaissance by Mosquitos was only in process of being attempted in the coverage of the Andaman Islands from Comilla and, a little later, of Bangkok in Siam. When the war with Japan ended in August, 1945, the range of P.R. aircraft in South East Asia Command was such that coverage of the Andaman and Nicobar Islands from Ceylon, flights deep into Siam and French Indo China from Rangoon, and a detailed coverage of targets in Sumatra, Southern Malaya, Singapore and Java by aircraft based on the Cocos Islands, had become normal routine.

304. The Mosquito indeed made amends for the structural defect which had curtailed its use in this Command, for it set up two records in 1945. Firstly, a Mosquito XVI broke the long distance record on March 22 for this type of aircraft in any theatre of war, with a flight of 2,493 miles in eight hours forty-five minutes, covering the Bangkok-Singapore railway to a point south of the Malayan frontier. This performance, however, was eclipsed by a Mosquito XXXIV based on the Cocos

Islands, which on 20th August, 1945, flew 1,240 miles to Penang Island and then went on to cover Taiping town and airfield at 17,000 feet. On the return home a survey run was made on the K8/12-inch camera. This was the longest P.R. flight to be made in the Command, and covered a total of 2,600 miles in nine hours five minutes.

Photographic Survey of Burma.

305. Possibly the two most outstanding contributions by photographic reconnaissance to the war in South East Asia were its survey photography of Burma at the beginning of 1944, and its detailed coverage of enemy occupied territories after the fall of Rangoon in May, 1945, in preparation for the large scale assault on Malaya.

306. The survey photography of Burma fulfilled a long-felt want by supplying accurate and up-to-date maps of Burma which were practically non-existent up to this time – the Air Force and Army having to use 1914-15 ground surveys which, as photographic reconnaissance proved, showed major errors. The new survey of Burma was one of the best examples of R.A.F. assistance to the Army in this Theatre.

307. Faced with the urgent and extensive programme of photographic reconnaissance in Malaya and Sumatra for Operation "Zipper" a detachment of 684 Squadron (Alipore) commenced operations from the Cocos Islands in July, 1945, with four Mk. XXXIV Mosquitos which had just been released for service use in temperate and tropical climates. The P.R. programme for "Zipper" went steadily forward and, by the end of July, was 60 per cent. completed. A second detachment of 684 Squadron Mosquitos was operating at this time from China Bay, Ceylon, for the coverage of the Andaman and Nicobar Islands.

P.R. organisation after fall of Rangoon.

308. At the time of Rangoon's capture in May, 1945, the Photographic Reconnaissance Force was commanded by Colonel Minton W. Kaye, United States Army Air Force, with Group Captain S.G. Wise, D.F.C., as Assistant Air Commander.

309. The Force controlled two R.A.F. Squadrons, No. 681 (Spitfires) and No. 684 (Mosquitos), while the Americans had a P.38 (F.5) Squadron, a P.40, and a B.24 Mapping Squadron. The American Units, however, had completed their task as a P.R. integrated force in the Command and, after carrying out a few P.R. sorties at the beginning of May, they then retired to prepare for withdrawal to China with the remainder of the American Air Forces in the Theatre. The two R.A.F. squadrons, therefore, were left to operate on their own.

310. It became apparent, after the fall of Rangoon, that Photographic Reconnaissance in the Command would have to be endowed with a mobility which would allow it to move forward with the tide of battle. Accordingly, No. 347 P.R. Wing, which was formed in April, became effective as a formation in May, 1945. The new Wing Headquarters absorbed all of the R.A.F. element of the Photographic Reconnaissance Force and certain sections of the Station Headquarters at Alipore and Bally (India), where the two R.A.F. Squadrons of Spitfires and Mosquitos were based.

311. In May, No. 684 Squadron continued to be based at Alipore, but No. 681 Squadron moved to Mingaladon, Rangoon and flew most of their sorties in support

of the Twelfth Army's mopping up operations along the Mawchi Road, the Sittang Bend and the road and river communications between Pegu and Moulmein.

312. On 9th June, 1945, the Wing passed to the Command of Group Captain C.E. St. J. Beamish, D.F.C

Working against the Monsoon in Operational Areas.

313. Bad weather was the enemy which photographic reconnaissance had to combat almost continuously. Only by dint of sheer perseverance were many of the most important covers accomplished.

314. With the arrival of the Monsoon in May over the operational areas in Southern Burma and Siam, coverage from a photographic point of view became extremely difficult and flying more hazardous.

315. The inter-tropical front appeared at the Isthmus of Kra and moved as far north as Mergui, but generally it kept more to the south. By the end of May, weather deteriorated considerably and the Monsoon entered into its own for the season.

316. While Spitfires, based in Southern Burma, were able to take advantage of local weather conditions for short P.R. sorties in support of the Army, the task was more difficult, long range Mosquitos undertaking many flights of more than 2,000 miles for each sortie. More than one aircraft on occasions returned to base with torn fabric and other evidence of severe climatic conditions.

317. In August, with the weeks drawing near for the assault on Malaya, No. 2 Mosquito Detachment of 684 Squadron (based on the Cocos Islands), succeeded in flying 282 operational hours with only four crews. Some of the beach targets necessary for operation "Zipper" were exceedingly exacting, since photography had to be done at low tide in order to secure a full picture of the state and condition of beaches in preparation for the landings.

318. Intimation of Japan's surrender was the signal for P.R. to work at greater pressure than ever. The "Zipper" programme, which was all but complete, was cancelled, and a new programme substituted entailing cover, three times a fortnight, by P.R. aircraft of all important targets ranging from Penang Island to Sourabaja in Java. It is worth noting that P.R. aircraft, during this period of uncertainty among Japanese units regarding their country's surrender, met with more opposition than at any other time. At Palembang, pilots reported that enemy A.A. fire was intense.

319. Probably the most outstanding P.R. sortie from a general and humane interest at this time was that undertaken by a pilot of 681 Squadron (Spitfires) when covering prisoner-of-war camps in the Kanchana Buri area of Siam, ten days after the declaration of Japan's surrender. Prisoners at one of the camps were crowded together and swarming over the watch towers, waving and cheering to the pilot of the aircraft. Signs were also laid on the ground, including a giant Union Jack to indicate to the pilot that the prisoners also knew of events which had caused excitement in the world outside.

PART III.
THE SURRENDER OF JAPAN.

THEATRE BOUNDARIES AND DEPLOYMENT OF AIR FORCES DECIDED AT MANILA CONFERENCE.

320. August, 1945 saw the war against Japan move with over-whelming speed towards its culmination.

321. Throughout the war, research in Britain, America and Germany had pursued the possibility of harnessing to war the potentialities of atomic energy, and the first atomic bombs were dropped with devastating effect on metropolitan Japan at Hiroshima and Nagasaki on 5th and 9th August, 1945, respectively. Adding further to the plight of Japan was the declaration of war by Russia on 8th August, followed by Soviet Forces crossing the Manchurian and Korean borders.

322. From these momentous events, and faced with certain Allied invasion of the homeland, for which air power had paved the way, Japan could see no escape. The end came in the form of surrender, which was broadcast from Tokio on 10th August, and the acceptance of the Allied terms on 14th August.

323. As the result of the Japanese intimation that they were prepared to discuss and to receive surrender terms, the Supreme Allied Commander, South East Asia, directed that a Mission representing himself and his three Commanders-in-Chief should be despatched to Manila in the Philippines. The primary object of this Mission was to discuss the terms of surrender with General MacArthur and his staff, with a view to co-ordinating measures to be adopted to implement the terms of surrender both in the South West Pacific area and in South East Asia.

324. As my representative on this Mission, I selected Air Commodore W.A.D. Brook, C.B.E., Deputy Senior Air Staff Officer. Other members of the Mission which left Kandy by York on 16th August, refuelling at Calcutta en route, and continuing the flight by night over enemy occupied territory, were:-

Major-General Penney, S.A.C.'s representative. Head of the Mission, and also representing C.-in-C, A.L.F.S.E.A.
Vice-Admiral C. Moody, representing C.-in-C, E.I.F.
Colonel Mitford-Slade, representing J.P.S., S.A.C.S.E.A.
Colonel Bull, representing J.P.L.C., S.A.C.S.E.A.
Lieut.-Colonel Maugham, representing Intelligence Branch, S.A.C.S.E.A.
Lieut-Commander Galley, R.N., Flag Lieutenant to Admiral Moody.
2nd Officer Price, W.R.N.S., Secretary to the Mission.

325. The Mission arrived at Manila shortly after dawn on 17th August. The return journey, following the same route, was completed on 21st August, crossing occupied territory once again by night.

Political Situation at Time of Surrender.

326. At the time of the S.A.C.S.E.A. Mission's arrival at Manila, the visit of the Japanese Mission to obtain the surrender terms was still awaited. It was thought that

some delay might have occurred arising out of the political confusion in Japan and the lack of communication facilities generally as the result of continuous and heavy bombing.

327. The general opinion in the South West Pacific Area appeared to be that the South East Asia Command Theatre was being far too precipitate in implementing the surrender terms which had not yet been agreed by the contracting parties. Furthermore, General MacArthur was adamant that any implementation of the surrender terms could only take place after the surrender terms had been formally agreed and signed by the Japanese Government either at Tokio or on board a ship in adjacent waters. This, it was calculated, would be at least a week after the presentation of the Allied terms to be collected by the Japanese Mission to Manila, to whom certain points would need clarification.

328. The Japanese Mission consisting of some eight Japanese officers arrived at Manila on the evening of August 19th, having flown in two Betty Bombers from Japan to Okinawa where they had transferred to a C.54. The Mission was led by Lt.-Gen. Kawaba Takashiro, Vice Chief of the Imperial General Staff. Altogether, the representatives were a dejected looking gathering of very small men, clad in shabby and ill-fitting uniforms. They were treated with respect and allowed to wear their swords throughout their visit – an uncomfortable privilege, as each member was carrying a sword nearly as tall as himself. The members of the Mission were housed in the same building as the S.A.C.S.E.A. Mission – a partially repaired building in which they were granted the hospitality of the top floor, the least repaired of all. After a brief meal on arrival they were summoned to a conference at G.H.Q. where they were presented with the terms of surrender for explanation and transmission to their Government. On their part, they provided full details of their Order of Battle, strength of garrisons and the necessary information regarding Prisoner-of-War camps in various Theatres.

329. The Japanese Mission returned to Okinawa from Manila at midday on 20th August. No untoward events occurred during their visit to the Philippines, but such was the mixture of feeling within their own country at that time regarding the peace terms that they were shot at by their own fighters when leaving Japan for Okinawa. A similar reception was contemplated on their return to Japan, and, in consequence, they took the precaution of approaching Japanese territory in the dark.

330. There is little doubt in my mind that the Japanese Government, at the time of surrender, was up against some very strong opposition from certain fanatical factions. It was stated that in Singapore, before our occupation in September, a group of young Japanese officers had planned to fly to Tokio and there weed out what they considered to be the "corrupt elements" around the Throne, where defeatist policies, they held, had greatly influenced the Emperor.

331. The conference at Manila revealed an exceedingly interesting feature. Opinion in the South West Pacific Area apparently attributed a far higher value to the enemy's fighting qualities than was attributed to those Japanese whom we fought and defeated in Burma. It appeared that the morale and determination of the enemy forces in the metropolitan area was on a far higher level than that experienced in the outer regions of Japanese conquest, where forces had been virtually isolated for

months and, in any case, were not directly involved in the defence of their homeland. For this reason, G.H.Q. Manila expected considerable opposition to their occupying forces in Japan proper, in the form of sabotage and other subversive activities by fanatical elements.

332. At this time, the American airborne division was standing by at Okinawa to fly into Japan. The ultimate figure for the build-up of U.S. Army Forces for occupation was put at some 18 Divisions together with the whole of the 5th Air Force, although it was not thought that this would include V.H.B. aircraft owing to the lack of suitable runways in Japan.

333. I think it is important to note the American attitude at that time towards the participation of Air Forces, other than American, in the initial occupation of Japan. General Kenney, Commanding General, Far Eastern Air Forces, was not disposed to discuss the occupation of Japan by Allied Air Forces, which he apparently regarded as unnecessary representation in a country where airfield facilities were limited. Furthermore, it seemed that any inclusion of British Air Forces in Japan would inevitably raise the question of Russian Air Forces in a similar role, to which the Americans were strongly averse in every way. On the other hand, the Americans favourably accepted the occupation of Hong Kong and elsewhere by our Air Forces, since they did not regard Hong Kong as their own problem. The fact that the British "Tiger Force" project for Okinawa was no longer contemplated, as the result of Japan's sudden surrender, also produced for the Americans a general feeling of relief, mainly on logistical grounds. The British airfield engineers, who were already in transit for "Tiger Force" constructional requirements, were delayed at the island of Quajalin in the Pacific, pending further instructions to proceed, and it was suggested to us that we might like to divert these forces for our own airfield requirements in Malaya and elsewhere.

334. Australia, however, let it be known that they had every intention of being represented in the forces of occupation of Japan. General MacArthur was informed, through General Blamey, that the Commonwealth proposed to provide a representative garrison for Japan, including three tactical squadrons of the Royal Australian Air Force. It is interesting to note that this was the first official intimation which had been received by Headquarters, South West Pacific Area regarding the representation of Allied Air Forces in Japan.

335. With Japan's surrender, H.Q. South West Pacific Area were not unnaturally anxious that we should accept full responsibility, as soon as possible, within the new Theatre boundaries originally discussed at a meeting between Admiral Mountbatten and General MacArthur, which had taken place at Manila during July.

336. In the division of responsibility for implementing the surrender terms, South East Asia Command was allotted the following:-

(*a*)	Andamans.	Nicobars.
	Burma.	Thailand.
	F.I.C. (South of 16° N.).	Malaya.
	Sumatra.	Java.
	Lombok.	Bali.

Australia accepted responsibility for:-

(*b*)	British New Guinea.	Borneo.
	Bismarck Islands.	Timor.
	Flores.	Ceram.
	Soemba.	Amboina.
	Boeros.	Tanimbar.
	Kai Aroe.	

Islands in the Arafura Sea.

337. This division, however, left a gap comprising the Celebes, Halmahora Islands and Dutch New Guinea, for which no forces were available to implement the surrender terms unless the Dutch did so – a commitment which would obviously have introduced a shipping problem to transfer the necessary forces from Europe. The Australians, too, were anxious to hand over Borneo to us as soon as possible.

THE SURRENDER IN SOUTH EAST ASIA.

Ceremonies at Rangoon and Singapore.

338. In accordance with the orders of the Supreme Allied Commander, South East Asia, Japanese envoys, headed by Lieutenant General Takazo Numata, Chief of Staff to Field Marshal Count Terauchi, Japanese Expeditionary Force, Southern Regions, arrived at Rangoon by air on August 26th to be given their instructions for the implementation of the local surrender terms. Thus, after inflicting on the Japanese one of the greatest defeats of the war in the Far East, in a campaign which had lasted for over three years and in which the enemy's losses amounted to 100,000 men, it was at Rangoon that the Japanese Generals arrived to take their orders from the Allied Forces in South East Asia.

339. The meetings in Rangoon with the Japanese plenipotentiaries were, in no sense, negotiations. There was no question of discussion of terms. The Japanese were there to accept Unconditional Surrender. It was intended also that a binding act of surrender should be signed at Rangoon and that the official ceremony of surrender would be carried out at Singapore after the Supreme Allied Commander's instructions had been completed at the Rangoon meetings.

340. The conditions insisted upon by the Supreme Allied Commander, South East Asia, included immediate relief to prisoners-of-war and internees; Allied aircraft to begin day and night reconnaissance flights over South East Asia; Allied vessels to begin mine-sweeping operations in hitherto Japanese-controlled waters, and also for Allied vessels to enter ports in Malaya and elsewhere with full facilities provided.

341. The meetings with the Japanese plenipotentiaries, which were resumed at Rangoon in the opening days of September, brought to light many positive facts concerning the plight of the Japanese Army in Burma from the time of the enemy's disastrous retreat at Imphal in June, 1944. It was apparent from one important statement read by Major General Ichida, at Rangoon on September 11th, that the Japanese in Burma had not reckoned with two important and vital factors which upset their calculations and placed their forces at disastrous disadvantages:-

(*a*) Allied air supply, which permitted ground forces in Burma to consolidate their positions without being forced to retreat, and thus rendered the enemy's infiltration and encircling tactics abortive.

(*b*) Allied air superiority, which so disrupted Japanese supply lines, both in Burma and further afield, that starvation and illness overtook thousands of Japanese troops facing Fourteenth Army, and also denied them the essential supplies of fuel, equipment and material with which to fight a superior equipped, and better supplied, Allied Force.

342. With the disruption of the enemy's lines of communication, and the systematic attacks on their rear supply bases, it was not surprising that Major General Ichida should declare:-

"From the time of the Imphal operation, last year, our Army in Burma carried on its operations continuously for a period of a year with its main force, and during that period the army hardly ever received any reinforcements in its manpower – none since December last year – the replenishment of military stores also being very meagre."

343. The situation of the Allied ground forces, ranged against them, presented a happier picture. Thanks mainly to Allied air superiority, and resulting air supply, they had withstood the siege of Imphal, and, on the siege being raised, had taken the offensive down through Burma with the knowledge that fuel, rations, ammunitions and miscellaneous equipment would be air-dropped or air-landed to them, throughout the advance, while casualties inflicted by the enemy would be taken care of and evacuated safely to base.

The Ceremony at Singapore.

344. With the Supreme Allied Commander, and other Commanders-in-Chief, it afforded considerable satisfaction to witness General Itagaki sign, for his defeated compatriots, Admiral Mountbatten's terms for Unconditional Surrender in the South East Asia Theatre at Singapore, on 12th September, 1945.

345. There was not displayed at that ceremony any deliberate outward show of pride in Allied military achievement. It was more, I consider, an atmosphere of confident achievement which reflected the mood of the three services in South East Asia that no matter how long the struggle against the Japanese might have taken, victory would be with us in the end. In South East Asia we had good reason to remember that unequal contest during the dark days of 1941 and 1942, when the enemy, powerful and well prepared, swept through Malaya, occupied Singapore and later Burma. But their ultimate and decisive defeat – when the tide turned against them, must surely have caused them to remember the sting of our air forces which, in due course, swept clear the skies over Burma, and disorganised the land communications of the Japanese army as the ground troops rolled the enemy back through Burma during the advance from Imphal to Rangoon.

346. The Instrument of Surrender was drawn up in English – the only authentic

version. In case of doubt as to the intention of our meaning in that Instrument of Surrender, the decision of the Supreme Allied Commander was unequivocal and final.

347. Under the terms of surrender, all Japanese Army, Navy and Air Forces in South East Asia passed to the control of the Supreme Allied Commander.

348. I was much impressed by one noticeable characteristic on the part of our enemies which was in striking contrast to their previous behaviour in this Theatre – some of it an exhibition of unmitigated barbarism. After the surrender there was a widespread attitude of subservient willingness by the Japanese to obey our orders. In Singapore, as in other parts of the Command, I observed that the Japanese, officers and men alike, conducted themselves with strict discipline in our presence. They were super-punctilious too, when paying respects to members of our forces. While this was no doubt correct, it did appear somewhat unreal.

349. If, at Singapore, the Japanese myth of invincibility still lurked in the midst of the more fanatical Japanese elements, the Supreme Allied Commander must have corrected sharply any such belief which was held, in so far as it concerned the campaign in South East Asia. Admiral Mountbatten made it clear and emphatic to Itagaki during the surrender ceremony that it was not a negotiated surrender, but complete capitulation by the Japanese, after total military defeat. He informed Itagaki that not only did he possess superior naval, military and air forces at Singapore, but, in addition, he had a large fleet anchored off Port Swettenham and Port Dickson where, three days previously, on September 9th, considerable forces had started disembarking at daylight. On the 10th, the strength of that force was 100,000 men ashore. Indeed, at the very time of the Japanese signing the Instrument of Surrender at Singapore, R.A.F. units were firmly established at strategic points throughout the vast territories of this Theatre which, a few weeks beforehand, had been held by the Japanese.

350. It was also emphasised at the Singapore ceremony that the invasion of Malaya would have taken place on September 9th whether the Japanese had resisted or not, and it was stressed for the particular benefit of General Itagaki, therefore, that the Japanese were surrendering to a superior Allied force in Malaya.

PART IV.
THE RE-OCCUPATION OF JAPANESE OCCUPIED TERRITORIES ON SURRENDER.

OPERATIONS "TIDERACE" AND "ZIPPER".

351. South East Asia Command's assault on Malaya, planned for 9th September, 1945, was forestalled by Japanese surrender, thus bringing about a last minute change in plan involving more than 500 aircraft of the Strategic, Tactical and General Reconnaissance units of the R.A.F. which had been assembled in India, Burma, Ceylon and the Cocos Islands for the attack.

352. While Operation "Zipper" went forward on 9th September as arranged, it did

so on a much modified scale, having quickly transferred a proportion of its original strength to Operation "Tiderace" and leaving itself more in the nature of a display to show the flag.

353. The sudden capitulation of Japan on August 14th had brought with it the gigantic task of effecting rapid occupation of the principal key points throughout the Japanese occupied territories in South East Asia and further afield.

354. South East Asia, in this respect, bore no comparison to the situation in Europe where, on the eve of Germany's capitulation, the armed might of the Allied forces could roll along the roads of the Reich to Berlin, and the Air Forces sweep over Germany at will from their bases behind the victorious troops. In South East Asia, the Japanese occupied territories were vast. They covered Siam, French Indo-China, the Tenasserim Coast of Southern Burma, Malaya, Singapore Island, Sumatra, Java and Borneo. Even far off Hong Kong became a commitment.

355. Headquarters, Air Command, South East Asia, based at Kandy, Ceylon, was 1,500 miles distant across the Bay of Bengal from its principal air bases in Burma. Yet, such was the flexibility of air power, and despite the many and intricate formalities with which the Command was confronted in implementing the surrender terms on the eve of the planned invasion of Malaya, that air formations occupied bases at Penang on September 5th, Singapore on the 6th, Bangkok on the 5th and Saigon and Hong Kong on September 12th.

356. More vital still was the fact that the air forces of my Command had also launched upon one of the greatest missions of mercy of the war – the relief and liberation of thousands of Allied prisoners-of-war from the misery and privations of their prison camps, and assisting in their transportation westwards.

The Advent of "Tiderace" for Occupation of Singapore.

357. Capitulation by Japan naturally rendered planning and preparations for the assault on Malaya somewhat abortive. But this was only on a limited scale.

358. At the end of July, the mounting curve of Allied air assaults on Japan was such that it did seem reasonable to presume that an early collapse was a distinct possibility. Accordingly, emergency planning was put in preparation for the rapid occupation of Singapore at an early date should the enemy agree to accept the terms of the Potsdam declaration of July 26th.

359. The wisdom of this planning made itself apparent early in August when the first atomic bomb was dropped on the Japanese homeland and Russia entered the war.

360. It was the possibility of Japanese treachery, however, which decided the course that planning would take, and the initial occupation of Singapore, known as Operation "Tiderace" was, therefore, mounted from resources other than those earmarked for Operation "Zipper". In this way, it was possible to counter any Japanese opposition to "Tiderace" which may have taken place, by continuing to mount the strong fighting "Zipper" operation as originally planned.

361. Although the first objective in the re-occupation plan was Singapore, a necessary step in order to establish an advanced air and naval base to clear the Straits

of Malacca for shipping, it became clear that Bangkok in Siam, and Saigon in French Indo-China, would also have to be occupied soon after the Japanese surrender.

362. Operations known as "Bibber", which involved the occupation of the Bangkok area, and "Masterdom", involving the re-entry into French Indo-China to gain control over the forces of Field Marshal Count Terauchi, whose Southern Army Headquarters were at Saigon, had therefore to be worked out in detail. Moreover, it had been indicated by the British Chiefs of Staff that the former British port of Hong Kong must also be occupied at an early date.

363. To meet these exigencies, therefore, it was found necessary to modify to some extent the air effort for Operation "Tiderace" so that the Dakota Squadrons, based in Rangoon, could be utilised for essential trooping and air lift during the occupation of Bangkok and subsequently of Saigon. This was exceedingly important, since a long voyage with troops from existing Allied bases to Siam and French Indo-China would almost certainly have prohibited the speedy occupation of these territories had not the ground forces been lifted by air.

364. That 14,000 Army and Air Force personnel for the garrison at Bangkok and Saigon were carried in by our Air Forces without loss after the Japanese surrender, was evidence of the additional role which the Air Forces of my Command were called upon to play on the cessation of hostilities, at a time when it was imperative to establish ground troops at key points within the scattered enemy-occupied territories in the quickest possible time.

Original "Zipper" Plan Forestalled.

365. The Surrender by Japan cut right across the ambitious air plan for Operation "Zipper" which had been so carefully conceived to support the landings by ground troops on the Southern region of the Malay Peninsula.

366. Landings on the beaches at Ports Swettenham and Dickson on D-Day, September 9th, were to have been made under air cover provided by carrier-borne aircraft of the Royal Navy, whose task would have included attacks on the enemy's lines of communication and troop concentrations until the fly-in of R.A.F. fighters was accomplished. Two aircraft carriers, H.M.S. SMITER and H.M.S. TRUMPETER, carrying short-range Spitfires and Sentinels and Austers for casualty evacuation, were to carry these aircraft to a point offshore for pilots to fly them from off the carriers and land them on the newly-occupied aerodromes.

367. The planned effort of the naval carrier-borne fighters was 190 sorties a day from the moment of their arrival in the areas of the bridgeheads for about a week. This would be further augmented, within six days, by an additional 72 sorties a day from the first land-based squadrons of R.A.F. Spitfires, arid six sorties per night from the night fighter Mosquitos. From the outset, therefore, air superiority was assured. The enemy was not expected to produce any serious air threat which could not be dealt with adequately by our fighters.

368. As more than a thousand miles separated the existing R.A.F. bases in Rangoon and the Cocos Islands from the landing beaches, and almost 1,500 miles in respect of other R.A.F. bases in Ceylon and Ramree Island, it was impossible for Light

bomber, fighter and fighter bomber squadrons to operate in immediate support of the bridgehead ground forces until the position ashore was consolidated, an airfield captured, repairs effected and runways made serviceable.

369. Basing its time-table on the speed of the Army's advance and the rapidity by which constructional engineers could repair damaged runways and taxi-tracks, it was estimated that strips could be brought into operation at the rate of approximately one per week. Once the newly-occupied airfields had been established, the long-range Thunderbolts, Mosquitos and Dakotas, flying a thousand miles from Rangoon, would then make the flight south to Malaya, being guided on the way by three navigational aid ships at specified positions off the Tenasserim Coast and Malayan Peninsula.

370. The first strip – Kelanang – was calculated to be operational by D plus 6; Port Swettenham by D plus 12 and Kuala Lumpur by D plus 20. It was possible that a fourth strip might be established at Batu Pahat, or Malacca, in order to accommodate a light Mosquito bomber and rocket-firing Beaufighter aircraft by D plus 40.

371. The value of the Cocos Islands prior to and during Operation "Zipper" would have been considerable. The Strategic and G.R. squadrons were to have taken part in large-scale pre-D-Day operations directed against radar installations covering the approaches to the assault area, and also to cutting the Bangkok-Singapore railway north of Kuala Lumpur. Other tasks included the neutralising of the Japanese Air Force, estimated at a little more than 170 aircraft in Malaya and Sumatra, also attacking enemy shipping employed in carrying supplies or reinforcements to Malaya to oppose our landing. The aerodromes at Kelanang, Port Swettenham and Kuala Lumpur were not to be bombed, since they were the first objectives on establishing the bridgehead.

372. Five R.A.F. Wings were detailed to operate in the tactical forces contained within Air Vice Marshal Bandon's 224 Group, whose advanced Headquarters were to be established ashore on D-Day to set up control communications and radar screens, as an early occupation of Kelanang air strip in a serviceable condition would allow Spitfires to be flown in the following day and made ready for action.

373. The R.A.F. Wings made available for the operation were Nos. 901 Wing, to be first located at Kuala Lumpur; 902 Wing at Kelanang; 904 Wing at an air strip to be sited and constructed; 905 Wing at Port Swettenham and 907 Wing at Batu Pahat or an alternative.

374. A prominent role in the "Zipper" operation was also allocated to the R.A.F. Regiment. Five Wings of nearly 2,500 officers and men, made up of nine Field Squadrons and five Light Anti-Aircraft Squadrons were to capture and hold the aerodromes and also to protect radar sites. The majority of the men had been on active service in India and Burma.

Other Operational Aspects of "Zipper".

375. Air operations in "Zipper", once our position ashore had been consolidated and airfields established, would have followed closely to plan thus:-

(*a*) Eight squadrons of Thunderbolts would have supported the drive on Singapore.

(*b*) Fighter Reconnaissance cover would have been provided by Spitfire F/R Mk. XIV's. and, as in Burma, they would have flown protective patrols over the traffic lanes of the supply dropping Dakotas.

(*c*) Two squadrons of Transport Command supply freighters were allocated to the task of carrying supplies from the beach head air strip at Port Swettenham to the forward troops. A start would first be made with a target of 150 tons per day from D plus 23.

(*d*) With the possibility of an airborne assault force deep behind enemy lines after the third or fourth week of the operation, six squadrons of Dakotas would have been flown in from Rangoon and out again immediately afterwards for this purpose.

(*e*) Mosquitos were to be employed as light bombers, night fighters and photographic reconnaissance aircraft.

(*f*) Air evacuation of casualties was to have been the task of Sentinel and Auster aircraft. As in Burma, they were to operate from a main strip flying as required to 400 yard clearings in the flight zone to pick up wounded and to carry them back to the Dakotas. The more seriously wounded were to have been ferried by Dakotas to Rangoon.

(*g*) Three D.D.T. spraying Dakotas operating from Kelanang were to spray mosquito infested zones over a wide area.

(*h*) To answer emergency calls from D plus 4, three Sunderland aircraft were to be available for air-sea rescue while three high-speed launches were also to be deck-carried to the beach head.

(*i*) Rocket firing Beaufighters were to be employed from about D plus 43 in attacks on shipping, enemy rolling stock, targets on Singapore Island and also in assisting in the bombardment plan for the crossing of the Johore Strait for the final assault on Singapore itself.

Modified Operation "Zipper" Goes Forward.

376. In the closing days of August, before even the "Zipper" convoys had left India for Malaya, the emergency operation "Tiderace" was ordered, since it was essential that air units should fly into Penang and Singapore without further delay. This brought No. 185 Wing, controlling Dakotas, Spitfires and Mosquitos from Burma to Penang, and No. 903 Wing from Akyab to Singapore, together with Nos. 152 and 155 Spitfire Squadrons flying Zayatkwin (Rangoon) – Penang – Singapore (Tengah), and 110 Squadron from Hmawbi (Burma) – Penang – Singapore (Seletar). No. 903 Wing elements reached Singapore on 6th September, some three days before the first "Zipper" elements arrived off the west coast of Malaya on September 9th.

377. With "Tiderace" operation completed, and air, ground and sea forces occupying Singapore, the modified "Zipper" operation went forward on September 9th with convoys standing off the beaches at Ports Swettenham and Dickson. The naval air support programme, however, had been called off.

378. The air effort for the original "Zipper" was considerably reduced and of the five R.A.F. Wings scheduled to take part in the operation, the following wings did not enter Malaya and were phased out:-

No. 901 Wing. No. 904 Wing. No. 907 Wing.

This left the Wing Order of Battle for "Zipper" as under:-

No. 902 Wing. Tengah.	No. 905 Wing. Kuala Lumpur.
No. 185 Wing. Penang.	No. 903 Wing. Kallang.
S.S. "Manela" Sunderland H.Q. Ship – Seletar.	

379. The following squadrons were also phased out:-

Spitfires	Squadrons No. 132 and 615.
Thunderbolts	Squadrons No. 530 and 261.
Dakotas	Squadrons No. 96 and 62.
Beaufighters	Squadrons No. 22, 217 and 45.
Mosquitos	Squadrons No. 82 and 211.

leaving the undernoted squadrons of the original plan:-

Spitfires	Squadrons No. 11, 17 and 681.
Thunderbolts	Squadrons No. 131, 258, 81 and 60.
Mosquitos	Squadrons No. 89, 684 and 84.
Austers	Squadron No. 656.
Sunderland Det.	Squadron No. 205.

The "Zipper" Landings which took place.

380. On D-Day, September 9th, the first of the "Zipper" landings under the modified plan took place, with ground forces and R.A.F. parties leaving the anchored convoys and going peacefully ashore in the Port Swettenham and Dickson areas.

381. This was the start of the large scale landing in Malaya – and under very different circumstances from what had been envisaged when the operation was first planned.

382. Included in the convoy was Headquarters ship H.M.S. BULOLO which carried Air Vice-Marshal Bandon and his advance H.Q. 224 Group staff who moved ashore to Kelanang airfield on September 10th; Telok Datok on September 14th; Kuala Lumpur on September 18th and Singapore on September 22nd.

383. The landing at Port Dickson, some fifty miles south of Swettenham, went forward as planned and without untoward incident.

384. On the eve of the 11th September, the D-plus-3 convoy dropped anchor among the great concentration of shipping already lying off Morib Beach. The scene, with every vessel twinkling lights, resembled more a Cowes regatta than one of the largest amphibious operations of the campaign.

385. The landings at Morib cannot be described as attaining the same degree of success as those experienced at Ports Swettenham and Dickson – due principally to the difficulties encountered on the water-covered beaches which, at that part of the coast, are nothing more than mud brought down by the Klang River. Morib is some 20 miles south of Port Swettenham and 30 miles north of Port Dickson. While there was much to commend Port Swettenham and Port Dickson for landings by a fighting force, this unfortunately, could not be said of Morib. A number of M.T. vehicles which were driven off the landing craft by their Army drivers into what was considered axle-deep water, later plunged into slime and mud while negotiating the shore and remained fast. There were several casualties.

386. These are important factors which might well have produced serious consequences had "Zipper" been mounted against opposing forces on dry land at this part of the coast.

SOME ASPECTS OF THE OCCUPATION OF SIAM, F.I.C. AND HONG KONG.

387. On the occupation of Siam, the Don Muang airfield at Bangkok provided two important functions. It enabled released Allied prisoners-of-war to be evacuated by our aircraft to Rangoon and Singapore, while it also formed a valuable staging post to Saigon in French Indo-China as well as a refuelling point for aircraft lifting there.

388. In Bangkok, the Siamese Air Force was found to be extraordinarily co-operative and markedly pro-R.A.F., since many of them had, in fact, been trained in England.

389. An unusual document, giving an outline of the activities and organisation of the Siamese Air Force, and also emphasising its attitude of passive resistance to the Japanese throughout the enemy's occupation of Siam, was handed over by the Siamese Air Force to R.A.F. Intelligence.

390. History must judge this document for itself. Whatever may have been happening politically behind the scenes in the Far East, in these dark days of December, 1941, there seems to be no doubt that units of the Siamese Air Force, on December 8th, took the air to resist the Japanese invader, only to be outnumbered and overwhelmed by units of the more superior Japanese Air Force. While this commendable spirit of resistance by the Siamese Air Force may have been evident, they were to learn sadly, the same day, that the Siamese Government in Bangkok was actually negotiating with the Japanese Ambassador.

391. "From outer appearances we played up to mislead the Japanese" is one comment in the Siamese document when discussing the defence of Siam during the period of Japanese occupation. In their participation in the defence of Don Muang airfield and Bangkok against Allied aircraft, it was maintained by the Siamese Air Force that "we just did it in a formal fashion. The United Nations aircraft would fly one way and our aircraft the other way, or at different heights. If by rare chance we had to meet we carried on just for appearances sake."

392. Such are some of the statements by the Siamese Air Force. But it is on fact, rather than on professions of loyalty, that any final assessment must be made. In this

respect, there is one incontrovertible fact concerning Allied prisoners-of-war, which does reveal the silent co-operation rendered by the Siamese Air Force from the time of their first prisoner-of-war, William MacClurry, an American pilot from the American Volunteer Group (Tiger Squadron), who bailed out at Cheing Mai at the onset of the war in the Far East, and whose custody by the Japanese was vigorously contested by the Siamese Air Force, until they finally confined him themselves to ensure his better treatment and safety.

393. It must also be marked to the credit of the Siamese Air Force that they did, to our knowledge, assist in furthering liaison and communication work within Siam, which included the conveyance of passengers in and out of the country; rendering assistance to, and providing safeguard for Allied personnel sent into Siam to gather information, and also indicating for our benefit, precise targets in the hands of the Japanese. Such acts of co-operation were fraught with grave risk, and it is not surprising that the Japanese ultimately adopted an attitude of suspicion.

The occupation of Saigon.

394. The outward welcome accorded to the Allied Forces from both the French and Annamese alike on our entry into French Indo-China was decidely embarrassing. Our Forces obviously found themselves in a divided house.

395. The main R.A.F. party flew into Saigon from Burma on September 12th, and was given a demonstrative reception by the French. At the same time, there were banners throughout Saigon's streets erected by the Annamese which welcomed the Allies but bore caustic anti-French slogans.

396. R.A.F. reconnaissance parties who inspected Japanese Air Force installations at Than Son Nhut and Saigon, found them most disappointing. Comparatively few aircraft were discovered, and none, indeed, were serviceable. It appeared that all serviceable aircraft had either been withdrawn for the defence of Japan or flown to Phu My aerodrome, twenty miles east of Saigon, after the cessation of hostilities. The majority of Japanese Air Force personnel previously at Saigon had also been withdrawn.

397. The Saigon-Than Son Nhut area was the maintenance and repair unit base for the Japanese in French Indo-China, but, since only two engine test benches were found, the normal capacity for engine repairs must have been very low. No sign of any centralised production line was apparent.

398. Of characteristic orderliness in Japanese storage equipment there was none. All kinds of equipment were found mixed together in each warehouse apparently without rhyme or reason, and there appeared to be little attempt to keep any detailed record of stock and issues. It is surprising how any items were found when required, or further commitments even calculated.

399. Arms discovered tallied with the list provided by the Japanese, but there was nothing to show that this list was, in fact, definite. Judging by the aggressive attitude of the Annamese towards the French at this period, it may well have been that considerable stocks of Japanese arms had not been declared.

The occupation of Hong Kong.

400. On August 29th a strong naval force under Rear Admiral C.H J. Harcourt, C.B., C.B.E. (Flag in H.M.S. SWIFTSURE) arrived off Hong Kong and landed a force on August 30th, being joined by Rear Admiral C.S. Daniel, C.B., C.B.E., D.S.C. (Flag in H.M.S. ANSON). The formal surrender of the Japanese at Hong Kong took place on September 16th. An air headquarters was established on September 12th.

401. One Spitfire squadron was conveyed in an aircraft carrier and the remainder of the air units, which included a Mosquito L.B. squadron, another Spitfire squadron, a Sunderland squadron, and one Dakota squadron, were flown in to Kaitak Airfield at Kowloon, on the mainland.

402. Air defence of Hong Kong, and the provision of air support for any operations which might be necessary by the ground forces involving security of the base, were the primary duties of the air forces as planned. In addition, however, Hong Kong provided a link in the chain of air communications for, and reinforcement of the British and Dominion Air Forces which would garrison Japan.

403. The "Shield" convoy, which was at sea at the conclusion of the Japanese war and, accordingly, was diverted while proceeding to Okinawa in connection with the Pacific "Tiger Force" operation, arrived in Hong Kong on September 4th with 3,400 officers and men of various R.A.F. units. A large percentage of "Shield" Force was composed of personnel of No. 5,358 Airfield Construction Wing, whose original task had been rendered redundant.

404. The variety of rehabilitation tasks undertaken by R.A.F. personnel on the occupation of Hong Kong and Kowloon on the mainland, and accomplished without any previous experience, showed that the Royal Air Force, apart from its qualities as a fighting service, could be extremely versatile in other spheres. It was gratifying to observe at Hong Kong how aircrew personnel, mainly fighter pilots, could apply themselves to ground duties varying from prison supervision to billeting and requisitioning, whereas those with greater technical knowledge, such as R.A.F. Airfield Construction Personnel, were largely responsible for the initiation and maintenance of the public services; power, light, transport, etc.

405. In the first few days of occupation, some 18,000 Japanese forces, including many senior officers, were rounded up, disarmed, and concentrated in Shamshui Po prison, previously a concentration camp on the mainland.

406. The first commandant of what, under British occupation, became a Japanese concentration camp, was a R.A.F. squadron leader whose previous experience had been limited to operational flying. He proved himself a competent prison governor during his short term of office before handing over his duties to an Army officer.

R.A.F. undertake many public services.

407. The total neglect of civic administration by the Japanese in Hong Kong and Kowloon, except in so far as it affected themselves, was all too apparent. Transport did not exist; electric power was unreliable and the supply severely limited; public health services had been totally ignored, and the streets stank with accumulated

rubbish and filth. There was, too, large scale looting by the Chinese who, until checked, literally stripped every house they entered of all furniture, fittings and every piece of wood including floor boards and window and door frames. Wood for fuel purposes, indeed, was at a premium in Hong Kong due to the absence of coal.

408. The problems of occupation which faced our forces on arrival were so numerous and varied that it was difficult to know where to make a start. Yet, at this time, when the R.A.F. personnel were busily engaged in establishing an occupation force, many important public services were undertaken with willingness.

409. To overcome the transport difficulties, every motor car available was requisitioned. This in itself involved considerable labour for R.A.F. personnel in rehabilitating and maintaining decrepit and mechanically unsound vehicles which had been left behind by the Japanese. In particular, restoration of the dock area to a standard capable of unloading the freight ships of "Shield" convoy presented big difficulties. The wharves were broken in many instances and covered with debris and dilapidated equipment. Sunken vessels in the bases were also hazards to navigation.

410. The power station at Kowloon was manned by a R.A.F. supervisory staff. While the plant did not work to full capacity, principally on account of fuel shortage, it was, nevertheless, made to function and supply all the requirements of light and power in Kowloon and the docks area. This work included the reconditioning of furnaces, boilers, and the repair of certain turbine power units.

411. In their search for wood as fuel, an R.A.F. reconnaissance party of ground personnel penetrated into the New Territories which were still occupied by the Japanese. Large stocks of wood were discovered at Taipo and Fanling, twenty and fifteen miles respectively. An incidental on this trip was that a chit was given to the Chinese Communist Army Troops which allowed the party to cross over the border to collect a number of abandoned railway trucks. A fuel supply for the Kowloon power station was thus assured, but the margin was so close that on one occasion the power house was within 15 minutes of closing down completely.

412. Railway workshops were also under the initial supervision of a R.A.F. staff, which was later augmented by suitable personnel through arrangements with Civil Affairs. Under R.A.F. supervision these workshops completed repair to three locomotives, some twenty goods wagons, and three passenger coaches. As a result, the rolling stock augmented by this output from the railway workshops was sufficient to meet the requirements of the railway within the colony.

413. Even Hong Kong's municipal water supply included an element of R.A.F. supervisory staff, though in this respect the water supply as a whole had suffered little during enemy occupation and therefore met existing requirements.

414. The morale of our Air Forces in the execution of these extraordinarily varied tasks was wonderfully high, and once the initial excitement and novelty associated with their misemployment in the role of shock troops, guards, policemen and municipal authorities had worn off, R.A.F. units took stock of the situation and turned their attention to the tasks of resuming their normal service duties.

THE LIBERATION OF ALLIED PRISONERS OF WAR AND INTERNEES

Operations "Birdcage" and "Mastiff".

415. The relief and liberation of almost 100,000 Allied prisoners-of-war and internees confined in Japanese prison camps throughout the vast territories of South East Asia, is an episode in the Far Eastern War which relied almost entirely upon Air Power for its success in the initial but vital stages of its operation.

416. It would be inaccurate to record that the Air Forces alone were responsible for the ultimate rescue and liberation of these thousands of prisoners, but the Air Forces of this Command carried out vital tasks as follows:-

(a) Spread the news of Japanese surrender in millions of leaflets dropped over the principal towns and known sites of Japanese prison camps scattered throughout South East Asia.

(b) Warned Allied prisoners-of-war and internees of their impending liberation.

(c) Dropped medical supplies, medical teams, administrative personnel and W/T operators to make first contact with prisoners and to signal back vital information regarding numbers imprisoned and supplies required.

(d) Air dropped, or air landed, quantities of food, clothing and other necessities to relieve the privations suffered at prison camps.

(e) Evacuated by air hundreds of prisoners from Malaya, Siam, French Indo-China, Sumatra and Java, including cases of very serious illness.

417. In a message to all formations of Air Command which took part in the inauguration of this task on August 28th, 1945, the operation was described as "the greatest mercy mission of the war".

418. It was a mission of paramount importance to thousands of families in Britain, the Dominions and, indeed, in Holland, who eagerly awaited information about relatives interned and captured during the Japanese conquest of Malaya in 1942.

419. In Singapore alone, about 35,000 prisoners were held in the various Japanese prison camps throughout Singapore Island the most notorious of which was the Changi Gaol. The inmates of these camps had been subjected to coarse indignities and even torture.

420. The feeling in Britain found expression in a message from the British Foreign Secretary to the Supreme Allied Commander, South East Asia, in which he drew Admiral Mountbatten's attention to the numerous enquiries which the Government had received since the publication of atrocity stories from Singapore and elsewhere, and saying that there was grave concern in respect of Sumatra, since deaths actually reported by the Japanese through the International Red Cross were much higher in proportion to numbers anywhere else in the Far East.

421. It can be seen, therefore, how well suited was Air Power to perform this vitally

important task involving great distances across great tracts of land – a task also in which speed was essential for its success.

Operation "Birdcage" launched.

422. As soon as the Japanese surrender had been universally accepted and confirmed, action was taken to issue instructions contained in specially prepared leaflets to:-

(*a*) Japanese Prison Guards.

(*b*) Allied Prisoners-of-war.

(*c*) Local Japanese forces.

(*d*) The local native population.

423. The operation to implement this action was allotted the code name of "Birdcage," and was launched by the Air Forces of Air Command on August 28th, operating from bases in Ceylon, Cocos Islands, Bengal and Burma.

424. Thereafter, Operation "Mastiff", was planned to ensure that medical aid, comforts, food, clothing, R.A.P.W.I. Control Staffs where necessary, and any other essential preliminary needs were introduced into the camps as early as possible.

425. Operation "Birdcage" was completed by August 31st. In the space of four days, leaflets had been dropped over 236 localities and 90 prisoner-of-war camps throughout Burma, Siam, French Indo-China, Malaya and Sumatra. Where sorties were at first rendered abortive by weather and by difficulty in locating targets or by mechanical trouble, they were persisted with on the following days. Very few priority targets remained uncovered. One group of towns in the hinterland of Malaya was successfully covered only at the third attempt.

426. In addition to Liberator sorties flown from bases in Ceylon, Cocos Islands and Bengal, Thunderbolts operating from Burma dropped one million leaflets on thirteen localities in Southern Burma extending as far south as the Kra Isthmus. No target was left uncovered. One Thunderbolt was lost during these operations – the aircraft crashing in flames at Kraburi.

427. I think it is worthy of note that Operation "Birdcage" was carried out in very indifferent conditions. Even more important still was the fact that an all round trip of many of the sorties was equivalent to a trans-Atlantic flight. Nevertheless, 75 per cent. of the crews reached their targets, which included towns and camps as far east as Hanoi, Tourane and Saigon.

Success of Leaflet Dropping.

428. The news of Japanese surrender contained in the millions of leaflets dropped met with great enthusiasm throughout the scattered territories of South East Asia. They were picked up on the streets of towns and read eagerly by the civilian population. The messages also dropped to the Allied prisoners-of-war stated, "We want to get you back home quickly, safe and sound".

429. Many of the prisoners had been Japanese forced labour for the building of

the notorious Bangkok-Moulmein railway – a slave task which will take its place among the list of incredible efforts carried out by captive men.

430. August, 1945, saw the greatest effort in leaflet dropping attempted by aircraft of the Command.

431. Prior to the surrender, and immediately after, some 33,000,000 leaflets were dropped over the enemy-occupied territories in South East Asia. This form of psychological warfare had been stepped up very considerably after the defeat of the Japanese in Burma, and in July the total dropped by aircraft of the Command reached 22,000,000.

432. One particular form of leaflet, dropped over the trapped Japanese forces in the PeguYomas of Southern Burma during July, not only called upon the enemy to surrender after telling them of the hopeless position of their homeland, but, on the reverse side offered them a safe conduct through the Allied lines with the added assurance that they would be given food, medical attention and honourable treatment.

Launching of Operation "Mastiff".

433. The saturating of towns and prison camps with leaflets announcing the Japanese surrender was, in itself, a laudable effort, but the main task which awaited the Air Forces was unquestionably that of Operation "Mastiff" in bringing practical relief and comfort to those who needed them most.

434. Hundreds of these prisoners were emaciated, gaunt and pitiful beings – some, indeed, were too weak to stand upon their legs. The majority of prisoners were deficient of proper clothing. There were instances too, where some were completely naked.

435. The need of medical supplies was perhaps the greatest, for the Japanese had shown little ability or willingness to appreciate the needs of prisoners-of-war in many cases. The immediate requirements in drugs, therefore, could only be taken to sufferers by air, and, as a large percentage of prisoners and internees, particularly in Singapore, were affected by malaria, it was estimated that 1.250,000 tablets of Atabrine, or substitute, were essential for delivery each week.

436. The "Mastiff" operation in the early stages was carried out by ten Liberator squadrons (including one R.A.A.F. squadron) and one Dakota squadron. Three Liberator squadrons operated from bases in Bengal – Jessore, Salbani and Digri – covering targets chiefly in Siam and French Indo-China. From bases in Ceylon another three Liberator squadrons operated over Malaya and Sumatra, while areas in Malaya and Java were supplied by three Liberator squadrons based in the Cocos Islands, though these were chiefly employed on targets in Sumatra.

437. The Dakota squadron operated from Rangoon over Siam and the Tenasserim Coastal Area of Southern Burma. The tasks undertaken by this Dakota squadron must not be confused with the all-out effort made by five Dakota squadrons of No. 232 Group, R.A.F., based on Rangoon, which were employed on the air-lift to Bangkok, where the Don Muang Airfield was quickly in use. The operations of these Dakota squadrons in the air landing of supplies and in the evacuation of prisoners-of-war was one of the outstanding features of the air operations associated with "Mastiff".

438. From 1st to 5th September, approximately 200 Dakota sorties were flown from Rangoon, and some 400 tons of stores were dropped or landed. The same aircraft carried back 4,000 prisoners-of-war and internees. On the following week the Dakotas carried out a further 360 sorties, and dropped or landed 600 tons of stores. On their return trips they carried back some 3,700 prisoners-of-war. It as a tribute to the enthusiasm shown by the Dakota aircrews at this time that 12th Army, by September 10th, was able to report that approximately 9,000 prisoners-of-war had been carried back to Rangoon from Bangkok. Early in the month, practically all the U.S. prisoners-of-war had been evacuated from the Bangkok area, the figure being approximately 162. This evacuation was carried out chiefly by U.S. airlift, which was also responsible for bringing out a number of British and Allied sick.

Use of Thunderbolts and R.A.A.F. Liberators.

439. Though not actually engaged upon Operation "Mastiff", a number of Thunderbolt aircraft flew from their bases in Burma and assisted in the problem of locating camps and determining their circumstances. Many of these Thunderbolt sorties were rendered abortive by weather, but other sorties resulted in the bringing back of valuable information. It was noted, for example, that several of the prison camps on the Burma-Siam railway, in the area stretching N.W. from Kanchanaburi, were deserted and empty, while prisoners-of-war in other scattered camps greeted the appearance of the Thunderbolts with understandable enthusiasm expressed by frantic cheering and waving.

440. The inclusion of a series of sorties by Liberators of the R.A.A.F. which took off from bases in North Western Australia to drop supplies over Magelang Airfield, in Java, also greatly assisted in the success of operations in the opening weeks. These aircraft landed in the Cocos Islands, loaded up with fresh supplies, and repeated the drop on Java en route back to Australia. The R.A.A.F. Liberators completed 21 sorties, all of which were successful. Other sorties of a similar nature were flown by these aircraft. At this time too, the presence in Singapore of Dakotas belonging to 31 Squadron, which operated over Sumatra, assisted materially in bringing out of Sumatra some of the first prisoners-of-war.

Target Area	August-September Week 30th-5th			September Week 6th-12th			September Week 13th-19th		
	Successful	Abortive	Missing	Successful	Abortive	Missing	Successful	Abortive	Missing
Siam	42	8	-	49	-	-	49	3	-
F.I.C.	13	1	1	11	-	-	11	1	2
Malaya	22	2	-	10	2	-	6	-	-
Sumatra	23	2	1	29	1	-	38	4	-
Java	-	-	-	2	-	-	22	1	-
	100	13	2	101	3	-	126	9	2

441. For purposes of comparison, the undernoted table shows the air effort over different target areas of South East Asia for the first three weeks during which Operation "Mastiff" was in progress, and which covers the particular period of my Despatch.

Working of RAPWI and the S.D. Squadrons.

442. The evacuation of prisoners-of-war and internees required the maximum co-operation between Naval, Land and Air Forces.

443. An Inter-Services Inter-Allied Committee was therefore established at the Headquarters of the Supreme Allied Commander, at Kandy, Ceylon, for planning and co-ordination of control. This Committee acted as the clearing house for information, and declared the decisions of the Supreme Allied Commander on policy, priorities, and allocation of responsibility.

444. The working organisation was known as RAPWI (Release Repatriation of Allied Prisoners-of-war and Internees), which had a Central Control for aid by air at Kandy, with Army and Air Force Officers, and Sub-Controls at Calcutta, Rangoon, Colombo and Cocos. As the necessity for air dropping decreased, these Controls were incorporated in the RAPWI Control Organisations with Naval, Army, Air and Allied representation. Subsequently a Control was opened at Singapore.

445. The RAPWI Controls were responsible for co-ordination of executive action in all matters of supplies for RAPWI, and the evacuation of personnel by aircraft and white and red ensign ships.

446. For the prodigious effort put up by the Cocos based squadrons engaged on operation "Mastiff", Red Cross and other stores for RAPWI were packed at Sigiriya, Ceylon, and handed over to the R.A.F. for delivery to the Cocos Islands. This demanded a very heavy ferrying commitment to the Cocos as two-thirds of the prison camps were supplied by the Cocos based squadrons. Every available Liberator and Sunderland aircraft was used during the inauguration of "Mastiff".

447. This extra effort by the S.D. Liberators based on the Cocos was due to the large loads which had to be carried to the prison camps at Singapore and Southern Sumatra – loads which averaged from 3,500 to 4,000 lbs.

448. No praise could be too high for the air and ground crew personnel of these Cocos based squadrons. Despite the severe shortage of experienced crews and, indeed, aircraft, a daily average of seven sorties, and sometimes nine, was maintained. One squadron flew to widely differing dropping zones throughout Malaya, Sumatra and Java. Ninety-five personnel were dropped on these sorties, of which 65 were doctors or medical orderlies, and all arrived safely despite the short notice at which most of the sorties were laid on. On the first day of the "Mastiff" operations, indeed, one of the aircraft dropped a medical team on Changi Airfield at dawn on August 29th, making a round trip of 3,400 miles.

449. The great distances covered and the adverse weather conditions encountered were difficulties which were not overcome lightly and without danger. A Liberator on a supply dropping mission to the prison camps at Palembang was seen to spin whilst executing a steep turn and all nine crew members were killed.

450. It became obvious that Operation "Mastiff" would continue for some considerable time until the last prisoner of war and internee had been evacuated from all areas by air and sea. As September advanced the numbers brought out mounted steadily. There has been praise on all sides for our squadrons co-operating with the other Services in this rescue of men and women who have endured untold hardships, indignities and, in some cases barbarous cruelties – comments of praise which I have confirmed myself during talks with repatriated prisoners of war flown out of the prison camp areas.

THE JAPANESE PLANNED COUNTER MEASURES TO INVASION OF MALAYA.

451. The the Allies' powerful "Zipper" operation for the landing in Malaya would have succeeded, and that mastery of the air covering the landing would have been secured almost from the start, seems a justifiable claim after careful examination of evidence made available through interrogation of Japanese officers following the surrender in South East Asia.

452. It was evident that the Japanese, in their defence of Malaya, were unable to conform to one of the first principles of modern warfare – that air superiority must be gained, and that the battle in the air must first be won, before ground forces can wage their operations with any likelihood of success.

453. The Japanese counter invasion plan was based on the fact that very few operational aircraft were available since it had been decided to concentrate all forces for the defence of the homeland. The aircraft available, therefore, were mainly trainers which were not easy to send back to Japan. In all, the enemy had, for the defence of Malaya, Sumatra and Java, approximately 800 serviceable aircraft all of which, in the last resort, were to be used as Tokkoki (special attacker suicide aircraft).

454. On D-Day, the enemy planned that there should be no daylight sorties whatever owing to the difficulty in providing sufficient fighter cover to break through the British fighter defences. About 50 to 60 suicide sorties were to be made at twilight with a fighter escort of 30 to 40 aircraft. The suicides were to fly in flights of about 5 aircraft and all attacks were to be concentrated on shipping. Even if balloons were used by the Allied convoys no other method of attack than that of suicide attack was considered feasible. Ground targets were also to be ignored and no fighter defence put up against R.A.F. bomber attacks. Once the Japanese fighters had fulfilled their escort tasks to the suicide aircraft they, in turn, were to be used as suicide aircraft themselves since there were not enough aircraft to use for both purposes.

455. One Japanese source of information, as the result of interrogation, was extremely revealing. This source declared that the whole of the aircraft available to the Japanese for the defence of Malaya against the Allied invasion would, as the result of the mass suicide attack policy, "have been knocked out in about a week".

Direct attack on Mainland not Expected.

456. Following upon the Allied victory in Burma, and the capture of Rangoon in

May, the Japanese expected attacks by the Allies on the Andamans, Nicobars, Mergui and Puket in August or September, with the main attack on Malaya coming at the end of October or nearly in November.

457. As soon as the airfields around Rangoon had been made serviceable by the Allies, the Japanese expected there would be a programme of softening-up attacks on Japanese bases by R.A.F. aircraft, with some 200 bomber sorties and 200 escorting fighter sorties daily. The enemy intended to put up little opposition on air attacks against Mergui, the Nicobars or Andamans, while no defensive fighter sorties were to be flown against the R.A.F. softening-up attacks unless Singapore itself were attacked.

458. A direct landing on the mainland of Malaya was not anticipated at the outset. Instead it was expected that the Allies would work gradually south, during which time there would be consolidation and the systematic building up of bases. In this connection, it is interesting to note that the Japanese considered any landing in the Puket area (an operation which we had earlier planned and then abandoned after the fall of Rangoon) would have proved exceedingly dangerous for them, as the short range of the available Japanese fighter aircraft would have made it most difficult to oppose a landing there. The area of Port Swettenham on the Peninsula, it was believed, would not be reached until the end of 1945.

459. As "Zipper" was planned for September, and would undoubtedly have taken place on that date but for the cessation of hostilities, it is evident that the dispositions by the Japanese for counteracting the Allied invasion would have been lamentably behind schedule.

Japanese Build up of Suicide Aircraft.

460. Taking into account the enemy's limited aircraft resources, the Japanese air strategy, on paper, was quite logically prepared.

461. In February, a little more than six months before surrender came, the Japanese Southern Area Army in South East Asia was informed by Tokio that there must be a change in air strategy in the Southern Area. The High Command had visualised that, before long, the Southern Area (French Indo-China, Siam, Malaya, Burma and Netherland East Indies) would be almost entirely cut off from the Empire and would have to develop their own air defence from an already diminishing air force in that area.

462. Training was accordingly speeded up, and all training aircraft and some operational and second line aircraft were ultimately modified to carry bombs.

463. As far back as February, 1945, the Japanese had already had some experience in the use of suicide attacks in the Philippines campaign and had seen how effective these suicide attacks could be against concentrations of shipping and, in particular, against large battleships and carriers.

464. It was the eventual plan of the Japanese, once the Allied invasion of Malaya had started, to use all their aircraft (first line, training and transport) as suicide aircraft against Allied shipping and then continue to fight on the land without an air force.

465. In the Southern Area, all Japanese aircraft were widely dispersed over the vast areas of Malaya, Sumatra and Java, while airfields were, in many instances, poor in condition. To effect this concentration of aircraft in Malaya, Sumatra and Java in preparation for the Allied invasion of Malaya, the Japanese had left Siam and French Indo-China almost bare of aircraft, except for some trainers, and it had not been thought possible to transfer to Malaya.

No Shortage of Suicide Pilots.

466. It seemed that there was no shortage of pilots in the Southern Area to man Japanese suicide aircraft, and that Major-General Kitagawa, G.O.C., 55th Air Training Division could, on his own admission, have called on 2,000 pilots for the 8/900 suicide aircraft at his disposal. On the other hand, few had any operational experience and consisted of training instructors and student pilots with little more than 100 hours flying. It was from these that only the best were selected as suicide pilots. Here, however, an exceedingly interesting and important factor must be noted. This special attack corps of suicide pilots was made up of ardent volunteers. They had determination to proceed to their doom elated in the thought that they were dying for their Emperor.

Major Factors Overlooked by Japanese.

467. The Japanese considered that they would have been able to defeat the Allies' first attempt at landing in Malaya by the use of their suicide aircraft, but considered that when the second attempt at landing was made by the Allies, they would have no more aircraft left and the second landing would therefore have been easy.

468. I refute the Japanese contention that the first attempt at landing by the Allies would have met with reverse. On impartial examination of the facts made available by the Japanese after surrender, there were several major factors which the Japanese most decidedly overlooked.

Briefly these factors were:-

    (i) No attacks were to have been made by Japanese suicide aircraft until dusk on D-Day, thus giving our air forces taking part in the large scale invasion of Malaya at least twelve hours to neutralise, as they would have done, Japanese aircraft in the Penang/North Sumatra area.

    (ii) R.A.F. Intelligence had estimated that 175 Japanese first line aircraft would be immediately available in Malaya and Sumatra. Of this number, only 20 were thought to be bombers, and 120 fighters – the remainder being reconnaissance and floatplanes.
    The general preparation of all the trainer units in these areas for suicide attacks was well known to the R.A.F., and the estimated number available in Malaya and Sumatra was 245 in Malaya and 20 in Sumatra. The estimated number of trainer aircraft in Java was 346.

By early September, the intended move of the Japanese trainer aircraft in Java to airfields in North Sumatra and Central Malaya had only just got under way, so that it seems fairly certain that many of these trainer aircraft would never have been able to leave Java, as the Japanese had quite overlooked the Allied threat by our air forces established in the Cocos Islands which had started operations in August.

(iii) It was unlikely that any reinforcements of aircraft could have been withdrawn from French Indo-China and Siam. In any event, the numbers and types of aircraft available from that source were negligible – a fact borne out on the entry of the R.A.F. into French Indo-China during the course of occupation after the surrender.

(iv) Without exception the Japanese officers interrogated after surrender were well aware of the fact that their communications were so unreliable that no High Command such as 3rd Air Army could have hoped to control operations once "Zipper" had started. Decisions, it should be noted, were to have been left to subordinate commanders and even to unit commanding officers. This undoubtedly would have meant a great deal of wasted effort.

(v) The Japanese had planned to rely on air reconnaissance for advance information on "Zipper" and the location of targets for suicide attacks in the preliminary stages of the invasion. They were so short of aircraft for this essential commitment, however, that it would have been exceedingly difficult for them to spot and hold any of the Allied Forces. Indeed, it is more likely that complete surprise would have been achieved on D-Day by the R.A.F. units taking part in "Zipper" and that large numbers of Japanese aircraft would most certainly have been destroyed on the ground.

(vi) Lastly, the Japanese Air Force had anticipated a breathing space between the air attacks on the Penang area and the attacks on Singapore. It is doubtful, however, if they could have withdrawn and redeployed many of their aircraft from that area as well as from Sumatra without our knowledge through superior photographic reconnaissance.

MAINTENANCE.

Meeting the needs of overhaul in face of advancing front.

469. The Maintenance Organisation in South East Asia was faced with two major issues during the period May to September, 1945, following upon the re-occupation of Rangoon and, later, the sudden termination of hostilities in August.

470. The influencing factors were:-

(*a*) The need for a re-orientation of the Maintenance Organisation as the result of the battle front having moved further away from the static repair and overhaul bases which had been built up in India.

(*b*) The termination of Lend/Lease by America to the United Nations following upon the surrender of Japan, this causing acute difficulties in providing replacements and spares for American types of aircraft an operational use within the Command.

471. On the one hand, the re-organisation of maintenance to meet the needs of the advancing front was not an insuperable task and soon righted itself once necessary changes had been effected, but the denial of spares, on the cessation of Lend/Lease, was distinctly serious as there were some 1,600 American aircraft and gliders in India and South East Asia for which spares were absolutely essential.

472. With the arrival in Southern Burma of the victorious Air Forces in May, it was considered that a reversion from the existing centralised system of maintenance in the Theatre should be initiated. The six months rapid advance down through Burma had been a testing time for every branch of maintenance. Burma could not be compared to the great flat desert stretches of the Middle East. Transport of the mobile units negotiated appalling roads after an equally difficult journey from India. At one time, indeed, it was doubtful if transport would last until Rangoon was reached.

473. These difficulties must be emphasised because it was to this mobile ground organisation, embracing Repair and Salvage Units, Air Stores Parks, Motor Transport, Maintenance Units and Motor Transport Light Repair Units, that the Air Forces in Burma were tied and were fully dependent upon for their servicing if not their very existence during operations.

474. The re-organisation of Maintenance which took place after our arrival in Southern Burma can be summarised as follows:-

(*a*) The Forward Repair Depots in the operational areas were abolished and Salvage units built up.

(*b*) Group Commanders were invested with the responsibility of repair and overhaul of their squadron's aircraft.

(*c*) Squadrons were given their full U.E. of aircraft instead of retaining a proportion of them in the Maintenance organisation as hitherto.

(*d*) Each Repair and Salvage Unit and Air Stores Park worked for a wing and specialised in the types of aircraft operated by the wing.

475. Re-organisation was necessary for yet another important reason. The great distance which, at that time, obtained between operational areas in Burma and bases in India, precluded the return of short range aircraft to Maintenance Units for major inspections and engine changes. Thus, it became necessary to transfer the responsibility for this maintenance work to the squadrons and other flying units. Owing to the different problems, including beaching facilities, involved in carrying

out major inspections on flying boats, this maintenance continued to be centralised at Koggala in Ceylon.

476. Hitherto, all repair and salvage units in the Command were controlled by Headquarters, Base Air Forces through Nos. 222, 226 and 230 Groups on a regional basis. In the re-organisation no change in policy, however, was effected in the case of units under 222 Group, Ceylon, and 226 Group, whose area extended throughout India, but excluded Bengal and Assam. The R. & S.U.s. on the other hand, had, of necessity, to be fully mobile and to move with the units they supported.

477. When the re-organisation was put into effect the establishments of flying units were increased by 25 per cent. in order to cover aircraft undergoing major inspections at units. This increase was effected by feeding in additional aircraft from the R. & S.U.s. as and when the squadron or unit became due for a major inspection.

478. The base at Rangoon carried heavy responsibilities – not only for the continuance of operations during the mopping up period in Burma, but in preparing its organisation to meet the coming operations against Malaya.

479. A Forward Equipment Unit and a Forward Repair Unit were maintained in Rangoon to support the Air Forces in Southern Burma and to act as backing, if necessary, for the "Zipper" forces which would deploy through Southern Burma bases. The pressure on maintenance at this crucial period is illustrated by the amount of work tackled. During the months from May to August, the Repair and Salvage Units returned to service 830 aircraft and dismantled a further 420 which had been written off. The heaviest month was May, after the entry into Rangoon, when 300 aircraft were repaired – an indication of the strenuous use to which they had been subjected during the last stage of the lightning advance to Rangoon.

480. It was thought that the Repair and Salvage Unit in Rangoon would build up a fairly extensive repair depot, but with the capitulation of the Japanese in August this was no longer necessary, and personnel were switched to Singapore to re-occupy and build up the original Repair Depot at Seletar on Singapore Island.

Difficulties arising from Lend/Lease termination.

481. President Truman's announcement of the Surrender of Japan brought with it the declaration that Lend/Lease to Allied Governments was at an end except for assistance to forces engaged against Japanese who had not surrendered.

482. The repercussions in Air Command, South East Asia were serious. There was a world-wide shortage of Dakota spares. The U.S.A.A.F., however, as a result of the termination of Lend/Lease had cancelled the production of spares for their earlier Marks I, II and III and there were 200 Dakotas included in this range within South East Asia Command.

483. To ascertain the position as it affected Air Command, investigation revealed that, excluding Dakotas, Expeditors, Thunderbolts and Cornells, there were some 1,600 American aircraft and gliders in India and South East Asia which would gradually become unserviceable through lack of spares.

484. The Command's most urgent attention at the beginning of September, therefore, was directed with the utmost speed to securing alternative arrangements

for supply of necessary spares. In some respects, but by no means all, the situation was partially alleviated by the arrangement reached at Washington that the U.S.A.A.F. would meet, on a cash basis, limited demands in respect of Liberator, Dakota and Skymaster aircraft only. No stock demands, however, were permitted. The literal interpretation of this ruling was that a demand could not be raised until an aircraft was actually grounded or until repair was held up. A period of from eight to ten weeks also must elapse before the necessary parts could be obtained from America.

485. What became quite certain was that no demand whatsoever would be met in other types of aircraft, which included the following:-

Thunderbolt.	Cornell.
Sentinel.	Vengeance.
Argus.	Catalina.
Expeditor.	Harvard.

486. It was clear, therefore, that as stocks for any particular item became exhausted, so also would the repair of aircraft, their engines, and associated equipment automatically cease. Cannibalisation, or robbing another aircraft, was of very limited value as the bulk of the spares required were rendered necessary by wear and tear or by climatic deterioration.

487. In a signal to the Air Member for Supply and Organisation, I stated that if we did not get the essential parts, I could foresee us falling down badly on our agreed commitments, and urged that dollars should be made available for purchase of our essential requirements for replacement arising from wear and tear.

488. But the difficulties in England over the termination of Lend/Lease were greater than it was at first realised. There were dollar quotas to be considered, and in this connection it was learned that demands on available dollars were extremely heavy, especially for foodstuffs. The situation in respect of aircraft spares and replacements, therefore, was not cheerful. As regards a British replacement for the Dakotas, we could no longer demand the highest priority for labour in Britain, now that the war had ended, thus making progress automatically slow in production.

R.A.F. REGIMENT OPERATIONS.

A record of achievements in the South East Asia Command.

489. In the various campaign stages of the war in South East Asia I have been left in no doubt whatsoever about the usefulness, efficiency and fine example of that most junior of all our forces – the R.A.F. Regiment.

490. The R.A.F. Regiment adequately carried out the task of close defence of airfields in Burma and in other operational areas in South-East Asia.

491. I have it on record from one of my Group Commanders who moved with Fourteenth Army all the way through Burma, that he considered it probable that the Group could not have occupied air strips as far forward as they did – with consequently better air support for the Army – had he not been confident that the R.A.F. Regiment could have maintained the necessary security.

492. In South East Asia the R.A.F. Regiment proved itself a force capable of carrying out more than the tasks which its originators claimed the Regiment could accomplish. It was not a force of men dressed up as guards and picqueted around some airfield or supply dump with guns propped in their hands. These men were so trained in the art and strategy of ground defence and of jungle warfare, that they were able to undertake with success counter measures against Japanese infiltration parties who might set themselves up near the perimeter of some airfield and constitute a menace until hunted down and destroyed.

493. When the advance through Burma began in January, 1945, there were ten Field Squadrons, seven A.A. Squadrons and seven Regiment Wing Headquarters working with the Tactical Air Forces. On the capture of Rangoon in May, 1945, these had been increased to fourteen Field Squadrons, nine A.A. Squadrons and eight Wing Headquarters.

494. For the D-Day operations planned for the assault on Malaya, the Regiment was also scheduled to play a prominent part. Five Regimental Wings of nearly 2,500 officers and men, made up of nine Field Squadrons and five A.A. Squadrons were available. One A.A. Squadron had been brought out of the Cocos Islands, where its twenty millimetre Hispano cannons had given protection to the heavy bomber and transport airfield there.

Defence of Airfields and Mopping Up.

495. When it is considered that few Japanese were ever taken prisoner in Burma, electing to face death rather than capture, and that the principal task of the R.A.F. Regiment was to protect our air strips rather than to make enemy captives, the effort of the Regiment between January and May, 1945, in all forms of service was exceedingly high. While operating at seven strips during that period, the A.A. Squadrons succeeded in destroying one enemy aircraft and registering hits on three others out of a total of nine enemy aircraft attacking these particular strips.

496. The most outstanding episode of the R.A.F. Regiment's service in this theatre was the assistance they gave in the defence of Meiktila airfield. It was essential to comb the airfield and its environs each morning for snipers before permitting aircraft to land. Every gully, fox-hole or other feasible hiding place of a sniper had to be examined. The patrols started just after daybreak and took almost two hours to complete. It was thorough and effective, but the only sure method of clearing the area of the enemy, to ensure the safety of our aircraft.

497. In mopping up isolated parties of Japanese in Burmese villages at the time of the advance on Rangoon, certain units of the R.A.F. Regiment gave considerable assistance to Civil Affairs Officers and also helped in the clearing and disposal of mortar bombs, booby-traps, mines and anti-tank traps. Extensive searches, including patrols up rivers, were also carried out by the Regiment in their efforts to arrest wanted and known collaborators and to enforce the surrendering of illegally held arms and ammunition. The river patrols on these occasions were necessary owing to the difficulties of communication and the nature of the country. During March and April, for example, one Field Squadron covered an area of 2,600 square miles, visited

or "raided" 250 villages, arrested 100 Japanese collaborators and recovered 26 rifles. Large quantities of ammunition of British and Japanese make were also recovered, together with clothing, equipment, parachutes and rations.

The Occupation of Singapore.

498. In the protection of newly captured airfields and the guarding of vital radar sites once the assault on Malaya had begun, the R.A.F. Regiment would have been indispensable to the Air Force and could have been relied upon to fulfil its task thoroughly and well. Even in the peaceful occupation of Singapore, units of the Regiment, within 24 hours, were maintaining the security of Kallang, Changi, Seletar and Tengah airfields – one of which had three hundred police in peacetime.

499. Up country in Malaya, during the early days of occupation by our forces, a squadron of the R.A.F. Regiment sent out a patrol into one of the thickly wooded areas and succeeded in recovering 600 gallons of petrol from a party of Malays and Chinese.

500. On September 10th, two days before the official surrender ceremony at Singapore, No. 1329 Wing R.A.F. Regiment, with four Field Squadrons, arrived at Penang and took over the entire garrison duties from the Royal Marines. On the day following it was decided that the Regiment should also occupy Port Butterworth and Prai area, Province Wellesley, as part of the Penang commitment.

501. If the R.A.F. Regiment in South East Asia had done nothing more than provide vital protection for our airfields, the record of its achievements would still read with commendable credit. That it was able to perform further additional services and maintain a smartness and discipline which called forth praise from Army and Navy alike, demonstrates the value of the Regiment as an adjunct to the Royal Air Force. In my many tours and inspections throughout this Theatre I have noted the almost "jealous-like" pride which the Regiment Squadrons have in their own service.

PART V.
ADMINISTRATIVE AND OTHER ASPECTS.

THE REPERCUSSIONS FELT BY AIR COMMAND AFTER DEFEAT OF GERMANY AND JAPAN.

502. The period May to September, 1945, witnessed a series of important changes associated with the administrative development of Air Command, South East Asia, and the recasting of plans already made to meet the changed conditions after the defeat of Germany and, later still, defeat of Japan.

503. The Command felt the full effects of the global shipping and manpower shortages; of pre-election uncertainties in England; of the change in emphasis of attacks on Japan's outlying conquests to the Japanese homeland; of the vastness of the task involved in building up the Southern Burma net of all-weather airfields in preparation for coming operations; of the monsoon; the sharp contraction in air supply

resources consequent upon the withdrawal of the American squadrons, and finally, the task of re-occupying liberated territories.

504. Following the reconquest of Burma in May, the future trend of the Command's administrative development was largely influenced by the following factors:-

    (i) Disbandment of the integrated Eastern Air Command Headquarters on 1st June, 1945 and the withdrawal of the United States Army Air Forces from the Command.

    (ii) Reorganisation of Headquarters, R.A.F., Burma, on the assumption of full operational and administrative control of the Air Forces in Burma.

    (iii) Administrative planning in anticipation of the forthcoming operations in South East Asia associated principally with the re-conquest of Malaya and the build-up of the strategic base of Singapore.

    (iv) Planning for the reorganisation of the Command, subsequent to the re-occupation of Singapore.

505. It was not unnatural, on the defeat of Germany, that attention should be focussed suddenly upon the impressive array of air power promised for South East Asia in Phase II of the war. Not only was the number of squadrons expected to be increased, but more modern and more powerfully armed aircraft were envisaged. There were expectations too, of plentiful supplies of spares and ancillary equipment calculated to abrogate, for the duration of the Far Eastern war, the parsimony of indigenous industrial resources. South East Asia, it was confidently hoped, would achieve a higher place in the list of priorities as from VE-Day. But this illusion was soon shattered. At the beginning of June it was officially revealed that the Pacific Tiger Force and post-war events in Europe would take priority over South East Asia's demands. The decision was occasioned not so much by the shortage of equipment as by the global deficiencies in shipping and manpower which implied that drastic cuts in the Phase II Target of 116 squadrons would have to be accepted. It became evident, therefore, that the basis for planning was not what the Command was entitled to expect, but what was actually available.

506. In spite of these difficulties – and they had been many in South East Asia – it was necessary to cut the administrative cloth to suit the operational coat. A target of 87 squadrons which, it was reckoned, would have to meet the air effort, both for "Zipper" and "Mailfist" and other commitments, was therefore accepted.

507. Although these factors did not seriously affect Operation "Zipper", the enforced economy would have had some bearing upon the final assault on Singapore itself and upon operations contemplated early in 1946 into Siam, had the war with Japan continued. Other tasks too, included action on the development of the air base in Southern Burma and the Cocos Islands, both closely associated with "Zipper" and the redeployment of the strategic forces, once heavy bomber bases further east and south east became available.

Important Changes After Fall of Rangoon.

508. The ease with which Rangoon fell caused future administrative planning to proceed along more ambitious lines. Before further operations could be undertaken, however, it was necessary to have a reshuffle of offensive and defensive units; introduce a revised maintenance policy and new equipment to meet conditions of the Malay Peninsula; to withdraw many air forces from Burma for rest, refit and concentration for "Zipper".

509. The most important change in Command organisation at this time was the departure of the American Air Forces which were withdrawn from the Theatre as from 1st June, 1945. The disintegration of the British and American Air Forces in Burma involved the disbandment of Headquarters, Eastern Air Command, and the transfer of the Air Staff from that Headquarters to H.Q. R.A.F., Burma, which then became an independent R.A.F. Command under H.Q. Air Command, South East Asia.

510. A series of other changes was brought about as a result of the revised responsibilities of Headquarters, R.A.F. Burma, upon disbandment of Eastern Air Command. Operational control of all R.A.F. formations and units, formerly under Eastern Air Command, was taken over by H.Q. R.A.F., Burma.

511. The title of "Strategic Air Force", which had included British and American squadrons, ceased to be used with effect from 1st June, 1945, and No. 231 Group, R.A.F., continued strategic operations alone. In the same way the disintegration of Combat Cargo Task Force was carried out and, on the departure of the American squadrons, No. 232 Group took over the full operational control of all R.A.F. transport units in the A.L.F.S.E.A. area.

512. Yet another important change at this time was the reorganisation of the R.A.F. Element of H.Q. Photographic Reconnaissance Force as a Wing (No. 347 Wing), after the withdrawal of the American Forces. Included in the wing's establishment was No.1 Photographic Interpretation Detachment. The object of the change was to give the former R.A.F. Element of Photographic Reconnaissance Force more mobility as a wing which could be moved forward as required for operational purposes.

513. Throughout the campaign in Burma, Headquarters 230 Group had been charged with the control of all maintenance and storage units in the area of Headquarters, R.A.F., Burma, but the Group itself was under the direct control of the C.M.O., Headquarters, Base Air Forces. This arrangement was unsatisfactory because it meant that the R.A.F. operational commander in Burma did not have complete control of his maintenance organisation. It was therefore decided to disband No. 230 Group and to absorb the Maintenance Staff of the Group into Headquarters, R.A.F., Burma, with effect from 15th May, 1945. The units under No. 230 Group were, at the same time, placed directly under the operational groups they served, and the staffs of these groups were increased to cope with this commitment by the addition of some of the posts thrown up from the disbandment of No. 230 Group.

Withdrawal of **224** *Group in Preparation for "Zipper".*

514. The main assault on Malaya, scheduled for early September, made necessary the withdrawal of No. 224 Group and units from the Arakan and Burma.

515. This was started early in May. The withdrawal was handled directly between Headquarters, R.A.F., Burma, and Headquarters, Base Air Forces. As from 1st June, 1945, H.Q. 224 Group was placed directly under the control of H.Q. Base Air Forces for the purpose of mounting operation "Zipper", but the A.O.C. 224 Group and his staff retained the right to visit all units during mounting and to advise on all matters concerning the training of units for their various tasks. Headquarters 224 Group undertook the responsibility for force planning.

516. It was decidedly unfortunate, if not serious, that owing to the acute shortage of shipping, the withdrawal of units from Burma did not go off as smoothly as might have been expected. Many of the units, indeed, came out of the Arakan with no equipment or M.T., while the equipment and M.T. of other units which arrived in India lay on the docks awaiting the arrival of the units for many weeks. When units ultimately reached India they were deployed on airfields which had been prepared for them, but owing to the non-arrival of equipment or personnel, the commencement of training was badly delayed.

Re-organisation of Air Command in **1945-46.**

517. In view of the extension of the responsibilities of Air Command, South East Asia, towards Singapore and beyond, the future organisation of formations in the Command required consideration.

518. The principal factors which necessitated reorganisation were as follows:-

(*a*) Mopping up operations of the enemy in Burma would continue for some time, but, so far as the Air Forces were concerned, these could be undertaken by one composite group (No. 221).

(*b*) Since No. 224 Group had been withdrawn from Burma for participation in Operation "Zipper", the Group would come directly under the operational control of Headquarters, Air Command, during the next stage of the Campaign.

(*c*) The Heavy Bomber Group (No. 231) was no longer suitably located in Burma. It would be based at the Cocos Islands for "Zipper" support.

(*d*) Photographic Reconnaissance, Special Duties and Air Supply Operations would no longer be concentrated on Burma, but would be required in widely separated areas. This called for direct control from the Headquarters of the Air Command of the groups engaged in these duties.

(*e*) The above factors reduced the responsibilities of H.Q. R.A.F. Burma, which had hitherto controlled several functional groups.

(f) The altered military situation had also called for the move of Headquarters, Allied Land Forces to Kandy, while Headquarters. Supreme Allied Command, together with the Headquarters of the three Commanders-in-Chief, would move to Singapore at the earliest practicable date.

(g) The 10th U.S.A.A.F. had been moved to China and Eastern Air Command dissolved. At the same time the R.A.F. Target Force for South East Asia in Phase II was not to be as large as originally planned.

519. These factors, it was considered, required revision of previous operational plans, and would enable a considerable reduction of planned overheads to be effected in Headquarters and Administrative Services.

520. On the fall of Singapore the following moves were scheduled to take place:-

(a) Headquarters, Air Command would move there in company with Headquarters, Supreme Allied Commander, H.Q. Allied Land Forces and part of the E.I.F. H.Q.

(b) Headquarters, No. 222 Group would move from Ceylon to Singapore and undertake responsibilities in that area similar to those undertaken by Mediterranean Allied Coastal Forces or Air Defences, Eastern Mediterranean.

(c) Headquarters, No. 231 Group would move to Singapore and be possibly employed either as a heavy Bomber Group Headquarters, the Headquarters of a Task Force, or be disbanded.

(d) Headquarters, No. 224 Group would also move to Singapore area and remain a composite group, being modelled as necessary to undertake further operations for the reconquest of Sumatra, Java and Borneo.

521. A small Headquarters, R.A.F. Ceylon, was also planned to take over area responsibilities for:-

a) Ceylon.

(b) Island Flying-boat, Emergency Landing Grounds and Met. Stations to the south.

(c) Cocos for administrative services.

522. Although the future strategy for South East Asia Command was not yet determined, making it impossible to forecast reliably for the future deployment of forces, it was considered that the reorganisation as planned would meet all the probable requirements.

THE MANPOWER SITUATION IN SOUTH EAST ASIA.

523. The energetic stepping up of operations in the Pacific directly against Japan, brought about a wide variety of circumstances which combined to deny Air

Command, South East Asia that priority in personnel which the Command had expected would be forthcoming.

524. Demands in Europe and the Pacific for shipping; the sudden announcement, preceding the General Election, to reduce the Overseas Tour for Army personnel by approximately 10 per cent; the operation of the Release Scheme, and the priority accorded to the Pacific "Tiger Force", all adversely reacted upon Air Command, South East Asia.

525. In May, 1945, the establishment and strength of the Command for British personnel were as follows:-

	Estab.	*Strength*	*Surplus/Deficiencies*	
Ground Officers	8,103	7,573	—	530
Other Ranks	105,470	110,459	4,989	—

526. The 6½ per cent. deficiency in ground officers affected principally the branches in Administration, Code and Cypher, Tech. (E) and Catering. On the other hand, the position as regards airmen was that the technical trades carried a surplus of 7,100, whilst the trade of

Clerk G.D. was deficient by not less than 36 per cent., equipment assistants by 20 per cent. and cooks by 28 per cent.

527. By September, 1945, the position had so deteriorated that an overall deficiency was shown, although certain trades continued to carry a surplus. The strength of personnel was as follows:-

	Estab.	*Strength*	*Surplus/Deficiencies*
Ground Officer	8,116	7,525	591
Other Ranks	123,466	114,419	9,047

528. The 7 per cent. deficiency in ground officers was spread over a great many branches. Physical Fitness carried a deficiency of 36 per cent. and Code and Cypher a deficiency of 22 per cent.

529. The overall 8 per cent. deficiency in other ranks, however, clouded the very large deficiencies carried in the following trades:-

	Per cent. deficiency.
Clerks G.D	43
Clerks Acctg.	36
Cooks	32
Driver M.T.	18
Equip. Asst.	36

530. The Command had clearly to take measures to rectify this weakness if it was to function administratively, and compulsory misemployment of surplus tradesmen and aircrew was therefore introduced. It was fortunate that, on the defeat of Japan, an opportunity was offered for a large scale reduction of establishments and disbandments to begin.

531. The Release Scheme, coming so soon after the cessation of the European

War, reacted very materially against the Command. It brought further grave losses in the difficult trades at a time when the efficient administration of the Command was essential for the prosecution of the war against Japan.

532. An even greater disadvantage was the fact that it withdrew from the Command the more senior and experienced personnel. Consequently, while the position in a branch or trade as far as actual personnel were concerned, may have appeared satisfactory on paper, it was not always so in actual performance of work, and efficiency thereby suffered.

Reduction in overseas tour for personnel.

533. On 6th June, 1945, the War Office suddenly announced a reduction in the overseas tour of Army personnel. This factor had every promise of producing serious repercussions in South East Asia, in which either coming operations, or morale, or both, might well have been affected. The fulfilment of the War Office announcement was rendered virtually impossible by the lack of homeward personnel shipping and the congestion in transit camps in India.

534. To avoid a parallel situation with regard to the Air Force in this Command, I signalled the Chief of Staff emphasising that any announcement of a reduction in overseas tour for the Air Force would be premature and impracticable at this juncture.

535. At the same time, I strongly recommended that shipping and air transport should be found in order to bring into effect, by 1st December, 1945, a reduction of tour from four to three and a half years, for all single officers and airmen. This reduction was agreed upon in August in principle, but was not fully implemented until December.

536. Between May and September, 1945, some 559 officers and 2,263 airmen left the Command under the Release Scheme. During the same period 2,201 officers and 12,932 airmen were repatriated in addition to those despatched on release.

537. The celebration of V.E.-Day in the Command was a sincere enough occasion for everyone, though it was only natural that it did not hold the same high spirit of enthusiasm for those in the East still fighting the last of the remaining Axis powers. The announcement that the Burma Star had been inaugurated gave general satisfaction to personnel serving in Burma – an award well merited – but personnel in India and Ceylon felt that the burden of their overseas service was not sufficiently recognised by the award of the Defence Medal.

538. The postal voting scheme for the General Election in July, 1945, was put into operation successfully during May and June, and ballot papers for personnel in South East Asia were flown out from England by transport aircraft. The papers were given priority over all other mails handled by R.A.F. Post Staffs. The total number of completed application forms for postal voting received by 25th June at R.A.F. Post Karachi was 33,500. A last minute supply of forms to the Cocos Islands, whose original consignment was mislaid in transit, produced satisfactory results.

539. Altogether, a total of 30,013 ballot papers was finally forwarded by air to the U.K. from the Command.

PART VI.
CONCLUSIONS.

Japan's defeat.

540. Japan, in her disastrous war against the Allied Powers, was defeated largely by her own misjudgement – embarking upon a policy of expansion which lengthened too far her lines of communication without providing adequately armed forces for their protection and maintenance.

541. Expansion brought the Japanese, in their initial flush of success, to the very threshold of India at a time when the Allies were least prepared to resist her westward march.

542. Defeat for the Japanese in South East Asia, I consider, had its begnning in the air battles over the Arakan in late 1943 and the opening months of 1944, when Allied air superiority was obtained.

543. It is my opinion that the cardinal weakness in Japan's war of aggression was undoubtedly a badly balanced war machine, which showed too heavy a bias in favour of land forces, and a much too weak air force, also air potential.

544. Without air support, the Japanese Army in South East Asia fought a losing battle after Allied air superiority had been won. The numbers actually killed during their campaign in Burma were enormous, whilst the number that perished in the jungle will never be known. This Japanese Army provided a grim reminder to any Army that embarks upon operations without adequate air support.

Close Support operations.

545. According to the Japanese, it is impossible to state definitely which of our Allied fighters had the greatest effect morally upon their ground forces in South East Asia, as each fighter had its own characteristics. The effect differed according to the nature of the target attacked and the time of the attack, whether by day or by night. On an assessment of the Allied fighter aircraft individually, however, it appears that the enemy considered the Spitfire, the Thunderbolt and the Mustang surpassed all others.

Fighter, and fighter/bomber offensive operations.

546. The effect of the Beaufighter and Mosquito attacks on Japanese shipping in the Gulf of Martaban during the early months of 1945 was such that the enemy stopped movement of shipping by day, and did movements only at night. In this way enemy shipping was conserved.

547. On the other hand, the harassing attacks these aircraft carried out on the enemy's road, rail and river transport areas was exceedingly effective. While it cost them few casualties to men, the air, attacks, according to the Japanese, made troop as well as supply movements virtually impossible. Materials and food, they stated, became difficult to move, and this had a bad effect upon the civilian population.

548. Our policy of surprise raids on the enemy's rear airfields was most effective.

In this respect the American fighter attacks, on these airfields were not only effective, but greatly helped to reduce the operational strength of the Japanese Army Air Force.

Heavy Bomber Operations.

549. The heavy bomber attacks which our aircraft carried out on Rangoon, and on supply dumps in the vicinity, cannot be compared, in effectiveness, to the heavy air attacks made on bridges, railway tracks, marshalling yards and important installations in other enemy occupied areas. The dumps in the Rangoon area which were targets of attack were, according to the enemy, destroyed to some extent, but they did not greatly affect Japanese morale. The bombing of Rangoon itself, however, which was continued for almost a month before the enemy's evacuation, had a marked effect upon their morale. The effect of the bombings on the civilian population appeared to be small because only military targets were bombed.

550. Bombing raids on military installations in the rear areas were admitted by the Japanese to be most effective, and many targets, some highly important to the Japanese war effort, were destroyed. The attacks, it appears, could have been even more effective had our bombers struck at the targets over a wider area, as enemy installations were immediately divided up into sections and scattered once a target area was hit.

Air Mining Operations Affect Supply.

551. I consider it exceedingly gratifying, and indeed, interesting, to have it confirmed by the Japanese themselves that the isolation of large sea transports, as the result of our air mining operations, seriously affected the Japanese supply situation. The mines were laid by our aircraft in the Rangoon River and off the Tenasserim and Malayan coasts. The sowing of these mines, the Japanese stated, was directly responsible for the sinking of important supply ships.

552. Our air mining programme, which began on 21st January, 1945, and was discontinued on 24th May, 1945, since the stage was then being set finally for the assault on Malaya, resulted in a total of 925 mines being dropped in the specified areas. The minelaying operations were 86.9 successful – only 29 mines being dropped foul, and 80 being brought back by aircraft to base.

553. From a tactical point of view, I was interested to learn that, of all the weapons which we used against the Japanese in Burma – rockets, machine-guns, cannon, bombs and Napalm – the machine-guns had the most effect, both morally and physically, upon their ground forces.

554. During the advance of our ground troops, the feints and dummy attacks by our supporting aircraft proved very effective in keeping the Japanese under cover – a highly important factor when troops are storming strongly-held positions.

555. Close support by the Japanese Army Air Force was negligible. Its development was dependent upon adequate air strength, and as the Japanese Army Air Force gradually dwindled away to nothing, close support for their ground forces was therefore impracticable.

556. While the Japanese also used Visual Control Posts to indicate targets to their aircraft, shortage of wireless equipment greatly hindered them in putting through demands for air support. This is in striking contrast to our own use of V.C.P.s., which we exploited to the full with excellent results.

Air supply.

557. Burma proved how an Army could march for a thousand miles through some of the worst country in the world so long as air supply was guaranteed by our retaining air superiority and having adequate air transport.

558. There is no doubt that the Japanese fully appreciated how vitally important Allied air supply was to the success of our operations. They confessed that all means possible were used to interfere with Allied air supply, but, due to the small size of their Air Force, they failed in their efforts.

559. Burma, I consider, has given us the classic example of an Army in the field existing on air supply, and the technique evolved from these air supply operations must surely command serious attention.

Lessons which emerged in South East Asia.

560. The war in South East Asia, has immeasurably enriched our experience in air operations in the East; quickened our perception to the dangers of a purely static defence system for these Empire territories, and shown how essential is air power for future defence.

The need for greater squadron mobility.

561. One of the most noticeable features of our operations in South East Asia was the clumsy and inadequate method which we had been forced to employ to maintain the mobility of our squadrons, their personnel and equipment.

562. This implies no reflection on the ground staff and maintenance organisation, who succeeded in achieving good results with the equipment and facilities available when moving the squadrons forward, month after month, through a country devoid of proper communications and faced with flooding during the monsoon, when roads turned into quagmires.

563. But a squadron working in support of front-line troops must have greater mobility to enable its ground organisation to move to its next base, and not find itself on some narrow inadequate road, choked for miles ahead with slow moving army transport.

564. It is on record that during April, 1945, when over 80 R.A.F. units moved forward in Burma to new bases in keeping with the overall plan of advance, one R.A.F. wing, having insufficient road transport, had to use bullock carts. Against this, there is the more logical instance of another R.A.F. wing which moved from Akyab to Rangoon by air, taking with it all its equipment and personnel and leaving behind only M.T., since it was picking up a new allotment of vehicles at its destination.

565. With so many moves by squadrons in the forward areas – many going ahead

with the bare minimum of staff to keep aircraft operational pending the arrival of the remainder of their ground personnel bringing up essential equipment – squadrons often found themselves separated from a proportion of their servicing echelons for several days due to lack of transport. Until the full staff of the echelons arrived, an enormous amount of work was thrown upon ground crew, since aircraft at the time were being pressed into service in support of the advance and had to be loaded with bombs and with ammunition. They also needed daily servicing.

566. This, I consider, is one of the most important lessons which emerged from operations in South East Asia. Experience has shown that Air Power, in the movement of its ground organisations, must have infinitely greater mobility in future, and be air-lifted by its own transports.

K. R. PARK,

Air Chief Marshal,

Allied Air Commander in Chief,

South East Asia.

August, 1946.

MAP

ABBREVIATIONS

AA	Anti-Aircraft
AAF	Auxiliary Air Force
A & SD	Admin and Special Duties
A/C	Army Co-operation
A/T	Anti-Tank
AAC-in-C	Allied Air Commander-in-Chief
ABDA	American-British-Dutch-Australian [Command]
AC	Army Co-operation
ACF	Air Commando Force
ACSEA	Air Command, South East Asia
ADC	Aide-De-Camp
AFC	Air Force Cross
ALF	Allied Land Forces
ALFSEA	Allied Land Forces South East Asia
AMES	Air Ministry Experimental Station
AMSO	Air Member for Supply and Organisation
AOA	Air Officer (Administration)
AOC	Air Officer Commanding
AOG	Aircraft On Ground
AOC-in-C	Air Officer Commanding-in-Chief
AP	Armour Piercing
AS	Air Staff
ASO	Air Staff Officer
ASP	Air Store Park
ASR	Air Sea Rescue
ASS	Airborne Salvage Section
ASU	Aircraft Storage Units
ATC	Air Transport Command

auw	all-up-weight
AVG	American Volunteer Group
AVM	Air-Vice Marshal
BAF	British Air Force
BAFSEA	British Air Force South-East Asia
BGS	Brigadier, General Staff
BOAC	British Overseas Airways Corporation
BOR	British Other Ranks
CAATO	Commander, Army-Air Transport Organisation
CAEUS	Casualty Air Evacuation Units
CB	Companion of the Most Honourable Order of the Bath
CBE	Commander of the Order of the British Empire
CCS	Casualty Clearing Station
CCTF	Combat Cargo Task Force
C-in-C	Commander-in-Chief
GD	General Duties
CMG	Companion of The Most Distinguished Order of Saint Michael and Saint George
CMU	Combined Maintenance Unit
COL	Chain Overseas Low
CVO	Commander of the Royal Victorian Order
DCAS	Deputy Chief of the Air Staff
DF	Direction Finding
DFC	Distinguished Flying Cross
DPMO	Deputy Principal Medical Officer
DSC	Distinguished Service Cross
DSO	Distinguished Service Order
EFTS	Elementary Flying Training School
EAC	Eastern Air Command/Eastern Army Command
EIF	East Indies Fleet
ENSA	Entertainments National Service Association
FEU	Forward Equipment Unit
FIC	French Indo-China
FRD	Forward Repair Depot
FRU	Forward Repair Unit
GAF	German Air Force

GBE	Knight Grand Cross of the Most Excellent Order of the British Empire
GCB	Knight Grand Cross of the Most Honourable Order of the Bath
GCI	Ground Controlled Intercept/Ground Control of Interception
GCVO	Knight Grand Cross of The Royal Victorian Order
GD	General Duties
GHQ	General Headquarters
GR	General Reconnaissance
HAA	Heavy Anti-Aircraft
HE	High Explosive
HF	High Frequency
HMIS	His Majesty's Indian Ship
HMT	His Majesty's Trawler/Troopship
HQ	Headquarters
IAF	Indian Air Force
IE	Initial Equipment
IMWOC	Indian Mobile Wireless Observer Companies
IOGROPS	Indian Ocean General Reconnaissance Operations
IOR	Indian Other Ranks
ISIAC	Inter-Services Inter-Allied Committee
ISLD	Inter-Service Liaison Department
ITW	Initial Training Wing
JAF	Japanese Air Force
JEF	Japanese Expeditionary Force
JPS	Joint Planning Staff
KBE	Knight Commander of the Most Excellent Order of the British Empire
KCB	Knight Commander of the Most Honourable Order of the Bath
LAA	Light Anti-Aircraft
LB	Light Bomber
L/Cpl	Lance Corporal
MAAF	Mediterranean Allied Air Forces
MC	Military Cross/Medium Capacity
MM	Military Medal
mph	miles per hour
MRU	Mobile Repair Unit/Mobile Radar Unit

MT	Motor Transport
MTLRU	Motor Transport Light Repair Unit
MU	Maintenance Unit
MVO	Member of the Royal Victorian Order
NAAFI	Navy, Army and Air Force Institutes
NAOR	Naval Air Operations Room
NCAC	Northern Combat Area Command
NCO	Non Commissioned Officer
NEI	Netherlands East Indies
NOIC	Naval Officer in Charge
OBE	Officer of the Most Excellent Order of the British Empire
OC	Officer Commanding
OSS	Office of Strategic Services
OTU	Operational Training Unit
PAC	Parachute And Cable
PMO	Principal Medical Officer
POL	Petrol, Oil, Lubricants
POW	Prisoner of War
PR	Photographic Reconnaissance
PRU	Photographic Reconnaissance Unit
PsOW	Prisoners of War
R/T	Receiver-Transmitter/Radio Transmitter
RAAF	Royal Australian Air Force
RAF	Royal Air Force
RAFVR	Royal Air Force Volunteer Reserve
RAMO	Rear Airfield Maintenance Organisation
R and SU	*see* RSU
RAP	Regimental Aid Post/River Air Patrol/Reserve Aircraft Pool
RAPWI	Recovery of Allied Prisoners of War and Internees
RDF	Radio Direction Finding (Radar)
RIASC	Royal Indian Army Service Corps
RN	Royal Navy
RP	Rocket Projectile
RSU	Repair and Salvage Unit
SAF	Strategic Air Force
SAAF	South African Air Force

SACSEA	Supreme Allied Commander South East Asia
S and T	Supply and Transport
SD	Special Duties
SEAC	South East Asia Command
SEF	Support Engineering Flight
SS	Steam Ship
SFTS	Service Flying Training School
TAF	Tactical Air Force
TF	Torpedo Fighter
UE	Unit Equipment
US	United States
USAAC	United States Army Air Corps
USAAF	United States Army Air Force
VCP	Visual/Vehicle Control Post
VHB	Very Heavy Bomber
VHF	Very High Frequency
W/OP AG	Wireless Operator/Air Gunner
WAAF	Women's Auxiliary Air Force
W/T	Wireless Telegraphy/Wireless
WAC	Women's Army Corps
WRNS	Women's Royal Naval Service

INDEX OF PERSONS

Index of Air Force and Military Units